A BOOK OF MASQUES

This book of seventeenth-century masques has been prepared by colleagues and former pupils of Allardyce Nicoll, historian of the drama, first editor of *Shakespeare Survey*, and founder of the Shakespeare Institute of the University of Birmingham. It is dedicated to him as a token of their esteem.

The Masque of Apes. From John Ogilby, *The Fables of Aesop
Paraphrased in Verse*, 1651.

A BOOK OF
MASQUES

IN HONOUR OF
ALLARDYCE NICOLL

CAMBRIDGE
AT THE UNIVERSITY PRESS
1967

Published by the Syndics of the Cambridge University Press
Bentley House, 200 Euston Road, London, N.W. 1
American Branch: 32 East 57th Street, New York, N.Y. 10022

© Cambridge University Press 1967

Library of Congress Catalogue Card Number: 66–14189

PN
6120.
M3
B6

54838

Printed in Great Britain
at the University Printing House, Cambridge
(Brooke Crutchley, University Printer)

CONTENTS

List of plates   *page* vii

General Editorial Note   xi

Notes on the Plates, prepared by Sybil Rosenfeld (Society   xiii
   for Theatre Research)

Plates between pages xv and 1

General Introduction, by Gerald Eades Bentley (Princeton   1
   University)

MASQUES

SAMUEL DANIEL, *The Vision of the Twelve Goddesses*   17
   (1604)
   edited by Joan Rees (University of Birmingham)

BEN JONSON, *Oberon, the Fairy Prince* (1611)   43
   edited by Richard Hosley (University of Arizona)

BEN JONSON, *Love Freed from Ignorance and Folly* (1611)   71
   edited by Norman Sanders (University of Tennessee)

THOMAS CAMPION, *The Lords' Masque* (1613)   95
   edited by I. A. Shapiro (University of Birmingham)

FRANCIS BEAUMONT, *The Masque of the Inner Temple*   125
   and Gray's Inn (1613)
   edited by Philip Edwards (University of Essex)

The Masque of Flowers (1614)   149
   edited by E. A. J. Honigmann (University of Glasgow)

WILLIAM BROWNE, *The Masque of the Inner Temple*   179
   (*Ulysses and Circe*) (1615)
   edited by R. F. Hill (King's College, University of
   London)

CONTENTS

BEN JONSON, *Lovers Made Men* (1617)   *page* 207
 edited by Stanley Wells (The Shakespeare Institute,
  University of Birmingham)

BEN JONSON, *Pleasure Reconciled to Virtue* (1618) 225
 edited by R. A. Foakes (University of Kent)

THOMAS MIDDLETON, *The Inner Temple Masque, or* 251
  Masque of Heroes (1619)
 edited by the late R. C. Bald (University of Chicago)

JAMES SHIRLEY, *The Triumph of Peace* (1634) 275
 edited by Clifford Leech (University of Toronto)

THOMAS NABBES, *The Spring's Glory* (1638) 315
 edited by John Russell Brown (University of Birmingham)

INIGO JONES AND WILLIAM DAVENANT, *Salmacida* 337
  Spolia (1640)
 edited by T. J. B. Spencer (The Shakespeare Institute,
  University of Birmingham)

JAMES SHIRLEY, *Cupid and Death* (1653) 371
 edited by B. A. Harris (University of York)

'These pretty devices': A Study of Masques in Plays, by 405
 Inga-Stina Ewbank (University of Liverpool)

LIST OF PLATES

Frontispiece The Masque of Apes. From John Ogilby,
The Fables of Aesop Paraphrased in Verse, 1651.

1   *Oberon*. Scene 1, Rocks. Inigo Jones. Walpole 40.

2   *Oberon*. Scene 2, Oberon's Palace. Inigo Jones. W. 42.

3   *Oberon*. Oberon's Palace in Rocks, another design.
    Inigo Jones. W. 44.

4   *Oberon*. Detail of Oberon's Palace. Inigo Jones. W. 45.

5   *Oberon*. Three Fays (?). Inigo Jones. W. 49.

6   *Oberon*. (*a*) One of the nation of Fays (?). (*b*) Two Fays (?).
    Inigo Jones. W. 48, 47.

7   *Oberon*. (*a*) Two Satyrs. (*b*) Two sketches for Oberon's head-
    dress (?). Inigo Jones. W. 41, 53.

8   *Oberon*. (*a*) Oberon (?). (*b*) Finished sketch of Oberon with
    altered head-dress (?). Inigo Jones. W. 50, 52.

9   *Oberon*. Two knights masquers. Inigo Jones. W. 54, 55.

10 *Love Freed from Ignorance and Folly* (?). Prison or castle
    gateway and cloud with eleven masquers. Inigo Jones. W. 17.

11 *The Lords' Masque*. (*a*) Entheus or Poetic Fury.
    (*b*) A masquer. Inigo Jones. W. 56, 57.

12 *The Lords' Masque*. (*a*) A masquer with hair in flames. (*b*) A
    page like a fiery spirit. Inigo Jones. W. 59, 58.

13 *The Masque of Flowers*. Kawasha. John White. Engraving
    from Thomas Hariot, *A Brief and True Report of the New
    Found Land of Virginia*, Frankfort, 1590.

14 *Pleasure Reconciled to Virtue*. Entry of Comus. Inigo Jones.
    W. 62.

15 *The Triumph of Peace.* Border of the scene. Inigo Jones. W. 180.

16 *The Triumph of Peace.* Scene 1, the Forum of Peace. Inigo Jones. W.183.

17 *The Triumph of Peace.* Scene 1, the Forum of Peace, another design. Inigo Jones. W. 184.

18 *The Triumph of Peace.* (*a*) Fat Bawd. (*b*) Plan for seating masquers. Inigo Jones. W. 186, 188.

19 *The Triumph of Peace.* (*a*) Sketches for head-dresses and masquer. (*b*) Sketch for masquer with alternative head-dresses. Inigo Jones. W. 189, 190.

20 *Salmacida Spolia.* Ground plan of stage and scenery. John Webb. W. 321.

21 *Salmacida Spolia.* Section of the stage and machinery. John Webb. W. 322.

22 *Salmacida Spolia.* Scene 1, Storm and tempest. Inigo Jones. W. 323.

23 *Salmacida Spolia.* Scene 2, Landscape with chariot. Inigo Jones. W. 328.

24 *Salmacida Spolia.* Scene 3, Mountains, the way to the Seat of Honour. Inigo Jones (copy by John Webb). W. 340.

25 *Salmacida Spolia.* The cloud open, disclosing the Queen with nine ladies; below, the Queen on a throne. Inigo Jones. W. 350.

26 *Salmacida Spolia.* Scene 5, Scene of architecture. Inigo Jones. W. 355.

27 *Salmacida Spolia.* Scene 5, Sketch for two lower lines of deities. Inigo Jones. W. 359.

28 *Salmacida Spolia.* Scene 5, Whole heaven with three lines of deities. Inigo Jones. W. 360.

29 *Salmacida Spolia*. Two studies of the bridge. Inigo Jones.
W. 356, 357.

30 *Salmacida Spolia*. (*a*) Furies. (*b*) Head of Fury and man with
cap and turban. Inigo Jones. W. 324, 326.

31 *Salmacida Spolia*. Two sketches of Wolfgangus Vandergoose.
Inigo Jones. W. 331, 332.

32 *Salmacida Spolia*. Irish, Scottish, and English habits.
Inigo Jones. W. 333, 334.

33 *Salmacida Spolia*. Two sketches for an old-fashioned
Englishwoman. Inigo Jones. W. 335, 336.

34 *Salmacida Spolia*. Two sketches for grotesques or drollities.
Inigo Jones. W. 337v., 338.

35 *Salmacida Spolia*. (*a*) Doctor Tartaglia and a Pedant of
Francolin. (*b*) Antique cavaliers. Inigo Jones. W. 337,
338v.

36 *Salmacida Spolia*. (*a*) Masquing dress for King Charles I.
(*b*) The King or a masquer. Inigo Jones. W. 341, 344.

37 *Salmacida Spolia*. The King or a masquer, two other designs.
Inigo Jones. W. 346, 348.

38 *Salmacida Spolia*. Lady in Amazonian habit, and alternative
design. Inigo Jones. W. 352v.

39 *Salmacida Spolia*. (*a*) King and Queen or masquer and lady.
(*b*) Queen Henrietta Maria, or lady, in an Amazonian habit.
Inigo Jones. W. 352, 354.

40 Unidentified Designs. Two masquers. Inigo Jones.
W. 430, 432.

41 Unidentified Designs. Two masquers. Inigo Jones.
W. 433, 437.

42 Unidentified Designs. Two lady masquers. Inigo Jones.
W. 420, 424.

43 Portrait of a lady, possibly in masque costume. Sitter and artist unknown.

44 Lucy, Countess of Bedford, in masque costume. Marcus Gheerhardts.

45 Miniatures. (*a*) Henry Frederick, Prince of Wales, in Roman costume. (*b*) Unknown lady in masque costume. (*c*) Queen Anne of Denmark in masque costume. (*d*) Unknown lady in masque costume. Isaac Oliver.

46 *Cupid and Death*. Death stealing the weapons of Cupid. Engraving after Mattheus Bril.

47 *Cupid and Death*. (*a*) Cupid and Death. (*b*) Cupid, Death, and Reputation. From J. Ogilby, *Fables of Aesop*, 1651.

48 Emblems. (*a*) *Cupid and Death*. Death stealing the weapons of Cupid. From Andreas Alciati, *Emblematum Libellus*, 1534. (*b*) *Pleasure Reconciled to Virtue*. Hercules at the cross-roads. From George Wither, *A Collection of Emblems*, 1635.

GENERAL EDITORIAL NOTE

Each editor of the masques in this volume has established his own text and modernized its spelling and punctuation. The same general principles have been followed throughout, but there may be some inconsistency of presentation in points of detail. In the Introductions, quotations from early printed works have generally been modernized, but quotations from manuscript sources follow the conventions of the original documents. We are grateful to Professor Samuel Schoenbaum of Northwestern University, Illinois, for reading the proofs of *The Masque of Heroes* edited by the late R. C. Bald.

T.J.B.S.; S.W.W.

The Shakespeare Institute,
University of Birmingham

NOTES ON THE PLATES

Editor's Note

The Inigo Jones designs at Chatsworth have been drawn on as fully as possible for the masques they illustrate in order 'to imagine them in action'. The attributions of the drawings to the various masques are those given in Percy Simpson and C. F. Bell, *Designs by Inigo Jones for Masques and Plays at Court*, Walpole and Malone Societies, 1924. The letter W with a number in the List of Plates refers to the numbers in this publication, which will enable readers to obtain further information about the designs and the reasons for the attributions. Some unidentified costume designs by Inigo Jones and other portraits and miniatures illustrate types of masquers' dress in general.

The editor is greatly indebted to the following for gracious permission to reproduce pictures in their possession: Her Majesty the Queen (Plate 45c); His Grace the Duke of Bedford (Plate 44); His Grace the Duke of Devonshire (Plates 1–12; 14; 16–19; 22–42); the Bristol City Art Gallery (Plate 43); the British Museum (Plates 20–1, 46); the Fitzwilliam Museum, Cambridge (Plate 45a); the Rijksmuseum, Amsterdam (Plate 45b); the Royal Institute of British Architects (Plate 15); the Victoria and Albert Museum (Plate 45d). Photographs of the Chatsworth designs were kindly supplied by the Courtauld Institute, the Witt Collection, and the Victoria and Albert Museum; those of the emblems by the British Museum and the Shakespeare Institute; and that of the miniature belonging to the Rijksmuseum by the Mauritshuis, the Hague.

S. R.

Notes on Individual Illustrations

Frontispiece For a discussion of this engraving see James G. McManaway, 'Notes on Two Pre-Restoration Stage-Curtains', *Philological Quarterly*, XLI (1962).

20 The inscription reads: 'Ground platt of a sceane where yᵉ side peeces of yᵉ sceane doe altogither change with yᵉ back shutters

comparted by yᵉ sceane of yᵉ King & Queen's Maᵗᵉ Masque of Salmacida Spolia in yᵉ new masquing howse Whitehall 1640.'

The key reads:

'A: Pilasters of the front:

B: The side shutters which runne in groues & change yᵉ sceane 4: seuerall tymes.

C: Engynes by which Deityes ascend and discend.

D: Backshutters below

E: Masquers seates

F: the great vpright gr[ou]es by which yᵉ seates were lett vpp and downe

G: a crosse peece of tymber which went in yᵉ groues to which yᵉ seate was fastened and was made camb[er] in yᵉ middle for greater strength.

H: Back Cloth

I: The space for Releiues betwixt yᵉ backshutters and backcloth when yᵉ seates were lett downe vnder yᵉ stage

K: yᵉ wall of yᵉ howse

L: peeces of tymber which bore vpp yᵉ groues of yᵉ backshutters, & yᵉ backcloth.

P: Engyne of yᵉ Kings seate see yᵉ vprights.'

21 The inscription reads: 'Profyle of yᵉ sceane when yᵉ sceane doth wholy change aswell on yᵉ sydes as at yᵉ back shutters, & when yᵉ syde peeces are made to change by running in groues. the Letters in this are countersigned by those of yᵉ ground platt, and those yᵗ are sett downe & marked in this and not expressed on yᵉ ground platt: are.'

The key reads:

'M: the ground lyne of yᵉ roome

N: yᵉ height of yᵉ stage before & behind

E.O: the Queenes seate drawne vpp to yᵉ height:

F: yᵉ Engyne by which yᵉ Queenes seate was lett vp & downe:

P: The peece of Tymber of yᵉ Engyne of yᵉ Kings seate which was strongly nayled & fastened to yᵉ vpright peece F: so yᵗ both yᵉ King & Queenes seate went in one grooue

The Capstalls for these Engynes were placed in yᵉ vault vnder yᵉ floore of yᵉ roome

Q: yᵉ freese of yᵉ front made to stand sloping

R: The peeces of Clouds which came downe from yᵉ roofe before yᵉ vpper part of yᵉ syde shutters whereby yᵉ grooues aboue were hidden & also yᵉ howse behind them: Then Clouds also went in grooues marked S: & changed with yᵉ sceanes below:

T: The Clouds of yᵉ heaven which went crosse yᵉ sceane & were hung betwixt the Clouds of yᵉ sydes whereby it appeared but one sole heaven

V: the vpper back shutters which were also hung in grooues and changed as yᵉ others did

W: The Capstall which belonged to the Engyne C: by which yᵉ Deityes were lett vpp & Downe it was placed vnder yᵉ stage vppon yᵉ floore of yᵉ Roome

X: braces which held vpp yᵉ Clouds & were fastned to yᵉ roofe of yᵉ sceane

Z: The roofe of yᵉ sceane.'

24 The inscription reads: '3 sceane of mountaynes the way to the seate of Honor K: & Q: masque 1640: a shutter'.

25 The inscription reads: 'raies of tinsell ou[e]r yᵉ Queene.'

27 The inscription reads: 'Releiue [sceane *struck out*] of Deityes belonging to yᵉ sceane of Architecture in yᵉ King and Queenes Masque 1640'.

32 The inscription reads: 'ould habites of yᵉ 3 nationes for yᵉ musicke. they must bee clencante and rich. Inglish & ould.'

43 The length of the dress makes it unlikely that this is a masque costume, but it is the kind of contemporary dress on which masquers' costumes were based.

44 For a discussion of this portrait, see Ben Jonson, *Works*, ed. Herford and Simpson, vii, p. xv.

1 *Oberon.* Scene 1, Rocks. Inigo Jones.

2 *Oberon*. Scene 2, Oberon's Palace. Inigo Jones.

3   *Oberon*. Oberon's Palace in Rocks, another design.
Inigo Jones.

4 *Oberon*. Detail of Oberon's Palace. Inigo Jones.

5 *Oberon.* Three Fays (?). Inigo Jones.

(*a*) One of the nation of Fays (?).

(*b*) Two Fays (?).

6   *Oberon*. Inigo Jones.

(*a*) Two Satyrs.

(*b*) Two sketches for Oberon's head-dress (?).

7   *Oberon*. Inigo Jones.

(a) Oberon (?).

(b) Finished sketch of Oberon
with altered head-dress (?).

8   *Oberon*. Inigo Jones.

9   *Oberon*. Two knights masquers. Inigo Jones.

10 *Love Freed from Ignorance and Folly* (?). Prison or castle gateway and cloud with eleven masquers. Inigo Jones.

(*a*) Entheus or Poetic Fury.

(*b*) A masquer.

11   *The Lords' Masque*. Inigo Jones.

(*a*) A masquer with hair in flames.

(*b*) A page like a fiery spirit.

12   *The Lords' Masque.* Inigo Jones.

13   *The Masque of Flowers*. Kawasha. John White. Engraving from Thomas Hariot, *A Brief and True Report of the New Found Land of Virginia*, Frankfort, 1590.

15 *The Triumph of Peace.* Border of the scene. Inigo Jones. The Royal Institute of British Architects.

16 *The Triumph of Peace*. Scene 1, the Forum of Peace. Inigo Jones.

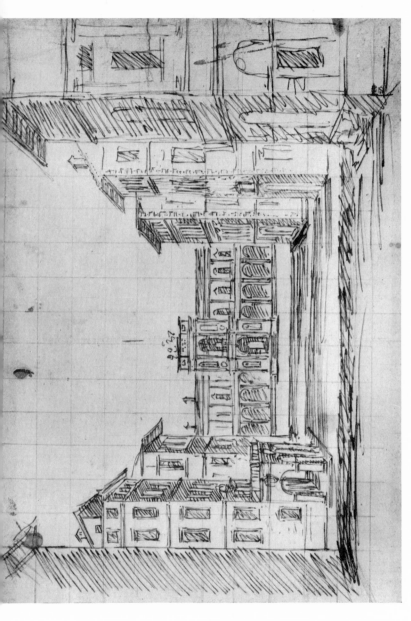

17 *The Triumph of Peace.* Scene 1, the Forum of Peace, another design. Inigo Jones.

(a) Fat Bawd.

(b) Plan for seating masquers.

18   *The Triumph of Peace*. Inigo Jones.

Sketches for head-dresses and masquer.

(*b*) Sketch for masquer with alternative
head-dresses.

19   *The Triumph of Peace*. Inigo Jones.

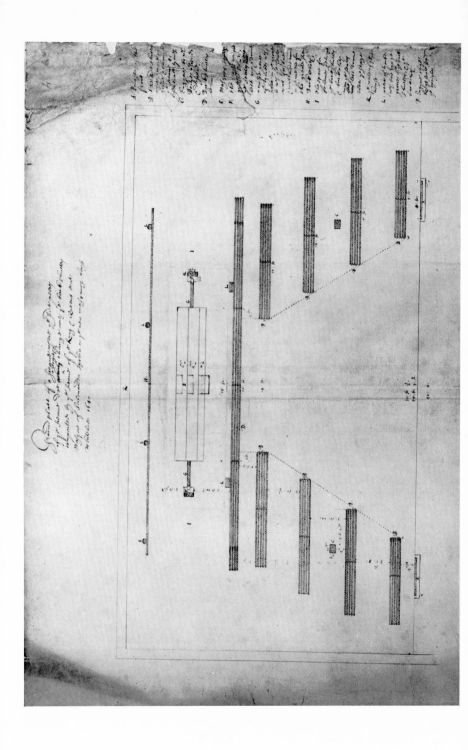

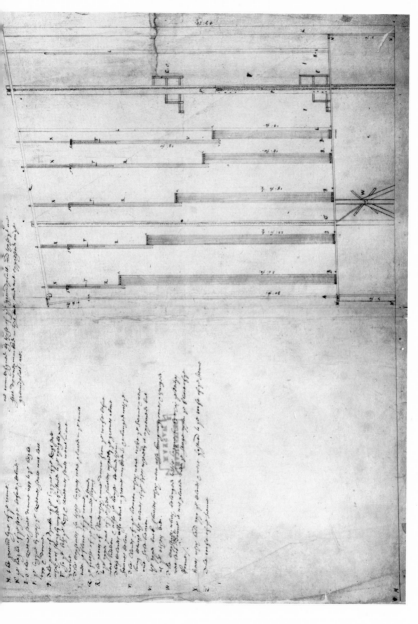

21 *Salmacida Spolia*. Section of the stage and machinery.
John Webb. (On the inscription, see Notes on the Plates, p. xiv.)

23 *Salmacida Spolia.* Scene 2, Landscape with chariot. Inigo Jones.

24 *Salmacida Spolia.* Scene 3, Mountains, the way to the Seat of Honour. Inigo Jones (copy by John Webb).

Salmacida Spolia. The cloud open, disclosing the Queen with nine ladies; below, the
Queen on a throne. Inigo Jones. (On the inscription, see Notes on the Plates, p. xv.)

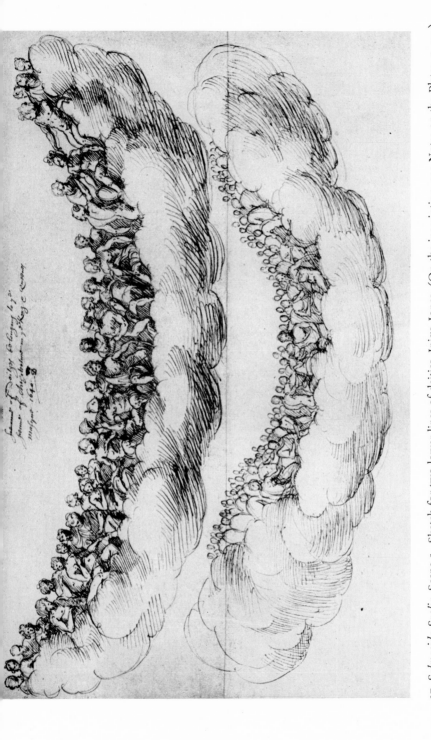

27 *Salmacida Spolia.* Scene 5, Sketch for two lower lines of deities. Inigo Jones. (On the inscription, see Notes on the Plates, p. xv.)

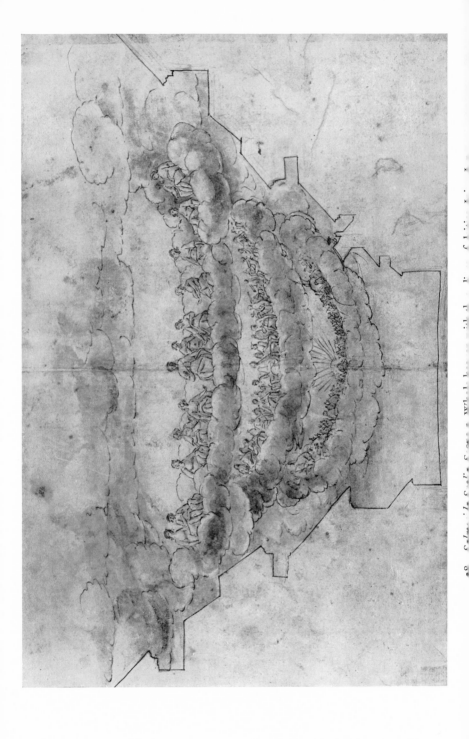

28 Coloni ola Carlo Fanana, Wha't here are mid del and er f limme him i. u.

W.356

29   *Salmacida Spolia.* Two studies of the bridge. Inigo Jones.

(a) Furies.

(b) Head of Fury and man with
cap and turban.

30   *Salmacida Spolia*. Inigo Jones.

31 *Salmacida Spolia*. Two sketches of Wolfgangus Vandergoose. Inigo Jones.

32 *Salmacida Spolia.* Irish, Scottish, and English habits. Inigo Jones. (On the inscription see Notes on the Plates, p. xv.)

33 *Salmacida Spolia.* Two sketches for an old-fashioned Englishwoman. Inigo Jones.

34 *Salmacida Spolia.* Two sketches for grotesques or drollities. Inigo Jones.

(*a*) Doctor Tartaglia and
a Pedant of Francolin.

(*b*) Antique cavaliers.

35   *Salmacida Spolia*. Inigo Jones.

(a) Masquing dress for King Charles I.

(b) The King or a masquer.

36 *Salmacida Spolia*. Inigo Jones.

37 *Salmacida Spolia*. The King or a masquer, two other designs. Inigo Jones.

38 *Salmacida Spolia*. Lady in Amazonian habit, and alternative design. Inigo Jones.

a) King and Queen or masquer and lady.

(*b*) Queen Henrietta Maria, or lady,
in an Amazonian habit.

39   *Salmacida Spolia.* Inigo Jones.

40   Unidentified Designs. Two masquers. Inigo Jones.

41   Unidentified Designs. Two masquers. Inigo Jones.

42   Unidentified Designs. Two lady masquers. Inigo Jones.

43   Portrait of a lady, possibly in masque costume. Sitter and artist unknown.
City Art Gallery, Bristol.

44   Lucy, Countess of Bedford, in masque costume. Marcus Gheerhardts. Woburn Abb

enry Frederick, Prince of Wales,
man costume. Fitzwilliam Museum,
ridge.

(*b*) Unknown lady in masque costume.
Rijksmuseum, Amsterdam.

ueen Anne of Denmark
sque costume. Windsor.

(*d*) Unknown lady in masque costume.
Victoria and Albert Museum.

45   Miniatures. Isaac Oliver.

Errabat focio Mors iuncta cupidine, serum Diuertere simul, simul una nocte cubarunt. Alter enim alteriu male prouida picula sumpsit
Mors pharetra, paruus tela gerebat Amor. Cerus Amor Mors hoc tempore cæca fuit. Mors aurata, tenet osea tela puer. A. aliæ.

ex ginnul. Bonef. *inu. Martin Bril.* *Ioh. Sadler sculp.*

(*a*) Cupid and Death.

(*b*) Cupid, Death, and Reputation.

47   *Cupid and Death*. From J. Ogilby, *Fables of Aesop*, 1651

(*a*) *Cupid and Death.* Death stealing t̄
weapons of Cupid. From Andreas Alc̄
Emblematum Libellus, 1534.

(*b*) *Pleasure Reconciled to Virtue.* Her̄
at the cross-roads. From George Wit̄
A Collection of Emblems, 1635.

48   Emblems.

GENERAL INTRODUCTION

By Gerald Eades Bentley

The Stuart masques, whose performance Allardyce Nicoll has so brilliantly illuminated for us, were enterprises noble in aspiration but all too often ignoble in their accomplishments. Since, in so many of the extant examples, it is easier for the modern reader to perceive the banality of the flattery, the trivial irrelevance of the humour, and the sometimes vulgar display of the spectacle, it is well to begin by noting those basic conceptions which Ben Jonson saw so clearly and often embodied in his masques, but which were more dimly perceived, and seldom realized, by his fellow masque poets.

The high function of the poet which Jonson envisaged, and which is frequently enunciated or implied in his plays, masques, poems, and prose works, is not unfamiliar. One of the better statements of it is that which appears in his *Timber: or Discoveries; Made upon Men and Matter, as they have flowed out of his daily readings, or had their reflux to his peculiar notion of the times.*

I could never think the study of wisdom confined only to the philosopher: or of piety to the divine: or of state to the politic. But that he which can feign a commonwealth (which is the poet) can govern it with counsels, strengthen it with laws, correct it with judgments, inform it with religion, and morals; is all these. We do not require in him mere elocution; or an excellent faculty in verse; but the exact knowledge of all virtues, and their contraries; with ability to render the one loved, the other hated, by his proper embattling them.

(*Ben Jonson*, ed. Herford and Simpson, VIII, 595)

To the reader of criticism this conception of the calling and function of the poet is familiar enough, but it is not always realized that to Jonson this high responsibility applied equally to the poet as masque-maker and to the poet as play-maker. Perhaps his most explicit assertion of his conception of the form of the masque and the task of its maker is the foreword with which he opens the printed text of one of his earliest and best masques, *Hymenaei*, danced on 5 January 1606. This piece had been prepared as a part of King James's celebration of the politically important marriage of the young Earl of Essex to Frances Howard, daughter of the Lord Chamberlain. Union is the theme, and it is characteristic of Jonson at his best that in this creation he carries his idea and its implications far beyond the simple union of the great families of Devereux and Howard.

It is a noble and just advantage that the things subjected to understanding have of those which are objected to sense, that the one sort are but momentary, and merely taking; the other impressing, and lasting: else the glory of all these solemnities had perished like a blaze, and gone out in the beholders' eyes, so short-lived are the bodies of all things, in comparison of their souls. And, though bodies oft-times have the ill luck to be sensually preferred, they find afterwards the good fortune (when souls live) to be utterly forgotten. This it is hath made the most royal princes and greatest persons (who are commonly the personators of these actions) not only studious of riches and magnificence in the outward celebration or show (which rightly becomes them) but curious after the most high and hearty inventions to furnish the inward parts (and those grounded upon antiquity, and solid learnings) which, though their voice be taught to sound to present occasions, their sense or doth or should always lay hold on more removed mysteries. And, howsoever some may squeamishly cry out that all endeavour of learning, and sharpness in these transitory devices, especially where it steps beyond their little or (let me not wrong 'em) no brain at all, is superfluous; I am contented, these fastidious stomachs should leave my full tables, and enjoy at home their clean empty trenchers, fittest for such airy tastes: where perhaps a few Italian herbs, picked up and made into a salad, may find sweeter acceptance than all the most nourishing and sound meats of the world.

For these men's palates, let not me answer, O Muses. It is not my fault if I fill them out nectar, and they run to metheglin.

Vaticana bibant, si delectentur.

All the courtesy I can do them, is to cry, again:

Praetereant, si quid non facit ad stomachum.

As I will, from the thought of them, to my better subject.

(*Ben Jonson*, VII, 209–10)

The composition which follows this introductory statement is a magnificent example of Jonson's deep concern with the soul of the masque and his determination to 'lay hold on more removed mysteries'. Union as he celebrates it here is not simply the union of Robert Devereux and Frances Howard, of two great English families, but the new union of England and Scotland, the union of King James and his kingdom, the cosmic union wrought by the power of love. These complex interrelationships are set forth in the speeches, the songs, the costumes, the carved and painted figures, the host of visual symbols and allusions, the ordering of the spectacle, and, one would assume, in the character of the dances. The intricate and learned developments of these aspects of his theme are impressive achievements of the mature Jonson. They have been thoughtfully analysed by D. J. Gordon in '*Hymenaei*: Ben Jonson's Masque of Union'.[1]

The scope and vigour of imagination, the extensive and gracefully manipulated learning, the implied control over architect, composer, choreographer, actors, and dancers displayed in *Hymenaei* are characteristic of Ben Jonson, but they can scarcely be expected of lesser masque writers. Not only did their performance fall short of his, but we have little evidence that they shared much of his high conception of the possibilities of the form or his insistence that the characters and their significances be 'grounded upon antiquity, and solid learnings'. This foundation of learning is perhaps most fully exhibited in the heavy annotations for the *Masque of Queens*, presented at court on 2 February 1609. Sixteen months later Samuel Daniel published his *Tethys' Festival*, danced on 5 June 1610, as a part of the festivities for the creation of Prince Henry as Prince of Wales. To introduce the descriptions and text of this masque Daniel prepared a 'Preface to the Reader', much of which seems to be a thinly veiled attack on the pretensions of Jonson. After saying that it is expected that he should publish 'a description and form of the late masque', Daniel continues:

which I do not out of a desire to be seen in pamphlets, or of forwardness to show my invention therein: for I thank God, I labour not with that disease of ostentation, nor affect to be known to be the man *digitoque monstrarier hic est*, having my name already wider in this kind than I desire, and more in the wind than I would. Neither do I seek in the

---

[1] *Journal of the Warburg and Courtauld Institutes*, VIII (1945), 107–45.

divulging hereof to give it other colours than those it wore, or to make an apology of what I have done...

And for these figures of mine, if they come not drawn in all proportions to the life of antiquity (from whose tyranny I see no reason why we may not emancipate our inventions, and be as free as they to use our own images) yet I know them such as were proper to the business, and discharged those parts for which they served, with as good correspondency as our appointed limitations would permit.

But in these things wherein the only life consists in show, the art and invention of the architect gives the greatest grace, and is of most importance: ours, the least part and of least note in the time of the performance thereof; and therefore I have interserted the description of the artificial part, which only speaks M. Inigo Jones.

(Grosart edition, III, 305–7)

These testy and pedestrian comments do not reveal the faintest hint of Jonson's high conception of the form and function of the masque, only a jealousy of the man who had propounded them and who had so recently displayed how his ideas were 'drawn in all proportions to the life of antiquity'. Daniel further reveals with commendable frankness his complete subservience to Inigo Jones, a subservience which Jonson saw as the foreshadowing of the decline of the masque. This preface recalls Jonson's remark about the author of *Tethys' Festival*, as recorded by Drummond of Hawthornden, 'Daniel was at jealousies with him'. In the light of Jonson's reiterated assertions of the high and holy function of the poet, the preface also provides grounds for another statement of Jonson's in the *Conversations*, 'Samuel Daniel was a good honest man...but no poet'.[1]

But the 'good honest man', Samuel Daniel, was by no means unique in his failure to appreciate Jonson's conception of the masque. No one else gives lip service to his ideal, and very few ever approach his accomplishment. Jonson's further judgment, recorded by Drummond, is sound, however arrogant: 'that next himself only Fletcher and Chapman could make a masque.' To Drummond, isolated in Edinburgh from the performances of the great court masques, this remark was no doubt simply a further example on which to base his final judgment of his visitor:

[1] *Ben Jonson*, I, 136 and 132.

4

He is a great lover and praiser of himself, a contemner and scorner of others...jealous of every word and action of those about him... thinketh nothing well bot what either he himself, or some of his friends and Countrymen hath said or done. (*Ibid.* 133 and 151)

Jonson's own writings—the 'apologetical dialogue' for his *Poetaster*, for instance—show that Drummond had reason for his estimate of the personality of his guest, yet most of the Jonsonian critical judgments recorded by the Laird of Hawthornden are sound, and as Jonson himself asserted in his pitiful epilogue for *The New Inn* (Blackfriars, January 1629):

> All strength must yield.
> Yet judgment would the last be, i' the field,
> With a true poet.

Yet even Jonson, for all his conviction and his belligerent assertiveness, could not continue to live up to the achievement of his earlier masques like *Hymenaei* and *Lord Haddington's Masque* and *The Masque of Queens*. The pressure of court taste and of his many collaborators in the co-operative enterprise of a great court production was overwhelming. Since his architect was a man of the stature and the great court influence of Inigo Jones, the conflict between the two was inevitable—and so was the victory of Jones. It should not be forgotten, however, as all too often it has been, that it was only after the break with his great architect-collaborator and after the humiliation of the lesser masques that Jonson could say in 'An Expostulation with Inigo Jones':

> O Shows! Shows! Mighty shows!
> The eloquence of masques! What need of prose
> Or verse or sense t' express immortal you?
> You are the spectacles of state! 'Tis true
> Court hieroglyphics! and all arts afford
> In the mere perspective of an inch board!
> You ask no more than certain politic eyes,
> Eyes that can pierce into the mysteries
> Of many colours! read them! and reveal
> Mythology there painted on slit deal!
> Oh, to make boards to speak! There is a task—
> Painting and carpentry are the soul of masque.

> (*Ben Jonson*, VIII, 403–4)

The decline from the assurance and idealism of the foreword for *Hymenaei* to the disillusionment of this poem, written after the performance of *Chloridia* on 22 February 1631, is some measure of the decline of the masque in the intervening quarter of a century: the taste of the Stuart court had discouraged the Jonsonian devotion to the 'more removed mysteries' and it had encouraged the excessive emphasis on the anti-masque and the development of spectacle for its own sake. In any endeavour requiring such complex co-operation of poet, choreographer, composer, and architect—to say nothing of the diverse artists and artisans they directed—a single success is remarkable. That such diverse individualists should go on year after year in a smoothly running hierarchy of authority and functioning in an intriguing and back-biting environment like the court of James I would have been miraculous. Of the minor conflicts we know little; the major clash was that between poet and architect.

Between two such titanic and self-conscious artists as Jonson and Jones, continued harmonious collaboration was surely impossible, even had each been endowed with the disposition of a saint, and neither was—certainly not Jonson. For each man his encompassing idea—invention for Jonson, design for Jones—was of overriding importance, and any deference to the other became a betrayal of his art.[1] The wonder is that they managed to collaborate effectively for so long as they did. By the beginning of the reign of Charles I, spectacle is usually dominant, as it had often been in the non-Jonsonian masques (such as Campion's *Lords' Masque*, 1613).

But equally conspicuous in the decline of the masque from Jonson's austere ideal is the burgeoning of the anti-masque. The form itself was not ill conceived; Jonson had used it effectively and harmoniously, and he had pointed out how it should function in the foreword for his *Masque of Queens* (2 February 1609):

It increasing, now, to the third time of my being used in these services to her Majesty's personal presentations, with the ladies whom she pleaseth to honour; it was my first and special regard, to see that the nobility of the invention should be answerable to the dignity of their persons. For which

---

[1] See D. J. Gordon, 'Poet and Architect: The Intellectual Setting of the Quarrel between Ben Jonson and Inigo Jones', *Journal of the Warburg and Courtauld Institutes*, XII (1949), 152–78.

reason, I chose the argument to be *A Celebration of honourable and true Fame, bred out of Virtue*: observing that rule of the best artist, to suffer no object of delight to pass without his mixture of profit and example.

And because her Majesty (best knowing that a principal part of life in these spectacles lay in their variety) had commanded me to think on some dance or show that might precede hers, and have the place of a foil, or false-masque; I was careful to decline not only from others, but mine own steps in that kind, since the last year I had an anti-masque of boys [*Lord Haddington's Masque*]: and therefore, now, devised that twelve women in the habits of hags, or witches, sustaining the persons of Ignorance, Suspicion, Credulity, etc. the opposites to good fame, should fill that part; not as a masque, but a spectacle of strangeness, producing multiplicity of gesture, and not unaptly sorting with the current, and whole fall of the device. *(Ben Jonson*, VII, 282)

Jonson's conception of this preliminary 'spectacle of strangeness' as a closely related introduction and contrast for the main entry of the masquers is dramatically sound, especially in a genre in which visual and aural impressions are even more important than they are in plays. Queen Anne was quite right in her implied perception that 'the nobility of the invention' and 'the dignity of their persons' could well make a masque too uniformly solemn, and she was well advised in her request for a 'foil, or false-masque' because 'a principal part of life in these spectacles lay in their variety'. Jonson's response in the *Masque of Queens* is an excellent example of what can be done with the device; not only do the twelve witches of his anti-masque display qualities antithetical to those virtues which are to follow, but their background, their costumes, their music, their words, and their actions, while all carefully based on the literature of witchcraft, are meticulously planned to present detailed contrasts to the appearance and actions of Queen Anne and the eleven ladies of the main masque which is to follow. Jonson describes the entry:

...that which presented itself was an ugly Hell which, flaming beneath, smoked unto the top of the roof. And, in respect all evils are (morally) said to come from Hell;...these witches, with a kind of hollow and infernal music, came forth from thence. First one, then two, and three, and more, till their number increased to eleven; all differently attired; some with rats on their heads; some, on their shoulders; others with

7

ointment-pots at their girdles; all with spindles, timbrels, rattles, or other venefical instruments, making a confused noise, with strange gestures.

(*Ibid.* 282–3)

After the chanting of their ninth charm, the witches dance, and the descriptions of their actions show how all aspects of the performance—choreography as well as verse, costume, music, spectacle —were controlled in accordance with Jonson's invention:

At which, with a strange and sudden music, they fell into a magical dance, full of preposterous change and gesticulation, but most applying to their property: who, at their meetings, do all things contrary to the custom of men, dancing back to back, hip to hip, their hands joined, and making their circles backward, to the left hand, with strange fantastic motions of their heads and bodies. All which were excellently imitated by the maker of the dance, Mr Hierome Herne, whose right it is here to be named.

(*Ibid.* 301)

Clearly, an anti-masque handled with such scrupulous regard to the main invention served to enhance the beauty of the spectacle and to emphasize the idea of the whole. At his best, Jonson was fertile in creating anti-masques and very skilful in ordering them. But the anti-masque had a fatal appeal to those barren spectators who were often prominent at court. They could scarcely be expected to repress their enthusiasm when their royal master so conspicuously exhibited his own taste. In *The Masque of the Inner Temple and Gray's Inn*, danced on 20 February 1613 as part of the celebrations for the wedding of Princess Elizabeth and the Count Palatine, the second anti-masque consisted of 'a Pedant, May Lord, May Lady, Servingman, Chambermaid, A Country Clown or Shepherd, Country Wench, an Host, Hostess, a He-baboon, She-baboon, a He-fool, She-fool, ushering them in'. This interlude was so taking that 'It pleased his Majesty to call for it again at the end, as he did likewise for the first anti-masque, but one of the Statues by that time was undressed' (p. 139 below). Even more emphatic was the King's expression of approval after *The Masque of Flowers*, presented at Whitehall by the gentlemen of Gray's Inn on Twelfth Night of the following year:

The masque ended, it pleased his Majesty to call for the antic-masque of song and dance, which was again presented; and then the Masquers uncovered their faces, and came up to the state, and kissed the King and Queen and Prince's hand with a great deal of grace and favour, and so were invited to the banquet (p. 171 below).

No more conspicuous advertising of the royal taste could be devised than the King's condescension to the Barber, the Pedlar, the Brewer, the Midwife, the Roaring Boy, the Bawd, the Chimney Sweeper, and the other characters of these two anti-masques from Gray's Inn. It can be no surprise that the writers and producers for the court took note and developed the anti-masque element; in subsequent masques this feature becomes longer and more irrelevant. Ben Jonson himself tended to elaborate the anti-masque in *Love Restored* (6 January 1612), *The Irish Masque* (29 December 1613), and *Mercury Vindicated from the Alchemists at Court* (6 January 1616). Orazio Busino's long description (pp. 232–4 below) of the performance of *Pleasure Reconciled to Virtue* (6 January 1618) not only shows that the comic preliminaries—including the two anti-masque dances—were extensive, but also indicates how much more elaborate the action was than the text suggests. Jonson's own attitude toward the degeneration to which he was contributing is to be seen in *Pan's Anniversary or the Shepherd's Holiday* (19 June[?] 1620). Here the Fencer has had the Tinker, the Mouse-trap Man, the Bellows Mender, the Toothdrawer, and the others dance their anti-masque in the revealed presence of the masquers above the Fountain of Light. After the dance he asks the Old Shepherd, 'How like you this, Shepherd? Was not this gear gotten on a holy-day?' And the Old Shepherd replies: 'Faith, your folly may deserve pardon, because it hath delighted: but beware of presuming, or how you offer comparison with persons so near the deities.'[1]

By the time of his *Masque of Augurs* (6 January 1622) Jonson seems resigned to the exaggerated and extraneous development of the anti-masque. Here Van-goose, 'the Projector of Masques', announces that

. . .me vould bring in some dainty new ting, dat never vas, nor never sall be in de *rebus natura*; dat has neder van de *materia*, nor de *forma*, nor de hossen, nor de voot but [is] a *mera devisa* of de brain,

[1] *Ben Jonson*, VII, 534.

9

and his device is the bear-ward, John Urson, and his three dancing bears. When the Groom of the Revels protests 'but what has all this to do with our masque?' Van-goose replies:

O Sir, all de better, vor an antic-masque, de more absurd it be, and vrom de purpose, it be ever all de better. If it go from de *Nature* of de ting, it is de more *Art*: for deare is *Art*, and deare is *Nature* yow sall see. *Hochos-pochos, Paucos Palabros.* (*Ben Jonson*, VII, 633 and 638)

Jonson's most extensive development of the anti-masque is in *The Gypsies Metamorphosed*, written for performance at Buckingham's seat at Burley-on-the-Hill on 3 August 1621, and twice repeated elsewhere. Here the anti-masque runs for more than forty pages, and the masquers proper are merely the anti-masquers with their faces washed. It can be argued, indeed, that *The Gypsies Metamorphosed* is scarcely a proper masque at all, since there is no set construction, scarcely any plot, and the cast consisted mostly of Buckingham's family, friends, and servants welcoming the visiting King and court. Yet the piece is eloquent testimony of the strong appeal of the anti-masque, for the number of extant texts, quotations, and allusions surpasses those for any other masque except Shirley's *The Triumph of Peace.*[1]

This masque of Shirley's, given by all four Inns of Court at Whitehall on 3 February 1634, was a very special occasion, widely advertised by a splendid procession through the streets of the city, and the large number of texts and references[2] testifies to the magnificence of the occasion and the procession as well as to the appeal of the masque itself. With all its dazzling effects both at Whitehall and in the London streets, *The Triumph of Peace* nonetheless illustrates the dominance of the anti-masque almost as fully as does *The Gypsies Metamorphosed*. Near the beginning Shirley makes his apologies in the dialogue of the ridiculous Fancy, Opinion, Jollity, and Laughter:

> *Fancy.* How many Anti-masques ha' they? Of what nature?
> For these are fancies that take most; your dull
> And phlegmatic inventions are exploded;
> Give me a nimble Anti-masque.
> *Opinion.* They have none, sir.

[1] See G. E. Bentley, *Jacobean and Caroline Stage*, IV, 645–7. [2] See *ibid.* V, 1154–63.

Laughter. No Anti-masque? I'd laugh at that, i' faith.
Jollity. What make we here? No jollity?
Fancy.   No Anti-masque!
  Bid 'em down with the Scene, and sell the timber,
  Send Jupiter to grass, and bid Apollo
  Keep cows again, take all their gods and goddesses
  (For these must farce up this night's entertainment),
  And pray the Court may have some mercy on 'em,
  They will be jeer'd to death else for their ignorance.
  The soul of wit moves here, yet there be some,
  If my intelligence fail not, mean to show
  Themselves jeer-majors; some tall critics have
  Planted artillery and wit-murderers.
  No Anti-masque! Let 'em look to't.   (p. 288 below)

To remedy this scandalous situation these presenters themselves perform the first anti-masque, and before the evening is over the court has been treated to a variety of different examples of the popular form, including those of the Presenters; the Tavern Folk; the Projectors; the Birds, Robbed Merchants, Nymphs and Satyrs, and Huntsmen; and the Windmill, Knight, Squire, Country Gentleman, and Bowlers. Finally, between the main masque and the final revels with the ladies, there is yet another anti-masque, of the Carpenter, Painter, Black Guard, Tailor, Tailor's Wife, Embroiderer's Wife, Feathermaker's Wife, and the Property Man's Wife.

In this most popular production the number and extent of the anti-masques are not only excessive, but most of them are barely relevant to the main idea. Jonson's insistence on the unity of the form and the dignity of the occasion has been lightly rejected.

The final production in the great series of Stuart court masques was William Davenant's *Salmacida Spolia*, danced on 21 January 1640, with the King appearing as the leader of the gentlemen masquers and Queen Henrietta Maria as the leader of the ladies. The social milieu of the occasion has been beautifully sketched by Miss C. V. Wedgwood in her essay, 'The Last Masque'.[1]

The masque itself, though entertaining and spectacular, is witness to the degeneration of the form. It could be said that *Salmacida*

---

[1] *Truth and Opinion* (1960), pp. 143–55.

Spolia has only two anti-masques, but the second has twenty different entries, and Davenant seems to treat each as a separate anti-masque, though their significance can seldom be deduced from the text. The spectacle is elaborate, with six or seven different sets or flying entries, and Davenant gives full credit for the whole conception to Jones: 'The invention, ornament, scenes, and apparitions with their descriptions, were made by Inigo Jones, Surveyor General of his Majesty's Works.' The work of the poet, which Jonson conceived of so highly, is here indicated by the modest sentence: 'What was spoken or sung, by William Davenant, her Majesty's Servant', with a final acknowledgment: 'The subject was set down by them both.'

So declined the great court masques, from Jonson's earlier master-pieces, which were

not only studious of riches and magnificence in the outward celebration or show, (which rightly becomes them) but curious after the most high and hearty inventions to furnish the inward parts (and those grounded upon antiquity, and solid learnings) which, though their voice be taught to sound to present occasions, their sense or doth or should always lay hold on more removed mysteries,

to those masques which delighted the cavaliers of Charles I, shows made up of funny but barely relevant variety turns combined with the astonishing spectacles of Inigo Jones and his ingenious carpenters.

*   *   *

The great splendour and expense of the Jacobean and Caroline court masques has sometimes led to the assumption that masques were rare. They were not. In the reigns of the first two Stuart sovereigns more than a hundred masque performances are recorded, and probably at least ninety different examples are involved. The difference between the small number of masques familiar to most readers and the rather large number written is, of course, largely a result of the indifference of the stationers: Shirley's *The Triumph of Peace* is really the only example of the form in which the printers seem to have shown much active interest; many of the occasions on which a masque is known to have been produced are now represented by no extant text.

A number of even the great court masques are lost: the 'Masque of Lords' presented at court on 1 January 1604 and the 'Masque of Scots' danced there on Twelfth Night following;[1] the masque for the wedding of Sir Philip Herbert and Lady Susan de Vere on 27 December 1604[2] and the masque for the wedding of Sir John Villiers and Lady Frances Coke at Hampton Court on 29 September 1617;[3] the masque at Hampton Court on 6 January 1621, in which a Puritan was ridiculed;[4] and Queen Henrietta Maria's masque at Denmark House on 14 January 1627[5] are examples of such lost court masques.

When we have no texts for well publicized court spectacles like these, it is not surprising that most of the masques presented in noble houses or in the halls of wealthy City companies have disappeared. Besides the few that are extant, there were many others for which we know only the occasion and sometimes a comment or two. On 3 January 1620 a number of English noblemen and gentlemen presented a lost masque at the house of the French Ambassador in London.[6] A year later, on 8 January 1621, a lost masque in honour of the French Ambassador was presented before the King and Queen at the house of Viscount Doncaster.[7] There are various records of the masque by John Maynard presented by Buckingham at York House before the King, Prince, and Spanish Ambassador on 18 November 1623, but no text has survived.[8] Another of the Duke of Buckingham's elaborate entertainments at York House included a masque on 5 November 1626 for the King and Queen and the French Ambassador, Bassompierre, but though the occasion is variously recorded, no text has been preserved.[9] On 12 January 1632 Lord Goring also presented to the Queen a masque, perhaps by William Davenant, but no text survives.[10]

---

[1] Unpublished Office of the Works Accounts E 351/3239.
[2] Reyher, *Les Masques Anglais*, p. 519.
[3] John Campbell, *Lives of the Chief Justices of England* (1874 ed.), I, 311.
[4] Chamberlain, *Letters*, II, 333 and *Finetti Philoxenis*, pp. 67–71.
[5] *C.S.P. Venetian*, XX (1626–8), 107. [6] Chamberlain, *Letters*, II, 282.
[7] *Ibid.* I, 333–4. [8] *Jacobean and Caroline Stage*, IV, 842–3.
[9] Thomas Birch, *Court and Times of Charles I*, I, 166.
[10] *Shakespeare Survey*, XI (1958), 108.

Masques were occasionally given in the great halls of wealthy City companies, but the texts have usually disappeared. Shirley's *The Triumph of Peace*, though planned by the lawyers for display at Whitehall, had another performance in the presence of the King and Queen in the Merchant Taylors' Hall in the City on 13 February 1634, but the tremendous public interest in this masque[1] brought about its publication even before the presentation for the Merchant Taylors and their guests. Other masques staged in their hall are lost: Middleton's *Masque of Cupid* for the wedding of the Earl of Somerset, performed there on 4 January 1614, is known only from allusions and City accounts.[2] John Chamberlain writes of another such occasion when, on 20 April 1619, the artillery company presented there 'a warlike dance or masque of twelve men in complete armour'.[3]

In these three categories of Jacobean and Caroline masques we probably have a fairly good survival rate (better than that for plays), though there may well be a number of lost ones to which we have no reference at all, or which are obscured under the blanket payments in the accounts in the Office of the Works. Much more obscure are the provincial masques, most of which have disappeared. A few texts for these country performances we do have, like that for Campion's masque given by 'the Lord Knowles, at Cawsome-House near Reading' for Queen Anne on 27 April 1613; and the very well-known texts for Jonson's *The Gypsies Metamorphosed* given for the King and Court at Burley-on-the-Hill and at Belvoir on 3 and 5 August 1621[4] and for *Comus* at Ludlow Castle on 29 September 1634.[5] But many other texts for such provincial occasions are lost. Examples are the masque presented by the Queen for Prince Henry at Winchester in late September or early October 1603;[6] the masque of Noblemen, Knights, Gentlemen, and Courtiers with which Nicholas Assheton says that the King was entertained at Houghton Tower in Lancashire, on 17 August 1617;[7] and 'the running masque [which] ranges all over the country' near Newmarket in early

[1] See *Jacobean and Caroline Stage*, v, 1154–63.
[2] E. K. Chambers, *Elizabethan Stage*, III, 442–3.
[3] Chamberlain, *Letters*, II, 233.
[4] *Jacobean and Caroline Stage*, IV, 645–7.　　　[5] *Ibid.* IV, 913–16.
[6] Nichols, *Progresses of King James*, I, 291.
[7] Chetham Society, Series I, vol. 14, 42–5.

February 1620;[1] the masque prepared by the daughters of Sir John Crofts at Saxham Parva near Bury St Edmunds for the court on 17 February 1620;[2] another masque by the same young ladies at the same place in mid-December 1621;[3] and the masque in which Queen Henrietta Maria danced and 'which was arranged and studied by her Majesty for this purpose in a country village, a pleasure resort not far from this city', in late September or early October 1632.[4]

Finally, one wonders how many dedicatory occasions were celebrated by masques now unknown, masques like Sir Francis Kynaston's *Corona Minervae*, presented before the royal children on 27 February 1636 for the opening of his college in Covent Garden.[5] The form—except for its expense—seems well suited to such inaugural ceremonies.

When considering the masque, therefore , it is well to bear in mind the fact that in the reigns of James I and Charles I the form was not rare; that masques were presented at court before the sovereign nearly every year, and sometimes twice or thrice a year; that masques for special entertainments at noble houses in London were not unusual; and that masques were presented at the great country seats probably much more often than the extant records of the occasions can now show.

[1] *Jacobean and Caroline Stage*, v, 1404.
[2] Chamberlain, *Letters*, II, 288.   [3] *Ibid.* 417.
[4] *C.S.P. Venetian*, XXIII (1632–6), 15–16.
[5] *Jacobean and Caroline Stage*, IV, 716–17.

THE VISION OF THE TWELVE GODDESSES

BY SAMUEL DANIEL

Edited by Joan Rees

INTRODUCTION

Jonson's gifts as a deviser of royal entertainments had already been demonstrated at Althorpe in the summer of 1603, but it was nevertheless Samuel Daniel who was chosen to provide the Queen's masque for the first Stuart Christmas in England. Court patronage was not new to Daniel, for Elizabeth had favoured him; but his life hitherto had been a private one, passed, after three years at Oxford, in the households of noble and distinguished patrons and employed, so far as appears, in tutoring and writing and collecting material for his historical poem, *The Civil Wars between the Houses of Lancaster and York*. From the time of the production of *The Vision of the Twelve Goddesses* onwards, however, he was closely associated with the Court and became a much more public figure. He wrote two pastoral plays for Queen Anne and was commissioned by her to provide a second masque in 1610 to celebrate the important occasion of Prince Henry's creation as Prince of Wales. He became licenser for the Children of the Queen's Revels and made a bid for success in the theatre with a refurbished version of his closet-drama, *Cleopatra*, and another play, *Philotas*. *Philotas*, indeed, in 1605, focused an unwelcome and even dangerous attention upon him, for he was suspected of having used the old story as a cover for critical comments on the Essex affair, but his credit at Court was good enough to enable him to ride out the storm. He died in October 1619 at the age of 57, having spent his last years working, under Anne's patronage, on a prose history of England.

Though Daniel enjoyed the Queen's favour and kept it until her death, it is probable that he had hoped initially to capture the interest of the King and to be employed on weightier matters. In 1603 he composed a *Panegyric Congratulatory* to be read to James on his progress south and in this poem he offered the new sovereign the benefit of his reflexions on statecraft based on his historical studies and also on his own deeply pondered experience of men and affairs. It was as a student of the arts of government both in their historical and their moral aspects that he primarily wished to present himself

2-2

to James; and he could justly claim this character, for his literary career as a whole shows a naturally sober and thoughtful mind turning increasingly in maturity to serious contemplation of the chequered pattern of human experience, past and present, and growing less and less interested in the play of fancy and the creation of beautiful trivia. It was inevitable that when called upon to prepare a masque for the new Court his mind should dwell upon the historic quality of the occasion and that he should conceive his task as being, above all, to contribute to state and greatness, to make, as he puts it, a 'hieroglyphic of empire and dominion'. He chose the theme as a corollary to his *Panegyric*: 'to present the figure of those blessings, with the wish of their increase and continuance, which this mighty kingdom now enjoys by the benefit of his most gracious Majesty, by whom we have this glory of peace with the accession of so great state and power.' It follows that his goddesses have political significances, his Graces have a strong sense of social duty, the music of the masque is emblematic of the concord of the united kingdom now become 'the land of civil music and of rest', and the final word is a prayer that the 'real' effects of the blessings only 'represented' in the masque will be vouchsafed to king and kingdom.

Historians of the masque dismiss *The Vision of the Twelve Goddesses* as old-fashioned and unimaginative in its structure and handling, and derogatory criticism in his own day stung Daniel to sharp retort. The flexibility, variety, and inventiveness of the Jonsonian masque are not to be found here and Daniel's work in no way anticipates the delicately poised and sophisticated artistry which other men were to create so soon after. Yet Daniel cannot be said to fail in what he sets out to do. He had in his youth been deeply interested in emblem literature and the art of visual representation of ideas, and this is the only possibility of the masque form which he cares to exploit. The action of the *Vision* is little more than a procession of 'devices' with the 'mot' spoken—for convenience—by the Sibyl, before their entry. His intention is simply to present the 'figures' of his ideas and to allow at the same time for the provision of the spectacle, music and dancing expected in shows of this nature. For the rest he has little interest in tilling what in 1595 he described as

imaginary ground
Of hungry shadows, which no profit breed;
Whence, music-like, instant delight may grow;
Yet, when men all do know, they nothing know.

So uninterested was he in the cultivation of the masque as a literary
form capable of new and rewarding development, that when in
Tethys' Festival, his second masque, he uses the term antemasque,
it may be that he is deliberately rejecting the Jonsonian anti-masque,
but it is equally likely that he is simply unacquainted with the
meaning of this new word. Only once do the magic and mystery of
the finer spirit of the masque really touch him and here the note he
strikes is a characteristically deep one:

Are they shadows that we see?
And can shadows pleasure give?
Pleasures only shadows be
Cast by bodies we conceive,
And are made the things we deem,
In those figures which they seem.
But these pleasures vanish fast,
Which by shadows are exprest:
Pleasures are not if they last,
In their passing is their best.
Glory is most bright and gay
In a flash and so away.
Feed apace then greedy eyes
On the wonder you behold.
Take it sudden as it flies
Though you take it not to hold:
When your eyes have done their part,
Thought must length it in the heart.

This is from *Tethys' Festival*. In *The Vision of the Twelve
Goddesses* the verse is serviceable but scarcely appealing, though the
songs of the Graces have some charm. When he wrote his earliest
poetry, the sonnet sequence *Delia* and the narrative *Rosamond*,
Daniel was a very considerable lyric poet, a master of beautiful
verbal harmonies, and *Hymen's Triumph*, as late as 1615, proves that

the gift remained with him; but in his middle years lyric was in general subordinated to substance, and in *The Vision of the Twelve Goddesses* musical effect is left almost entirely to the musicians while Daniel pursues his serious allegory of state.

The Countess of Bedford had recommended Daniel's services to the Queen and the published masque is dedicated to her in an epistle which contains a useful description of the actual performance on 8 January 1604. Supplementary detail is provided in a lively account of the proceedings by that invaluable correspondent, Sir Dudley Carleton. The scene was the Great Hall at Hampton Court, Christmas being celebrated there because of an outbreak of the plague in London. The old system of dispersed setting was used, with Sleep's cave and the Temple of Peace at one end of the hall and the mountain at the other. This kind of arrangement inevitably took up a good deal of room, with a consequent reduction of the number of spectators, and it was soon abandoned, though Daniel used it again for *Tethys' Festival*. The dresses, for which Queen Elizabeth's wardrobe was drawn upon, were splendid and the jewels most costly, and altogether as spectacle it seems to have been a great success. The munificence with which it was presented and the majesty before which it was performed gave it an importance the political aspects of which the French and Spanish ambassadors realized as keenly as Daniel, and their wrangles over invitations were rather more spirited on this occasion than usual. With its close reference to state for the satisfaction of the stronger minds and its provision of spectacle to gratify a more frivolous appetite for novelty and display it fulfilled all that, as Daniel understood it, could reasonably be expected of a masque. Others were to reveal further possibilities, and the attitudes expressed in Daniel's dedication to Lady Bedford contrast very sharply with those of Jonson in particular and of the others, poets, artists, musicians, architects, who combined under James to make a brief golden age of sister arts. When Daniel wrote *The Vision of the Twelve Goddesses* the masque had not yet flowered. What he himself achieved in the *Vision* perhaps deserves no other reproach than that it is merely adequate. But his critical comments and his attitude to his work have implications beyond the immediate subject, and at the heart of them is some deep-seated lack of confidence in the imagination itself, a rationalizing tendency which leads him to reject in anticipation all the 'unprofitable' beauty so soon to be created. For him the splendid subtleties of the masque are but shadows of a shadow, a dream of a dream, and—the voice of disenchantment at the brilliant and fragile and swiftly passing show—'better dream asleep, than dream awake'.

[DRAMATIS PERSONAE

Night
Somnus, *her Son*
A Sibylla
Iris
The Three Graces
Juno
Pallas
Venus
Vesta
Diana
Proserpina
Macaria
Concordia
Astraea
Flora
Ceres
Tethys

} The Masquers

Torchbearers and Musicians]

THE VISION OF THE TWELVE
GODDESSES

presented in a Masque,
the eighth of January, at Hampton Court:
by the Queen's most excellent Majesty,
and her Ladies.

*   *   *

To the Right Honourable the Lady Lucy,
Countess of Bedford

Madam,

In respect of the unmannerly presumption of an indiscreet printer, who
without warrant hath divulged the late show at Court, presented the 5
eighth of January, by the Queen's Majesty and her Ladies, and the same
very disorderly set forth: I thought it not amiss, seeing it would otherwise
pass abroad to the prejudice both of the masque and the invention, to
describe the whole form thereof in all points as it was then performed, and
as the world well knows very worthily performed, by a most magnificent 10
Queen, whose heroical spirit and bounty only gave it so fair an execution
as it had. Seeing also that these ornaments and delights of peace are in
their season as fit to entertain the world and deserve to be made memorable
as well as graver actions, both of them concurring to the decking and
furnishing of glory and majesty as the necessary complements requisite 15
for state and greatness.

And therefore first I will deliver the intent and scope of the project:
which was only to present the figure of those blessings, with the wish of
their increase and continuance, which this mighty kingdom now enjoys
by the benefit of his most gracious Majesty, by whom we have this glory 20
of peace, with the accession of so great state and power. And to express
the same, there were devised twelve Goddesses, under whose images
former times have represented the several gifts of heaven, and erected
temples, altars and figures unto them, as unto divine powers, in the shape

and name of women. As unto Juno, the Goddess of empire and *regnorum* 25
praesidi, they attributed that blessing of power: to Pallas, wisdom and
defence: to Venus, love and amity: to Vesta, religion: to Diana, the gift
of chastity: to Proserpina, riches: to Macaria, felicity: to Concordia, the
union of hearts: Astraea, justice: Flora, the beauties of the earth: Ceres,
plenty: to Tethys, power by sea.   30

And though these images have oftentimes divers significations, yet it
being not our purpose to represent them with all those curious and
superfluous observations, we took them only to serve as hieroglyphics for
our present intention, according to some one property that fitted our
occasion, without observing other their mystical interpretations, wherein 35
the authors themselves are so irregular and confused as the best mytho-
logers, who will make somewhat to seem anything, are so unfaithful to
themselves as they have left us no certain way at all, but a tract of confusion to take our course at adventure. And, therefore, owing no homage
to their intricate observations, we were left at liberty to take no other 40
knowledge of them than fitted our present purpose nor were tied by any
laws of heraldry to range them otherwise in their precedencies than they
fell out to stand with the nature of the matter in hand. And in these cases
it may well seem *ingenerosum sapere solum ex commentariis quasi maiorum
inventa industriae nostrae viam precluserint, quasi in nobis effoeta sit vis* 45
naturae, nihil ex se parere, or that there can be nothing done authentical
unless we observe all the strict rules of the book.

And therefore we took their aptest representations that lay best and
easiest for us. And first presented the hieroglyphic of empire and dominion,
as the ground and matter whereon this glory of state is built. Then those 50
blessings and beauties that preserve and adorn it: as armed policy, love,
religion, chastity, wealth, happiness, concord, justice, flourishing seasons,
plenty: and lastly power by sea, as to imbound and circle this greatness of
dominion by land.

And to this purpose were these Goddesses thus presented in their 55
proper and several attires, bringing in their hands the particular figures of
their power which they gave to the Temple of Peace, erected upon four
pillars, representing the four Virtues that supported a globe of the earth.

I

First Juno, in a sky-colour mantle embroidered with gold and figured 60
with peacocks' feathers, wearing a crown of gold on her head, presents a
sceptre.

2

Pallas (which was the person her Majesty chose to represent) was attired in
a blue mantle with a silver embroidery of all weapons and engines of war, 65
with a helmet-dressing on her head, and presents a lance and target.

3

Venus, in a mantle of dove-colour and silver embroidered with doves,
presented (instead of her *cestus*, the girdle of amity) a scarf of divers
colours.   70

4

Vesta, in a white mantle embroidered with gold-flames, with a dressing
like a nun, presented a burning lamp in one hand, and a book in the other.

5

Diana, in a green mantle embroidered with silver half moons and a 75
croissant of pearl on her head, presents a bow and a quiver.

6

Proserpina, in a black mantle embroidered with gold-flames, with a crown
of gold on her head, presented a mine of gold ore.

7   80

Macaria, the Goddess of felicity, in a mantle of purple and silver embroidered with the figures of Plenty and Wisdom (which concur to the
making of true happiness), presents a caduceum with the figure of
Abundance.

8   85

Concordia, in a parti-coloured mantle of crimson and white (the colours
of England and Scotland joined) embroidered with silver hands in hand,
with a dressing likewise of parti-coloured roses, a branch whereof in a
wreath or knot she presented.

9   90

Astraea, in a mantle crimson with a silver embroidery, figuring the sword
and balance as the characters of justice, which she represented.

10

Flora, in a mantle of divers colours embroidered with all sorts of flowers,
presents a pot of flowers.   95

27

11

Ceres, in straw colour and silver embroidery with ears of corn and a dressing of the same, presents a sickle.

12

Tethys, in a mantle of sea-green, with a silver embroidery of waves and a 10 dressing of reeds, presents a trident.

Now for the introducing this show: It was devised that the Night, represented in a black vesture set with stars, should arise from below and come towards the upper end of the hall, there to waken her son, Somnus, sleeping in his cave, as the proëm to the vision. Which figures when they 10 are thus presented in human bodies, as all virtues, vices, passions, knowledges and whatsoever abstracts else in imagination are, which we would make visible, we produce them using human actions, and even sleep itself (which might seem improperly to exercise waking motions) hath been often shewed us in that manner, with speech and gesture. As for 11 example:

> *Excussit tandem sibi se; cubitoque levatus*
> *Quid veniat (cognovit enim) scitatur.*

> *Intanto sopravenne, e gli occhi chiuse*
> *A i Signori, ed a i sergenti il pigro Sonno.*　　　　　11

And in another place:
> *Il Sonno viene, e sparso il corpo stanco*
> *Col ramo intriso nel liquor di Lethe.*

So there Sleep is brought in as a body, using speech and motion: and it was no more improper in this form to make him walk and stand or speak 12 than it is to give voice or passion to dead men, ghosts, trees and stones: and therefore in such matters of shows, these like characters (in what form soever they be drawn) serve us but to read the intention of what we would represent: as in this project of ours, Night and Sleep were to produce a vision, an effect proper to their power and fit to shadow our purpose, for 12 that these apparitions and shows are but as imaginations and dreams that portend our affections, and dreams are never in all points agreeing right with waking actions: and therefore were they aptest to shadow whatsoever error might be herein presented. And therefore was Sleep (as he is described by Philostratus in *Amphiarai imagine*) apparelled in a white thin 13 vesture cast over a black, to signify both the day and the night, with wings of the same colour, a garland of poppy on his head and, instead of his ivory and transparent horn, he was shewed bearing a black wand in the

28

left hand and a white in the other to effect either confused or significant
dreams, according to that invocation of Statius: 135

> *Nec te totas infundere pennas*
> *Luminibus compello meis, hoc turba precatur*
> *Laetior, extremo me tange cacumine virgae.*

And also agreeing to that of Silius Italicus:

> *... Tangens Lethaea tempora virga.*   140

And in this action did he here use his white wand as to infuse significant
visions to entertain the spectators and so made them seem to see there a
temple with a Sibylla therein attending upon the sacrifices; which done,
Iris (the messenger of Juno) descends from the top of a mountain raised
at the lower end of the hall, and marching up to the Temple of Peace,   145
gives notice to the Sibylla of the coming of the Goddesses and withal
delivers her a prospective wherein she might behold the figures of their
deities and thereby describe them; to the end that at their descending
there might be no stay or hindrance of their motion which was to be
carried without any interruption to the action of other entertainments   150
that were to depend one of another, during the whole show, and that
the eyes of the spectators might not beguile their ears, as in such cases it
ever happens, whiles the pomp and splendour of the sight takes up all the
intention without regard what is spoken; and therefore was it thought
fit their descriptions should be delivered by the Sibylla.   155

Which as soon as she had ended, the three Graces in silver robes with
white torches appeared on the top of the mountain, descending hand in
hand before the Goddesses; who likewise followed three and three, as in a
number dedicated unto sanctity and an incorporeal nature, whereas the
dual, *Hierogliphicè pro immundis accipitur*. And between every rank of   160
Goddesses marched three torch-bearers in the like several colours, their
heads and robes all decked with stars and in their descending the cornets
sitting in the concaves of the mountain and seen but to their breasts in the
habit of satyrs sounded a stately march which continued until the Goddesses were approached just before the temple and then ceased, when the   165
consort music (placed in the cupola thereof, out of sight) began: where-
unto the three Graces, retiring themselves aside, sang whiles the Goddesses
one after another with solemn pace ascended up into the temple and
delivering their presents to the Sibylla (as it were but in passing by)
returned down into the midst of the hall, preparing themselves to their   170
dance, which, as soon as the Graces had ended their song, they began to
the music of the viols and lutes placed on one side of the hall. Which dance

being performed with great majesty and art, consisting of divers strains framed unto motions circular, square, triangular, with other proportions exceeding rare and full of variety, the Goddesses made a pause, casting 175 themselves into a circle, whilst the Graces again sang to the music of the temple and prepared to take out the Lords to dance. With whom after they had performed certain measures, galliards, and corantos, Iris again comes and gives notice of their pleasure to depart: whose speech ended, they drew themselves again into another short dance with some few pleasant changes 180 still retiring them toward the foot of the mountain, which they ascended in that same manner as they came down, whilst the cornets taking their notes from the ceasing of the music below, sounded another delightful march.

And thus, Madam, have I briefly delivered both the reason and manner of this masque, as well to satisfy the desire of those who could not well 185 note the carriage of these passages by reason (as I said) the present pomp and splendour entertained them otherwise (as that which is most regardful in these shows) wherein (by the unpartial opinion of all the beholders, strangers and others) it was not inferior to the best that ever was presented in Christendom: as also to give up my account hereof unto your Honour, 190 whereby I might clear the reckoning of any imputation that might be laid upon your judgment for preferring such a one to her Majesty in this employment as could give no reason for what was done.

And for the captious censurers, I regard not what they can say, who 195 commonly can do little else but say; and if their deep judgments ever serve them to produce anything, they must stand on the same stage of censure with other men and peradventure perform no such great wonders as they would make us believe: and I comfort myself in this, that in Court I know not any, under him who acts the greatest parts, that is not ob- 200 noxious to envy and a sinister interpretation. And whosoever strives to show most wit about these punctilios of dreams and shows are sure sick of a disease they cannot hide and would fain have the world to think them very deeply learned in all mysteries whatsoever. And peradventure they think themselves so, which if they do, they are in a far worse case than they imagine; *Non potest non indoctus esse qui se doctum credit.* And let us labour 205 to show never so much skill or art, our weaknesses and ignorance will be seen, whatsoever covering we cast over it. And yet in these matters of shows (though they be that which most entertain the world) there needs no such exact sufficiency in this kind. For, *Ludit istis animus, non proficit.* And therefore, Madam, I will no longer idly hold you therein but refer you to 210 the speeches, and so to your better delights, as one who must ever acknow-ledge myself especially bound unto your Honour.   Sam. Daniel

[The Masque]

The Night, represented in a black vesture set with stars, comes and wakens her son, Somnus (sleeping in his cave), with this speech.

Awake dark Sleep, rouse thee from out this cave,   215
Thy mother Night that bred thee in her womb
And fed thee first with silence and with ease,
Doth here thy shadowing operations crave:
And therefore wake my son, awake, and come
Strike with thy horny wand the spirits of these   220
That here expect some pleasing novelties:
And make their slumber to beget strange sights,
Strange visions and unusual properties,
Unseen of latter ages, ancient rites
Of gifts divine, wrapp'd up in mysteries.   225
Make this to seem a temple in their sight,
Whose main support, holy Religion frame:
And 1 Wisdom, 2 Courage, 3 Temperance, and 4 Right,
Make seem the pillars that sustain the same.
Shadow some Sibyl to attend the rites,   230
And to describe the Powers that shall resort,
With th'interpretation of the benefits
They bring in clouds and what they do import.
Yet make them to portend the true desire
Of those that wish them waking, real things: 235
Whilst I will hov'ring here aloof retire
And cover all things with my sable wings.
Somnus. Dear mother Night, I your commandèment
Obey, and dreams t'interpret dreams will make,
As waking curiosity is wont,   240
Though better dream asleep than dream awake.
And this white horny wand shall work the deed
Whose power doth figures of the light present:
When from this sable radius doth proceed
Nought but confused shows to no intent.   245
Be this a temple, there Sibylla stand,
Preparing reverent rites with holy hand,

And so, bright visions, go, and entertain
All round about whilst I'll to sleep again.

Iris, the messenger of the Goddesses descending from the mount where 250
they were assembled (decked like the rainbow) spake as followeth.

I, the daughter of wonder (now made the messenger of Power) am
here descended to signify the coming of a celestial presence of
Goddesses determined to visit this fair Temple of Peace which holy
hands and devout desires have dedicated to unity and concord. And 255
leaving to show themselves any more in Samos, Ida, Paphos, their
ancient delighting places of Greece and Asia, made now the seats of
barbarism and spoil, vouchsafe to recreate themselves upon this
western mount of mighty Brittany, the land of civil music and of
rest, and are pleased to appear in the self-same figures wherein 260
antiquity hath formerly clothed them and as they have been cast in
the imagination of piety, who hath given mortal shapes to the gifts
and effects of an eternal power for that those beautiful characters of
sense were easier to be read than their mystical *Ideas* dispersed in
that wide and incomprehensible volume of nature. 265

And well have mortal men apparelled all the graces, all the
blessings, all virtues, with that shape wherein themselves are much
delighted and which work the best motions and best represent the
beauty of heavenly powers.

And therefore, reverend prophetess, that here attendest upon the 270
devotions of this place, prepare thyself for those rites that appertain
to thy function and the honour of such Deities and to the end thou
mayst have a fore-notion what Powers and who they are that
come, take here this prospective and therein note and tell what thou
seest: for well may'st thou there observe their shadows, but their 275
presence will bereave thee of all save admiration and amazement,
for who can look upon such Powers and speak? And so I leave thee.

Sibylla, having received this message and the prospective, useth these
words.

What have I seen? where am I, or do I see at all? or am I any where? 280
was this Iris (the messenger of Juno) or else but a phantasm or
imagination? will the divine Goddesses vouchsafe to visit this poor

32

temple? Shall I be blest, to entertain so great Powers? It can be but a
dream: yet so great Powers have blest as humble roofs, and use, out
of no other respect than their own gracefulness, to shine where they 285
will. But what prospective is this? or what shall I herein see?
O admirable Powers! What sights are these?

Juno

First here imperial Juno in her chair,
With sceptre of command for kingdoms large,   290
Descends all clad in colours of the air,
Crown'd with bright stars, to signify her charge.

Pallas

Next war-like Pallas in her helmet dressed
With lance of winning, target of defence: 295
In whom both wit and courage are expressed,
To get with glory, hold with providence.

Venus

Then lovely Venus in bright majesty
Appears with mild aspect in dove-like hue: 300
With th'all-combining scarf of amity
T'engird strange nations with affections true.

Vesta

Next holy Vesta with her flames of zeal
Presents herself clad in white purity: 305
Whose book the soul's sweet comfort doth reveal
By the ever-burning lamp of piety.

Diana

Then chaste Diana, in her robes of green,
With weapons of the wood her self addrests   310
To bless the forests where her power is seen,
In peace with all the world but savage beasts.

Proserpina

Next rich Proserpina, with flames of gold,
Whose state although within the earth, yet she   315
Comes from above and in her hand doth hold
The mine of wealth, with cheerful majesty.

Macaria

Then all in purple robes, rich Happiness
Next her appears, bearing in either hand   320
Th'ensigns both of wealth and wits, t'express
That by them both her majesty doth stand.

Concordia

Next all in parti-colour'd robes appears
In white and crimson graceful Concord dress'd   325
With knots of union, and in hand she bears
The happy joined roses of our rest.

Astraea

Clear-eyed Astraea next with reverent brow
Clad in celestial hue (which best she likes)   330
Comes with her balance and her sword to show
That first her judgment weighs before it strikes.

Flora

Then cheerful Flora, all adorn'd with flowers,
Who clothes the earth with beauty and delight   335
In thousand sundry suits whilst shining hours
Will scarce afford a darkness to the night.

Ceres

Next plenteous Ceres in her harvest weed
Crown'd with th'increase of what she gave to keep   340
To gratitude and faith: in whom we read,
Who sows on Virtue shall with glory reap.

Tethys

Lastly comes Tethys, Albion's fairest love,
Whom she in faithful arms doth deign t'embrace   345
And brings the trident of her power t'approve
The kind respect she hath to do him grace.

Thus have I read their shadows, but behold!
In glory where they come as Iris told!

The three Graces, coming to the upper part of the hall, sang this song 350
while the Goddesses delivered their presents. Gratiae sunt 1 dantium,
2 reddentium, 3 et promerentium.

1. Desert, Reward and Gratitude,
    The Graces of society,
    Do here with hand in hand conclude   355
    The blessed chain of amity:
    For we deserve, we give, we thank,
    Thanks, gifts, deserts, thus join in rank.

2. We yield the splendent rays of light,
    Unto these blessings that descend: 360
    The grace whereof with more delight
    The well disposing doth commend;
    Whilst Gratitude, Rewards, Deserts,
    Please, win, draw on, and couple hearts.

3. For worth and power and due respect,   365
    Deserves, bestows, returns with grace
    The meed, reward, the kind effect
    That give the world a cheerful face,
    And turning in this course of right,
    Make virtue move with true delight.   370

The song being ended and the Masquers in the midst of the hall,
disposing themselves to their dance, Sibylla, having placed their
several presents on the altar, uttereth these words:

O Power of Powers, grant to our vows we pray,
That these fair blessings which we now erect   375

In figures left us here, in substance may
Be those great props of glory and respect.
1 Let kingdoms large, 2 let armed policy,
3 Mild love, 4 true zeal, 5 right shooting at the white
Of brave designs: 6 let wealth, 7 felicity,   38
8 Justice, 9 and concord, 10 pleasure, 11 plenty, 12 might
And power by sea, with grace proportionate,
Make glorious both the sovereign and his state.

*After this the Masquers danced their own measures, which being ended
and they ready to take out the Lords, the three Graces sang.*   38

Whiles worth with honour make their choice
For measur'd motions order'd right,
Now let us likewise give a voice
Unto the touch of our delight.

For comforts lock'd up without sound,   39
Are th'unborn children of the thought:
Like unto treasures never found
That buried low are left forgot.

Where words our glory do not show,
There like brave actions without fame,   39
It seems as plants not set to grow,
Or as a tomb without a name.

*The Masquers having ended their dancing with the Lords, Iris gives
warning of their departure.*

Iris. As I was the joyful messenger to notify the coming so am I now 40
the same of the departure of these divine Powers. Who having
clothed themselves with these appearances do now return back
again to the spheres of their own being from whence they came.
But yet, of myself, this much I must reveal (though against the
warrant of a messenger, who, I know, had better to fail in obedience 40
than in presumpti on) that these deities by the motion of the all-
directing Pallas, the glorious patroness of this mighty monarchy,
descending in the majesty of their invisible essence upon yonder
mountain found there the best (and most worthily the best) of

36

ladies, disporting with her choicest attendants whose forms they 410
presently undertook as delighting to be in the best-built temples
of beauty and honour. And in them vouchsafed to appear in this
manner, being otherwise no objects for mortal eyes. And no doubt
but that, in respect of the persons under whose beautiful coverings
they have thus presented themselves, these deities will be pleased 415
the rather at their invocation (knowing all their desires to be such)
as ever more to grace this glorious monarchy with the real effects
of these blessings represented.

After this, they fell to a short departing dance and so ascend the
mountain.   420

FINIS

THE TEXT

There are three versions of the text to be taken into account:

(1) A small quarto edition printed in 1604 with the following title: *The True Description of a Royal Masque presented at Hampton Court upon Sunday night being the eighth of January 1604 and personated by the Queen's most excellent Majesty, attended by eleven Ladies of Honour.* This is the surreptitious edition referred to by Daniel in the opening lines of his dedication of the authorized edition to the Countess of Bedford. It contains many mistakes of a kind likely to arise from hasty and not very intelligent reading of a roughly written manuscript. At one or two points it corrects errors which creep into the authorized text, but its principal interest is that it includes rather fuller stage directions than the later editions. Daniel's dedicatory letter to Lady Bedford which first appears in the authorized edition of 1604 describes in some detail how the masque was staged and dressed, and this is no doubt the reason why he pruned the directions in the text he himself prepared for publication.

(2) The octavo edition of 1604 printed under Daniel's supervision with the intent of correcting the errors of the quarto, and containing the dedication to Lady Bedford.

(3) The text included in the 1623 posthumous edition of Daniel's poetical works published under the auspices of the poet's brother. This edition contains minor and insignificant variants from the octavo of 1604.

COPIES COLLATED

1604 Q (surreptitious edition): Bodleian and British Museum. The B.M. copy (press mark 161. a. 41) is of special interest because it contains notes in a contemporary hand of the names of the ladies who 'personated' the goddesses.

1604 Octavo (authorized edition) here designated O: Bodleian and Huntington. The Bodleian copy has been used as control text.

1623 folio: Bodleian and Taunton Public Library (lent by the Borough Librarian).

COLLATION

I have recorded variants only where: (1) Q prints correctly what is evidently erroneous in the copy text; (2) Q offers a reading of equal value with that of the copy text and may represent the original version; (3) Q

has a stage direction which usefully amplifies that of O. In the editions of
Evans (*English Masques*, 1897) and Parks and Beatty (*The English Drama
900–1642*, New York, 1935) the Q stage directions are incorporated into
what is basically the 1623 text. (Parks and Beatty's edition is based on
Evans's, with some errors.) There appears to be some advantage in leaving
the O directions as they stand and printing additions among the variants
since (i) this represents the text as Daniel intended it to be read, and (ii)
there is no modern edition which prints the text as Daniel prepared it:
Evans and Parks and Beatty take 1623 as the copy text with the modifica-
tions specified, and Law's edition of 1880 and Grosart's of 1885 are also
based on 1623.

The extra-metrical numbers at lines 228 (O and Q) and 351–2 (O only)
have been retained since they function as stage directions; e.g. at line 228
the numbers would not be spoken but Night would point to the appropriate pillar. See also Collation and Commentary on lines 357–8.

COLLATION

118 *intriso*] *this ed.*; intimo Q *and* O.

213–14 *The Night...this speech*] O; *The Night, apparelled in a black vesture set with stars coming from below and approaching near unto the temple erected toward the upper end of the hall, wakens her son, Somnus, that there lies sleeping in a cave, with this speech* Q.

218 shadowing] O; shadowed Q.

224 latter] Q; latters O.

241 dream asleep than dream awake] O; dreams asleep than dreams awake Q.

245 confused shows] O; confus'd dark shows Q.

246–7] *not in* Q.

251 *decked like the rainbow*] O; *decked in the colour of the rainbow* Q.

278–9 *Sibylla...these words*] O; *Sybilla decked as a nun, in black upon white, having received this message and the prospective, useth these words* Q.

312 In peace with all the world, but savage beasts] O; T'hold peace with all the world but with wild beasts Q.

345 doth deign] Q; deign O.

347 The kind respect she hath] O; Her favour and respect Q.

350–1 *The three Graces...presents*] O; *The three Graces march before the Goddesses, descending down the mountain with loud music, and, coming up to the upper end, stay and sing this song, whilst the Goddesses go up to the temple with presents and from thence march down the hall.* Q.

351–2] *Gratiae sunt...promerentium*] *not in* Q.

357 we deserve, we give, we thank] O; 1, I deserve. 2, I give. 3, I thank Q.

358] Q *inserts* All *at beginning of line.*

378–81] *numbering not in* Q.

383 the sovereign and his state] O; this kingdom and estate Q.

394 do] Q; doth O.

419–20 *ascend the mountain*] O; *ascended the mountain in the same order as they came down.* Q.

40

COMMENTARY

4–7] The reference is to the 1604 quarto.

25–6 *regnorum praesidi*] the protectress of kingdoms.

44–6 *ingenerosum...parere*] ignoble to know only what can be gleaned from commentaries and to produce nothing of one's own as though the discoveries of our ancestors had closed the way to our industry and the force of nature were worn out in us.

55–6 their proper and several attires] They all wore, according to Dudley Carleton, loose mantles and petticoats of different colours, the material embroidered satin and cloth of gold and silver. 'Only Pallas', he adds, 'had a trick by herself, for her clothes were not so much below the knee that we might see a woman had both feet and legs which I never knew before.' Her costume was very rich, for: 'She had a pair of buskins set with rich stones, a helmet full of jewels, and her whole attire embossed with jewels of several fashions'.

87 embroidered with silver hands in hand] silver embroidery representing hands clasped together.

103 from below] i.e. through a trap door.

112–13] At last he shook himself; and raising himself on his elbow asked why she came (for he recognized her). Ovid, *Metamorphoses*, XI, 621.

114–15] In the meantime lazy sleep came and closed the eyes of both lords and sergeants.

117–18] Sleep came and having sprinkled the weary body with a rod steeped in the waters of Lethe.

130] Philostratus, *Imagines* I. 27.

136–8] I do not call upon you to spread the whole of your wings over my eyes—this more light-hearted people pray for—just touch me with the tip of your wand. Statius, *Silvae*, v. iv. 16.

140] Touching his temples with a Lethean wand. Silius Italicus, *Punica*, x. 356.

147 prospective] a spy-glass, or perhaps a magic mirror in which distant or future events could be seen.

160 *Hierogliphicè...accipitur*] is taken to denote the impure. Of the descent of the Goddesses as a spectacular effect, Dudley Carleton notes that it was 'the best presentation I have at any time seen'.

161 in the like several colours] Carleton says the torch-bearers were dressed in 'white satin loose gowns', but perhaps he is confusing them with the Graces who also carried torches.

174–5 motions... variety] dance figures specially arranged for the occasion.

178 measures, galliards, and corantos] slow stately dances, lively dances with a hopping step, and lively dances with a gliding step. Among the lords

taken out for these dances was the young Prince Henry whom the ladies tossed from hand to hand like a tennis ball, as Carleton reports. He adds that the Spanish ambassador 'for his Spanish galliard showed himself a lusty old reveller' and of the ladies 'for good grace and good footmanship, Pallas bare the bell away'.

205 *Non potest...credit*] he cannot but be ignorant who believes himself to be learned.

209 *Ludit...proficit*] The mind plays with these things, does not profit from them.

244 When from this sable radius] Whereas from this black wand.

287] Notes in a contemporary hand on a B.M. copy of the 1604 Q give the names of the ladies who 'personated' the Goddesses as follows: The Countess of Suffolk (Juno), the Queen (Pallas), Lady Rich (Venus), the Countess of Hertford (Diana), the Countess of Bedford (Vesta), the Countess of Derby (Proserpina), Lady Hatton (Macaria), the Countess of Nottingham (Concordia), Lady Walsingham (Astraea), Lady Susan Vere (Flora), Lady Dorothy Hastings (Ceres), Lady Elizabeth Howard (Tethys).

310 addrests] addresses; a nonce word for the sake of rhyme, remarkable in 'well-languaged Daniel'.

351–2] The Graces are 1 of giving, 2 of requiting, 3 of deserving.

357–8] Q's reading makes it clear that the Graces first spoke in turn, then in chorus.

379 right shooting at the white] an image from archery. The white is the white target usually placed on the butt.

389 touch] sense, feeling.

OBERON, THE FAIRY PRINCE

BY BEN JONSON

Edited by Richard Hosley

INTRODUCTION

Oberon, the Fairy Prince was performed before King James, Queen Anne, and the Princess Elizabeth on 1 January 1611. The theatre was the 'new' Banqueting House at Whitehall, built by James in 1606 to replace the 'old' House of 1581.[1] The part of Oberon was danced by Henry Prince of Wales, and his Knights Masquers are said by Stow to have included two earls (one of whom was Southampton), three barons, five knights, and two esquires. There is reason to believe that the parts of the Anti-masquers were taken by the King's Men. The Spanish and Venetian ambassadors were present, and the latter, who sat next to the Queen, tells us that the masque was 'most remarkable for the grace of the Prince's every movement'.[2]

Prince Henry Frederick was born at Stirling Castle on 19 February 1594, four years after his father, James VI of Scotland, had married Anne, sister of Christian IV of Denmark.[3] Queen Elizabeth I of England stood godmother to Henry, giving him (through a proxy) the name of her own father and grandfather. Nine years later, in the summer of 1603, Prince Henry accompanied Queen Anne on her progress from Edinburgh to London in the wake of the new king of England. Toward the end of June the Queen and Prince sojourned four days at the house of Sir Robert Spencer at Althorp (near Northampton), where they were received with an entertainment written by Ben Jonson. Thus began the association of prince and poet which led to Jonson's dedicating *The Masque of Queens* to Henry in 1609 and writing for him *The Speeches at Prince Henry's Barriers* in 1610, *Oberon* in 1611, and *Love Restored* in 1612.

Henry once said that the two things which most delighted him

---

[1] John Smythson's plan of the 1606 Banqueting House is reproduced by Per Palme in his study of Inigo Jones's Banqueting House of 1622: *Triumph of Peace* (1956), p. 116. The room was 53 feet wide and 120 feet long.

[2] *C.S.P. Venetian*, XII (1905), 106.

[3] Elkin Calhoun Wilson, *Prince Henry and English Literature* (1946). The fullest biographical account is by Thomas Birch, *The Life of Henry Prince of Wales* (1760). The miniature by Isaac Oliver is reproduced as Plate 45 (*a*).

45

were arms and horses. His attitude (managing a pike) in the frontispiece to Drayton's *Poly-Olbion* (1612) is evidently characteristic. Thus he developed a keen interest in the Navy, not surprising in the young friend of Sir Walter Raleigh. But his tastes were varied. He liked music and was taught by Ferrabosco, who dedicated his *Ayres* to Henry in 1609. He was a good dancer, appearing in Jonson's *Hymenaei* in 1606. He took the Admiral's Men under his patronage as the Prince's Servants. He received the dedication of Chapman's *Homer* (1609) and collected one of the most valuable libraries in England. He was strongly Protestant. Not much detected for women, he suffered a nip from the Blatant Beast when his name was lightly linked with that of Frances Howard in 1611. He had a sense of humour, once remarking, when reminded by James that Prince Charles seemed likely to prove the better scholar, that in that case he would make his brother Archbishop of Canterbury. Henry was created Prince of Wales in the summer of 1610. He died, apparently of typhoid fever, on 6 November 1612, at the age of eighteen. He had been sixteen when he danced as Oberon at Whitehall on New Year's Night of 1611.

An eyewitness account of the performance of *Oberon*, written in Spanish, is preserved among the Papers of William Trumbull the Elder.[1] It contains several details not found in the text of the masque. For example, it mentions the 'very large curtain' which concealed the first scene until the King and Queen had taken their places in the hall and the masque was permitted to begin. It records that, in the Revels, Prince Henry danced thrice with the Queen, and that the Earl of Southampton (Shakespeare's patron) danced with the Princess Elizabeth. And it notes that the Anti-masquers joined with the Masquers in the 'ballet of the sortie'. The description also conflates the two scene-openings of the text, failing to mention the discovery of the sleeping Sylvans at the opening of scene 1 and recording that Oberon and his Knights were discovered at the opening of scene 1 (Rocks) instead of at the opening of scene 2 (Oberon's Palace).

---

[1] Historical Manuscripts Commission, *Report on the Manuscripts of the Marquess of Downshire* (1938), III, 1–2; reprinted by C. H. Herford and Percy Simpson, *Ben Jonson*, X (1950), 522–3.

Samuel Daniel's *The Vision of the Twelve Goddesses*, performed in the old Banqueting House at Whitehall in 1604, employed the old scenic technique of structures dispersed about the hall. In the next few years the scenery of masques tended to become concentrated at the lower end of the hall, and changeable scenery was introduced.[1] Jonson's *Masque of Queens* (1609) required one scene-opening, the shutters of the first scene being drawn aside to reveal a second. Daniel's *Tethys' Festival* (1610) had two scene-openings, the opening of the second scene discovering a third scene. *Oberon* also calls for two scene-openings, consequently for three scenes. At least one of these (possibly all three) is represented among the extant scenic designs from the hand of Inigo Jones.

Among the drawings by Jones preserved in the collection of the Duke of Devonshire at Chatsworth are sixteen which Percy Simpson and C. F. Bell have associated with *Oberon*. None of the identifications is implausible and most are probable; but only two are certain, those of nos. 42 and 43 as variant draughts of the design for scene 2, Oberon's Palace. Five of the drawings are designs for scenes:

40. Scene 1, Rocks (?). Plate 1. The absence of caverns (shown in nos. 42 and 44 and reflected in a stage-direction recording that the Satyrs '*came running forth severally from divers parts of the rock*') suggests either that this design is not for *Oberon* or that the caverns were cut in non-moving side pieces, the design relating only to shutters intended to stand behind the side pieces.

42. Scene 2, Oberon's Palace. Plate 2. The drawing is inscribed '2 sceane K: Oberons Pallace'. The scene is described in a stage-direction as '*the frontispiece of a bright and glorious palace whose gates and walls were transparent*'. Both this design and its earlier draught no. 43 show two rectangular spaces and an arched doorway between them which apparently constituted the transparency of gates and walls. Presumably a display of lights was seen through these spaces, which may have been translucent rather than transparent. Such a display would account for Jonson's description of the palace as '*bright and glorious*', and it would also accord with the words of Silenus: 'Look! Does not his palace show | Like another sky of lights?' If side pieces were used for the rocks and caverns, this design would represent a scene in at least two planes.

[1] Richard Southern, *Changeable Scenery* (1952).

43. Original sketch of the frontispiece of Oberon's Palace in no. 42. A set of accompanying dimensions is printed by Simpson and Bell. Some of the dimensions are slightly altered in no. 42.

44. Oberon's Palace in Rocks (?). Plate 3. A connexion with no. 42 is indicated by the moon, the cupola, the chimneys, the rocks, and the caverns. Simpson and Bell suggest that this design may be a remodelling of no. 42, 'for some later and unidentified masque'; and Enid Welsford (*The Court Masque*, p. 224) identifies the later masque as Aurelian Townshend's *Albion's Triumph* (1632), which requires the scene of a temple in a grove. It may be, however, that no. 44 represents a third (non-moving) scene for *Oberon*, a sort of loggia as backing for Oberon and his Knights when they are discovered '*within afar off in perspective*', within an arch of rocks and sky. Thus the scene would have been in two planes or, if the caverns were cut in standing side pieces, in three planes.

45. Alternate design for a detail of Oberon's Palace in Rocks (?) in no. 44. Plate 4. A connexion with no. 44 is indicated by the cupola, the three arches supported by columns, the decorative deer and hounds, and the ogival shape of the drawing. This design may represent a backing intended for use with an 'interior' arch (instead of an arch of rocks and sky as presumably in no. 44).

Of the remaining designs by Inigo Jones which have been ascribed to *Oberon*, five are for costumes of Satyrs and Fays (nos. 41, 46–9), six for costumes of Oberon and his Knights Masquers (nos. 50–5). Most of these designs are reproduced in the present volume (Plates 5–9).

Records (printed by Herford and Simpson, X, 519–22) of the expenses for *Oberon* reveal that the production cost in the neighbourhood of £2,100. The sum of about £1,100 was paid for costumes; £350 presumably for scenery; about £300 for preparation of the hall; about £230 for miscellaneous expenses, including £15 for 'Players' (presumably the King's Men), 40s. 'for heades & beards' (surely not *forheades*, as printed in Herford and Simpson), £20 to Robert Johnson for music, and £40 to Thomas Giles for dances; and £140 'in reward' to the 'inventors' and their other collaborators in music and dance—£40 each to Ben Jonson and Inigo Jones, £20 each to Alfonso Ferrabosco, Monsieur Confesse, and Jerome Herne.

Because of these records and the survival of four pieces of music we are especially well informed about the music and dances for *Oberon*. Alfonso Ferrabosco, who had been Prince Henry's music-master and who wrote music for Jonson's *Hymenaei*, *The Haddington Masque*, *The Masque of Queens*, and *Love Freed from Ignorance and Folly*, composed the music for at least two of the songs: 'Nay, nay, | You must not stay' and 'Gentle Knights, | Know some measure.'[1] Robert Johnson, Musician both to King James and to Prince Henry, composed the music for at least two of the dances: 'The Satyrs' Masque' (the Anti-masquers' dance) and, though less certainly, 'The Fairy Masque' (the dance of the Lesser Fays).[2] Thomas Lupo arranged Johnson's music for the violin. Jerome Herne, who was Musician to Prince Henry and had 'made' dances for *The Haddington Masque* and *The Masque of Queens*, apparently contributed to the dances (their music, choreography, or teaching); and so too did Thomas Giles, who had 'made' (and, in at least one instance, 'taught') dances in *The Masque of Beauty*, *Hymenaei*, *The Haddington Masque*, and *The Masque of Queens*. Monsieur Confesse, who was paid for 'teaching' the dances of *Love Freed*, seems to have served also as dancing-master in the production of *Oberon*. There was a 'Companie of violins', and this was supported by three named violinists, Thomas Lupo the Elder, Alexander Chisan, and Roland Rubidge; all three were King's Musicians. (May their distinction have consisted in playing the treble violin?) Ten singers and six lutanists were 'provided' by Ferrabosco, twenty lutanists by Johnson ('for the Prince's Dance'). The thirteen 'Holt boyes' of the Pell Order Book were certainly (as Cutts points out) hautboys. There were two cornets, and sixteen 'other instruments for the Satires & faeries'.

The world is divided into people who believe and who dis-believe in the proposition that live bears were used on the Eliza-bethan stage. It seems to me impossible to determine whether live or artificial bears were used to draw forth Oberon's chariot, but I have a strong prejudice that the bears were artificial—despite the possible

---

[1] The music has been published by John P. Cutts, 'Le rôle de la musique dans les Masques de Ben Jonson et notamment dans *Obéron*', in *Les Fêtes de la Renaissance*, ed. Jean Jacquot (1956), pp. 298–300; and by Andrew J. Sabol, *Songs and Dances for the Stuart Masque* (1959), nos. 14–15.

[2] Cutts, pp. 294–7; Sabol, nos. 48–9.

use of live bears for a dance in Jonson's *Masque of Augurs* (1622).
I am influenced by a number of considerations: that the Revels
Accounts record such properties as a hound's head, an artificial lion,
and a horse of wood; that the Henslowe Papers record such
properties as a bear's skin and a lion's head; that a lion's head alone
afforded sufficient characterization for a sword-carrying imper-
sonator of that beast in Aurelian Townshend's *Tempe Restored*
(1632), as is shown by Inigo Jones's design no. 156, reproduced by
Allardyce Nicoll (*Stuart Masques*, fig. 185); that artificial eagles,
griffons, and lions were employed to draw forth chariots in Jonson's
Masque of Queens (1609); that the Welsh Goats which dance in
Jonson's *For the Honour of Wales* (1618) must have been artificial;
and that an 'artificial ass'—surely a manageable enough beast if one
wished to stage live animals—is ridden on stage by Silenus in the
anonymous *Masque of Flowers* (1614).

In *Oberon* Jonson struck a happy balance in his use of the anti-
masque, avoiding the excessive contrast of the earlier *Masque of
Queens* (1609), yet stopping short of the comic realism of the later
Love Restored (1612). The basic contrast between Satyrs and Fays
in *Oberon* may be compared with that between Satyr and Fairies in
the *Althorp Entertainment* of 1603. In each piece the tendency
toward Disorder or Misrule is imaged by the traditionally mocking
Satyrs or Satyr. But the Fays of the masque are both less and more
than the Fairies of the entertainment. They are not true Fairies (like
those of the entertainment or of *A Midsummer-Night's Dream*), but
simply Knights referred to by poetic convention as Fays (like the
Knights of 'grave and diligent' Spenser's *Fairy Queen*). The Fays
and the Fairy Prince represent the concept of Rule which had been
represented in the entertainment by the 'audience' composed of
Queen Anne and Prince Henry. Accordingly there cannot be, as in
the entertainment, a direct conflict between the Satyrs and Fays of
Oberon: the Satyrs, despite their eternal impulse to kick over the
traces, venerate and pay homage to the Fairy Prince. What small
conflict there is in *Oberon* is between Satyrs and Sylvans—the
servants of (and spokesmen for) the Fays. In attempting to persecute
the Sylvans, the Satyrs come close to committing a crime against
Oberon and the Fays; but inevitably they desist, checked by Silenus

their 'governor', and ultimately they join with both Sylvans and
Fays in the harmony of the Closing Dance. Thus Jonson, in imaging
control of Misrule and its corollary the acceptance of Rule, reflects a
major theme of the speeches and songs praising King James as an
ideal ruler.[1]

[1] On Jonson's treatment of monarchy, see W. Todd Furniss, 'Ben Jonson's
Masques', in *Three Studies in the Renaissance* (1958). Interesting criticism of *Oberon*
may be found in *The Jonsonian Masque* (1965) by Stephen Orgel.

[DRAMATIS PERSONAE

Satyrs
Silenus
Sylvans
Fays
Knights Masquers
Prince Oberon
Phosphorus]

OBERON,
THE FAIRY PRINCE.

A MASQUE OF PRINCE HENRY'S

*   *   *

*The first face of the scene appeared all obscure, and nothing perceived
but a dark rock, with trees beyond it and all wildness that could be
presented; till at one corner of the cliff, above the horizon, the Moon
began to show and, rising, a Satyr was seen (by her light) to put forth
his head and call.*   5

> *1 Satyr.* Chromis, Mnasyl? None appear?
> See you not who riseth here?
> You saw Silenus late, I fear!
> I'll prove if this can reach your ear.

He wound his cornet and thought himself answered, but was deceived 10
by the echo.

> O you wake then: come away,
> Times be short are made for play;
> The hum'rous Moon too will not stay;
> What doth make you thus delay?   15
> Hath his tankard touch'd your brain?
> Sure, they're fall'n asleep again,
> Or I doubt it was the vain
> Echo did me entertain.
> Prove again.   20

>   *He wound the second time, and found it.*

>   I thought 'twas she.
> Idle Nymph, I pray thee, be
> Modest and not follow me;
> I nor love myself nor thee.   25

Here he wound the third time and was answered by another Satyr, who likewise showed himself. To which he spoke.

> Ay, this sound I better know.
> List! I would I could hear mo.

At this they came running forth severally from divers parts of the rock, leaping and making antic action and gestures, to the number of ten; some of them speaking, some admiring; and amongst them a Silene, who is ever the prefect of the Satyrs and so presented in all their chori and meetings. 30

> *2 Satyr.* Thank us, and you shall do so. 35
> *3 Satyr.* Ay, our number soon will grow.
> *2 Satyr.* See Silenus!
> *3 Satyr.*   Cercops too!
> *4 Satyr.* Yes. What is there now to do?
> *5 Satyr.* Are there any Nymphs to woo? 40
> *4 Satyr.* If there be, let me have two.
> *Silenus.* Chaster language. These are nights
>   Solemn to the shining rites
>   Of the Fairy Prince and Knights,
>   While the Moon their orgies lights. 45
> *2 Satyr.* Will they come abroad anon?
> *3 Satyr.* Shall we see young Oberon?
> *4 Satyr.* Is he such a princely one
>   As you speak him long agone?
> *Silenus.* Satyrs, he doth fill with grace 50
>   Every season, every place;
>   Beauty dwells but in his face:
>   He's the height of all our race.
>   Our Pan's father, god of tongue,
>   Bacchus, though he still be young, 55
>   Phoebus, when he crowned sung,
>   Nor Mars, when first his armour rung,
>   Might with him be nam'd, that day.
>   He is lovelier than in May
>   Is the Spring, and there can stay 60

As little as he can decay.
Chorus. O that he would come away!
3 Satyr. Grandsire, we shall leave to play
  With Lyaeus now, and serve
  Only Ob'ron.   65
Silenus.   He'll deserve
  All you can and more, my boys.
4 Satyr. Will he give us pretty toys
  To beguile the girls withal?
3 Satyr. And to make 'em quickly fall?   70
Silenus. Peace, my wantons: he will do
  More than you can aim unto.
4 Satyr. Will he build us larger caves?
Silenus. Yes, and give you ivory staves
  When you hunt, and better wine—   75
1 Satyr. Than the Master of the Vine?
2 Satyr. And rich prizes to be won
  When we leap or when we run?
1 Satyr. Ay, and gild our cloven feet?
3 Satyr. Strew our heads with powders sweet?   80
1 Satyr. Bind our crooked legs in hoops
  Made of shells, with silver loops?
2 Satyr. Tie about our tawny wrists
  Bracelets of the Fairy twists?
4 Satyr. And, to spite the coy Nymphs' scorns,   85
  Hang upon our stubbed horns
  Garlands, ribbons, and fine posies—
3 Satyr. Fresh as when the flower discloses?
1 Satyr. Yes, and stick our pricking ears
  With the pearl that Tethys wears.   90
2 Satyr. And, to answer all things else,
  Trap our shaggy thighs with bells
  That, as we do strike a time
  In our dance, shall make a chime—
3 Satyr. Louder than the rattling pipes   95
  Of the Wood-gods—
1 Satyr.   Or the stripes

Of the tabor, when we carry
Bacchus up, his pomp to vary.
Chorus. O that he so long doth tarry! 100
Silenus. See, the rock begins to ope,
Now you shall enjoy your hope;
'Tis about the hour, I know.

There the whole scene opened and within was discovered the frontispiece
of a bright and glorious palace whose gates and walls were transparent. 105
Before the gates lay two Sylvans, armed with their clubs and dressed in
leaves, asleep. At this, the Satyrs wondering, Silenus proceeds.

Look! Does not his palace show
Like another sky of lights?
Yonder, with him, live the Knights, 110
Once the noblest of the earth,
Quick'ned by a second birth,
Who for prowess and for truth
There are crown'd with lasting youth,
And do hold, by Fates' command, 115
Seats of bliss in Fairy Land.
But their guards (methinks) do sleep!
Let us wake 'em. Sirs, you keep
Proper watch, that thus do lie
Drown'd in sloth. 120
1 Satyr.   They ha' ne'er an eye
To wake withal.
2 Satyr.   Nor sense, I fear,
For they sleep in either ear.
3 Satyr. Holla, Sylvans! Sure, they're caves 125
Of sleep, these—or else they're graves.
4 Satyr. Hear you, friends, who keeps the keepers?
1 Satyr. They're the eighth and ninth sleepers!
2 Satyr. Shall we cramp 'em?
Silenus.   Satyrs, no. 130
3 Satyr. Would we'd Boreas here, to blow
Off their leafy coats and strip 'em.
4 Satyr. Ay, ay, ay, that we might whip 'em.

3 Satyr. Or that we had a wasp or two
  For their nostrils.   135
1 Satyr.   Hairs will do
  Even as well: take my tail.
2 Satyr. What d'you say to a good nail
  Through their temples?
3 Satyr.   Or an eel   140
  In their guts, to make 'em feel?
4 Satyr. Shall we steal away their beards?
3 Satyr. For Pan's goat, that leads the herds?
2 Satyr. Or try whether is more dead,
  His club or th'other's head?   145
Silenus. Wags, no more: you grow too bold.
1 Satyr. I would fain, now, see 'em roll'd
  Down a hill, or from a bridge
  Headlong cast, to break their ridge-
  Bones; or to some river take 'em: 150
  Plump; and see if that would wake 'em.
2 Satyr. There no motion, yet, appears.
Silenus. Strike a charm into their ears.

At which the Satyrs fell suddenly into this catch.

      Buzz, quoth the blue fly,   155
         Hum, quoth the bee;
      Buzz and hum, they cry,
         And so do we.
      In his ear, in his nose,
         Thus, do you see?   160
      He eat the dormouse,
         Else it was he.

The two Sylvans, starting up amazed and betaking themselves to their arms, were thus questioned by Silenus.

      How now, Sylvans! Can you wake?   165
      I commend the care you take
      I' your watch. Is this your guise,
      To have both your ears and eyes

Seal'd so fast, as these mine Elves
Might have stol'n you from yourselves?   17

3 Satyr. We had thought we must have got
Stakes, and heated 'em red-hot,
And have bor'd you through the eyes
(With the Cyclops) ere you'ld rise.

2 Satyr. Or have fetch'd some trees to heave   17
Up your bulks, that so did cleave
To the ground there.

4 Satyr.   Are you free
Yet of sleep, and can you see
Who is yonder up, aloof?   18

1 Satyr. Be your eyes yet Moon-proof?

Sylvan. Satyrs, leave your petulance
And go frisk about and dance,
Or else rail upon the Moon:
Your expectance is too soon.   18
For before the second cock
Crow, the gates will not unlock.
And till then we know we keep
Guard enough, although we sleep.

1 Satyr. Say you so? Then let us fall   19
To a song or to a brawl.
Shall we, grandsire? Let us sport,
And make expectation short.

Silenus. Do, my wantons, what you please.
I'll lie down and take my ease.   19

1 Satyr. Brothers, sing then, and upbraid
(As we use) yond seeming maid.

Song

Now my cunning lady, Moon,
Can you leave the side, so soon,   20
 Of the boy you keep so hid?
Midwife Juno sure will say
This is not the proper way
 Of your paleness to be rid.

58

But perhaps it is your grace 205
To wear sickness i' your face,
   That there might be wagers laid
   Still, by fools, you are a maid.

Come, your changes overthrow
What your look would carry so. 210
   Moon, confess then what you are.
And be wise and free to use
Pleasures that you now do lose;
   Let us Satyrs have a share.
Though our forms be rough and rude, 215
Yet our acts may be endued
   With more virtue: everyone
   Cannot be Endymion.

*The song ended, they fell suddenly into an antic dance, full of gesture
and swift motion, and continued it till the crowing of the cock, at which* 220
they were interrupted by Silenus.

   Silenus. Stay, the cheerful Chanticleer
   Tells you that the time is near:
   See, the gates already spread!
   Every Satyr bow his head. 225

*There the whole palace opened, and the nation of Fays were discovered,
some with instruments, some bearing lights, others singing; and within,
afar off in perspective, the Knights Masquers sitting in their several
sieges. At the further end of all, Oberon in a chariot, which to a loud
triumphant music began to move forward, drawn by two white bears and* 230
on either side guarded by three Sylvans, with one going in front.

Song

   Melt earth to sea, sea flow to air,
      And air fly into fire,
   Whilst we, in tunes, to Arthur's chair 235
      Bear Oberon's desire;
     Than which there nothing can be higher
   Save James, to whom it flies:
   But he the wonder is of tongues, of ears, of eyes.

59

Who hath not heard, who hath not seen, 24

   Who hath not sung his name?

The soul that hath not, hath not been,

   But is the very same

   With buried sloth and knows not fame,

Which doth him best comprise: 24

For he the wonder is of tongues, of ears, of eyes.

By this time the chariot was come as far forth as the face of the scene.
And the Satyrs beginning to leap and express their joy for the unused
state and solemnity, the foremost Sylvan began to speak.

Sylvan. Give place, and silence; you were rude too late: 25

   This is a night of greatness and of state,

   Not to be mix'd with light and skipping sport—

   A night of homage to the British court,

   And ceremony, due to Arthur's chair,

   From our bright master, Oberon the fair; 25

   Who with these Knights Attendants, here preserved

   In Fairy Land for good they have deserved

   Of yond high throne, are come of right to pay

   Their annual vows, and all their glories lay

   At's feet, and tender to this only great, 26

   True majesty, restored in this seat;

   To whose sole power and magic they do give

   The honour of their being, that they live

   Sustain'd in form, fame, and felicity,

   From rage of fortune or the fear to die. 26

Silenus. And may they well. For this indeed is he,

   My boys, whom you must quake at, when you see.

   He is above your reach, and neither doth

   Nor can he think within a Satyr's tooth;

   Before his presence you must fall or fly. 27

   He is the matter of virtue, and plac'd high.

   His meditations, to his height, are even,

   And all their issue is akin to heaven.

   He is a god, o'er kings; yet stoops he then

   Nearest a man when he doth govern men, 27

To teach them by the sweetness of his sway,
And not by force. He's such a king as they
Who're tyrants' subjects or ne'er tasted peace
Would, in their wishes, form for their release.
'Tis he that stays the time from turning old   280
And keeps the age up in a head of gold;
That in his own true circle still doth run
And holds his course, as certain as the sun.
He makes it ever day and ever spring
Where he doth shine, and quickens every thing   285
Like a new nature; so that true to call
Him by his title is to say, He's all.
Sylvan. I thank the wise Silenus for this praise.
Stand forth, bright Fays and Elves, and tune your lays
Unto his name; then let your nimble feet   290
Tread subtle circles that may always meet
In point to him; and figures, to express
The grace of him and his great emperess;
That all that shall tonight behold the rites
Perform'd by princely Ob'ron and these Knights   295
May, without stop, point out the proper heir
Design'd so long to Arthur's crowns and chair.

The song, by two Fays

1.   Seek you majesty, to strike?
      Bid the world produce his like.
                                                        300

2.   Seek you glory, to amaze?
      Here let all eyes stand at gaze.

1, 2. Seek you wisdom, to inspire?
      Touch then at no other's fire.

1.   Seek you knowledge, to direct?   305
      Trust to his, without suspect.

2.   Seek you piety, to lead?
      In his footsteps, only, tread.

Chorus. Every virtue of a king,
And of all, in him, we sing. 310

Then the lesser Fays dance forth their dance; which ended, a full song follows, by all the voices.

Song

The solemn rites are well begun,
And though but lighted by the moon 315
They show as rich, as if the sun
Had made this night his noon.
But may none wonder that they are so bright,
The moon now borrows from a greater light.
Then, princely Oberon, 320
Go on,
This is not every night.

There Oberon and the Knights dance out the first masque-dance; which was followed with this song.

Song 325

Nay, nay,
You must not stay,
Nor be weary yet;
This's no time to cast away,
Or for Fays so to forget 330
The virtue of their feet.
Knotty legs and plants of clay
Seek for ease or love delay.
But with you it still should fare
As with the air of which you are. 335

After which they danced forth their second masque-dance, and were again excited by a song.

Song

1. Nor yet, nor yet, O you in this night blest,
Must you have will or hope to rest. 340

2. If you use the smallest stay,
   You'll be overta'en by day.

1. And these beauties will suspect
   That their forms you do neglect,
   If you do not call them forth.   345

2. Or that you have no more worth
   Than the coarse and country Fairy
   That doth haunt the hearth or dairy.

*Then followed the measures, corantos, galliards, etc., till Phosphorus
the day-star appeared and called them away; but first they were invited* 350
home, by one of the Sylvans, with this song.

Song

Gentle Knights,
Know some measure of your nights.
Tell the high-grac'd Oberon   355
It is time that we were gone.
Here be forms so bright and airy,
   And their motions so they vary
As they will enchant the Fairy
   If you longer, here, should tarry.   360

Phosphorus. To rest, to rest. The herald of the Day,
Bright Phosphorus, commands you hence; obey.
The Moon is pale and spent, and winged Night
Makes headlong haste to fly the Morning's sight;
Who now is rising from her blushing wars   365
And with her rosy hand puts back the stars.
Of which myself, the last, her harbinger,
But stay to warn you that you not defer
Your parting longer. Then do I give way,
As Night hath done, and so must you, to Day.   370

*After this, they danced their last dance, into the work. And with a full
song the Star vanished, and the whole machine closed.*

Song

O yet how early and before her time
The envious Morning up doth climb,   37
   Though she not love her bed!
What haste the jealous Sun doth make
His fiery horses up to take,
   And once more show his head!
Lest, taken with the brightness of this night,   38
The world should wish it last, and never miss his light.

THE TEXT

The source of the text of *Oberon* is the print in the Jonson Folio of 1616, which requires no emendation of any consequence. (There were numerous press-corrections during the printing of F 1, but none that improves the sense.) The Second Folio (1640) introduces one emendation which, if accepted, would affect interpretation of the staging (see Collation note and Commentary at line 372). A few minor variants occur in the texts of the songs accompanying the music printed by Cutts and by Sabol. Jonson's annotation, omitted from the present edition, may be consulted in Herford and Simpson's *Ben Jonson*, VII; a few excerpts are given in the Commentary below.

COLLATION

65 Ob'ron.] OB'RON? F 1.

240 seen] seene F 1 (*uncorr.*); beene F 1 (*corr.*).

249 *Sylvan*] SYLVANE F 1 (*uncorr.*); SYLVANI F 1 (*corr.*).

260 At's] At F 1.

293 emperess] Emperesse F 2; empresse F 1.

372 *song the Star*] *song, the* | *starre* F 1 (*uncorr.*); *Song,* | *starre* F 1 (*corr.*); | *song, straight* F 2.

COMMENTARY

2 *a dark rock*]   This scene (1) may be represented by Inigo Jones's design no. 40 (Plate 1). The scene was a standard one; Herford and Simpson compare Chapman's satire in his *Masque of the Middle Temple and Lincoln's Inn* (1613): '*Plu[tus]*. Rockes? Nothing but Rockes in these masking devices! Is Invention so poore that shee must needes ever dwell amongst Rocks?'

6 Chromis, Mnasyl]   'They are the names of two yong *Satyres*, I find in *Vir. Eclog. 6.* that took *Silenus* sleeping; who is fain'd to bee the *Paedagoge* of *Bacchus*: As the *Satyres* are his Collusores, or Play-fellowes' (Jonson).

6–9 appear...ear]   The Satyrs' speeches are in the same stanza as those of the Satyr, Fairy, and Elves in Jonson's *Althorp Entertainment* (1603): four lines of trochaic tetrameter (the last syllable usually apocopated), rhyming AAAA. Jonson uses the same heptasyllabic line for the couplets of *Love Freed from Ignorance and Folly* (1611).

8 saw Silenus late]   i.e. were drinking.

10 *wound*]   winded.

25 myself nor thee]   'Respecting that knowne fable of *Echo's* following *Narcissus*; and his self-Love' (Jonson).

32 *Silene*]   The name is used generally for an older satyr, 'over-seer, or governour' of a company of satyrs (Jonson), and specifically for the fat, jovial, hard-drinking tutor of Bacchus. Compare the description of Silenus in *The Masque of Flowers* (1614), p. 164 below.

38 Cercops]   one of the gnomes (later changed into apes) who robbed Hercules in his sleep.

41 let me have two]   'The nature of the *Satyres* the wise *Horace* express'd wel, in the word, when hee called them *Risores & Dicaces* [*Ars poetica*, 225]' (Jonson).

42 Chaster language]   'But in the *Silenes*, was nothing of this petulance, and lightnesse; but on the contrarie, all gravitie, and profound knowledge, of most secret mysteries' (Jonson, who compares, among other authorities, Plato for his description in the *Symposium* of the Silenus-mask of Socrates).

45 orgies]   ceremonies, rites (not necessarily bacchanalian).

47 Oberon]   Dwarf King of the Fairies in *Huon of Bordeaux* (tr. Berners, c. 1530). The name (Fr. *Auberon*) apparently derives from *Alberich*, the elf of the *Heldenbuch* and the *Nibelungenlied*. Oberon appears as the Fairy King in Greene's *James IV* (c. 1591) and in *A Midsummer-Night's Dream* (c. 1595).

49 speak]   spoke.

54 Pan's father]   Mercury, who, 'in the translated figure of a goate', begot

Pan 'on the faire *Spartan* PENELOPE' (Jonson, *Highgate Entertainment*, 1604, 181–3).

57 when first his armour rung] 'He was then lovely, as being not yet stayn'd with blood' (Jonson).

60–1 stay As little] 'i.e. must advance to further beauty' (Herford and Simpson).

64 Lyaeus] Bacchus.

84 twists] threads.

90 Tethys] wife of Oceanus.

97 stripes] sounds (produced by striking).

99 up] aloft.

104 *the whole scene opened*] That is, the shutters of scene 1 were drawn apart, discovering the sleeping Sylvans and scene 2.

105 *a bright and glorious palace*] This scene (2) is represented by Inigo Jones's design no. 42 (Plate 2).

106 *Sylvans*] In Campion's *Lord Hay's Masque* (1607), Sylvans are '*attired in changeable Taffatie, with wreaths of flowers on their heads*'; and in his *Caversham Masque* (1613) Sylvanus is '*shaped after the description of the ancient Writers, his lower parts like a Goate and his upper parts in an anticke habit of rich Taffatie cut into Leaves; and on his head he had a false Hair, with a wreath of long Boughes and Lillies that hung dangling about his necke, and in his hand a Cypresse branch*'.

124 in either ear] i.e. soundly (a latinism; Herford and Simpson compare Terence's 'in aurem utramvis').

127 who keeps the keepers?] proverbial (after Juvenal's 'quis custodiet ipsos custodes?').

128 eighth and ninth sleepers] 'A reference to the Seven Sleepers of Ephesus hidden under the persecution of Diocletian in a cave (A.D. 250) and found alive in 479 in the reign of Theodosius' (Herford and Simpson).

144 whether] which (of two).

153 charm] incantation.

172 Stakes] Compare the *Odyssey*, IX, 382 ff.

191 brawl] the French dance (Fr. *bransle*, *branle*).

201 the boy] Endymion.

202 Midwife Juno] Juno Lucina presided over the birth of children. Glycerium invokes her aid in Terence's *Andria*: 'Iuno Lucina, fer opem, serva me, obsecro' (III, i).

206 sickness] green-sickness.

219 *an antic dance*] Robert Johnson's music for this dance, 'The Satyrs' Masque', has been published by Cutts, pp. 294–5, and by Sabol, no. 48. Sabol, in a discussion of the characteristically grotesque and fanciful music of the anti-masque in general, makes an interesting observation: 'Particularly noteworthy in Robert Johnson's music for this dance (no. 48) are the sustained notes of the second strain, which suggest that the executants had

assumed stands, or poses, in the midst of the dance' (p. 2). The dance may have been a brawl or branle (compare line 191); see Walter Sorell, 'Shakespeare and the Dance', *Shakespeare Quarterly*, VIII (1957), 380. It is generally supposed that Johnson's music for the Satyrs' dance was used also for the '*dance of twelve Satyrs*' in *The Winter's Tale* (IV, iv), written probably during the early months of 1611; see the new Arden edition, by J. H. P. Pafford (1963), p. xxii. If so, it seems likely that some at least of the dancers in the masque performed also in the play—a theory that lends special point to the Servant's statement in *The Winter's Tale* that 'one three' of the twelve Satyrs 'hath danced before the king'. Thus the parts of the Anti-masquers in *Oberon* would have been taken by the King's Men (the 'Players' mentioned in the Pell Order Book). A year later the King's Men performed in Prince Henry's *Love Restored* (1612).

226 *the whole palace opened*] That is, the shutters of scene 2 were drawn apart, discovering the Nation of Fays. The discovered scene (3) may be represented by Inigo Jones's design no. 44 (Plate 3).

229 *a chariot*] Compare Inigo Jones's design no. 62 (Plate 14) for the chariot of Comus in Jonson's *Pleasure Reconciled to Virtue* (1618); also Nicoll, *Stuart Masques*, figs. 85–90.

230 *two white bears*] Presumably artificial, like the beasts that draw forth chariots in Jonson's *Masque of Queens* (1609), lines 711–17.

269 think within a Satyr's tooth] i.e. contemplate sensuality.

287 He's all] a play on the Greek *pan*.

293 empress] i.e. Queen Anne.

297 Arthur's crowns] England and Scotland.

311 *lesser*] i.e. in size (the dancers being boys).

311 *their dance*] Robert Johnson's (?) music for this dance, 'The Fairy Masque', has been published by Cutts, pp. 296–7, and by Sabol, no. 49.

326 Nay, nay] Alfonso Ferrabosco's music for this song has been published by Cutts, p. 300, and by Sabol, no. 14.

332 plants] feet (a latinism; *planta pedis*, sole of the foot).

337 *excited*] incited (to dance again).

343 these beauties] the ladies of the audience with whom the Masquers will dance in the Revels of line 349.

349 *Phosphorus*] the planet Venus when appearing before sunrise. Compare the appearance of Hesperus in Davenant's *Luminalia* (1638): '*The morning Starre appeares in the Aire, sitting on a bright Cloud, in forme of a beautifull youth*'; and of Amphiluche in Shirley's *The Triumph of Peace* (see p. 303 below).

353 Gentle Knights] Ferrabosco's music for this song has been published by Cutts, pp. 298–9, and by Sabol, no. 15.

371 *the work*] the scenic frame or arch.

372 *the Star vanished*] It is possible that F2 (1640) rightly completes an intended alteration in the uncorrected state of F1 (1616) which was only

partly effected in the corrected state (see Collation note). If this were the case, not Phosphorus but the Masquers would 'vanish'.

372 *machine*]   contrivance.

375 Morning]   Aurora.

376 Though]   as though. Aurora *does* love her bed, since it contains Tithonus. To assume ellipsis of *as* (*N.E.D.*, 'though', 4*b*) seems preferable to emending the text (e.g. *not* to *doth*).

377 Sun]   Sol.

LOVE FREED FROM IGNORANCE AND FOLLY

BY BEN JONSON

Edited by Norman Sanders

INTRODUCTION

In December 1610 the court of James I was awaiting the arrival of
Maria de' Medici's ambassador extraordinary, Marshal Lavendin,
who was to bring to England for signature the Anglo-French treaty
negotiated by Henri IV before his assassination earlier in the year.
One result of the preparations made for his entertainment was that
two of Jonson's masques, *Oberon* for Prince Henry and *Love Freed
from Ignorance and Folly* for the Queen, which had been planned as
part of the Christmas festivities, were postponed so that they could
be mounted in Lavendin's honour (*C.S.P. Venetian*, XII, 101).
Unfortunately, the Marshal was delayed, much to the King's dis-
pleasure, and Prince Henry's masque was presented on 1 January
1611 in the presence of the ambassadors of Spain and Venice (*ibid.*
p. 106). The Queen's masque, however, was again put off because,
according to the Venetian ambassador, Marc' Antonio Correr, 'the
stage machinery is not in order or because their Majesties thought it
well to let the Marshal depart first' (*ibid.* p. 110). It was finally
produced on 3 February in Lavendin's presence, for Correr again
reports, on 1 February, that after the signing of the treaty 'the
Marshal is hurrying his departure...[and] nothing keeps him but
the Queen's masque which takes place the day after to-morrow'
(*ibid.* p. 115).

Jonson's stage-directions in the 1616 folio text are unusually brief
and give but little information about the staging, and none about
the sets or costumes. However, the fact that the entertainment cost
the Exchequer something over £600 indicates that the production
was a lavish one; and the entries relating to the expenditure of this
sum in the Accounts of the Exchequer of Receipt (Miscellanea,
E 407/57 (1), ff. 1, 2) enable us to make good some of the details not
supplied by Jonson.

The *décor* and production were in the hands of Inigo Jones who
received, as did Jonson, £40 for 'his pains and his invention'.
Among Jones's extant drawings there are none which may con-
fidently be linked with this masque, but no. 17 of his *Designs* may

73

represent the scene for the release of the eleven Daughters of the Morn from the Prison of Night. Alfonso Ferrabosco wrote the settings for the songs, two of which, namely 'O what a fault' (lines 299–307) and 'How near to good is what is fair!' (lines 310–17), are extant in the Tenbury MS (1018, ff. 36ᵛ–37ᵛ) at St Michael's College, Worcester. Robert Johnson scored the songs for the lutes, a Mr Confess arranged the dances and played the part of one of the Muses' Priests, Thomas Lupo set the dances to the violins, and Jacques Cordier (or Bochan) taught the choreography to the Queen and her ladies. In all, sixty-six musicians were employed for the performance to play sackbuts, lutes, violins, flutes and hautboys.

From the same set of accounts some idea of how the performers were dressed can also be gained. Cupid, to appear 'the naked boy', was in a suit of flesh-coloured satin decorated with lace and puffs; the twelve Follies wore coats of several-coloured taffeta, which perhaps were parti-coloured garments reminiscent of the stage Fool's costume; and the three Graces, also in coloured taffeta, may have resembled their counterparts in *The Magnificent Entertainment* with their 'long robes of sundry colours hanging loose'. The Muses' Priests were splendidly decked out in robes of crimson taffeta with scarves of sarsenet and copper lace, and wore hoods and gorgets of light blue satin lined with calico.

For the action of the masque Jonson again adopts the wandering pilgrim motif that he had used earlier with so much success in *The Masque of Beauty*. The opening depicts the moment of crisis in the journey of the Daughters of the Morn who, led by the Queen of the Orient and under the guidance of Cupid, have set out from their home in the east to seek Phoebus where he dines nightly with the Ocean in his western palace. On landing in Ultima Thule they have been captured by the Sphinx, Ignorance, and incarcerated in the Prison of Night. Cupid has offered on their behalf to subject himself to a test in the form of a riddle, on the understanding that should he fail to elucidate its meaning he will die to redeem the lady prisoners from captivity.

From his marginal notes on the action it is clear that Jonson conceived Ignorance as a monstrous enemy of Love and Beauty who hinders all noble actions, and as a perverter of truth who

74

'covets to enwrap herself in dark and obscure terms'. In this respect
she is seen as the antithesis of Love who ever attends on Beauty and
expresses himself 'with all clearness and simplicity'. In emphasizing
the monstrous nature of Ignorance Jonson is, of course, in the
Renaissance tradition which lies behind Holofernes's words 'O, thou
monster Ignorance, how deformed dost thou look!'. However, in
representing the quality specifically as a sphinx he was probably
indebted to the emblematists whose works were in part designed,
according to Fabricii da Teramo, to expel the 'monstrous sphinx of
ignorance unleashed in this century'. His immediate source for this
identification may well have been either Alciati's *Emblemata* or
Ripa's *Iconologia* both of which Jonson is known to have used.
Emblem no. 187 (Antwerp Edition 1574) 'Ignorantia' in Alciati's
collection is headed 'Submovendam ignorantiam' and is illustrated
by a picture of a sphinx which except for its lack of wings has all the
features found in Jonson's marginal gloss. Beneath are some verses,
also quoted by Ripa in the 1603 edition of his book, which include
the following lines:

> Quod monstruum id? Sphinx est. Cur candida virginis ora,
> Et volucrum pennas, crura leonis habet?
> Hanc faciem assumpsit rerum ignorantia:...

For the purpose of the masque, however, Jonson appears to have
added to this creature from Alciati the wings, riddle and rocky
perch of the Theban Sphinx of Seneca or Apollodorus, together
with the qualities of 'fierceness and swiftness to evil' which he may
have found in the *Mythologiae* of Natalis Comes.

In his handling of the central device Jonson draws as close to
truly dramatizing the masque as he had managed up to this time.
Once the previous events and present situation have been outlined
in the opening dialogue and the riddle has been posed, Cupid, in a
succession of plausible guesses, gives an interpretation which is seen
to fail only at the penultimate couplet. The Sphinx claims him as her
prey, and her offspring, the Follies, preparatory to dragging him
away to his death, perform a wild dance which constitutes the
climax of both the anti-masque and the dramatic element itself. This
crisis is resolved not by some device of sudden visual splendour but

by the appearance of the Muses' Priests who are necessary aids because, as Jonson probably learnt from Apollodorus,

> It is true that Sphinx their dame
> Had the sense first from the Muses,
> Which in uttering she doth lame,
> Perplexeth, and abuses.

Therefore it is only they who can advise Love that the solution is to be found by looking into the 'brightest face here shining', that is the face of King James.

Cupid's failure to solve the Sphinx's puzzle is due to his inability to reconcile his solution of 'A mistress' with the

> Two contraries which Time, till now,
> Nor Fate knew where to join, or how.

This paradox as well as the others contained in the riddle is ultimately based upon certain Christian exercises which Jonson adapted for his own purpose in the masque. As Edgar Wind has shown in his *Pagan Mysteries in the Renaissance* (1958, Ch. XIV), they derive from the *serio ludere* of Cusanus who, in order to direct the mind to the hidden God, invented a series of experiments in metaphor or semi-magical exercises, which consisted of finding in an unusual object within human experience those apparent contradictions which are combined in the Godhead. For example, the motionless eye of God is said to follow us everywhere, and so the eyes of a portrait are used by Cusanus in his *De Visione Dei* to illustrate an eye 'which still moves and still is fix'd'. Similarly, in his *De beryllo* and *De ludo globii* a lens and a newly invented toy are cited to show how immanence and transcendence may be combined, how an object within the world can embrace the world from without. Strictly speaking, therefore, the Sphinx's riddle should have the answer 'God', but for Jonson the transference of such divine traits to the King, God's agent on earth, and by extension to Albion, the country he governs, was but an easy step.

The identification of James with Phoebus has also behind it a comparable profound philosophical substance. The analogy between the King's position in society and the sun's in the heavens was, of course, a commonplace; and the imagery based upon it provided ready-made illustrative materials for the political theorist and court panegyrist alike. But, as D. J. Gordon has demonstrated in *The Journal of the Warburg and Courtauld Institutes*, IV (1943), 122–41, behind Jonson's use of the sun/light symbolism of kingship in his masques there lies a knowledge of the theory of beauty developed by the Florentine Platonists. The Love of *Love Freed* is, therefore, the 'seeing Cupid' concerned with the Idea of Beauty and not the blind, wanton boy associated with earthly sensual love as he is depicted in the Sphinx's speeches. Beauty is personified in the Daughters of the Morn who grieve that they might not ever see Phoebus 'that glorious star, | For whose love [they] came so far'. And it is James-Phoebus alone that can inspire Cupid to rescue Beauty both from the Prison of Night and from the clutches of Time who 'Is eating, every piece of hour, | Some object of the rarest worth'.

Thus, while in *Love Freed* we can see Jonson characteristically developing the masque's dramatic elements so as to provide an exquisite poetic framework for the formal climax, he preserves at the same time the standards of decorum, hierarchical unity and moral truth which he held to be the governing principles of the masque as a literary form. It stands as one of those 'high and hearty inventions' which accords with his own criteria: an entertainment whose voice is 'taught to sound to present occasions' but whose 'sense or doth or should always lay hold on more removed mysteries'.

[DRAMATIS PERSONAE

Love (Cupid)
Sphinx (Ignorance)
Twelve Follies
Twelve Muses' Priests
The Graces
Eleven Daughters of the Morn
Chorus]

A MASQUE OF HER MAJESTY'S.
LOVE FREED FROM IGNORANCE
AND FOLLY

*   *   *

So soon as the King's majesty was set and in expectation, there was
heard a strange music of wild instruments, to which a Sphinx came
forth dancing, leading Love bound.

Sphinx. Come, sir tyrant, lordly Love,
   You that awe the gods above,   5
   As their creatures here below,
   With the sceptre call'd your bow;
   And do all their forces bear
   In the quiver that you wear,
   Whence no sooner you do draw   10
   Forth a shaft, but is a law.
   Now they shall not need to tremble,
   When you threaten or dissemble,
   Any more; and, though you see
   Whom to hurt, you ha'not free   15
   Will to act your rage. The bands
   Of your eyes now tie your hands.
   All the triumphs, all the spoils,
   Gotten by your arts and toils
   Over foe and over friend,   20
   O'er your mother, here must end;
   And you, now, that thought to lay
   The world waste, must be my prey.
Love. Cruel Sphinx, I rather strive
   How to keep the world alive   25
   And uphold it; without me
   All again would Chaos be.
   Tell me, monster, what should move

79

Thy despite thus against Love?
Is there nothing fair and good,   30
Nothing bright but burns thy blood?
Still, thou art thyself, and made
All of practice to invade
Clearest bosoms. Hath this place
None will pity Cupid's case?   35
Some soft eye (while I can see
Who it is that melts for me)
Weep a fit? Are all eyes here
Made of marble? But a tear,
Though a false one, it may make   40
Others true compassion take.
I would tell you all the story
If I thought you could be sorry;
And, in truth, there's none have reason
Like yourselves to hate the treason;   45
For it practis'd was on beauty,
Unto whom Love owes all duty.
Let your favour but affright
Sphinx here, I shall soon recite
Every passage how it was.   50
Sphinx. Do, I'll laugh, or cry alas.
Thinks poor Love, can ladies' looks
Save him from the Sphinx's hooks?
Love. No, but these can witness bear
Of my candour, when they hear   55
What thy malice is, or how
I became thy captive now;
And it is no small content,
Falling, to fall innocent.
        Know then, all you glories here,   60
In the utmost east there were
Eleven Daughters of the Morn;
Ne'er were brighter bevy born,
Nor more perfect beauties seen.
The eldest of them was the Queen   65

Of the Orient, and 'twas said
That she should with Phoebus wed;
For which high-vouchsafed grace
He was lov'd of all their race.
And they would, when he did rise,   70
Do him early sacrifice
Of the rich and purest gum,
That from any plant could come;
And would look at him as far
As they could discern his car,   75
Grieving that they might not ever
See him; and when night did sever
Their aspects, they sat and wept
Till he came, and never slept.
Insomuch, that at the length   80
This their fervour got such strength
As they would a journey prove,
By the guard and aid of Love,
Hither to the farthest west;
Where, they heard, as in the east,   85
He a palace no less bright
Had, to feast in every night
With the Ocean, where he rested
Safe and in all state invested.

   I, that never left the side   90
Of the fair, became their guide.
But behold, no sooner landing
On this isle, but this commanding
Monster Sphinx, the enemy
Of all actions great and high,   95
Knowing that these rites were done
To the wisdom of the sun,
From a cliff surpris'd them all.
And, though I did humbly fall
At her lion's feet, and pray'd   100
As she had the face of maid,
That she would compassion take

Of these ladies, for whose sake
Love would give himself up; she,
Swift to evil, as you see   10
By her wings and hooked hands,
First did take my offer'd bands,
Then to prison of the night
Did condemn those sisters bright,
There for ever to remain   11
'Less they could the knot unstrain
Of a riddle, which she put
Darker than where they'are shut;
Or, from thence, their freedoms prove
With the utter loss of Love.   11
   They, unwilling to forego
One who had deserved so
Of all beauty in their names,
Were content to have their flames
Hid in lasting night, ere I   12
Should for them untimely die.
I, on th'other side, as glad
That I such advantage had
To assure them mine, engaged
Willingly myself, and waged   12
With the monster that if I
Did her riddle not untie,
I would freely give my life
To redeem them and the strife.
Sphinx. Ha' you said, sir? Will you try   13
Now your known dexterity?
You presume upon your arts
Of tying and untying hearts;
And it makes you confident,
But anon you will repent.   13
Love. No, Sphinx, I do not presume,
But some little heart assume
From my judges here, that sit
As they would not lose Love yet.

82

Sphinx. You are pleasant, sir; 'tis good.   140
Love. Love does often change his mood.
Sphinx. I shall make you sad again.
Love. I shall be the sorrier then.
Sphinx. Come, sir, lend it your best ear.
Love. I begin t'have half a fear.   145
Sphinx. First, Cupid, you must cast about
  To find a world, the world without,
  Wherein what's done, the eye doth do,
  And is the light and treasure too.
  This eye still moves and still is fixed,   150
  And in the powers thereof are mixed
  Two contraries which Time, till now,
  Nor Fate knew where to join, or how.
  Yet, if you hit the right upon,
  You must resolve these all by one.   155
Love. Sphinx, you are too quick of tongue;
  Say't again, and take me'along.
Sphinx. I say, you first must cast about
  To find a world, the world without.
Love. I say, that is already done,   160
  And is the new world i' the moon.
Sphinx. Cupid, you do cast too far,
  This world is nearer by a star:
  So much light I'll give you to't.
Love. Without a glass? Well, I shall do't.   165
  Your world's a lady, then; each creature
  Human is a world in feature,
  Is it not?
Sphinx.   Yes, but find out
  A world you must, the world without.   170
Love. Why, if her servant be not here,
  She doth a single world appear
  Without her world.
Sphinx.   Well, you shall run.
Love. Nay, Sphinx, thus far is well begun.   175
Sphinx. Wherein what's done, the eye doth do,

And is the light and treasure too.
Love. That's clear as light: for wherein lies
A lady's power but in her eyes?
And not alone her grace and power,
But oftentimes her wealth and dower.
Sphinx. I spake but of an eye, not eyes.
Love. A one-eyed mistress that unties.
Sphinx. This eye still moves and still is fixed.
Love. A rolling eye that, native there,
Yet throws her glances everywhere;
And, being but single, fain would do
The offices and arts of two.
Sphinx. And in the powers thereof are mixed
Two contraries.
Love.   That's smiles and tears,
Or fire and frost; for either bears
Resemblance apt.
Sphinx.   Which Time, till now,
Nor Fate knew where to join, or how.
How now, Cupid? At a stay?
Not another word to say?
Do you find, by this, how long
You have been at a fault and wrong?
Love. Sphinx, it is your pride to vex
Whom you deal with, and perplex
Things most easy. Ignorance
Thinks she doth herself advance,
If of problems clear she make
Riddles, and the sense forsake,
Which came gentle from the Muses,
Till her uttering it abuses.
Sphinx. Nay, your railing will not save you;
Cupid, I of right must have you.
Come my fruitful issue forth,
Dance, and show a gladness, worth
Such a captive as is Love,
And your mother's triumph prove.

[*Enter*] *the Follies* [*and*] *dance, which were twelve she-fools.*

    Now, go take him up and bear him   215
    To the cliff, where I will tear him
    Piece-meal, and give each a part
    Of his raw and bleeding heart.
  Love. Ladies, have your looks no power
    To help Love at such an hour?   220
    Will you lose him thus? Adieu.
    Think what will become of you:
    Who shall praise you, who admire?
    Who shall whisper, by the fire
    As you stand, soft tales? Who bring you   225
    Pretty news, in rhymes who sing you?
    Who shall bathe him in the streams
    Of your blood, and send you dreams
    Of delight?
  Sphinx.   Away, go bear him   230
    Hence; they shall no longer hear him.

[*Enter*] *the Muses' Priests, their number twelve,* [*and sing*]
             their song, to a measure.

    Gentle Love, be not dismay'd;
      See, the Muses pure and holy,   235
    By their Priests have sent thee aid
      Against this brood of Folly.

    It is true that Sphinx their dame
      Had the sense first from the Muses,
    Which in uttering she doth lame,   240
      Perplexeth, and abuses.

    But they bid that thou should'st look
      In the brightest face here shining,
    And the same, as would a book,
      Shall help thee in divining.   245

  Love. 'Tis done, 'tis done, I have found it out:
    Britain's the world, the world without;

The King's the eye, as we do call
The sun the eye of this great all;
And is the light and treasure too. 250
For 'tis his wisdom all doth do,
Which still is fixed in his breast,
Yet still doth move to guide the rest.
The contraries which Time, till now,
Nor Fate knew where to join, or how, 255
Are Majesty and Love which there,
And nowhere else, have their true sphere.
Now, Sphinx, I've hit the right upon
And do resolve these all by one:
That is, that you meant Albion. 260
Priest. 'Tis true in him and in no other;
      Love, thou art clear absolved.
      Vanish, Follies, with your mother,
        The riddle is resolved.
      Sphinx must fly when Phoebus shines, 265
      And to aid of Love inclines.
Love. Appear then you my brighter charge,
And to light yourselves enlarge
To behold that glorious star,
For whose love you came so far, 270
While the monster with her elves
Do precipitate themselves. [*Exeunt Sphinx and Follies.*]

[*Enter the*] Graces. *Their song crowning Cupid.*

A crown, a crown for Love's bright head,
    Without whose happy wit 275
All form and beauty had been dead,
    And we had died with it.
For what are all the graces
Without good forms and faces?
Then, Love, receive the due reward 280
    Those Graces have prepar'd.
Chorus. And may no hand, no tongue, no eye
Thy merit or their thanks envy.

[*The Daughters of the Morn, led by the Queen of the Orient,*
         enter from their prison.]   285
   A dialogue between the Chorus and the Graces.

Chorus. What gentle forms are these that move
      To honour Love?
Graces. They are the bright and golden lights
      That grace his nights;   290
Chorus. And shot from beauty's eyes,
      They look like fair Aurora's streams;
Graces. They are her fairer daughter's beams
      Who now doth rise.
Chorus. Then night is lost or fled away,   295
      For where such beauty shines is ever day.

   The masque dance followed. That done, one of the
         Priests alone sang.

   1 Priest. O what a fault, nay, what a sin
   In Fate or Fortune had it been,   300
   So much beauty to have lost!
   Could the world with all her cost
   Have redeem'd it?
   Chorus.   No, no, no.
   1 Priest. How so?   305
   Chorus. It would Nature quite undo,
      For losing these, you lost her too.

   The measures and revels follow. Then another of the
         Priests alone [*sang*].

2 Priest. How near to good is what is fair!   310
      Which we no sooner see,
   But with the lines and outward air
      Our senses taken be.
   We wish to see it still, and prove
      What ways we may deserve: 315
   We court, we praise, we more than love,
      We are not griev'd to serve.

The last masque dance. And after it this full song.

What just excuse had aged Time
   His weary limbs now to have eased, 320
And sat him down without his crime,
    While every thought was so much pleased!
But he so greedy to devour
   His own and all that he brings forth,
Is eating, every piece of hour, 325
    Some object of the rarest worth.
Yet this is rescued from his rage,
As not to die by time or age;
    For beauty hath a living name,
    And will to heav'n from whence it came. 330

The going out.

Now, now, gentle Love is free, and beauty bless'd
   With the sight it so much long'd to see;
Let us the Muses' Priests and Graces go to rest,
   For in them our labours happy be. 335
Then, then, airy music sound, and teach our feet
   How to move in time and measure meet:
Thus should the Muses' Priests and Graces go to rest
   Bowing to the sun thron'd in the west.

THE TEXT

The masque was first printed in the folio of 1616, having been entered in the Stationers' Register on 20 January 1615 by William Stansby presumably among 'certayne Masques at the Court never yet printed' (*Arber*, III, 562). The text is clean and contains only two substantive errors: 'lives' for 'lines' at line 312, and the meaningless 'angry' at line 336. Twenty-one copies of the folio were collated for the present edition: British Museum (G. 11630, c. 39. k. 9); Royal Shakespeare Theatre Library (4615, 4616); Cambridge University Library; Birmingham University Library; University College Library, London; John Rylands Library, Manchester; Cosin Library, Durham; New York Public Library; Huntington Library, California (62100, 62101, 62104, 62105); Folger Library, Washington (Copies 1, 3, 4, 5, 6 of *S.T.C.* 14751; Copies 1, 2 of *S.T.C.* 14751. 2). The variants between these copies are mainly in punctuation, spacing, spelling and typography, some being the result of press correction and others due to the resetting of certain formes. The one substantive press variant is found at line 56 and is noted in the Collation (p. 90).

The text in the second folio of 1640 was almost certainly set up from that in the first, and a collation of the copies in the libraries of the Royal Shakespeare Theatre and the Shakespeare Birthplace Trust revealed only minor changes and corrections in punctuation, differences in spelling and the introduction of one error. Texts of the songs at lines 299–307 and 310–17 are also found in Tenbury MS 1018, ff. 36ᵛ–37ᵛ, which contains Ferrabosco's setting; these include two variant readings of little importance, one correction of a folio reading and seven lines not in the folio text, the details of which are included in the Collation and the Commentary. Jonson's marginal glosses are also included in the Commentary.

The punctuation of the copy-text has been modernized in the present edition except that wherever the folio punctuation appears to aim at an obvious rhetorical effect it has been retained. The apostrophes in the copy-text indicating elision have also been kept.

COLLATION

3]   F 1 *has an extra stage direction* SPHINX leading LOVE bound.

56 is]   *omitted in some copies of* F 1, *vi҉. B.M. c. 39. k. 9, Royal Shakespeare Theatre 4616, John Rylands, Cosin, Cambridge University, Huntington 62105, Folger Copy 5 of S.T.C. 14751.*

287–95]   *Speech prefixes conj. Gifford; not in* F 1, F 2.

301 to have]   had been *Tenbury MS.*

312 lines]   *Tenbury MS; conj. Whalley;* lives F 1, F 2.

314 to see it still]   it still to see *Tenbury MS.*

336 airy]   *conj. Swinburne;* angry F 1, F 2.

COMMENTARY

2 *a strange...instruments*]　The music was probably produced by the thirteen sackbuts and hautboys which are listed among the expense items for the masque in the Accounts of the Exchequer of Receipt. The Witches in *The Masque of Queens* also enter with 'a kind of hollow and infernal music' (lines 29–30).

2 *Sphinx*]　'By this Sphinx was understood Ignorance who is always the enemy of Love and Beauty, and lies still in wait to entrap them. For which Antiquity hath given her the upper parts and face of a woman, the nether parts of a lion, the wings of an eagle to show her fierceness and swiftness to evil where she hath power' (Jonson). See Introduction, pp. 74–5.

4–11 *Come...law*]　In his masques this is Jonson's usual conception of Cupid and his trappings; cf. *The Haddington Masque*, lines 86–126.

16 *to act your rage*]　to perpetrate your wild folly.

19 *toils*]　snares, traps.

21 *your mother*]　i.e. Venus; the reference is to Cupid's using his golden arrow on his mother; cf. *The Haddington Masque*, lines 124–6.

26–7 *without me...Chaos be*]　The allusion is to the legend that Love was the first of the gods to spring out of Chaos, an idea Jonson uses frequently in his masques; cf. *The Masque of Beauty*, lines 282–5, 326–8; *A Challenge at Tilt*, lines 162–5; *Love's Triumph through Callipolis*, lines 155–8.

33 *practice*]　trickery, treachery.

35 *case*]　plight.

38 *a fit*]　a short period, a spell.

45 *treason*]　breach of faith.

53 *hooks*]　claws; see lines 106, 215–18.

55 *candour*]　stainlessness of character, integrity; cf. *The Alchemist*, v, v, 152.

60–129 *Know then...strife*]　'The meaning of this is that these ladies being the perfect issue of Beauty and all worldly grace were carried by Love to celebrate the majesty and wisdom of the King, figured in the sun, and seated in these extreme parts of the world, where they were rudely received by Ignorance on their first approach, to the hazard of their affection, it being her nature to hinder all noble actions; but that the Love which brought them thither was not willing to forsake them, no more than they were to abandon it. Yet was it enough perplexed in that the monster Ignorance still covets to enwrap itself in dark and obscure terms, and betray that way; whereas true Love affects to express itself with all clearness and simplicity' (Jonson).

65–6 *The eldest...Orient*]　i.e. Queen Anne, wife of James I.

67 *Phoebus*]　i.e. James I; see Introduction, pp. 76–7.

72 Of the rich...gum] A compressed superlative meaning 'richest and purest'. Cedar wood, bays, and junipers were all used for sacrifice in classical times.

82 prove] try, essay.

86–9 He a palace...invested] Cf. *The Masque of Beauty*, lines 388–91.

98 From a cliff] Cf. the Theban Sphinx which delivered its riddle from a rock; see Introduction, p. 75.

107 First...bands] See lines 16–17.

108–13 Then...shut] Cf. *Twelfth Night*, IV, ii, 47 'there is no darkness but ignorance'.

111 unstrain] unravel, untie.

114 prove] make good, establish.

125 waged] wagered, bargained.

129 strife] dispute, quarrel.

146–55 First, Cupid...all by one] See Introduction, p. 76.

157 take me'along] go no faster than I can follow, let me understand you.

161 the new world i' the moon] The reference is to Galileo's *Nuntius Sidereus* (1610).

163 star] This term was applied to any of the heavenly bodies including the earth and the moon.

165 glass] telescope.

166–7 each creature...feature] The allusion is to the Pythagorean doctrine of man as microcosm; cf. *Hymenaei*, line 125.

174 you shall run] you shall proceed.

183 unties] releases from allegiance.

196 At a stay] unable to go any further.

202–7 Ignorance...abuses] The Sphinx's riddle, being a species of poetry, was ultimately derived from the Muses but was mangled by her distorted method of utterance; cf. Apollodorus, III, v, 7–8.

214–18 [*Enter*]...heart] 'This shows that Love's expositions are not always serious till it be divinely instructed and that sometimes it may be in the danger of Ignorance and Folly, who are the mother and issue, for no folly but is born of ignorance' (Jonson).

216 cliff] See note to line 98.

232–45 *Enter...divining*] 'Here is understood the power of wisdom in the Muses' ministers, by which name all that have the spirit of prophecy are styled, and such they are that need to encounter Ignorance and Folly, and are ever ready to assist Love in any action of honour and virtue, and inspire him with their own soul' (Jonson).

247 the world without] Cf. *The King's Entertainment*, lines 41–50: '...and in her lap a little globe, inscrib'd upon ORBIS BRITANNICUS. And beneath, the word DIVISUS AB ORBE. To shew, that this empire is a world divided from the world, and alluding to that of CLAU[DIUS]—*Et nostro diducta Britannia mundo.* And VIRG[IL]—*Et penitus toto divisos orbe Britannos.*'

254–6 The contraries...Love] Cf. Ovid, *Metamorphoses*, II, 846–7: 'non bene conveniunt nec in una sede morantur maiestas et amor.'

259 all by one] The pun is more accurate in the folio spelling 'all by on'.

267 Appear...charge] This is addressed to the Queen and her lady masquers, not to the three Graces.

271 elves] malignant beings.

272 precipitate] As did the Theban Sphinx when Oedipus had solved her riddle.

299–317 O what...serve] In Alfonso Ferrabosco's setting of these verses (Tenbury MS, 1018, ff. 36ᵛ–37ᵛ, and printed in A. J. Sabol, *Songs and Dances for the Stuart Masque* (1959), no. 16), lines 304–7 'No, no, no... lost her too' are omitted, and seven extra lines inserted after 'redeem'd it' in line 303, these being:

> Senses by unjust force banish'd
> From the object of you[r] pleasure,
> Now of you is all end vanish'd;
> You who late possess'd more treasure,
> When eyes fed on what did shine
> And ears drank what was divine,
> Than earth's broad arms could measure.

312 lines] lineaments. The folio reading 'lives' is obviously wrong, and is the result probably of either foul case or the compositor's misreading of the minims in the MS copy. In the Tenbury MS of Ferrabosco's setting the spelling is quite clearly 'lynes'.

319–26 What...worth] The identification of Time with Saturn was a conventional Roman concept, and there are many references to Saturn devouring his children. Jonson's source might have been any of the following: Cicero, *De Natura Deorum*, R. Stephanus, *Dictionarium*, L. G. Gyraldus, *De Deis Gentium*, or N. Comes, *Mythologiae*.

329–30 For beauty...came] Cf. Ficino, *In Convivium Platonis, De Amore, Commentarium* (Paris, 1641), Or. 5, Cap. 4, p. 298: 'Pulchritudo est splendor divini vultus.'

336 airy] Swinburne's conjecture has been generally accepted. The folio reading 'angry' is obviously inappropriate, although it has been defended by F. Cunningham in his edition of 1871.

THE LORDS' MASQUE

BY THOMAS CAMPION

Edited by I. A. Shapiro

INTRODUCTION

Festivities to celebrate the wedding of Princess Elizabeth, only daughter of King James I of England, were extravagant, even by Jacobean standards, and numerous. They included three masques, the first of which, Campion's *The Lords' Masque*, was commissioned by the King[1] for presentation on the night of the wedding, 14 February 1613, and paid for out of the Exchequer. The two others, Chapman's *Masque of the Middle Temple and Lincoln's Inn* and Francis Beaumont's *Masque of the Inner Temple and Gray's Inn* (see pp. 125–48), were organized and paid for by the Inns of Court presenting them. The texts of all three were reprinted by John Nichols in his *Progresses of James I* (1828), vol. II, pp. 527–626, together with contemporary accounts of all the other wedding festivities; this was the first reprint of *The Lords' Masque* since its original publication in 1613.

Thomas Campion (1567–1620), who wrote the dialogue and songs for *The Lords' Masque*, was one of the best English lyric poets of his time, or, indeed, of any other. He was also an amateur musician of note. Since 1605, when he obtained an M.D. at the University of Caen, he had practised medicine, but that seems not to have interrupted his verse-writing or music-making, or to have diminished his reputation as poet and composer. In 1607 he had been called on to write a masque for Lord Hay's wedding and in 1614 he was to write another for the wedding of James's favourite, the Earl of Somerset. He was also commissioned to write two 'Entertainments' to welcome royalty on progress.

The staging of *The Lords' Masque*, its scenery, dresses, lighting-effects and everything else pertaining to *décor*, were designed by Inigo Jones. It seems likely that in addition Jones collaborated with Campion in devising certain details of the masque's action, for it presents 'something much more elaborate than any masque had previously offered' (Nicoll, *Stuart Masques*, p. 74); the much admired devices of the dancing stars (lines 123–8, 173–4), the

---

[1] The warrant is printed in J. P. Collier's *Annals of the Stage*, I, 378.

moving lights (lines 190–1), and Sibylla's pulling on of a large obelisk (lines 334–45) could not have been included by Campion, perhaps not even conceived, without consultation with Jones.

The choice of Orpheus as the prime mover of the action is an interesting reflexion of Campion's personal preoccupations. Apparently it did not occur to him that his audience might wonder why Orpheus, rather than Mercury or another of Jove's usual messengers, should be employed to release Entheus (Poetic Inspiration) from Mania's cave, though it is possible that he meant us to infer that Entheus could be released only by that Orphean music which could tame wild beasts and move trees, rocks, and rivers, as Elizabethan writers frequently remind us. Unity of action, with logical and explicit connexion between episodes, is not, however, among the merits of *The Lords' Masque*, great as those are. Why, for example, does Poetic Inspiration, after accepting the command 'to create | Inventions rare' (lines 89–90), exercise instead a supernatural ability to detect the hidden presence of Prometheus? One might suppose that Campion had accidentally omitted to explain that in what follows Prometheus and his creatures are embodiments of Entheus's imaginings, did not that conflict with Prometheus's announcement that he comes to make a third presenter 'In equal balance' with Orpheus and Entheus (lines 136–7). However, such inconsistencies, if noticed, must have been immediately forgotten as the audience admired the splendid spectacles that followed in the Prometheus episodes. These are based on the legend as it is found in Elizabethan reference books, in which Prometheus is described as the first maker of human images, to whom he gave life by means of fire stolen from heaven, so creating the first men and thereby incurring the wrath of Jove. As the Prometheus scenes were concluding (lines 323–5) the audience must have supposed that the show was over; nothing had led them to expect yet another change of scene or the introduction of the new speaker, Sibylla. The lack of any connexion between the Prometheus scenes and this final episode may, however, have been deliberate. The prophetess and her 'trophy' may have been introduced thus abruptly for greater theatrical effect.

In spectacle and in stage-effects, the latter still something of a novelty in England at that date, *The Lords' Masque* was unusually rich, as Campion's 'description' shows. The technical means by which such effects were produced have been discussed in detail by Allardyce Nicoll (*Stuart Masques*, esp. pp. 72–5, 135–6) and need not be noticed again here, but what Campion means by 'the Scene' requires elucidation. Above what would now be called the stage there was an upper stage, provided with its own curtain (cf. lines 5, 123–4). The upper stage did not project as far forward as the lower; that is indicated in line 96, which Entheus must have spoken from the front of the lower stage while pointing back to the still undrawn curtain, 'that veil', before the upper stage. It seems that scenery on the lower stage, e.g. Orpheus's thicket and Mania's cave (lines 8–9), was all underneath the upper stage, and that the front of the lower stage was left conveniently clear for action. Such an arrangement is required by lines 204–9, which show that the 'cloud, which reached from the top of the heavens to the earth' was drawn across the lower stage, but was close enough to the front of the upper stage to allow the masquers to step on to it and so descend, while at the same time it masked 'the wood, being the under-part of the Scene' and also, presumably, the thicket and cave, during the scene-changing described in lines 211 *et seq.* If the 'under-part of the Scene' was provided with its own curtain, this must have hung just below that which covered the upper stage. Such curtaining would be consistent with Campion's 'description', and seems likely to have been employed to mask 'the whole scene' until performance began. Had it been necessary during the performance, these curtains could have been drawn to mask a change of scene at either stage-level, or on both together, while action continued on the front of the lower stage. If the 'under-part of the Scene' was curtained, as assumed above, no proscenium curtain would have been needed. A proscenium frame, however, or alternatively, permanent wings, must have been employed; though nowhere mentioned, this would have been necessary to conceal (until line 204 and again after line 209) the cloud 'from the side of the Scene' that passed 'overthwart' the stage, and perhaps also to mask the obelisk that Sibylla drew on to the stage (cf. line 345 and Commentary thereon). It is probable therefore that in Campion's 'description' the phrase 'the whole Scene' refers not to the whole of the acting area but only to those portions on which scenery was set, i.e. the upper stage and the area immediately below it.

Campion's description of the scenery, dresses, dances, and 'artifices' was written after the masque's presentation, as several passages prove (cf. lines 57–64; 123–9; 173–90). It can nearly always be distinguished from the original stage-directions because it is written in the past tense, whereas the present was used, as one would expect, in the stage-directions. For example, in lines 18–20 the original direction obviously was 'The consorts...cave; she as one amazed speaks', into which was inserted the description: 'Her habit...graceful.' In lines 69–73, the opening sentence down to 'behind them' must be an original stage-direction, to which a 'description' has been appended. Again, in lines 203–26, the opening sentence (to 'lights') is clearly the original direction; after it two distinct pieces of the 'description' have been run together; the second, lines 210–26, would be more appropriately located after line 237. Since two other 'descriptions' are undoubtedly misplaced in the original edition (lines 278–9 and 339–48; cf. Collation), this suggests that they, and possibly others also, were supplied in a form not easy for the printer to relate correctly to the text, and that Campion did not correct the proofs.

Dancing was originally, with music, 'the soul of masque' and it continued prominent in all, despite the development of spectacle. A space between the stage and the King's 'state' was specially carpeted and kept clear for the dances. Here was danced, for example, the 'lively measure' of the 'Sixteen Pages, like fiery spirits' (line 196), and that is why they 'return toward the Scene' (line 203) to attend the masquers. As usual, special 'new' dances were devised for the masquers (cf. lines 296, 435; the dances mentioned in lines 62, 200, 380 were probably also 'new').

The dances were devised and taught and music set for them by the most eminent masters and composers of the day. They are named in a writ[1] for payment of fees to Campion, Inigo Jones and the musicians, composers, and actors employed. Of the 'states' (line

---

[1] Printed by F. Devon, *Issues of Exchequer* (1836), p. 165; and by Reyher, pp. 508–9; summary in Chambers, *Elizabethan Stage*, III, 244.

183) who danced in this masque we know the names of only four: the Earls of Montgomery and of Salisbury, Lord Hay and Miss Ann Dudley (cf. Chambers, *op. cit.* III, 242). The last was chief lady of honour to the bride and accompanied her to Heidelberg (Mary A. E. Green, *Elizabeth...Queen of Bohemia* (ed. S. C. Lomas, 1909), pp. 9, 44). A clue to the identities of the other 'states' lies in Sir Edward Phelips's reference to this as 'the Erles and Ladyes Maske' (P.R.O., S.P. 14, vol. 72, fo. 93).

Inigo Jones's preliminary sketch for the costume of the eight male Masquers is reproduced in Plate 11*b*, and his final, and coloured, version in Plate 12*a* (cf. *Designs*, nos. 57–8, and plate VI). The Pages' costume illustrated in Plate 12*b* (*ibid.* no. 59, and frontispiece) may have been designed only for half of them; there are indications, in the list quoted below, that the attire of the eight 'Ladies' Pages' may have differed from that of the eight male Masquers' Pages. The only other design known, that for Entheus, Plate 11*a* (*ibid.* no. 56), was based on a woodcut of 'Furor Poeticus' in Ripa's *Iconologia* (cf. Nicoll, *Stuart Masques*, figs. 150–1).

Some idea of the magnificent mounting of *The Lords' Masque* can be got from a long statement of materials and workmanship 'employed at the Marriage of...the Lady Elizabeth' found in a warrant dated 4 May 1613, and printed in full (in the original spelling) in *Archaeologia* (1836), vol. XXVI, pp. 383–94. The list includes materials and clothes for the masque, but does not always distinguish those from what was supplied for the bride's trousseau. Among items for the masque specified or identifiable as such are:

755½ yards of tawny, white, crimson, colour de roy and black satin, employed upon suits for Masquers, and furniture for Bedsteads; 25 yards of white cloth of silver, employed upon 8 Masquers; 511¾ yards of several coloured taffeta to line sundry gowns, and employed in Masquers' apparel; 14 yards of black Perpetuana, for a suit for a Madman; 37 yards of sarsenet to line Masquing Pages' suits, and to make scarves; 1 lb. 4 oz. of fine Venice gold and spangles...to be employed upon 8 plumes of feathers; 232 lbs 5¼ oz. and a drachm of rich gold and silver spangled lace of sundry sorts for 8 Women Masquers; 12 oz. of white sewing silk, 8 yards of Venice ribbon, and 8 dozen of drumwork points for 8 Masquing Pages; making 8 Masquing suits of striped tinsel for Ladies' Pages, with small furnishings, as canvas, buckram, baize, pasteboard and wire, lined with taffeta sarsenet, and sewed with silk; making 5 suits for . . . 5 Speakers in the Masque, viz. Orpheus' antic coat-armour, with bases, labels, breeches and mantle, Mania's robe, with double sleeves and petticoat, Entheus' robe and mantle, and a pair of double sleeves, Prometheus' robe and mantle, Sibylla's robe, petticoat and veil, and for fustian, baize, coarse canvas, bumbast, for tinsel copper lace and fringes, for buskins, shoes, curl hair-wire and one pound of silk, for the [aforementioned 5 speakers]; 204 yards of copper stuffs, and 318 yards of tinsels of gold and silver, employed upon Masquers' apparel; 294 oz. of copper lace, containing 880 yards, employed upon 8 suits for 8 Pages in the Masque; 22 pair of silk stockings and 4 pair of worsted stockings for Pages, Speakers and footmen . . .

Almost certainly these items do not comprise all relating to the masque; for example, it seems highly probable that the following was provided for one or other set of '8 Masquing Pages':

8 pair of fine pumps for 8 pages, with 8 pair of roses edged with copper to them; 96 hanging buttons, with pendants, 44 dozen of little buttons and 8 caps for Pages.

It is thus not surprising that the few contemporary comments on *The Lords' Masque* which have come down to us should be mostly about its splendour. 'Very rich and sumptuous, yet it was very long and tedious, and with many devices, more like a play than a masque', reported John Chamberlain (*Letters*, ed. McClure, I, 428). But Chamberlain did not care for plays or masques, and had not been in the audience; we do not know who his informants were, or whether their views were representative. Sir John Finett, whose court functions took him to all masques, wrote that

The Maske of Lordes and honourable maydes . . . was performed wth exceeding charge and commendable discharge but why should the world expect in a busynes of no wayghtye consequence, more then ordinarye good performance frô such extraordinary great persons. It was the richest show but not showde the rychest that I haue seene, wch seemed to be a singularity of some in the affectatiô (though perhaps unseasonable) [of][1] conceald brauery: howsoeuer, the deuyse was ingeniously cast, the dances

[1] Paper torn; reading not certain.

well figured and euery Lord and Ladyes parte most mesurably caryed, and, this may sufficiently commend it (P.R.O., S.P. 14, vol. 72, fo. 64ʳ).

The Venetian Ambassador, Antonio Foscarini, reported that the masque 'was very beautiful, with three changes of scene...certain stars danced in the heavens by a most ingenious device...' (*C.S.P. Venetian*, XII, p. 498). He also had been present at the performance; in his report home he was presumably comparing it with what he had seen in this kind in Italy.

[DRAMATIS PERSONAE

Speakers
Orpheus
Mania, goddess of madness
Entheus
Prometheus
Sibylla, a prophetess

Non-speaking participants
Twelve 'frantics'
Eight male Masquers
Sixteen Pages (torchbearers)
Eight female Masquers]

The Description, Speeches and Songs of

THE LORDS' MASQUE

presented in the Banqueting House
on the marriage night
of the high and mighty COUNT PALATINE
and the royally descended
the LADY ELIZABETH,
14 February 1613

*   *   *

I have now taken occasion to satisfy many, who long since were desirous
that the Lords' Masque should be published, which, but for some private
lets, had in due time come forth.

*The Scene was divided into two parts from the roof to the floor. The
lower part being first discovered (upon the sound of a double consort,* 5
*expressed by several instruments, placed on either side of the room)
there appeared a wood in perspective, the innermost part being of relief
or whole round, the rest painted. On the left hand from the seat was a
cave, and on the right a thicket, out of which came Orpheus, who was
attired after the old Greek manner, his hair curled and long, a laurel* 10
*wreath on his head, and in his hand he bare a silver bird; about him
tamely paced several wild beasts: and upon the ceasing of the consort
Orpheus spake.*

> *Orpheus.* Again, again, fresh kindle Phoebus' sounds
>   T'exhale Mania from her earthy den;   15
> Allay the fury that her sense confounds,
>   And call her gently forth; sound, sound again.

*The consorts both sound again, and Mania, the goddess of madness,
appears wildly out of her cave. Her habit was confused and strange, but
yet graceful; she as one amazed speaks.*   20

Mania. What powerful noise is this importunes me
    T'abandon darkness which my humour fits?
Jove's hand in it I feel, and ever he
    Must be obey'd ev'n of the frantic'st wits.
Orpheus. Mania!   25
Mania.   Hah!
Orpheus.   Brain-sick, why start'st thou so?
  Approach yet nearer, and thou then shalt know
  The will of Jove, which he will breathe from me.
Mania. Who art thou? if my dazzled eyes can see,   30
  Thou art the sweet enchanter heav'nly Orpheus.
Orpheus. The same, Mania, and Jove greets thee thus:
  Though several power to thee and charge he gave
  T'enclose in thy dominions such as rave
  Through blood's distemper, how durst thou attempt   35
  T'imprison Entheus, whose rage is exempt
  From vulgar censure? It is all divine,
  Full of celestial rapture, that can shine
  Through darkest shadows: therefore Jove by me
  Commands thy power straight to set Entheus free.   40
Mania. How can I? Frantics with him many more
  In one cave are lock'd up; ope once the door,
  All will fly out and through the world disturb
  The peace of Jove; for what power then can curb
  Their reinless fury?   45
Orpheus.   Let not fear in vain
  Trouble thy crazed fancy; all again,
  Save Entheus, to thy safeguard shall retire,
  For Jove into our music will inspire
  The power of passion, that their thoughts shall bend   50
  To any form or motion we intend.
  Obey Jove's will then; go, set Entheus free.
Mania. I willing go, so Jove obey'd must be.
Orpheus. Let music put on protean changes now;
  Wild beasts it once tam'd, now let Frantics bow.   55

*At the sound of a strange music twelve Frantics enter, six men and six
women, all presented in sundry habits and humours: there was the Lover,*

*the Self-Lover, the Melancholic-Man full of fear, the School-Man
over-come with fantasy, the over-watched Usurer, with others that
made an absolute medley of madness; in midst of whom Entheus (or* 60
*Poetic Fury) was hurried forth and tossed up and down, till by virtue of
a new change in the music the Lunatics fell into a mad measure, fitted
to a loud fantastic tune; but in the end thereof the music changed into a
very solemn air, which they softly played while Orpheus spake.*

> *Orpheus.* Through these soft and calm sounds, Mania, pass 65
> With thy Fantastics hence; here is no place
> Longer for them or thee; Entheus alone
> Must do Jove's bidding now, all else be gone.

*During this speech Mania with her Frantics depart, leaving Entheus
behind them, who was attired in a close cuirass of the antic fashion,* 70
*bases with labels, a robe fastened to his shoulders, and hanging down
behind; on his head a wreath of laurel, out of which grew a pair of wings;
in the one hand he held a book, and in the other a pen.*

> *Entheus.* Divinest Orpheus, O how all from thee
> Proceed with wondrous sweetness! Am I free? 75
> Is my affliction vanish'd?
> *Orpheus.*   Too too long,
> Alas, good Entheus, hast thou brook'd this wrong.
> What! number thee with madmen! O mad age,
> Senseless of thee, and thy celestial rage. 80
> For thy excelling rapture, ev'n through things
> That seem most light, is borne with sacred wings:
> Nor are these musics, shows, or revels vain,
> When thou adorn'st them with thy Phoebean brain.
> They're palate-sick of much more vanity, 85
> That cannot taste them in their dignity.
> Jove therefore lets thy prison'd sprite obtain
> Her liberty and fiery scope again;
> And here by me commands thee to create
> Inventions rare, this night to celebrate, 90
> Such as become a nuptial by his will
> Begun and ended.

Entheus.   Jove I honour still,
And must obey. Orpheus, I feel the fires
Are ready in my brain, which Jove inspires.
Lo, through that veil I see Prometheus stand
Before those glorious lights which his false hand
Stole out of heav'n, the dull earth to inflame
With the affects of love and honour'd fame.
I view them plain in pomp and majesty
Such as, being seen, might hold rivality
With the best triumphs. Orpheus, give a call
With thy charm'd music, and discover all.
Orpheus. Fly, cheerful voices, through the air, and clear
These clouds, that yon hid beauty may appear.

A Song

1. Come away; bring thy golden theft,
        Bring, bright Prometheus, all thy lights;
    Thy fires from heav'n bereft
        Shew now to human sights.

Come quickly, come; thy stars to our stars straight present,
For pleasure being too much deferr'd loseth her best content.
What fair dames wish, should swift as their own thoughts appear;
To loving and to longing hearts every hour seems a year.

2. See how fair, O how fair they shine!
        What yields more pomp beneath the skies?
    Their birth is yet divine,
        And such their form implies.

Large grow their beams, their near approach afford them so
By nature; sights that pleasing are, cannot too amply show.
O might these flames in human shapes descend this place,
How lovely would their presence be, how full of grace!

*In the end of the first part of this song, the upper part of the Scene was
discovered by the sudden fall of a curtain; then in clouds of several
colours (the upper part of them being fiery, and the middle heightened
with silver) appeared eight Stars of extraordinary bigness, which so*

were placed, as that they seemed to be fixed between the firmament and the earth; in the front of the Scene stood Prometheus, attired as one of the ancient heroes.

Entheus. Patron of mankind, powerful and bounteous,   130
  Rich in thy flames, reverend Prometheus,
  In Hymen's place aid us to solemnize
  These royal nuptials; fill the lookers' eyes
  With admiration of thy fire and light,
  And from thy hand let wonders flow tonight.   135
Prometheus. Entheus and Orpheus, names both dear to me,
  In equal balance I your third will be
  In this night's honour. View these heav'n-born stars,
  Who by my stealth are become sublunars.
  How well their native beauties fit this place,   140
  Which with a choral dance they first shall grace;
  Then shall their forms to human figures turn,
  And these bright fires within their bosoms burn.
  Orpheus, apply thy music, for it well
  Helps to induce a courtly miracle.   145
Orpheus. Sound, best of musics, raise yet higher our sprites,
  While we admire Prometheus' dancing lights.

A Song

1. Advance your choral motions now
    You music-loving lights;   150
  This night concludes the nuptial vow,
    Make this the best of nights.
  So bravely crown it with your beams
    That it may live in fame
  As long as Rhenus or the Thames   155
    Are known by either name.

2. Once move again, yet nearer move
    Your forms at willing view;
  Such fair effects of joy and love
    None can express but you.   160

Then revel midst your airy bowers
  Till all the clouds do sweat,
That pleasure may be pour'd in showers
  On this triumphant seat.

3. Long since hath lovely Flora thrown   16
      Her flowers and garlands here;
    Rich Ceres all her wealth hath shown,
      Proud of her dainty cheer.
    Chang'd then to human shape, descend,
      Clad in familiar weed,   17
    That every eye may here commend
      The kind delights you breed.

*According to the humour of this song, the Stars moved in an exceeding
strange and delightful manner, and I suppose few have ever seen more
neat artifice than Master Inigo Jones showed in contriving their* 17
*motion, who in all the rest of the workmanship which belonged to the
whole invention showed extraordinary industry and skill, which if it be
not as lively expressed in writing as it appeared in view, rob not him of
his due, but lay the blame on my want of right apprehending his
instructions for the adorning of his art. But to return to our purpose;* 18
*about the end of this song, the stars suddenly vanished, as if they had
been drowned amongst the clouds, and the eight Masquers appeared in
their habits, which were infinitely rich, befitting states (such as indeed
they all were) as also a time so far heightened the day before, with all
the richest show of solemnity that could be invented. The ground of their* 18
*attires was massy cloth of silver, embossed with flames of embroidery;
on their heads, they had crowns, flames made all of gold-plate enamelled,
and on the top a feather of silk, representing a cloud of smoke. Upon
their new transformation, the whole Scene being clouds dispersed, and
there appeared an element of artificial fires, with several circles of lights,* 19
*in continual motion, representing the house of Prometheus, who then
thus applies his speech to the Masquers.*

They are transformed.

Prometheus. So, pause awhile, and come, ye fiery sprites,
  Break forth the earth like sparks t'attend these knights.   19

Sixteen Pages, like fiery spirits, all their attires being alike composed of flames, with fiery wings and bases, bearing in either hand a torch of virgin wax, come forth below dancing a lively measure, and the dance being ended, Prometheus speaks to them from above.

The Torch-bearers' dance.

      200

Prometheus. Wait, spirits, wait, while through the clouds we pace,
  And by descending gain a higher place.

The Pages return toward the Scene, to give their attendance to the Masquers with their lights: from the side of the Scene appeared a bright and transparent cloud, which reached from the top of the heavens 205 to the earth: on this cloud the Masquers led by Prometheus descended with the music of a full song; and at the end of their descent, the cloud brake in twain, and one part of it (as with a wind) was blown overthwart the Scene.

While this cloud was vanishing, the wood, being the under-part of 210 the Scene, was insensibly changed, and in place thereof appeared four noble women-statues of silver, standing in several niches, accompanied with ornaments of architecture, which filled all the end of the house, and seemed to be all of goldsmith's work. The first order consisted of pilasters all of gold, set with rubies, sapphires, emeralds, opals and such 215 like. The capitals were composed, and of a new invention. Over this was a bastard order with cartouches reversed, coming from the capitals of every pilaster, which made the upper part rich and full of ornament. Over every statue was placed a history in gold, which seemed to be of bas-relief; the conceits which were figured in them were these. In the 220 first was Prometheus, embossing in clay the figure of a woman; in the second he was represented stealing fire from the chariot-wheel of the sun; in the third he is expressed putting life with this fire into his figure of clay; and in the fourth square Jupiter, enraged, turns these new-made women into statues. Above all, for finishing, ran a cornice, which 225 returned over every pilaster, seeming all of gold and richly carved.

A full Song

    Supported now by clouds, descend
    Divine Prometheus, Hymen's friend;
    Lead down the new transformed fires   230

III

And fill their breasts with love's desires,
That they may revel with delight
And celebrate this nuptial night,
So celebrate this nuptial night,
   That all which see may say
They never view'd so fair a sight
   Even on the clearest day.

Entheus. See, see, Prometheus, four of these first dames
  Which thou long since out of thy purchas'd flames
  Didst forge with heav'nly fire, as they were then
  By Jove transform'd to statues, so again
  They suddenly appear by his command
  At thy arrival. Lo, how fix'd they stand;
  So did Jove's wrath too long, but now at last
  It by degrees relents, and he hath plac'd
  These statues, that we might his aid implore,
  First for the life of these, and then for more.
Prometheus. Entheus, thy counsels are divine and just,
  Let Orpheus deck thy hymn, since pray we must.

     The first invocation in a full song

     Powerful Jove, that of bright stars
     Now hast made men fit for wars,
     Thy power in these statues prove
     And make them women fit for love.

Orpheus. See, Jove is pleas'd; statues have life and move.
  Go, new-born men, and entertain with love
  These new-born women; though your number yet
  Exceeds theirs double, they are arm'd with wit
  To bear your best encounters. Court them fair:
  When words and music speak, let none despair.

     The Song

  1. Woo her, and win her, he that can:
     Each woman hath two lovers,
    So she must take and leave a man,
     Till time more grace discovers.

This doth Jove to show that want
　　Makes beauty most respected;
If fair women were more scant,
　　They would be more affected.

2. Courtship and music suit with love,　　　　　270
　　They both are works of passion;
Happy is he whose words can move,
　　Yet sweet notes help persuasion.
Mix your words with music then,
　　That they the more may enter;　　　　　275
Bold assaults are fit for men,
　　That on strange beauties venture.

While this song is sung, and the Masquers court the four new-trans-
formed Ladies, four other Statues appear in their places.

Prometheus. Cease, cease your wooing strife; see, Jove intends　280
To fill your number up, and make all friends.
Orpheus, and Entheus, join your skills once more,
And with a hymn the Deity implore.

The second invocation to the tune of the first

Powerful Jove, that hast given four,　　　　　285
Raise this number but once more,
That complete, their numerous feet
May aptly in just measures meet.

The other four Statues are transformed into women, in the time of this
invocation.　　　　　290

Entheus. The number's now complete, thanks be to Jove,
No man needs fear a rival in his love;
For all are sped, and now begins delight
To fill with glory this triumphant night.

The Masquers having every one entertained his Lady, begin their first 295
new entering dance: after it, while they breathe, the time is entertained
with a dialogue song.

Breathe you now, while 'Io Hymen'
  To the bride we sing:
O how many joys and honours   30
  From this match will spring!
Ever firm the league will prove
Where only goodness causeth love.
Some for profit seek
What their fancies most disleek;   30
These love for virtue's sake alone:
Beauty and youth unite them both in one.

Chorus. Live with thy bridegroom happy, sacred bride;
  How blest is he that is for love envied.

The Masquers' second dance.   31

Breathe again, while we with music
  Fill the empty space:
O but do not in your dances
  Your selves only grace.
Ev'ry one fetch out your fere   31
Whom chiefly you will honour here.
Sights most pleasure breed
When their numbers most exceed:
Choose then, for choice to all is free;
Taken or left, none discontent must be.   32

Chorus. Now in thy revels frolic, fair delight,
  To heap joy on this ever-honour'd night.

*The Masquers during this dialogue take out others to dance with them,
men women, and women men, and first of all the princely Bridegroom
and Bride were drawn into these solemn revels, which continued a long* 32
space, but in the end were broken off with this short song.

A Song

Cease, cease, you revels, rest a space;
New pleasures press into this place,
Full of beauty and of grace.   33

Entheus. Make clear the passage to Sibylla's sight,
  Who with her trophy comes to crown this night;
  And, as her self with music shall be led,
  So shall she pull on with a golden thread
  A high vast obelisk, dedicate to fame,   335
  Which immortality itself did frame.
  Raise high your voices now; like trumpets fill
  The room with sounds of triumph, sweet and shrill.

*The whole Scene was now again changed, and became a perspective with
porticoes on each side, which seemed to go in a great way. In the middle* 340
*was erected an obelisk, all of silver, and in it lights of several colours;
on the side of this obelisk, standing on pedestals, were the statues of the
Bridegroom and Bride, all of gold, in gracious postures. This obelisk
was of that height, that the top thereof touched the highest clouds, and
yet Sibylla did draw it forth with a thread of gold. The grave Sage was* 345
*in a robe of gold tucked up before to her girdle, a kirtle gathered full,
and of silver; with a veil on her head, being bare-necked, and bearing in
her hand a scroll of parchment.*

A Song

  Come triumphing, come with state,   350
    Old Sibylla, reverend dame;
  Thou keep'st the secret key of fate,
    Preventing swiftest fame.
  This night breathe only words of joy
  And speak them plain, now be not coy.   355

Sibylla. Debetur alto iure principium Iovi,
  Votis det ipse vim meis, dictis fidem.
  Utrinque decoris splendet egregium iubar,
  Medio triumphus mole stat dignus sua,
  Caelumque summo capite dilectum petit.   360
  Quam pulchra pulchro sponsa respondet viro!
  Quam plena numinis! Patrem vultu exprimit,
  Parens futura masculae prolis, parens
  Regum, imperatorum: additur Germaniae
  Robur Britannicum; ecquid esse par potest?   365

Utramque iunget una mens gentem, fides,
Deique cultus unus, et simplex amor.
Idem erit utrique hostis, sodalis idem, idem
Votum periclitantium, atque eadem manus.
Favebit illis pax, favebit bellica   3
Fortuna, semper aderit adiutor Deus.
Sic, sic Sibylla; vocibus nec his deest
Pondus, nec hoc inane monumentum trahit.
Et aureum est, et quale nec flammas timet,
Nec fulgura, ipsi quippe sacratur Ioui.   3

Prometheus. The good old sage is silenc'd, her free tongue
That made such melody, is now unstrung:
Then grace her trophy with a dance triumphant;
Where Orpheus is, none can fit music want.

A song and dance triumphant of the Masquers   3

1. Dance, dance, and visit now the shadows of our joy,
    All in height and pleasing state, your changed forms employ.
    And as the bird of Jove salutes with lofty wing the morn,
    So mount, so fly, these trophies to adorn.
    Grace them with all the sounds and motions of delight,   3
    Since all the earth cannot express a lovelier sight.
    View them with triumph, and in shades the truth adore;
    No pomp or sacrifice can please Jove's greatness more.

2. Turn, turn, and honour now the life these figures bear;
    Lo, how heav'nly natures far above all art appear!   3
    Let their aspects revive in you the fire that shin'd so late,
    Still mount and still retain your heavenly state.
    Gods were with dance and with music serv'd of old,
    Those happy days deriv'd their glorious style from gold:
    This pair, by Hymen join'd, grace you with measures then,   3
    Since they are both divine and you are more than men.

> *Orpheus.* Let here Sibylla's trophy stand;
> Lead her now by either hand
> That she may approach yet nearer
> And the bride and bridegroom hear her   4

Bless them in her native tongue,
Wherein old prophecies she sung
Which time to light hath brought:
She speaks that which Jove hath taught.
Well may he inspire her now,   405
To make a joyful and true vow.
Sibylla. Sponsam, sponse, toro tene pudicam,
Sponsum, sponsa, tene toro pudicum.
Non haec unica nox datur beatis,
At vos perpetuo haec beabit una   410
Prole multiplici, parique amore.
Laeta, ac vera refert Sibylla; ab alto
Ipse Iuppiter annuit loquenti.
Prometheus. So be it ever, joy and peace,
And mutual love give you increase,   415
That your posterity may grow
In fame as long as seas do flow.
Entheus. Live you long to see your joys
In fair nymphs and princely boys:
Breeding like the garden flowers,   420
Which kind heav'n draws with her warm showers.
Orpheus. Enough of blessing, though too much
Never can be said to such;
But night doth waste, and Hymen chides,
Kind to bridegrooms and to brides.   425
Then, singing, the last dance induce,
So let 'Good-night' prevent excuse.

The Song

No longer wrong the night
Of her Hymenaean right;   430
A thousand Cupids call 'Away!'
Fearing the approaching day;
The cocks already crow:
Dance then and go.

The last new dance of the Masquers, which concludes all with a lively 435
strain at their going out.

THE TEXT

The Lords' Masque was appended to Campion's *Relation of the late Royal Entertainment...at Cawsome House...upon the 27th and 28th April, 1613*,[1] and published with that in '1613'. Neither item was entered in the Stationers' Register. The booklet is a quarto, unpaginated. *The Entertainment* ends on B 4ᵛ, which has no catchword; *The Lords' Masque* begins on C 1ᵛ and ends on D 4ᵛ. This might encourage the inference that originally it was intended to publish *The Entertainment* by itself, and that *The Lords' Masque* may have been 'annexed', in the words of the title-page, subsequently. If, however, independent publication of *The Entertainment* was ever contemplated, that intention must have been abandoned before the joint title-page (A 1) was set up, for A 1 is demonstrably conjugate with A 4 in many of the copies examined. The British Museum possesses a copy containing *The Entertainment* alone, but it is in a modern binding and there is no evidence that it was ever issued separately. The following copies contain both items:

Bodley 1 (Wood 537 (8)); Bodley 2 (Gough, Berks 3 (30)); Bodley 3 (Malone 187 (5)); B.M. 1 (C. 21. c. 48); B.M. 2 (C. 33. c. 7 (8)); Bristol Public Library; Harvard; Huntington.

Of these all but the third Bodleian copy (which was not available) have been collated for the present edition, but no variants were found other than the two already noted in Greg's *Bibliography*, neither of which occurs in the text of the masque.

[1] *S.T.C.* 4545; Greg, *Bibliography of Drama to Restoration*, nos. 318–19.

COLLATION

The Lords' Masque was reprinted by: John Nichols in *Progresses of James I* (1828), II, 554–65; A. H. Bullen in (1) *The Works of Dr Thomas Campion* (1889) and in (2) *Thomas Campion: Songs and Masques* (1903); H. A. Evans in *English Masques* (1897); P. S. Vivian in (1) *Campion's Poetical Works* (Muses' Library), 1907 and in (2) *Campion's Works* (Oxford, 1909). The last of these, Vivian (2), reproduces the original text, spelling and capitalization with almost complete accuracy (including the misprints in lines 180 and 194, though not those in 52 and 235), but treats the punctuation with some freedom, especially in verse passages. Most of the obvious emendations were introduced by Nichols; in what follows 'Nichols +' indicates an emendation adopted by all subsequent editors.

2 which,] which Q.
12 paced] *This ed.*; placed Q.
45 reinless] rainelesse Q; brainelesse *Nichols*.
52 will] *Nichols* +; willing Q.
82 seem] *Nichols*; seems Q.
120 nature;] *This ed.*; nature Q.
121 descend this] Q; descend to grace this *Nichols*.
122 be, how] Q; be, their forms how *Nichols*.
180 *adorning*] *Nichols*; adoring Q.
194 sprites] *Nichols* +; spirits Q.
235 say] *Nichols* +; stay Q.
278–9] *Transferred here by Evans; between lines 237 and 238 in* Q.
282 Entheus] *Nichols* +; Eutheus Q.
321 frolic, fair] *Nichols* +; frolicke-faire Q.
339–48] *Transferred here in this edition; found between lines 330 and 331 in* Q.
373 monumentum] *Nichols* +; momumentum Q.

COMMENTARY

Title] from the joint title-page in Q; there is no divisional half-title. The head-title of the masque has the same wording down to 'Elizabeth'.

3 lets] occasions of delay.

3 in due time] The other two masques given at these festivities were sent to press immediately after performance. Campion's cannot have been printed earlier than May 1613.

4 *Scene*] see Introduction, p. 99.

4 *divided*] i.e. horizontally; see Introduction, p. 99.

5 *discovered*] revealed.

5 *sound*] music.

5 *consort*] orchestra.

6 *expressed by several instruments*] played by a variety of instruments.

7 *in perspective*] contrived to appear solid.

8 *whole round*] wholly in the round.

8 *the seat*] the King's 'state', in the 'upper hall'.

12 *paced*] The Quarto's reading, *placed*, must be wrong; had the beasts been static, 'tamely' would be pointless. Moreover, an eye-witness account (Reyher, p. 512) tells us that Orpheus was *followed about* by a camel, a bear and other savage beasts. For Campion's use of pace = 'walk', cf. line 201, and *Works*, ed. Vivian, p. 69, line 20.

15 exhale] draw out.

15 Mania] a trisyllable, accented Manía.

18 *goddess*] not found in Elizabethan mythological handbooks. Cooper's *Thesaurus* gives *mania* as a noun, meaning 'madness', but not as a name.

19 *habit...confused*] clothes were a medley.

19 *strange*] 'foreign' or 'exotic'.

20 *graceful*] pleasing.

20 *amazed*] 'crazy' or 'bewildered'.

33 several] special.

35 Through blood's distemper] Blood was believed to be the link between body and mind; disease of the blood would therefore affect a man's mind. Cooper, s.v. *mania*, expresses the common belief that madness is 'a disease rising of too much...blood'.

36 Entheus] Latin (from Greek) for 'divinely inspired'; here used as a name for 'poetic fury' personified.

36 rage] poetic fury; inspiration.

37 vulgar censure] ordinary judgments.

41 Frantics] lunatics.

47 crazed] 'diseased' or 'morbid'.

50 passion] according to the Elizabethans, the driving force of all men not governed by their rational soul.

50–1 bend | To] comply with.

51 motion] 'suggestion' or 'direction'.

52 will] Nichols's emendation of the Quarto's *willing*, an error doubtless induced by 'willing' in the next line.

54 put on] induce.

57 *in sundry habits and humours*] different in dress and disposition.

58 *Melancholic-Man...fear*] Ungrounded fear was considered a primary symptom of morbid depression.

58 *School-Man*] Academic.

59 *fantasy*] illusions.

59 *over-watched*] 'too vigilant' or 'suspicious'.

60 *absolute*] perfect, complete.

62 *measure*] dance.

63 *fantastic*] 'eccentric' or 'grotesque'.

70 *attired*] Inigo Jones's design for Entheus's dress is reproduced in our Plate 11 (*a*).

70 *antic*] grotesque.

71 *bases*] a kilt-like garment.

71 *labels*] strips of material hanging loose (from the waist of Entheus's 'bases').

81 excelling rapture] sublime ecstasy.

84 Phoebean] because inspired by Phoebus Apollo.

85 palate-sick] 'sated' or 'nauseated'.

88 fiery] cf. line 94.

93 still] ever.

96 that veil] the curtain screening the upper stage; it was made to resemble clouds (line 105).

97 false] disloyal.

99 affects] emotions.

102 triumphs] ceremonial spectacles.

103 discover] 'uncover' or 'open up'.

119–20 approach...nature] as they approach nearer their divine nature [cf. line 117] is manifested.

134 admiration] 'wonder' or 'awe'.

139 stealth] stealing (i.e. from heaven).

139 sublunars] dwellers below the moon, i.e. on earth.

149 motions] movements, i.e. dances.

155 Rhenus] The Rhine flows through the bridegroom's realm.

158 at willing] text corrupt?

168 dainty] 'choice' or 'precious'.

170 weed] clothing.

173 *humour*] properly 'mood', but here it must mean 'rhythm'.

175 *neat artifice*]   extreme ingenuity.

179–80 *my want...instructions*]   my incomplete comprehension of his explanations.

183 *states*]   persons of great estate or place.

184 *so far...before*]   so enhanced by the events of the day.

185 *solemnity*]   ceremonial.

186 *embossed...embroidery*]   on which raised patterns of flames were embroidered.

190–1 *element...house of Prometheus*]   The element of fire was the sphere of fixed stars; this obsolete meaning of 'element' is better illustrated here than in *N.E.D.* (*q.v.* sb. 10). Apparently there was now revealed a representation of a starry sky; some of the moving 'circles of lights' may have represented the planets, for certain mythographers make Prometheus the discoverer of the planetary motions. On 'circles of lights' see Nicoll, *Stuart Masques*, p. 136.

198 *below*]   possibly from under the stage, though that seems a dangerous waiting-place for torch-bearers. Such an entry would have had the advantage of giving immediate access to the carpeted dancing-place.

202 a higher place]   because nearer the king's seat.

207 *with the music*]   to the music.

207 *a full song*]   see lines 227 ff. The 'description' that follows (lines 210–26) would have been better placed between lines 237 and 238.

212–13 *accompanied...architecture*]   in an architectural setting.

213 *end...house*]   presumably 'the back of the stage'.

215–16 *rubies...such like*]   Probably the gems were simulated by coloured lights; cf. Nicoll, *Stuart Masques*, pp. 129–30, 135–6, and C. F. Bell in Herford and Simpson's *Jonson*, x, 413–20.

216 *composed*]   composite.

219 *history*]   story, here, of course, in picture-form.

220 *conceits*]   subjects.

221 *embossing*]   modelling.

227 *full*]   presumably it was sung by all singers and choir.

239 purchas'd]   stolen.

244 did]   *sc.* stand.

249 deck]   adorn, i.e. with music and song.

261 *The Song*]   This song was set by Campion himself, who printed the music on a spare page of his *Masque at the Marriage of the Earl of Somerset* (1614). A facsimile of the original, with transcription in modern notation, was published by F. W. Sternfeld in *Journal of Warburg Institute*, xx (1957), 373–5. Another transcription into modern notation is found in Andrew J. Sabol's *Songs and Dances for the Stuart Masque* (Brown University Press, 1959), no. 17. Sabol's concise but comprehensive introduction has an interesting discussion of Campion's three surviving masque songs (pp. 10–11), but there are no grounds for his assertion (p. 138) that the anonymous dance music for *The Pages' Masque* (no. 50) was composed for the pages in

Campion's *Lords' Masque*. With more appropriate caution he advances this as a conjecture on pp. 3 and 170.

287 numerous] rhythmical, i.e. keeping time to music.

293 sped] provided for.

295 *entertained*] greeted and paired with; in line 296 the meaning is 'taken up with'.

296 *new entering dance*] The 'new' dances were those specially devised for the masque; in 'entering' dances the masquers presumably went from the stage to the dancing-place.

296 *breathe*] pause for breath.

315 fetch...fere] take out as your partner.

323 *dialogue*] *sc.* song (cf. line 297).

325 *solemn*] 'formal', or 'ceremonial'.

325 *revels*] the technical name for the 'mixed' dancing of masquers and members of the audience.

331 clear the passage] i.e. 'clear the space between stage and king's chair'. This seems to prove that the dancing space was not built up above the floor, as was occasionally done for other masques, for in that case the end of the dancing would automatically have 'cleared the passage'.

332 trophy] the obelisk (cf. lines 341–5).

339–48] This description is found between lines 330 and 331 in Q.

339 *now again changed*] Not necessarily to be taken literally. The change of scene might have been effected at leisure while the masquers, with their torch-bearers, were concentrating the audience's attention on the dancing-place.

345 *forth*] Normally this would imply that Sibylla drew on the obelisk sideways from the wings, and that may have been done. However, taken with lines 340–1, *forth* may here mean 'forward'.

353 Preventing] anticipating; cf. line 427.

367 cultus unus] Frederick and his bride were both protestants.

374 aureum] Campion's description says it was silver (line 341). Was the colour changed (for contrast with the golden statues) during production?

377 such melody] This suggests that Sibylla's lines were chanted, or spoken to music like Orpheus's speech at lines 65–8.

381 shadows...joy] the statues on the obelisk.

382 your...employ] encircle, in your changed shapes; *changed* may allude to their 'transformations' earlier, or possibly to an 'unmasking' at this point.

384 mount] *sc.* the stage, where the obelisk stood.

387 shades] representations; cf. line 381, *shadows*.

389 the life] the living originals.

392] suggests that the masquers may have mounted to the upper stage, or been somehow raised to it.

398 Lead her...hand] Presumably Sibylla was now led forward by Prometheus and Entheus.

THE MASQUE OF THE INNER
TEMPLE AND GRAY'S INN

BY FRANCIS BEAUMONT

Edited by Philip Edwards

INTRODUCTION

The Masque of the Inner Temple and Gray's Inn, performed at
Whitehall on Saturday, 20 February 1613, was the last of the three
masques given in honour of the wedding of Princess Elizabeth and
the Elector Palatine; the others being Campion's *The Lords' Masque*
(q.v.), 14 February, and Chapman's *Masque of the Middle Temple
and Lincoln's Inn*, 15 February. The masque was to have been given
on the night of 16 February, but, when everything was ready, the
presentation was suddenly postponed.

The original title-page of the Quarto (1613) describes the masque
as 'By Francis Beamont, Gent.'. A cancel was printed to replace this
title-page (Greg, *Bibliography*, I, no. 309), and the only alteration
was the removal of Beaumont's name. Because the spelling 'Beamont' also appears at the head of the Folio text (1647), it seems
clear that the name, so spelt, was in the original manuscript from
which both texts independently derive (see below), and was carried
over into the expanded manuscript which is the immediate source of
the Quarto. But someone (perhaps Beaumont himself) must have
thought it inappropriate for the poet's name to head a work which,
now that it gave a full account of the dancing, the music, the settings,
and the costumes, was so obviously an entertainment brought into
being by many people working together. This is the only masque
written by Beaumont, though there is the masque in *The Maid's
Tragedy*. 1613, which is about the time of his marriage, is supposed
to mark the slackening off of his dramatic work in association with
Fletcher. It is presumably as a former member of the Inner Temple
that he was asked to write the verse for the masque.

The only other person actually named in connexion with the
masque was closely associated with Gray's Inn—Sir Francis Bacon.
John Chamberlain called him the 'chief contriver', and he is
mentioned in two other places as directing affairs;[1] the dedication
speaks of his 'advancing' the masque by his 'countenance and

[1] Chamberlain, *Letters*, I, 425; *Pension Book of Gray's Inn*, ed. R. J. Fletcher
(1901), p. 202; Phineas Pett's autobiography (see p. 129).

loving affection'. Dyce (Beaumont and Fletcher, *Works*, I (1843), p. xxxviii) said that 'its machinery and contrivances were by Inigo Jones'. There seems to be no evidence for this, but Inigo Jones was responsible for the other two wedding masques, and the use of the double traverse or curtains in both Beaumont's and Campion's masques might indicate a common artificer. Reyher (pp. 178–9) thought a French hand might have been responsible for the innovation of the divided entry of the first anti-masque. Reyher also noted that the music had been attributed ('*sans preuves*') to Giovanni Coperario (John Cooper). Among the tantalizingly vague titles to music from Stuart masques in a manuscript in the British Museum (Add. MS 10444) occurs, on folio 28^v, 'Cuperaree or Grays in' and, on folio 29^r, 'The second'. A. J. Sabol (*Songs and Dances for the Stuart Masque* (1959), nos. 46 and 47; Introd. p. 2) thinks that these were by Coperario, and were 'probably used' in Beaumont's masque. But it is also interesting that pieces on folio 28^r and 28^v are entitled 'Sr Francis Bacons Masque. 1.' and 'Sr Fra: Bacons second Masque' (see *The Masque of Flowers*).

The masque put both Inns deeply into debt. In May, Gray's Inn was trying to get back from the masquers their costumes 'or else the value thereof', since these had been at the charge of the house, and had cost 'above an hundred marks' each. In June, it was noted that a great part of the cost of the masque was still unpaid—and the masquers had still not returned their suits: they were to pay £30 or run the risk of expulsion. In November, the court had to order that all the admittance money 'of this term and the next' should go towards paying off the outstanding debt. The Inner Temple was no better off. On 4 May the records of a parliament note that the house was in debt over the masque 'not so little as 1,200 *li*.'.[1] This figure is not surprising, when we are told that the journey to Whitehall by water alone cost 'better than three hundred pound' (Chamberlain, *Letters*, I, 426).

The argument of the masque is fully described in the text, and needs little comment. The theme is the marriage of the rivers Thames and Rhine, and the journey of the masquers by water to the

[1] *Pension Book of Gray's Inn*, pp. 201, 205, 206, 208; *Calendar of the Inner Temple Records*, ed. F. A. Inderwick, II (1898), 72.

palace was an important part of the design. The action of the masque is apparently supposed to take place at the foot of a hill near Olympia in the Peloponnese; the presenters are Mercury and Iris. The first anti-masque is divided into four entries: first, nymphs or naiads, then the Hyades or stars, then cupids, then statues; the four dances are 'cumulative' as each new group enters: the first of four dancers, the second of nine, the third of thirteen, the last of seventeen. This is Mercury's anti-masque. Iris provides a second anti-masque, of particular interest as a parody of the traditional country dances at the ancient may-games, or summer 'maying' festivals (see Chambers, *Medieval Stage*, chs. VIII and IX). Many of the characters, including pedant and baboon, reappear in Gerrold's morris-dance in *The Two Noble Kinsmen*, III, v, 137–48. The 'main masque' is of 'Olympian' knights and musician priests, supposed to be a prelude to a revival of the Olympic games.

We have a full account of the circumstances of the masque, both from the Quarto and from contemporary reports. The procession by boat from Southwark to Whitehall, with its great display of wax lights and torches, provoked a good deal of admiring comment,[1] though the person responsible for organizing it, the famous Master Shipwright Phineas Pett, gives a cool account.

I was intreated by diverse Gentlemen of ye Inns of Court whereof S^r ffrancis Baconn was Cheife to attend ye bringing of a Mask by water in the night from St Mary Overyes to Whitehall in some of the Gallies but ye Tide falling out very contrary & the Company attending the Maskers very unruely ye project could not be performed so Exactly as was purposed & Expected but yet they were safely landed at the Pryving staires at Whitehall for which my paines ye Gentle. gave me a faire recompence.[2]

The extraordinary disappointment of the postponement of the masque after the triumphal arrival is candidly discussed by Chamberlain; he mentions the reason given in the Quarto (the crowding in the hall), but goes on:

but the worst of all was that the King was so wearied and sleepie with sitting up almost two whole nights before, that he had no edge to yt,

---

[1] E.g. *C.S.P. Venetian*, XII (1610–13), 533; Howes's ed. of Stow's *Chronicle* (1615), pp. 916–18; *Cal. of Inner Temple Records*, pp. xl, 76.

[2] B.M. Harl. MS 6279. An inferior version is printed in Chambers, *Elizabethan Stage*, III, 234.

wherupon Sir Fra Bacon adventured to intreat his Majestie, that by this disgrace he wold not as yt were bury them quicke: and I hear the King shold aunswer, that then they must burie him quicke for he could last no longer... (*Letters*, I, 426; letter to Alice Carleton, 18 Feb. 1613).

The masquers were 'much discouraged, and out of countenance', their devices and apparel now being known. The one advantage they gained by the postponement was the change of the room from the Great Hall (where Chapman's masque was given) to the Banqueting House (that built in 1607 and burned in 1619), 'graunted to them,' says Chamberlain, 'though with much repining and contradiction of theyre emulators' (p. 429; letter to Winwood, 23 Feb. 1613). Further amends were made by the King in inviting the masquers on the next day 'to a solemne supper in the new mariage roome, where they were well treated and much graced with kissing his Majesties hand' (p. 431). This supper was in addition to the usual feast after the masque; concerning that, Foscarini (the Venetian Ambassador) noted that 'after the King had made the round of the table, everything was in a moment rapaciously swept away' (*C.S.P. Venetian*, XII (1610–13), p. 533).

[DRAMATIS PERSONAE

Mercury
Iris
Four Naiads ⎫
Five Hyades ⎪ The first anti-masque
Four Cupids ⎬
Statues ⎭
A Pedant ⎫
A May Lord ⎪
A May Lady ⎪
A Servingman ⎪
A Chambermaid ⎪
A Country Clown or Shepherd ⎪ The second
A Country Wench ⎬ anti-masque
An Host ⎪
An Hostess ⎪
A He-Baboon ⎪
A She-Baboon ⎪
A He-Fool ⎪
A She-Fool ⎭

Fifteen Olympian Knights; the masquers
Chorus of Twelve Priests of Jupiter]

THE MASQUE

OF THE INNER TEMPLE AND GRAY'S INN, GRAY'S INN AND THE INNER TEMPLE:

presented before his Majesty, the Queen's Majesty,

the Prince, Count Palatine and the Lady Elizabeth their

Highnesses, in the Banqueting House at Whitehall

on Saturday the twentieth day of February, 1613

*   *   *

To the worthy Sir Francis Bacon, his Majesty's Solicitor-General, and the grave and learned Bench of the anciently allied houses of Gray's Inn and the Inner Temple, the Inner Temple and Gray's Inn.

Ye that spared no time nor travail in the setting forth, ordering, and furnishing of this masque, being the first fruits of honour in this kind 5 which these two societies have offered to his Majesty, will not think much now to look back upon the effects of your own care and work; for that whereof the success was then doubtful, is now happily performed and graciously accepted. And that which you were then to think of in straits of time, you may now peruse at leisure. And you Sir Francis Bacon 10 especially, as you did then by your countenance and loving affection advance it, so let your good word grace it and defend it, which is able to add value to the greatest and least matters.

This Masque was appointed to have been presented the Shrove Tuesday before, at which time the masquers, with their attendants and divers 15 others, gallant young gentlemen of both houses, as their convoy, set forth from Winchester House, which was the rendezvous, towards the Court, about seven of the clock at night.

This voyage by water was performed in great triumph. The gentlemen masquers being placed by themselves in the King's royal barge with the 20 rich furniture of state, and adorned with a great number of lights placed in such order as might make best show.

They were attended with a multitude of barges and galleys, with all

variety of loud music, and several peals of ordnance. And led by two
admirals.   25

Of this show his Majesty was graciously pleased to take view, with the
Prince, the Count Palatine and the Lady Elizabeth their Highnesses, at
the windows of his privy gallery upon the water, till their landing, which
was at the privy stairs; where they were most honourably received by the
Lord Chamberlain, and so conducted to the vestry.   30

The hall was by that time filled with company of very good fashion,
but yet so as a very great number of principal ladies and other noble
persons were not yet come in, whereby it was foreseen that the room
would be so scanted as might have been inconvenient. And thereupon his
Majesty was most graciously pleased, with the consent of the gentlemen 35
masquers, to put off the night until Saturday following, with this special
favour and privilege, that there should be no let as to the outward
ceremony of magnificence until that time.

At the day that it was presented, there was a choice room reserved for
the gentlemen of both their houses, who coming in troop about seven of 40
the clock, received that special honour and noble favour, as to be brought
to their places by the Right Honourable the Earl of Northampton,
Lord Privy Seal.

The Device or Argument of the Masque

Jupiter and Juno, willing to do honour to the marriage of the two famous 45
rivers Thamesis and Rhene, employ their messengers severally, Mercury
and Iris, for that purpose. They meet and contend: then Mercury for his
part brings forth an anti-masque all of spirits or divine natures: but yet
not of one kind or livery (because that had been so much in use heretofore)
but as it were in consort like to broken music. And preserving the 50
propriety of the device (for that rivers in nature are maintained either by
springs from beneath, or showers from above), he raiseth four of the
Naiads out of the fountains, and bringeth down five of the Hyades out of
the clouds to dance. Hereupon Iris scoffs at Mercury for that he had
devised a dance but of one sex, which could have no life: but Mercury, 55
who was provided for that exception, and in token that the match should
be blessed both with love and riches, calleth forth out of the groves four
Cupids, and brings down from Jupiter's altar four Statues of gold and
silver, to dance with the Nymphs and Stars: in which dance, the Cupids
being blind, and the Statues having but half life put into them, and re- 60
taining still somewhat of their old nature, giveth fit occasion to new and

strange varieties both in the music and paces. This was the first anti-masque.

Then Iris for her part, in scorn of this high-flying device, and in token that the match shall likewise be blessed with the love of the common 65 people, calls to Flora her confederate (for that the months of flowers are likewise the months of sweet showers and rainbows) to bring in a May-dance, or rural dance, consisting likewise not of any suited persons, but of a confusion or commixture of all such persons as are natural and proper for country sports. This is the second anti-masque. 70

Then Mercury and Iris, after this vying one upon the other, seem to leave their contention: and Mercury, by the consent of Iris, brings down the Olympian Knights, intimating that Jupiter, having after a long discontinuance revived the Olympian games, and summoned thereunto from all parts the liveliest and activest persons that were, had enjoined 75 them, before they fell to their games, to do honour to these nuptials. The Olympian games portend to the match celebrity, victory, and felicity. This was the main masque.

The fabric was a mountain with two descents, and severed with two
traverses. 80

At the entrance of the King

The first traverse was drawn, and the lower descent of the mountain
discovered; which was the pendant of a hill to life, with divers boscages
and grovets upon the steep or hanging grounds thereof, and at the foot
of the hill, four delicate fountains running with water and bordered with 85
sedges and water-flowers.

Iris first appeared, and, presently after, Mercury, striving to
overtake her.

Iris apparelled in a robe of discoloured taffeta figured in variable
colours, like the rainbow, a cloudy wreath on her head, and tresses. 90

Mercury in doublet and hose of white taffeta, a white hat, wings on his
shoulders and feet, his caduceus in his hand, speaking to Iris as followeth.

   Mercury. Stay, stay!
   Stay light-foot Iris, for thou strivest in vain,
   My wings are nimbler than thy feet. 95
   Iris.   Away,
   Dissembling Mercury; my messages

Ask honest haste, not like those wanton ones
Your thund'ring father sends.
Mercury.   Stay foolish maid,   100
  Or I will take my rise upon a hill,
  When I perceive thee seated in a cloud
  In all the painted glory that thou hast,
  And never cease to clap my willing wings
  Till I catch hold of thy discolour'd bow,   105
  And shiver it beyond the angry power
  Of your curst mistress to make up again.
Iris. Hermes forbear, Juno will chide and strike;
  Is great Jove jealous that I am employ'd
  On her love-errands? she did never yet   110
  Clasp weak mortality in her white arms,
  As he hath often done: I only come
  To celebrate the long-wish'd nuptials,
  Here in Olympia, which are now perform'd
  Betwixt two goodly rivers, which have mix'd   115
  Their gentle-rising waves, and are to grow
  Into a thousand streams, great as themselves;
  I need not name them, for the sound is loud
  In heaven and earth; and I am sent from her,
  The queen of marriage, that was present here,   120
  And smil'd to see them join, and hath not chid
  Since it was done: good Hermes let me go.
Mercury. Nay you must stay; Jove's message is the same,
  Whose eyes are lightning, and whose voice is thunder,
  Whose breath is any wind he will, who knows   125
  How to be first on earth as well as heaven.
Iris. But what hath he to do with nuptial rites?
  Let him keep state upon his starry throne,
  And fright poor mortals with his thunderbolts,
  Leaving to us the mutual darts of eyes.   130
Mercury. Alas, when ever offer'd he t'abridge
  Your lady's power, but only now in these,
  Whose match concerns his general government?
  Hath not each god a part in these high joys?

135

And shall not he, the king of gods, presume   135
Without proud Juno's licence? Let her know
That when enamour'd Jove first gave her power
To link soft hearts in undissolved bonds,
He then foresaw, and to himself reserv'd
The honour of this marriage: thou shalt stand   140
Still as a rock, while I, to bless this feast,
Will summon up with my all-charming rod
The Nymphs of fountains, from whose wat'ry locks,
Hung with the dew of blessing and increase,
The greedy rivers take their nourishment.   145
You Nymphs, who bathing in your loved springs,
Beheld these rivers in their infancy,
And joy'd to see them, when their circled heads
Refresh'd the air, and spread the ground with flowers:
Rise from your wells, and with your nimble feet   150
Perform that office to this happy pair,
Which in these plains you to Alpheus did,
When passing hence through many seas unmix'd,
He gain'd the favour of his Arethuse.

Immediately upon which speech, four Naiads arise gently out of their 155
several fountains, and present themselves upon the stage, attired in
long habits of sea-green taffeta, with bubbles of crystal intermixed with
powdering of silver, resembling drops of water, bluish tresses on their
heads, garlands of water-lilies. They fall into a measure, dance a little,
then make a stand.   160

Iris. Is Hermes grown a lover? by what power,
Unknown to us, calls he the Naiades?
Mercury. Presumptuous Iris, I could make thee dance
Till thou forgott'st thy lady's messages,
And rann'st back crying to her; thou shalt know   165
My power is more: only my breath, and this,
Shall move fix'd stars, and force the firmament
To yield the Hyades, who govern showers
And dewy clouds, in whose dispersed drops
Thou form'st the shape of thy deceitful bow.   170

You maids, who yearly at appointed times
Advance with kindly tears the gentle floods,
Descend, and pour your blessings on these streams,
Which rolling down from heaven-aspiring hills,
And now united in the fruitful vales,   175
Bear all before them, ravish'd with their joy,
And swell in glory till they know no bounds.

*Five Hyades descend softly in a cloud from the firmament to the middle
part of the hill, apparelled in sky-coloured taffeta robes, spangled like
the heavens, golden tresses, and each a fair star on their head; from* 180
*thence descend to the stage, at whose sight the Naiads seeming to
rejoice, meet and join in a dance.*

 Iris. Great wit and power hath Hermes, to contrive
  A lifeless dance, which of one sex consists.
 Mercury. Alas poor Iris, Venus hath in store   185
  A secret ambush of her winged boys,
  Who lurking long within these pleasant groves,
  First struck these lovers with their equal darts;
  Those Cupids shall come forth, and join with these,
  To honour that which they themselves begun.   190

*Enter four Cupids from each side of the boscage, attired in flame-
coloured taffeta close to their body like naked boys, with bows, arrows,
and wings of gold, chaplets of flowers on their heads, hoodwinked with
tiffany scarfs; who join with the Nymphs and the Hyades in another
dance. That ended, Mercury speaks.*   195

 Mercury. Behold, the Statues which wise Vulcan plac'd
  Under the altar of Olympian Jove,
  And gave to them an artificial life,
  Shall dance for joy of these great nuptials:
  See how they move, drawn by this heavenly joy,   200
  Like the wild trees which follow'd Orpheus' harp.

*The Statues enter, supposed to be before descended from Jove's altar, and
to have been prepared in the covert with the Cupids, attending their call.
 These Statues were attired in cases of gold and silver close to their*

body, faces, hands and feet, nothing seen but gold and silver, as if they 201
had been solid images of metal, tresses of hair as they had been of metal
embossed, girdles and small aprons of oaken leaves, as if they likewise
had been carved or moulded out of the metal: at their coming, the music
changed from violins to hoboys, cornets, etc. And the air of the music
was utterly turned into a soft time, with drawing notes, excellently 210
expressing their natures, and the measure likewise was fitted unto the
same, and the Statues placed in such several postures, sometimes all
together in the centre of the dance, and sometimes in the four utmost
angles, as was very graceful besides the novelty. And so concluded the
first anti-masque. 215

    Mercury. And what will Juno's Iris do for her?
    Iris. Just match this show, or my invention fails;
      Had it been worthier, I would have invok'd
      The blazing comets, clouds, and falling stars,
      And all my kindred meteors of the air, 220
      To have excell'd it, but I now must strive
      To imitate confusion: therefore thou,
      Delightful Flora, if thou ever felt'st
      Increase of sweetness in those blooming plants
      On which the horns of my fair bow decline, 225
      Send hither all the rural company,
      Which deck the May-games with their country sports;
      Juno will have it so.

The second anti-masque rush in, dance their measure, and as rudely
depart: consisting of 230
                    A Pedant,

May Lord,	*May Lady,*
Servingman,	*Chambermaid,*
A Country Clown, or Shepherd,	*Country Wench,*
An Host,	*Hostess,*
A He-Baboon,	*She-Baboon,*
A He-Fool,	*She-Fool, ushering them in.*

All these persons apparelled to the life, the men issuing out of one side of
the boscage, and the women from the other; the music was extremely

138

well fitted, having such a spirit of country jollity as can hardly be 240
imagined, but the perpetual laughter and applause was above the
music.

The dance likewise was of the same strain, and the dancers, or rather
actors, expressed every one their part so naturally and aptly, as when a
man's eye was caught with the one, and then passed on to the other, he 245
could not satisfy himself which did best. It pleased his Majesty to call
for it again at the end, as he did likewise for the first anti-masque, but
one of the Statues by that time was undressed.

Mercury.	Iris, we strive	
Like winds at liberty, who should do worst		250
Ere we return. If Juno be the queen		
Of marriage, let her give happy way		
To what is done, in honour of the state		
She governs.		
Iris.	Hermes, so it may be done	255
Merely in honour of the state, and these		
That now have prov'd it, not to satisfy		
The lust of Jupiter in having thanks		
More than his Juno, if thy snaky rod		
Have power to search the heavens, or sound the sea,		260
Or call together all the ends of earth,		
To bring in anything that may do grace		
To us, and these; do it, we shall be pleas'd.		
Mercury. Then know that from the mouth of Jove himself,		
Whose words have wings, and need not to be borne,		265
I took a message, and I bare it through		
A thousand yielding clouds, and never stay'd		
Till his high will was done: the Olympian games		
Which long have slept, at these wish'd nuptials		
He pleas'd to have renew'd, and all his knights		270
Are gather'd hither, who within their tents		
Rest on this hill, upon whose rising head		
Behold Jove's altar, and his blessed priests		
Moving about it: come you holy men,		
And with your voices draw these youths along,		275

That till Jove's music call them to their games,
Their active sports may give a blest content
To those, for whom they are again begun.

The Main Masque

The second traverse is drawn, and the higher ascent of the mountain is 2&
*discovered, wherein, upon a level after a great rise of the hill, were
placed two pavilions, open in the front of them; the pavilions were to
sight as of cloth of gold, and they were trimmed on the inside with rich
armour and military furniture hanged up as upon the walls, and behind
the tents there were represented in perspective the tops of divers other* 2&
*tents, as if it had been a camp. In these pavilions were placed fifteen
Olympian Knights, upon seats a little embowed near the form of a
croisant; and the Knights appeared first as consecrated persons, all in
veils, like to copes, of silver tiffany, gathered, and falling a large
compass about them, and over their heads high mitres with long pendants* 2
*behind falling from them: the mitres were so high that they received
their hats and feathers, that nothing was seen but veil. In the midst,
between both the tents upon the very top of the hill, being a higher level
than that of the tents, was placed Jupiter's altar, gilt, with three great
tapers upon golden candle-sticks burning upon it: and the four Statues,* 2&
*two of gold and two of silver, as supporters, and Jupiter's Priests in
white robes about it.*

*Upon the sight of the King, the veils of the Knights did fall easily
from them, and they appeared in their own habit.*

The Knights' attire 3&

*Arming doublets of carnation satin, embroidered with blazing stars of
silver plate, with powderings of smaller stars betwixt; gorgets of silver
mail; long hose of the same with the doublets, laid with silver lace
spangled, and enriched with embroidery between the lace; carnation silk
stockings embroidered all over, garters and roses suitable; pumps of* 3&
*carnation satin, embroidered as the doublets; hats of the same stuff and
embroidery, cut like a helmet before, the hinder part cut into scallops,
answering the skirts of their doublets; the bands of the hats were wreaths
of silver in form of garlands of wild olives; white feathers with one fall*

of carnation; belts of the same stuff and embroidered with the doublet; 310
silver swords; little Italian bands and cuffs embroidered with silver; fair
long tresses of hair.

The Priests' habits

Long robes of white taffeta, long white heads of hair; the High Priest a
cap of white silk shag close to his head, with two labels at the ears, the 315
midst rising in form of a pyramis, in the top thereof a branch of silver;
every Priest playing upon a lute: twelve in number.

The Priests descend and sing this song following, after whom the
Knights likewise descend, first laying aside their veils, belts, and
swords. 320

The first song

Shake off your heavy trance,
And leap into a dance
Such as no mortals use to tread,
Fit only for Apollo
325
To play to, for the moon to lead,
And all the stars to follow.

The Knights by this time are all descended and fallen into their place,
and then dance their first measure.

The second song 330

On blessed youths, for Jove doth pause,
Laying aside his graver laws
For this device;
And at the wedding such a pair,
Each dance is taken for a prayer, 335
Each song a sacrifice.

The Knights dance their second measure.

The third song

Single. More pleasing were these sweet delights,
If ladies mov'd as well as knights; 340
Run ev'ry one of you and catch
A nymph, in honour of this match,

141

And whisper boldly in her ear.
Jove will but laugh, if you forswear.
All. And this day's sins he doth resolve 34
That we his priests should all absolve.

The Knights take their ladies to dance with them galliards, durets, corantoes, etc., and lead them to their places. Then loud music sounds, supposed to call them to their Olympian games.

The fourth song 35

Ye should stay longer if we durst:
Away! Alas that he that first
Gave Time wild wings to fly away,
Hath now no power to make him stay.
But though these games must needs be play'd, 35
I would this pair, when they are laid,
    And not a creature nigh them,
Could catch his scythe, as he doth pass,
And cut his wings, and break his glass,
    And keep him ever by them. 36

The Knights dance their parting measure and ascend, put on their swords and belts, during which time the Priests sing the fifth and last song.

Peace and silence be the guide
To the man, and to the bride! 36
If there be a joy yet new
In marriage, let it fall on you,
    That all the world may wonder!
If we should stay, we should do worse,
And turn our blessing to a curse, 37
    By keeping you asunder.

FINIS

142

THE TEXT

The text of the masque exists in two versions. The fullest is in a quarto (Q), entered in the Stationers' Register to George Norton, together with Chapman's wedding masque, on 27 February 1613 (wrongly put down as 27 January); the printer was Felix Kingston. It is fully described by Greg in his *Bibliography*, vol. I, no. 309; the cancel title-page has already been mentioned. The other version (F) was printed in the 1647 folio of Beaumont and Fletcher's *Comedies and Tragedies*. The verse of the masque shows forty variant readings from Q; all the introductory prose is missing, and, instead of the elaborate descriptions of the scenery, action and costumes, there are only brief stage-directions.

Humphrey Moseley, the publisher of the Folio, acquired the masque, with four other plays, during the course of printing; the masque appears towards the end of the volume, on *8 D 2 recto and verso. Although Moseley's troubles with his printers were causing a good deal of tucking in and improvising in the book's final stages,[1] I do not think that printing difficulties are in any way the reason for the brevity of F. F must represent the manuscript of the verse of the masque before that same manuscript was used to compile the extended version which lies behind Q. F is clearly not a truncated redaction of Q.

In the first place, F's stage-directions (the more important of which are given in the Commentary) supply details not present in Q; in particular, of the way in which the presenters first entered (lines 87–8), of the abrupt end of the second dance (line 182), of the action of the third and fourth dances (lines 194–5, 202–15). The wording of F's directions is often echoed in Q's fuller accounts; that F has the priority seems clear from the second anti-masque (lines 229–48), where Q gives a smoother version of F's words, and then lamely tacks on *consisting of* to introduce the list of the persons in the dance. Then, for the verse, the misreading *maides* for *Naiades* (line 162, and note to lines 178–82) is perhaps enough to show that F derives from manuscript and not the clear print of Q.

But the manuscript cannot have been the author's; by comparison with Q, F's alternative readings are in almost every case declensions, and we

[1] See R. C. Bald, *Bibliographical Studies in the Beaumont and Fletcher Folio of 1647* (1938), esp. pp. 1, 36–7; Greg, *Bibliography*, III, 1015–17; J. Gerritsen, *The Library 5*, III (1949), 233–64.

must suppose scribal interference to account for their weakness. We must suppose a scribe who had difficulty with his author's handwriting, whose inattention and haste caused him both to make sheer mistakes and to substitute weaker alternatives (see text-notes at lines 107, 116, 184, 188, 262, for example), and who freely 'improved' when he did not like the wording or the grammar, or failed to understand them (e.g. lines 138, 190). All the same, one has to consider each variant very carefully indeed, because there is obviously the chance that, in spite of carelessness and sophistication, F's scribe might have preserved original readings which failed to reach Q. Dyce preferred F to Q in seven readings. To my mind, there is uncertainty only about four. At line 359, we have *cut his wings* (Q), or *clip his wings* (F); here *clip* is the more expected verb, and it is easier to think of it as a substitution for the less usual *cut* than vice versa. At line 128, there is the problem of whether Jove is to *keepe state* upon his throne (Q), or *sit pleasd* (F). Here, the argument of the 'harder reading' used for *cut* will certainly favour F. But in secretary hand 'keepstate' could be misread as 'sitpleasd', and, in view of other misreadings in F, one may prefer Q. More evenly balanced are the variants at line 227, *Countrey sports* (Q), or *clownish sports* (F). Q is perhaps slightly preferable, but the origin of F's reading is hard to explain. Finally, F surely has the original reading in the fourth song (lines 357, 360), *nigh 'em...by 'em*, where Q's *nie them...by them* seems a polite scribal improvement. But, since Q is, throughout, the better text and the obvious one to follow, I have allowed its reading here to stand rather than, for the sake of one variant, produce an eclectic text.

To sum up, both Q and F derive ultimately from the same manuscript, at the head of which stood the name 'Francis Beamont' (see above, p. 127); this manuscript was carefully copied by someone closely connected with the masque, who greatly amplified its brief notes on the dancing and action, for publication immediately after the performance. For his Folio, Moseley acquires a late transcript of the manuscript (or causes it to be made) which is so careless as to be almost useless, except for its preservation of the original stage-directions.[1]

The shorter folio version was used in Beaumont's *Poems*, 1653, in the enlarged Folio of 1679, in *Works*, 1711 and 1750. George Colman first discovered and reprinted the full quarto text, in Beaumont and Fletcher's

---

[1] The hypothesis of a common MS seems to be borne out by the blunders in both F and Q at lines 198–9. Q transposes these lines, and F omits the second of them. If line 199 had been added in the margin of the original MS, it might have been inserted in the wrong place by Q's scribe, and overlooked or ignored by F's scribe.

Dramatick Works, 1778, x, 487–503. The folio text then disappeared, except that Dyce used some of its readings in 1843.

The Bodleian Library copy of the Quarto has been used for this edition, checked against the British Museum copy, which contains the cancel title-page.

93 Stay, stay!] Q; *not in* F.

105 of] Q; on F.

107 curst] Q; mad F.

112 hath] Q; has F.

115 which] Q; that F, *Dyce.*

116 gentle-rising] Q; gentle winding F.

125 any] Q; aiery F.

128 keep state] Q; sit pleasd F.

133 his] Q; the F, *Dyce.*

138 undissolved bonds] Q; undissolving bands F, *Dyce.*

142 my] Q; mine F.

146 You] Q; Yea F.

162 Naiades] Q; maides F.

171 You] Q; Yea F.

184 lifeless] Q (liuelesse); lively F.

188 struck] Q; stuck F.

190 begun] Q; began F, *Dyce.*

195, 196 *Mercury*] *Colman*; Iris F, Q.

199 Shall...nuptials:] *Colman*; *precedes* 198 *in* Q; *not in* F.

217 my invention fails] Q; mine inventions faile F.

226 the] Q; that F.

227 country] Q; clownish F, *Dyce.*

252 marriage] Q; marriages F.

262 in] Q; thee F.

266 bare] Q; bore F.

269 have] Q; had F, *Dyce.*

303 *the same with the doublets, laid*] *this ed.*; the same, with the doublets laide Q.

351 Ye] Q; You F.

354 Hath] Q; Ha's F.

357 them] Q; 'em F.

359 cut] Q; clip F.

360 them] Q; 'em F.

370 blessing] Q; blessings F.

COMMENTARY

Title]   From the title-page; the date is there '1612' (Old style); the equality of the Inns is tactfully suggested by the repetition of names; *the Prince* is Charles. F has a differently worded title.

1–13]   The dedication originally followed the account of the postponement of the masque.

14, 15 Masque...masquers]   spelt *mask, maskers* in this section; elsewhere *masque*.

17 Winchester House]   in Southwark, by London Bridge.

24 peals of ordnance]   from the banks: as they embarked, as they passed the Temple, and on arrival.

29–30 the Lord Chamberlain]   Thomas Howard, 1st Earl of Suffolk.

34 scanted]   restricted.

38 until]   extending to; therefore, 'at'.

42 Earl of Northampton]   the unprincipled Henry Howard, now aged 73.

50 in consort like to broken music]   harmonizing like music for instruments of different types.

53 Naiads]   the nymphs of rivers, etc.; they had appeared in Daniel's *Tethys' Festival*, 1610.

53 Hyades]   daughters of Atlas, turned into stars whose rising and setting could portend rain.

56 exception]   objection.

79–80 *severed with two traverses*]   The curtains divided the scene horizontally.

82–3]   Foscarini wrote: 'One saw the scene, with forests; on a sudden, half of it changed to a great mountain with four springs at its foot.'

83 *pendant*]   slope.

83–4 *boscages and grovets*]   thickets and little groves.

87–8]   F reads: 'Enter Iris running, Mercury following and catching hold of her' (confirmed by line 122). Mercury usually enters by a descent.

89 *discoloured*]   many-coloured.

90 *like the rainbow*]   Iris was goddess of the rainbow.

106 shiver]   shatter.

152–4]   The river Alpheus flowed through the plain of Olympia, and was supposed to go undersea to Sicily to the fountain of Arethuse, with whom the river had fallen in love.

155–60]   F reads: 'The Nymphs rise and dance a little, and then make a stand.'

178–82]   F reads: 'The Cloud descends with the Hyades, at which the maids [*read* Naiades] seem to be rejoiced; they all dance a while together, then make another stand, as if they wanted something.'

188 equal] either 'impartial' or 'just'.

191–5] F reads: 'The Cupids come forth and dance [until] they are weary with their blind pursuing the Nymphs, and the Nymphs weary with flying them.'

191–2 *flame-coloured*] signifying love or desire.

193 *chaplets*] garlands.

193 *hoodwinked*] blindfold.

194 *tiffany*] a thin silk.

195–6] The ascription of this speech to Iris in Q and F would be more acceptable (two scribes carrying over a mistake from the one MS) if the compiler of the description had not repeated the error. But error it is: this is still Mercury's 'show'.

196–7] The golden robots who helped Vulcan at his forge (*Iliad*, XVIII) are freely treated here.

202–15] F reads: 'The Statues come down, and they all dance till the Nymphs out-run them and lose them, then the Cupids go off, and last the Statues.'

229–48] F reads: 'The second Antimasque rusheth in, they dance their measure, and as rudely depart.'

236] Baboons appeared also in the anti-masque of Chapman's wedding masque.

272] F's stage-direction for the discovery of the Knights, etc., follows this line.

288 *croisant*] crescent.

291 *received*] enclosed, covered.

295 *the four Statues*] As one of the live Statues is now undressing, these must be real statues.

301 *Arming*] military.

302 *gorgets*] throat armour.

305 *roses*] rosettes.

311 *Italian bands*] falling-bands, or collars, of Italian cut-work lace.

315 *shag*] cloth with a velvety nap.

315 *labels*] short strips of cloth.

337] F reads: 'The third song, after their many dances, when they are to take out the Ladies.'

344] Ovid, *Art of Love*, I, 632: *Iuppiter ex alto periuria ridet amantum.*

347–8 *galliards, durets, corantoes*] The first and last are usual dances; *durets* are otherwise unknown except for their mention in *The Masque of Flowers* (q.v., p. 170).

THE MASQUE OF FLOWERS

Edited by E. A. J. Honigmann

INTRODUCTION

When the favourite of James I, the Earl of Somerset, formerly Robert Carr of Ferniehurst, married the Lady Frances Howard, daughter of the Earl of Suffolk, the Lord Chamberlain, on 26 December 1613, contemporary England was shocked—as various extant private letters testify. Only three months earlier a commission had pronounced in favour of the nullity of the bride's marriage to her then husband, the Earl of Essex, a decision influenced by political pressures which gave rise to 'many rumours, and strong feelings'. Publicly, however, the Somerset marriage passed off as a splendid spectacle. The fashionable world paid tribute to the favourite with presents of every description, including the performance of several masques—the last of which was *The Masque of Flowers*, produced by the gentlemen of Gray's Inn, in the Banqueting House at Whitehall, on Twelfth Night (6 January), 1614.[1]

Like most masques, *Flowers* proved a costly affair: and we have it on contemporary evidence that the great Sir Francis Bacon not only 'encouraged' the Grayans (in the words of the dedication), but paid all expenses out of his own purse.

Sir Fra: Bacon prepares a maske to honor this mariage which will stand him in above 2000^{li}, and though he have ben offered some helpe by the house [i.e. Gray's Inn], and specially by Master Sollicitor Sir Hen: Yelverton, who wold have sent him 500^{li} yet he wold not accept yt, but offers them the whole charge with the honor: mary his obligations are such as well to his Majestie as to the great Lord [i.e. Somerset], and to the whole house of Howards as he can admit no partners (Chamberlain, *Letters*, I, 493; to Carleton, 23 Dec. 1613).

An undated letter signed 'Fr. Bacon' and addressed to an unspecified lord probably throws further light on Bacon's anxiety to please on this important occasion.

[1] For the Somerset marriage and the masques celebrating it cf. John Nichols, *The Progresses, Processions, and Magnificent Festivities, of King James the First* (4 vols., 1828), II, 704 ff.; James Spedding, *The Letters and the Life of Francis Bacon* (7 vols., 1861–74), IV, 391 ff., and E. K. Chambers, *The Elizabethan Stage*, III, 246–7; IV, 59–60. *Flowers* was entered in the Stationers' Register on 21 January 1614.

Yt may please yor good L. I am sory the joynt maske from the fowr Innes of Cowrt faileth. whearin I conceyue thear is no other grownd of that euent, but impossibility. Neuerthelesse bycause it falleth owt that at this tyme Graies Inne is well furnyshed, of galant yowng gentlemen, yor lp may be pleased to know, that rather then this occasion shall passe withowt some demonstration of affection from the Inns of Cowrt, Thear are a dozen gentlemen of Graies Inne, that owt of the honor which they bear to yor l., and my l. Chamberlayne to whome at theyr last maske they were so much bownde, will be ready to furnysh a maske wyshing it were in their powers to performe it according to theyr mynd. And so for the p^rsent I humbly take my leaue resting

yor lp̃s very humbly
and much bownde

[Endorsed: M^r Fr. Bacon] FR. BACON[1]

Spedding, the learned biographer of Bacon, suggested that this letter refers to *Flowers*, for the 'Lord Chamberlain was the Earl of Suffolk, who was the bride's father: so that everything seems to fit'.[2] Yet Sir Edmund Chambers raised objections in 1903, and, less forcefully, in 1923: 'The weakness of this theory is that the letter is bound up in the Lansdowne collection with Burghley's papers [Burghley died in 1598], and is endorsed "Mr. Fr. Bacon", whereas Bacon was knighted on July 23, 1603.'[3] In 1940, however, the Historical Manuscripts Commission printed the summary of a letter from Samuel Calvert, dated 14 December 1613, which seems to confirm Spedding's brilliant conjecture.

My lord of Somerset's marriage takes place on St. Stephen's day in Henry VII's chapel, Westminster. A supper in the Banqueting House, and three masks intended, one by the queen, the second by the Lords, the last at Sir F. Bacon's *etc.* charge of Gray's Inn, for some private obliga-

---

[1] Lansdowne MS 107, f. 13, art. 8, as printed in the Malone Society's *Collections* (I, 2), 1908, pp. 214–15.

[2] Spedding, IV, 393–4. The thirteen masquers who took part in *Flowers* (line 330) agree with Bacon's no doubt loosely-meant 'dozen'. Bacon's reference to the Grayans' obligation to the Lord Chamberlain 'at theyr last maske' also supports Spedding, for it is specially mentioned in Beaumont's masque of 1613 (presumably the last masque of the Grayans before 1614) that the gentlemen of the Inner Temple and Gray's Inn 'were most honourably received by the Lord Chamberlain' (cf. p. 133).

[3] In the Malone Society's *Collections* (I, 2), p. 214, and Chambers, *Elizabethan Stage*, III, 213–14. Cf. note 2, p. 153, below.

tion; the other Houses all refusing to spend more money, their expenses having been already extraordinary in shows, which they performed with greater affection than they can afford.[1]

This letter agrees with Bacon's in depicting *Flowers* as a substitute for another venture involving 'the other Houses', a matter possibly also hinted at in the dedication of 1614 ('that one Inn of Court by itself. . .'): and such a retreat from a 'joynt maske' cannot have been a common occurrence. We know, in fact, that 'the other Houses' incurred 'extraordinary expenses' in 1613 in celebrating the marriage of Princess Elizabeth 'in shows' (masques)—so that, even more than before, 'everything seems to fit'.[2]

Why did Bacon rise to such extravagance to honour a man who was never an intimate of his? Spedding argued that Somerset (then Viscount Rochester) helped to bring about Bacon's promotion to the Attorney-Generalship in 1613, and that Bacon could not repay this obligation by any present which might be turned into money, since this would be tantamount to a 'sale of office', and therefore grasped at the opportunity offered by a masque, 'costly to the giver, not negotiable by the receiver; valuable as a compliment, but as nothing else'.[3] The gossip that Yelverton wished to join Bacon in

[1] *Report on the Manuscripts of the Marquess of Downshire Preserved at Easthamstead Park Berks*, ed. A. B. Hinds, vol. 4 (H.M.C. vol. 75), 1940, p. 267. By permission of the Marquess of Downshire and of the Berkshire Record Office I was able to inspect the original, now at Reading. The curious phrasing 'at Sir F. Bacon's *etc.* charge of' resulted, apparently, from a deletion: 'by Sʳ Francis Bacon &c of' was altered by Calvert to 'at Sʳ Francis Bacon charge &c of' [*at* and *charge* interlined]. Mr Hinds's summary, incidentally, omitted three words immediately following my excerpt: 'with greater affeĉion, then they can affoord, *this in question.*' (My italics.) Compare the claim made in the dedication that *Flowers* was produced in three weeks.

[2] For the expenses of the 1613 masques, and the difficulties of the Inns in meeting them, cf. Chambers, *Elizabethan Stage*, III, 235, 262. Chambers's doubts about Bacon's letter (cf. note 3, p. 152) need not be taken too seriously. The endorsement 'Mʳ Fr. Bacon' was not necessarily contemporary (the Lansdowne *Catalogue*, 1812, described the volume containing the letter as made up of 'miscellaneous papers without dates'); and Burghley's papers were kept by no means as carefully separated from later ones in the Lansdowne collection as Chambers implied.

[3] Spedding, IV, 392–5. Both Chamberlain's letter and Calvert's refer to Bacon's 'obligations'. Ironically, Bacon later prosecuted both the 'principal persons' in celebration of whose 'happy alliance' *Flowers* came into being. The notorious murder of Overbury was discovered in 1615, and led to the trial of both Somerset and his countess in 1616; Suffolk lost his staff as Lord Treasurer in 1618, and proceedings against him soon followed (cf. Spedding, V, 208 ff., VII, 1 ff.).

financing *Flowers* bears out Spedding's guess, for Yelverton's promotion to the Solicitor-Generalship coincided with Bacon's: if Rochester backed the one, as Bacon acknowledged, it is likely enough that he backed the other as well.

If we agree to Spedding's dating of Bacon's letter we can the more readily accept the assurance in the dedication of *Flowers* that the whole entertainment was prepared 'in the space of three weeks', for the letter suggests a belated change of plans (cf. note 1, p. 153). Shortness of time would then explain the masque's comparative unoriginality.

Structurally *Flowers* consists of two traditional masque-devices loosely strung together, the contest or challenge and the transformation. Winter and Spring, and then Silenus and Kawasha, act out two contests, and the main masque, which gave its title to the piece, centred on the 'device of the transforming'. Practically all the principal 'characters' had, in addition, figured in Jacobean masques before 1614, not to mention French and Italian ones. The debate between Winter and Spring (or Summer) goes back much further, of course, but was still a popular motif—as in Nashe's *Summer's Last Will and Testament* and the anonymous *Masque of the Four Seasons* (before 1612); and possibly Winter in *Flowers* owes something to Jonson's Januarius in *The Masque of Beauty*, 1608. A Silene or Silenus had a speaking part in Jonson's *Oberon* (before 1612); as for Red Indians, the inspiration for Kawasha,[1] these figured as 'the chief masquers' in Chapman's *Masque of the Middle Temple and Lincoln's Inn*, 1613, while in Campion's masque for the Somerset marriage, performed exactly twelve days before *Flowers*, 'America' appeared as one of the 'four parts of the earth' in a similar guise. The contest between Silenus and Kawasha, again, simply echoes, without much sophistication, the popular debate about the merits of

[1] Evans, *English Masques* (p. 102) recognized Kawasha as the Virginian idol Kiwasa described in De Bry's voyages (*America*, Part I, 1590). De Bry gave an illustration of 'Ther Idol Kiwasa' (no. 21); see Plate 13 of this volume. Yet it seems more likely that the authors of *Flowers* were inspired by the more recent *Purchas his Pilgrimage*, 1613, though Purchas copied almost verbatim from his predecessor: 'Their Idol called *Kiwasa*, is made of wood fower foote high, the face resembling the inhabitants of Florida, painted with flesh colour, the brest white, the other parts blacke, except the legges which are spotted with white; hee hath chaines or strings of beades about his necke' (Book 8, ch. 6).

wine and tobacco—for the many 'tobacconists' of the time classed the 'Virginian weed' as an intoxicant comparable to the grape (some even held that it cured all diseases, or was 'the philosopher's stone').[1] Indeed, the one element in the masque claimed as an original idea, the transformation of flowers to men ('For never writer's pen | Yet told of flowers re-turn'd to men' (lines 316–17)), emerges as derivative as well, for (leaving aside the reverse process as illustrated by Narcissus, etc.) in Campion's *Lord Hay's Masque*, 1607, trees were magically changed to men, a not dissimilar metamorphosis.

Though unoriginal, *Flowers* reaches a fair level of competence in its blank verse dialogue, if not, perhaps, in its songs and prose commentary. In view of the three sets of initials appended to the dedication one might divide the authorship according to these three obvious units, more especially since the commentary also exhibits a distinctive feature not found in the other two: it was either written by the author of the commentary accompanying Beaumont's masque of 1613, or by someone impressed by this predecessor's example.[2] Unfortunately the registers of Gray's Inn admissions offer several candidates for each set of initials, so that we cannot identify the authors with their help;[3] indeed, it must remain doubtful whether or not there were three authors, for the initials might represent officials of the Society, or of the revels of that year. Moreover, as Spedding recognized, in promoting a masque in 1613 Bacon 'would have a good deal to say about all the arrangements',

[1] For the commonplace comparison of tobacco and wine cf. Sir John Beaumont's *The Metamorphosis of Tabacco*, 1602, *passim*, e.g. the description of tobacco as 'this *Americk* grape' (sig. E1ᵇ).

[2] The commentary on Beaumont's masque need not have been his own, of course. Both Beaumont's masque and *Flowers*, be it observed, include a 'device' or 'argument', and begin and end this with the same words: 'Jupiter and Juno, *willing to do honour to the marriage of...At the entrance of the King* the first traverse was drawn...', 'The Sun, *willing to do honour to a marriage between...At the entrance of the King...* appeared a traverse...' (cf. pp. 133–4, 160); and a number of (not very uncommon) phrases appear in both masques. Perhaps the substitution of 'priests' for 'gods' (line 350) resulted from too much attention to Beaumont's masque (cf. p. 141), for in both masques 'the priests descend' at the same point, before the 'transforming'. The 'device', almost identical with the letter brought by Gallus, must be the synopsis of *Flowers* prepared for the Lord Chamberlain.

[3] Cf. Joseph Foster, *The Register of Admissions to Gray's Inn, 1521–1889* (1889).

for he had been actively concerned in the preparation of masques over a period of twenty years; if he was 'the chief contriver' of Beaumont's masque of 1613, as Chamberlain reported and as the Gray's Inn records corroborate, the terms of the dedications to Bacon of that masque and of *Flowers* are so similar that we may once more follow Spedding's lead and assume Bacon to have planned, or at least discussed and approved, the 'argument' of *Flowers*.[1]

One other possibility suggests itself as regards the masque's authorship. In December 1613 one of the many gentlemen who served in Bacon's household was Thomas Bushell, a youth of about twenty who, according to Aubrey, 'had a good wit and a working and contemplative head. His lord much loved him'. Much later, in 1636, Bushell produced, and apparently himself composed, an entertainment consisting of verse speeches and songs, *The Several Speeches and Songs, at the Presentment of Mr Bushell's Rock to the Queen's Most Excellent Majesty*. His connexion with Bacon and his interest in 'shows' make it tempting to identify Bushell with the 'T.B.' who signed the dedication of *Flowers*.[2]

In some copies four-part music for five of the Kawasha–Silenus songs is found appended to *Flowers*, without any composer's name. In the edition of the masque privately printed for Gray's Inn in 1887, in commemoration of its first revival since 1614, A. W. à Beckett observed: 'Much of the original music of the Maske, which was composed by Coperario, Master of Music to the Children of James the First, has also been discovered and prepared for modern interpretation.' *Grove's Dictionary of Music and Musicians* (ed. 1954) added that John Coperario (or Cooper) 'supplied much of the music in "The Masque of Flowers"', that some of Coperario's masque-tunes, including one for *Flowers*, can be seen in Add. MS 10444, and gave a cross-reference to John Wilson, who published some songs from *Flowers* as his own in three-part arrangement in

---

[1] Cf. Spedding, IV, 343. For Bacon's participation in masques cf. Chambers, *Elizabethan Stage*, III, 211 ff. If three men collaborated on *Flowers* another possible division would be (i) the Invierno–Primavera introduction (to line 158), (ii) the two antic-masques (to line 258), (iii) the main masque.

[2] There is a life of Bushell by J. W. Gough, *The Superlative Prodigall: A Life of Thomas Bushell* (1932).

Cheerfull Ayres, 1660.[1] *Grove* concluded that Coperario and Lanier and Wilson collaborated in the music. Coperario and Lanier, it will be remembered, supplied music for Campion's *Masque of Squires*, the first of the masques presented at the Somerset marriage.

[1] Add. MS 10444 may contain more than one tune from *Flowers*: cf. articles by W. J. Lawrence and J. P. Cutts in *Music and Letters*, III and XXXV (1922 and 1954).

[DRAMATIS PERSONAE

Invierno
Primavera
Gallus
Silenus
Kawasha
Twelve Garden-gods
Thirteen Masquers

Antic-masque I ⎧ Silenus' Ass, Satyr, four Singers (Miller, Wine
⎪ Cooper, Vintner's Boy, Brewer), five Musicians,
⎨ and Sergeant; Kawasha's two Red Indians, four
⎪ Singers (Skipper, Fencer, Pedlar, Barber), five
⎩ Musicians and Boy, and Sergeant

Antic-masque II ⎧ Pantaloon, Courtesan; Swiss and his Wife;
⎪ Usurer, Midwife; Smug and his Wench; Frete-
⎨ lyne, Bawd; Roaring Boy, Citizen's Wife;
⎪ Mountebank, Jewess of Portugal; Chimney-
⎩ sweeper and his Wench]

THE MASQUE OF FLOWERS.

PRESENTED BY THE GENTLEMEN OF GRAY'S INN,

AT THE COURT OF WHITEHALL, IN THE BANQUETING HOUSE, UPON TWELFTH NIGHT, 1613.

Being the last of the Solemnities and Magnificences which
were performed at the Marriage of the Right Honourable the
Earl of Somerset, and the Lady Frances, daughter of the
Earl of Suffolk, Lord Chamberlain.

*   *   *

To the very honourable knight, Sir Francis Bacon,
His Majesty's Attorney-General.

Honourable Sir,

This last masque, presented by gentlemen of Gray's Inn, before his
Majesty, in honour of the marriage and happy alliance between two such 5
principal persons of the kingdom as are the Earl of Suffolk and the Earl of
Somerset, hath received such grace from his Majesty, the Queen and
Prince, and such approbation from the general, as it may well deserve to
be repeated to those that were present, and represented to those that were
absent, by committing the same to the press, as others have been. The 10
dedication of it could not be doubtful, you having been the principal, and
in effect the only person, that did both encourage and warrant the
gentlemen to show their good affection towards so noble a conjunction,
in a time of such magnificence; wherein we conceive, without giving you
false attributes (which little need where so many are true), that you have 15
graced in general the Societies of the Inns of Court, in continuing them
still as third persons with the Nobility and Court in doing the King
honour. And particularly Gray's Inn, which as you have formerly
brought to flourish both in the ancienter and younger sort, by countenanc-

ing virtue in every quality, so now you have made a notable demonstration 20
thereof in the later and less serious kind by this, that one Inn of Court by
itself, in time of a vacation, and in the space of three weeks, could perform
that which hath been performed, which could not have been done but
that every man's exceeding love and respect to you gave him wings to
overtake Time, which is the swiftest of things. This which we allege for 25
your honour we may allege indifferently for our excuse, if anything were
amiss or wanting; for your times did scarce afford moments, and our
experience went not beyond the compass of some former employment of
that nature, which our graver studies mought have made us by this time
to have forgotten. And so, wishing you all increase of honour, we rest, 30

Humbly to do you service,

I.G.　　W.D.　　T.B.

The Device of the Masque

The Sun, willing to do honour to a marriage between two noble persons
of the greatest island of his universal empire, writeth his letter of commis- 35
sion to the two seasons of the year, the Winter and the Spring, to visit and
present them on his part; directing the Winter to present them with
sports, such as are commonly called by the name of Christmas sports, or
Carnival sports, and the Spring, with other sports of more magnificence.

And more especially, that Winter for his part take knowledge of a 40
certain challenge which had been lately sent and accepted between
Silenus and Kawasha upon this point, that wine was more worthy than
tobacco, and did more cheer and relieve the spirits of man (this to be tried
at two weapons, at song and at dance); and requiring the Winter to give
order that the same challenge be performed in the days of solemnity of 45
the same marriage.

The same letter containeth a second special direction to the Spring, that
whereas of ancient time certain beautiful youths had been transformed
from men to flowers, and had so continued till this time, that now they
should be returned again into men, and present themselves in masque at 50
the same marriage.

All this is accordingly performed. And first the two seasons Invierno
and Primavera come in, and receive their dispatch from the Sun by
Gallus, the Sun's messenger; thereupon Winter brings in the challenge,
consisting of two antic-masques, the antic-masque of the song and the 55
antic-masque of the dance.

160

Then the Spring brings in the masque itself, and there is first seen in the fabric a fair garden upon a descending ground, and at the height thereof there is a stately long arbour or bower arched upon pillars, wherein the masquers are placed, but are not discovered at the first, but there appear 60 only certain great tufts of flowers betwixt the columns. Those flowers upon the charm do vanish, and so the masquers appear every one in the space or inter-column of his arch.

The Masque

At the entrance of the King, at the lower end of the Banqueting House 65
appeared a traverse painted in perspective, like the wall of a city with
battlements, over which were seen the tops of houses. In the middle
whereof was a great gate, and on either side a temple, the one dedicated
to Silenus and the other to Kawasha, in either of which opened a little
gate. 70
Out of the great gate in the middle of the city entered Invierno or
Winter, attired like an old man, in a short gown of silk shag, like
withered grass all frosted and snowed over, and his cap, gown, gamashes
and mittens furred crimson, with long white hair and beard, hung with
icicles. He marcheth up to the middle of the hall, and looks round about 75
him.

> *Invierno.* Why, thus it should be; such a night as this
>   Puts down a thousand weary longsome days
>   Of Summer, when a sun and moon and stars
>   Are met within the palace of a king, 80
>   In sev'ral glory shining each on other
>   With rays of comfort and benign aspects;
>   When hearts are warm. 'Tis for the seely birds
>   To sacrifice their pipes unto the Spring,
>   And let the pilgrim bless the Summer's day; 85
>   But courts and youth and ladies needs must praise
>   The Winter's reign.

While Invierno was thus speaking entereth the Spring or Primavera,
attired like a nymph, a high tire on her head, antic with knots of fair hair
and cobweb lawns rising one above another, garnished with flowers to 90

*some height, and behind falling down in a pendant; an upper-body of
cloth of silver flory, naked neck, and breast, decked with pearls; a
kirtle of yellow cloth of gold, branched with leaves; a mantle of green
and silver stuff cut out in leaves; white buskins, tied with green ribbons
fringed with flowers. She overtaking Invierno claps him on the shoulder.* 95

Primavera. Well overtaken, Winter.
Invierno.   Primavera!
  What's that I see? why, how dare you approach
  In Janus' month? D'ye mean to give the lie
  To all the almanacs that are come forth,   10
  As if they had not lied enough besides?
  Provoke me not; fly hence, you wanton girl,
  Stay not one minute!
Primavera. Good old lad, I know you a merry one
  Within doors; bluster not, I'll choose thee for   10
  My Valentine, and tell thee tales and riddles
  These livelong nights. Thou'rt ever borrowing
  Some days of me, then let this one day pass,
  Good frost-beard, now. But stay, methinks I see
  The trumpet of the Sun, he'll stint this strife.   11

*Gallus comes in post, attired like a post, in yellow damask doublet and
bases, the doublet with close wings, cut like feathers; a pouch of carnation satin, wherein was his packet, hung in a baldric of the same; a pair
of yellow boots; spurs with one long prick like a cock; a little hat of
yellow damask, with a plume of red feathers like a crest.* 11

Invierno. Gallus, mine own brave bird! welcome in troth!
  Thou art no peeping creature that attends
  This gaudy wench, thou wak'st the feather'd hours,
  And call'st to labour; tell us, what's the news?
Primavera. What, crest and spur! welcome, thou com'st in time, 12
  Winter hath almost giv'n me the ague, faith,
  He is so bitter; but thou shalt end our quarrel.
Gallus. Seasons both, God save you in your times!
  I know you both so well, as if I should
  Give leave for you to chirp, and you to chat,   12

How you make all things green,
And you make all things fat.
Time would away; peace, then, read this dispatch,
For I must back to my accustom'd watch.

Winter reads the letter. The letter superscribed: To our faithful and 130
never-failing quarter-waiters, Invierno and Primavera.

Invierno. We have taken knowledge of a marriage to be solemnized
between two noble persons, in the principal island of our universal
empire, unto which we are pleased to do honour, and thereupon
have directed our several letters to you the seasons of the year to 135
visit and present them on your part. To this purpose we would
have you, Invierno, to present them with such sports as are
commonly known by the name of Christmas sports, or Carnival
sports; and you, Primavera, with sports of a more delicate nature;
either of you according to your quality. And for your better 140
instruction and enablement towards the due execution of this your
commission we require you, Invierno, that, whereas we understand
that Silenus hath lately sent a challenge to Kawasha, upon this
point, to maintain that wine is more worthy than tobacco and
cheereth man's spirit more, the same to be tried at two several 145
weapons, song and dance; which challenge the said Kawasha hath
also accepted;—you take order that the said challenge be performed
at this marriage, taking your convenient time. And we require
you, Primavera, for your part, that whereas of ancient time there
were certain fair youths turned into flowers, which have so con- 150
tinued until this time, that you deal with Flora by virtue of this
commission that they be now returned to men, and present a
dance at this marriage. Hereof fail you not.
  Given at our palace, your lord and master,
                    I, the Sun.   155

Postscript. We have also directed our letters to the Summer and the
Harvest, the one to present them with length of days, and the
other with fruit, but those letters come with the next dispatch.

Antic-Masque of the Song

Hereupon they depart all three, and presently entered Silenus at a little 16₄
gate on the right hand, mounted upon an artificial Ass, which some-
times being taken with the strain of the music did bow down his ears and
listen with great attention; the trappings were of ivy;—attended by a
Satyr for his palfreiner, who led the Ass.

At the same instant entered Kawasha at the other little gate, riding 16
upon a cowl-staff covered with a footcloth of pied stuff, borne upon two
Indians' shoulders attired like Floridans.

Silenus an old fat man, attired in a crimson satin doublet without
wings, collar or skirts; a great paunch, so as his doublet, though drawn
with a lace, would not meet together by a handful; sleeves of cloth of 17
gold, bases and gamashes of the same; a red swollen face with a bunched
nose, grey beard, bald head, prick-ears and little horns.

Kawasha had on his head a night-cap of red cloth of gold close to his
skull, tied under his chin, two holes cut in the top out of which his ears
appeared, hung with two great pendants; on the crown of his cap a 17
chimney; a glass chain about his neck; his body and legs of olive-colour
stuff, made close like the skin; bases of tobacco-colour stuff cut like
tobacco leaves, sprinkled with orsidue; in his hand an Indian bow and
arrows.

Before either of these went a Sergeant. The Sergeant of Silenus 18
carried a copper mace, and a bunch of grapes carved at the upper end;
the Sergeant of Kawasha carried on his shoulder a great tobacco-pipe as
big as a caliver.

Before Silenus marched four Singers, and behind him five Fiddlers;
before and behind Kawasha as many of each kind. The Singers on 18
Silenus' part were a Miller, a Wine Cooper, a Vintner's Boy, a
Brewer. His music, a tabor and a pipe, a bass violin, a treble violin, a
sackbut, a mandora. Kawasha's Singers, a Skipper, a Fencer, a
Pedlar, a Barber. His music, a bobtail, a blind harper and his boy, a
bass violin, a tenor cornet, a sackbut. 19

Upon their entrance the music on both sides played till they came to
the middle of the stage. Then Silenus' Singers began his catch, and so
marched forward towards the state.

The Catch

Silenus. Ahay for and a ho,   195
  Let's make this great potan
  Drink off Silenus' can,
  And when that he well drunk is
  Return him to his monkeys,
    From whence he came.   200

Then Kawasha's side answered:

Kawasha. Ahay for and a ho,
  We'll make Silen fall down
  And cast him in a sown,
  To see my men of ire   205
  All snuffing, puffing smoke and fire,
    Like fell dragon.

The Freeman's Song

Silenus. Kawasha comes in majesty,
  Was never such a god as he,   210
  He is come from a far country
  To make our noses a chimney.
Chorus. Silenus' ass doth leer to see
  His well-appointed company.

The Fiddlers of Silenus frumpled over the last verses.   215

Kawasha. The wine takes the contrary way
  To get into the hood,
  But good tobacco makes no stay
  But seizeth where it should.
  More incense hath been burn'd   220
    At great Kawasha's foot
  Than to Silen and Bacchus both,
    And take in Jove to boot.
Chorus. Therefore do yield
  And quit the field,   225
  Or else I'll smoke ye!

These verses frumpled over by the music of Kawasha.

> *Silenus.* The Worthies they were nine, 'tis true,
> And lately Arthur's knights I knew,
> But now are come up worthies new,   230
> The roaring boys, Kawasha's crew.
> *Chorus.* But if Silenus' ass should bray,
> 'Twould make them roar and run away.
> *Kawasha.* Silenus taps the barrel, but
> Tobacco taps the brain,   235
> And makes the vapours fine and soot
> That man revives again.
> Nothing but fumigation
> Doth chase away ill sprites,
> Kawasha and his nation   240
> Found out these holy rites.
> *Chorus.* Therefore do yield
> And quit the field,
> Or else I'll smoke ye!

This song all join and sing.   245

> Ahay for and a ho,
> The ass still looks askance-a;
> But strife in song
> It is too long,
> Let's end it in a dance-a.   250

After the song ended they marched all out in the same order they came in, their music playing.

[Antic-Masque of the Dance]

Then entered the antic-masque of dance, consisting on Silenus' side of a Pantaloon, Courtesan; Swiss and his Wife; Usurer, Midwife; Smug 255 and his Wench; Kawasha's of a Fretelyne, Bawd; Roaring Boy, Citizen's Wife; Mountebank, Jewess of Portugal; Chimney-sweeper and his Wench.

[The Main Masque]

The dance ended, the loud music sounded. The traverse being drawn, 260
was seen a garden of a glorious and strange beauty, cast into four
quarters, with a cross-walk, and alleys compassing each quarter. In the
middle of the cross-walk stood a goodly fountain raised on four columns
of silver; on the tops whereof stood four statues of silver, which supported
a bowl, in circuit containing four and twenty foot, and was raised from 265
the ground nine foot in height; in the middle whereof, upon scrolls of
silver and gold, was placed a globe garnished with four golden mask-
heads, out of which issued water into the bowl; above stood a golden
Neptune, in height three foot, holding in his hand a trident, and riding
on a dolphin so cunningly framed that a river seemed to stream out of 270
his mouth.

The garden-walls were of brick artificially painted in perspective, all
along which were placed fruit trees with artificial leaves and fruit. The
garden within the wall was railed about with rails of three foot high,
adorned with balusters of silver, between which were placed pedestals 275
beautified with transparent lights of variable colours; upon the pedestals
stood silver columns, upon the tops whereof were personages of gold,
lions of gold and unicorns of silver; every personage and beast did hold
a torchet burning that gave light and lustre to the whole fabric.

Every quarter of the garden was finely hedged about with a low hedge 280
of cypress and juniper; the knots within set with artificial green herbs,
embellished with all sorts of artificial flowers. In the two first quarters
were two pyramids garnished with gold and silver, and glistering with
transparent lights, resembling carbuncles, sapphires and rubies. In every
corner of each quarter were great pots of gilly-flowers, which shadowed 285
certain lights placed behind them and made a resplendent and admirable
lustre.

The two farther quarters were beautified with tulippas of diverse
colours, and in the middle and in the corners of the said quarters were
set great tufts of several kinds of flowers, receiving lustre from secret 290
lights placed behind them.

At the farther end of the garden was a mount raised by degrees,
resembling banks of earth covered with grass; on the top of the mount
stood a goodly arbour substantially made, and covered with artificial

trees and with arbour-flowers, as eglantine, honeysuckles and the 29⁹ like.

The arbour was in length three and thirty foot, in height one and twenty, supported with terms of gold and silver; it was divided into six double arches, and three doors answerable to the three walks of the garden. In the middle part of the arbour rose a goodly large turret, and 30⁰ at either end a smaller.

Upon the top of the mount on the front thereof was a bank of flowers curiously painted, behind which, within the arches, the Masquers sat unseen. Behind the garden, over the top of the arbour, were set artificial trees appearing like an orchard joining to the garden, and over all was 30⁵ drawn in perspective a firmament like the skies in a clear night.

Upon a grassy seat under the arbour sat the Garden-gods, in number twelve, apparelled in long robes of green rich taffeta, caps on their heads and chaplets of flowers. In the midst of them sat Primavera, at whose entreaty they descended to the stage and, marching up to the King, sang 31⁰ to lutes and theorboes.

The Song that Induced the Charm

Cantus I

Give place, you ancient powers,
That turned men to flowers; 31⁵
For never writer's pen
Yet told of flowers re-turn'd to men.
Chorus. But miracles of new event
Follow the great Sun of our firmament.

The Charm 32⁰

Hearken, ye fresh and springing flowers,
The Sun shines full upon your earth;
Disclose out of your shady bowers,
He will not blast your tender birth.
Descend you from your hill, 32⁵
Take spirit at his will,
No flowers, but flourish still.

The charm ended, the Gods retire to their places. The loud music again sounded. The banks of flowers softly descending and vanishing, the

Masquers, in number thirteen, appeared, seated in their arches, 330
apparelled in doublets and round hose of white satin, long white silk
stockings, white satin pumps; the doublet richly embroidered in curious
panes with embossed flowers of silver, the panes bordered with em-
broidery of carnation silk and silver; the hose cut in panes answerable
to the embroidery of the doublets; the skirts of the doublets embroidered 335
and cut into lilies, and the wings set forth with flowers of several
colours, made in silk and frosted with silver; ruff-bands edged with a
lace of carnation silk and silver, spangled very thick and stuck full of
flowers of several kinds; fair vizards and tresses; delicate caps of silk
and silver flowers of sundry kinds, with plumes of the same, in the top 340
whereof stuck a great bunch of aigrettes; every Masquer's pump
fastened with a flower suitable to his cap; on their left arms a white
scarf fairly embroidered sent them by the bride, and on their hands a rich
pair of embroidered gloves sent them by the bridegroom.

The loud music ceasing, the Masquers descend in a gallant march 345
through three several doors of the arbour to the three several alleys of
the garden, marching till they all met in the middle alley under the
fountain, and from thence to the stage, where they fell into their first
measure.

That ended, the Priests descend again, and sang the second song. 350

The Song referring to the Device of the Transforming

Cantus II

Thrice happy flowers!
Your leaves are turn'd into fine hair,
Your stalks to bodies straight and fair,   355
Your sprigs to limbs, as once they were,
Your verdure to fresh blood, your smell
To breath; your blooms, your seedy cell,
All have a lovely parallel.
Chorus. The nymphs that on their heads did wear you   360
Henceforth in their hearts will bear you.

That done, they dance their second measure, after which follows the
third song, referring to the ladies.

Cantus III

Of creatures are the flowers, fair ladies,   3⁶
    The prettiest, if we shall speak true;
The earth's coronet, the sun's babies,
    Enamell'd cups of heaven's sweet dew;
Your fairer hands have often blest them
When your needles have express'd them.   37
   Chorus. Therefore though their shapes be changed
    Let not your favours be estranged.

*This ended, they took their ladies, with whom they danced measures,
corantos, durettos, moriscos, galliards. Then was sung the fourth song,
having reference to the King.*   37

Cantus IV

    All things return with time,
    But seldom do they higher climb;
    Yet virtue sovereign
    Mends all things, as they come again.   3⁸
    This isle was Britain in times past,
    But then was Britain rude and waste;
    But now is Britain fit to be
    A seat for a fifth monarchy.
   Chorus. Offer we to his high deserts   3⁹
    Praises of truth, incense of hearts,
    By whom each thing with gain reverts.

*Then they danced their parting measure, at the end whereof followed
this last song, having reference to the married couple.*

Cantus V   3⁹

    Lovely couple, seasons two
    Have perform'd what they can do;
    If the gods inspire our song
    The other two will not stay long;

Receive our flowers with gracious hand 395
As a small wreath to your garland.
Chorus. Flowers of honour, flowers of beauty
Are your own; we only bring
Flowers of affection, flowers of duty.

The masque ended, it pleased his Majesty to call for the antic-masque of 400
song and dance, which was again presented; and then the Masquers
uncovered their faces, and came up to the state, and kissed the King and
Queen and Prince's hand with a great deal of grace and favour, and so
were invited to the banquet.

THE TEXT

I have collated all nine copies of the 1614 edition listed in Greg's *Bibliography*. Despite its many obvious misprints, so far as I can see only two changes were made in the text: the title-page was re-set (to improve its appearance, without any alteration in the phrasing), and one error was corrected (cf. line 157). Nevertheless, we have to take into account variant readings in some of the songs, for the words printed with the music in 1614, and also the words as printed by Wilson in 1660, differ slightly from those printed in the masque proper. In the Collation, therefore, I cite the masque itself as 'Q', the second version of the songs accompanying the 1614 text as 'A', and Wilson as 'B'.[1]

It seems, incidentally, that the speakers' names, or at least some of them, were not found in the printer's copy. This would explain the tangle in lines 97–8, the catchwords which wrongly give the first word of the next speech instead of the speech prefix, and, perhaps, the placing of the speakers' names in the outer margin, an unusual procedure.

H. A. Evans included *Flowers* in his *English Masques*, 1897, and this is the only 'modern' edition. Unfortunately, Evans based his text on Nichols's old-spelling version of 1828 and failed to correct Nichols's frequent misprints and omissions. The text issued for Gray's Inn in 1887 suffers from more drastic changes, interpolations as well as omissions, and therefore the present reprint may claim to be the first one to have received some care.

---

[1] In the Collation of the texts of the songs I ignore mere verbal repetition.

COLLATION

4 by]   Q; by the *Evans*.
26 your]   Q; our *Nichols*.
29 mought]   Q; ought *Nichols*.
65 *King,...House*]   *This ed.*; *King,...*house, Q.
97–8 *Invierno*. Primavera! | What's]   *Nichols*; *Inuierno? Primauera?* |
    Inuierno. Whats Q.
107 Thou'rt]   *Nichols*; Th'art Q.
112 *with*]   *Nichols*; not in Q.
132 *Invierno*]   Not in Q.
156–7 and...one to]   and...one Q (*Yale copy*); &...one to Q.
162 *with the*]   *Evans*; with Q.
164 *palfreneir*]   *This ed.*; Palfreueir Q; *palfreveir Nichols*.
178 *orsidue*]   *This ed.*; orcedure Q; ochre-dust *conj. Evans*.
195 Ahay...ho]   Q; Ahey, ahey...hoe A; A Hey a Hey a Hey for and a
    Hoe, a Hey for and a Hoe B.
196 Let's]   Q; weell A,B.
199 Return]   Q; Weel turn A; returne him turne B.
202]   *As line 195* Q,A,B.
205 my]   Q; his A; our B.
212 noses]   Q, A (*Medius, Contratenor*); nose A (*Tenor, Bassus*), B.
214 His]   Q; This A,B.
220 been burn'd]   A,B; burne Q; burned *Nichols*.
222 and]   Q,A; or B.
223 And]   Q,A; or B.
224 *Chorus*]   *With line 225* Q.
224 Therefore]   Q; Wherefore A,B.
224 do]   Q,A; then B.
225 And]   QA; or B.
226]   Q; *not in* A; Or else I'le smoake you B (*Bassus only*).
229 I]   Q; we B.
230 up]   Q; up of B.
234 *Kawasha*]   *Nichols*; not in Q.
239 sprites]   *This ed.*; spirits Q.
247 The]   A; Tee Q.
247 still looks]   Q; lookes yet A.
249 It is]   Q; Will be A.
253]   *Nichols*.
257 *Citizen's Wife*]   *Conj. Evans*; *Citizen* Q.
259]   *This ed.*

328–9 *places...sounded*]   *This   ed.*;   places,...sounded   Q;   *places,...
sounding Nichols.*
336 *lilies*]   *This ed.*; Lillies flowers Q; lily-flowers *Evans.*
350 *sang*]   *This ed.*; sung Q; *sing Nichols.*
385 *Chorus*] *Evans; with line 386* Q.
390] *Evans; not in* Q.
397 *Chorus*]   *This ed.; not in* Q.

COMMENTARY

Head-title 1613] Old Style, i.e. 1614.

4 last] the last masque at the Somerset marriage: cf. head-title.

33 *Device*] i.e. the 'argument'.

42 Silenus] The foster-father of Bacchus and leader of the satyrs.

42 Kawasha] Cf. p. 154 and Plate 13.

54 Gallus] i.e. the cock.

55 antic-masques] anti-masques. An early use of the word (*antic* because of the grotesques). There are no directions in Q for Winter to bring in the antic-masques.

63 inter-column] the space between two columns. First recorded in *N.E.D.* in 1665.

65 *lower end*] It is not clear in Q whether the king enters at the lower end, or whether the performance took place there; but Campion's masque, played in the same hall twelve days before *Flowers*, had the stage at 'the lower end of the Hall'.

66 *traverse*] curtain.

72 *shag*] a cloth having a velvet nap on one side, usually of worsted but sometimes of silk.

73 *gamashes*] a kind of leggings or gaiters.

79 sun...moon...stars] king, queen and courtiers? Cf. line 155.

83 seely] innocent, harmless; foolish.

89 *tire*] head-dress.

90 *cobweb lawns*] fine transparent lawns or linens.

91 *upper-body*] clothing for the upper body, i.e. for chest and shoulders.

92 *flory*] fleury, decorated with fleurs-de-lis.

92 *neck,...breast,*] So Q. It is not clear whether Spring's breast was naked (on boy-actors playing naked female rôles cf. H. Prunières, *Le Ballet de Cour en France*, 1914, p. 181), or whether her breast was simply decked with pearls. But in Inigo Jones's design for Spring in Jonson's *Chloridia*, 1631, she is naked-breasted.

93 *kirtle*] gown.

93 *branched*] adorned with a figured pattern.

110 trumpet] trumpeter.

111 *doublet*] a close-fitting body-garment worn by men.

112 *bases*] a plaited skirt appended to the doublet, reaching from waist to knee.

112 *wings*] a pair of lateral projecting pieces on or near the shoulders on a doublet, etc.

126 green] One expects *lean* in antithesis to *fat*. Or does *fat* refer to Winter (= dull, slow-witted)?

131 *quarter-waiters*] A nonce-word. A *waiter* was a regular member of a noble household; *quarter* refers to the four quarters, or seasons.

155 Sun] James I was *le roi soleil* to his courtiers (cf. lines 79 and 322, Chapman's masque of 1613, Jonson's *Love Freed* (p. 86)), and sometimes commanded entertainments from his subjects.

164 *palfreneir*] groom.

166 *cowl-staff*] a stout stick used to carry a cowl (tub), being thrust through its two handles. *To ride on a cowl-staff* = to be set astride a pole and carried about in derision.

166 *footcloth*] a rich cloth laid over the back of a horse and hanging down to the ground on either side.

171 *bunched*] bulging; protuberant.

172 *prick-ears*] the erect, pointed ears of some beasts.

178 *orsidue*] a gold-coloured alloy of copper and zinc, rolled into very thin leaf, used to ornament toys, etc.

180 *Sergeant*] an inferior executive officer, such as the *sergeant of the mace* who carried a mace as a badge of office.

183 *caliver*] light musket.

184 *Fiddlers*] musicians. Presumably tabor and pipe belonged to one man, and the harper's boy did not play.

187 *tabor*] drum.

188 *sackbut*] trombone.

188 *mandora*] i.e. mandola, a small lute.

188 *Skipper*] In Campion's masque for the Somerset marriage there was a dance of twelve skippers (seamen).

189 *bobtail*] Unexplained. If an instrument 'it must signify a "kit" or small fiddle, so called probably from its curtailed shape, for there is no other treble instrument in the group of Kawasha's music' (Evans).

192 *catch*] round.

193 *state*] chair of state.

196 potan] Unexplained, but Q, A and B all concur. Perhaps an American Indian word. 'Petun' was well known in England as Indian for tobacco (cf. 'Sig. Petoune' in Sharpham's *Fleire*, 1607); 'Powhatan', the Virginian 'emperor' described in many pamphlets before 1614, might be thus contracted, or 'pocan' (poke-weed, smoked by N. American Indians: cf. *N.E.D.*) misread.

204 sown] swoon.

208 *Freeman's Song*] a lively vocal composition.

215 *frumpled*] rumpled, tumbled.

220 been burn'd] Q is clearly wrong, but A,B give a short line which fails to rhyme with its partner: *in troth* after *burn'd* would patch the gap.

229 lately] Perhaps a reference to the knights in Campion's *Masque of Squires* or (less likely) to Jonson's *Speeches at Prince Henry's Barriers*.

231 roaring boys] riotous fellows.

232 bray] 'In that memorable expedition of the gods against the giants the braying of Silenus's ass had a principal stroke in putting the giants to flight' (Bacon, *Wisdom of the Ancients*, Preface).

236 soot] sweet.

255 *Smug*] cant for blacksmith.

256 *Fretelyne*] From *Fritellino*, the stage-name of P. M. Cecchini (K. M. Lea, *Italian Popular Comedy*, 1934, II, 390).

257 *Citizen's Wife*] 'As the other couples consist of a man and a woman, this [Q's "Citizen"] should probably be Citizen's wife' (Evans). 'Citizen' could refer to either sex.

275 *balusters*] banisters.

279 *torchet*] small torch.

281 *knots*] formal flower-beds.

285 *gilly-flowers*] clove-scented pinks.

292 *degrees*] steps.

298 *terms*] busts or statues of the upper body terminating in a pillar or pedestal. Cf. Jonson's *Chloridia*: 'An arbour...borne up with terms of satyrs.'

307 *Garden-gods*] Probably twelve gods of this particular garden rather than traditional 'garden-gods' (such as Priapus) are meant.

311 *theorboes*] large lutes.

319 Sun] James I: cf. line 155 n.

331 *hose*] breeches.

333 *panes*] a piece of cloth, several of which were joined together side by side to make one cloth or garment.

336 *lilies*] Perhaps *lilies* and *flowers* were alternatives in the MS. Or did the author write *Iilli-flowers* (as in line 285)?

341 *aigrettes*] a tuft of feathers, such as that borne by the egret (lesser white heron); a spray of gems, etc., worn on the head.

343–4 *scarf...gloves*] traditional presents at marriages.

349 *measure*] dance.

350 *Priests*] i.e. garden-gods. Cf. p. 155 n. 2.

350 *sang*] I retain the past tense since Q's style and tenses (cf. lines 328–9) are muddled elsewhere.

374 *corantos*] quick dances.

374 *durettos*] Unexplained. Cf. p. 142, lines 347–8, and note.

374 *moriscos*] morris dances.

374 *galliards*] lively dances.

384 fifth monarchy] the last of the five great empires referred to in the prophecy of Daniel, in the seventeenth century identified with the millennial reign of Christ predicted in the Apocalypse.

385 *Chorus*] Misplaced by one line in Q, as in line 224.

394 other two] Cf. lines 156–8.

397 *Chorus*] Indented like the other choruses in Q.

THE MASQUE OF THE INNER TEMPLE
(ULYSSES AND CIRCE)

BY WILLIAM BROWNE

Edited by R. F. Hill

INTRODUCTION

The title-page of the Emmanuel MS (see 'The Text', p. 200 below) provides information absent from the Newnham MS, namely that the Inner Temple masque was 'presented by the gentlemen there Jan: 13. 1614'. It thus fell in the last (4th) week of the Christmas festivities. Bullen doubted whether the masque was in fact ever performed, since he could discover no record of expenses for the production in the Inner Temple accounts. An answer to Bullen involves a discussion of date. It is always assumed that January 1614/15 is meant, since one would expect the year given to be that of the Christmas to which the masque belonged (i.e. 1614). But this reasoning does not always apply, for the anonymous *Masque of Flowers* is dated Twelfth Night 1614 although part of the celebrations of a marriage which took place on 26 December 1613. However, January 1614/15 is the more likely interpretation because it accords with the one clue we have as to the performance. Records of an Inner Temple parliament held 21 April 1616 tell us that George Lowe, chief cook, petitioned for reimbursement of charges incurred for the repair of a little chamber he had in the cloisters,

by reason the same or a great part thereof and the chimney therein was at Christmas was a twelvemonth broken down by such as climbed up at the windows of the hall to see the mask, which then was.[1]

'Christmas was a twelvemonth' would have been Christmas 1614. The concurrence of the two dates makes it almost certain that the performance of Browne's masque is being referred to.[2] Evidently it was enthusiastically attended.

---

[1] F. A. Inderwick, *A Calendar of the Inner Temple Records* (1898), II, 95.

[2] Inderwick (Introduction, pp. xl–xliv) warmly refutes Bullen's suggestion (*Poems*, 1894) that the masque was never performed. But Inderwick is an unreliable interpreter of the accounts. There is, in fact, no unusual expenditure in the Christmas accounts for 1614/15, and the same is true of Middleton's *Masque of Heroes*, Inner Temple, Christmas 1618/19. This should occasion no surprise, since both were private entertainments for which the expenses were presumably borne by the gentlemen themselves, whereas for the two public masques with which the society was associated, *The Masque of the Inner Temple and Gray's Inn* (1613) and *The Triumph of Peace* (1634), expenses are recorded.

Campion, in the opening description of his *Masque at the Marriage of the Earl of Somerset*, 26 December 1613 (Q, 1614), remarks that satyrs, nymphs, and the like, are the outmoded inventive devices of ancient writers, and that the moderns have transferred their fictions to 'enchanters and commanders of spirits'. His masque relates the journey of a company of knights to England, their assault by enchanters and enchantresses, their shipwreck, transformation into golden pillars and eventual restoration to human shape by a touch from a golden branch. There are obvious parallels to the story of Ulysses and Circe and, since it is to be presumed that Browne acquainted himself with recent masque literature before setting to work, I believe that this masque guided him in his choice of subject. The story of Ulysses and Circe was common literary property and Browne as a scholar was unlikely to have had recourse to English treatments of the legend. In any case, marginal notes and details in the masque make it clear that he was well acquainted with the primary classical sources, that is *Odyssey*, Books X and XII and *Metamorphoses*, Book XIV. In *Britannia's Pastorals*, Book I (1613), Song 5, line 128, Browne alludes to his friend's (that is, Chapman's) translation of Homer, and later in the same song uses the episode of Ulysses and the Sirens as illustration (lines 335–46). It seems likely, therefore, that the subject-matter of his masque was fresh in his mind from a re-reading stimulated by Chapman's forthcoming translation of the *Odyssey* (S.R. 2 November 1614). Finally, his Devon boyhood fostered a delight in streams and shores which is as apparent in the watery preoccupations of his *Pastorals* as in his choice of a sea subject for his masque.

If Browne's subject-matter is commonplace his treatment of it is individual. Circe is transformed from a wicked enchantress, bent on the ruin of Ulysses and his companions, into a resolute but amiable pursuer of his love, whose art, according to her own claims (lines 196–206), brought him safe through various perils to her island. This claim necessitates an astute vindication of her innocence in the matter of changing some of Ulysses's men into monsters (lines 307–30). Another deviation from classical authority is Browne's presentation of the Sirens as maidens of Circe; in *Odyssey*, Book XII, it is Circe's advice which saves Ulysses's party from destruction at their hands. Another refashioning is the rivalry of Tethys and Circe in the protection of Ulysses, by which means Browne achieves a lively clash for the opening of his masque.

But his handling of the legendary material aims only at the creation of an amatory pastoral work. He completely ignores the traditional interpretation of the Circe and Siren episodes as allegories of the brutalizing and destructive influence of sensual indulgence. Indeed, his spirited concluding song 'On and imitate the sun' is a strenuous call to love. All this is of a piece with the unusual character of Browne's masque; he eschews personified abstractions and makes no gesture towards moral instruction. True, it was a private entertainment, but even Middleton's boisterous *Masque of Heroes* (1619) contrives an edifying climax, and Aurelian Townshend's *Tempe Restored* (1631) makes the expected moral allegory of the Circe legend. Evidently Browne meant his title-page motto seriously; his masque was a holiday from his ambitious endeavours in the line of Spenser and Drayton.

The masque is comparatively simply mounted and it is a point worthy of note that by absolving Circe from the responsibility of having transformed Ulysses's men into animals Browne sidetracks a complicated re-transformation scene before the eyes of the audience. Circe's only deliberate action has been to charm Ulysses's men to sleep, and they are finally discovered as the masquers, and awakened by a touch of Circe's wand. I agree with Nicoll (*Stuart Masques*, p. 81) that the set was probably divided vertically, the first discovery revealing the cliff of Circe's island on one side of the stage, the second revealing the main set, to form a composite pastoral and sea-shore setting. For the third and fourth discoveries only 'doors' were required, hinged flats painted as foliage. It is a traditional set, at once attractive and functional with its variety of woodland concealment for players and singers. Apart from the vertical division Browne's setting is very similar in essentials to that of two Inns of Court masques which he may well have seen, *The Masque of the Inner Temple and Gray's Inn* (1613) and *The Masque of Flowers* (1614).

Ulysses and Circe has the character of a short play interspersed with songs and dances. The well-knit little action is played out by characters of credible human attributes. The anti-masque is so neatly integrated—the animals are thought to be some of Ulysses's companions and the cause of his grief—that it forms a part rather than an interruption of the masque action. This structural neatness is surprising since it is the vice of his *Pastorals* to be diffuse and inconclusive in action. The discipline of the short dramatic form also cured his muse of the prolix ornamentation which so dazes one in the *Pastorals*. His talent was for song rather than narrative as is apparent in the often delicately modulated examples in this masque.

Warton conjectured that Browne's treatment of the story of Circe suggested to Milton the subject of *Comus*. This is unlikely. Whereas *Comus* is demonstrably indebted to Spenser, Shakespeare and Fletcher, there are no parallels with *Ulysses and Circe*.[1] But Browne's masque is an engaging example of the genre—not least because of its untypical moral-holiday air—and needs no other claim to the attention of posterity.

[1] None of the 'parallelisms' discussed by Warton in his notes to *Comus* (ed. of Milton's *Poems upon Several Occasions*, 1791) is convincing. H. C. H. Candy, 'Milton's Early Reading of Browne', *N. & Q.* CLVIII (1930), 310–12, does not link *Comus* with *Ulysses and Circe*.

[DRAMATIS PERSONAE

Two Sirens
Triton
Circe
Nymphs of the Wood
Ulysses
A woodman
First anti-masquers: two with harts' heads and bodies;
                          two like Midas, with ass's ears;
                          two like wolves;
                          two like baboons;
                          Grillus, in the shape of a hog
Second anti-masquers: seven Nymphs
Knights: the Masquers
Musicians]

THE INNER
TEMPLE MASQUE

Presented by the gentlemen there Jan. 13 1614.

Ovid ad Pisonem
nec semper Gnosius arcum
destinat, exempto sed laxat cornua nervo.

*   *   *

To the honourable society of the
Inner Temple.

Gentlemen,

I give you but your own; if you refuse to foster it I know not who will;
by your means it may live. If it degenerate in kind from those other our
society hath produced blame yourselves for not seeking to a happier muse.
I know it is not without faults, yet such as your loves or at least *Poetica* 5
Licentia (the common salve) will make tolerable. What is good in it that
is yours, what bad mine, what indifferent both, and that will suffice, since
it was done to please ourselves in private by him that is

All yours

W. Browne 10

The description of the first scene.

*On one side the hall towards the lower end was discovered a cliff of
the sea done over in part white according to that of Virgil, lib. 5:*

> *Iamque adeo scopulos Sirenum advecta subibat*
> *Difficiles quondam multorumque ossibus albos.* 15

*Upon it were seated two Sirens as they are described by Hyginus and
Servius with their upper parts like women to the navel and the rest like
a hen. One of these at the first discovery of the scene, a sea being done in
perspective on one side the cliff, began to sing this song, being as*

186

lascivious proper to them and beginning as that of theirs in Homer, 20
lib. μ *Od.*

Δεῦρ' ἄγ' ἰών, πολύαιν' 'Οδυσεῦ, μέγα κῦδος 'Αχαιῶν.

   Siren. Steer hither, steer, your winged pines
      All beaten mariners,
    Here lie love's undiscover'd mines   25
      A prey to passengers;
    Perfumes far sweeter than the best
    Which make the Phoenix urn and nest.
      Fear not your ships
    Nor any to oppose you save our lips,   30
      But come on shore
    Where no joy dies till love hath gotten more.

The last two lines were repeated, as from a grove near, by a full chorus;
and the Siren about to sing again, Triton, in all parts as Apollonius,
lib. 4 Argonautica, shows him, was seen interrupting her thus: 35

   Triton. Leave, leave, alluring Siren, with thy song
    To hasten what the Fates would fain prolong;
    Your sweetest tunes but groans of mandrakes be,
    He his own traitor is that heareth thee.
    Tethys commands; nor is it fit that you   40
    Should ever glory you did him subdue
    By wiles whose policies were never spread
    Till flaming Troy gave light to have them read.
    Ulysses now furrows the liquid plain
    Doubtful of seeing Ithaca again,   45
    For in his way more stops are thrust by time
    Than in the path where virtue comes to climb.
    She that with silver springs for ever fills
    The shady groves, sweet meadows and the hills,
    From whose continual store such pools are fed   50
    As in the land for seas are famosed,
    'Tis she whose favour to this Grecian tends
    And to remove his ruin Triton sends.

Siren. But 'tis not Tethys, nor a greater power,
  Cynthia, that rules the waves: scarce he, each hour,
  That wields the thunderbolts, can things begun
  By mighty Circe, daughter to the sun,
  Check or control; she that by charms can make
  The scaled fish to leave the briny lake,
  And on the seas walk as on land she were;
  She that can pull the pale moon from her sphere,
  And at midday the world's all-glorious eye
  Muffle with clouds in long obscurity;
  She that can cold December set on fire
  And from the grave bodies with life inspire;
  She that can cleave the centre and with ease
  A prospect make to our antipodes;
  Whose mystic spells have fearful thunders made
  And forc'd brave rivers to run retrograde.
  She, without storms, that sturdy oaks can tear
  And turn their roots where late their curl'd tops were;
  She that can with the winter solstice bring
  All Flora's dainties. Circe bids me sing,
  And till some greater hand her power can stay,
  Whoe'er command, I none but her obey.
Triton. Then Nereus' daughter thus you'll have me tell?
Siren. You may.
Triton.   Think on her wrath.
Siren.   I shall.
Triton.   Farewell. [*Exit*]
Siren. Vain was thy message, vain her hest, for I
  Must tune again my wanton melody.

Here she went on with her song thus:

For swelling waves, our panting breasts
        Where never storms arise
Exchange; and be a while our guests:
        For stars, gaze on our eyes.
The compass, love shall hourly sing,
And as he goes about the ring,

We will not miss 90
To tell each point he nameth with a kiss.
Chorus. Then come on shore
Where no joy dies till love hath gotten more.

*At the end of this song Circe was seen upon the rock, quaintly attired,
her hair loose about her shoulders, an anadem of flowers on her head,* 95
*with a wand in her hand; and then making towards the Sirens called
them thence with this speech:*

   Circe. Sirens, enough; cease; Circe hath prevail'd.
   The Greeks which on the dancing billows sail'd,
   About whose ships a hundred dolphins clung 100
   Rapt with the music of Ulysses' tongue,
   Have with their guide by powerful Circe's hand
   Cast their hook'd anchors on Æaea's strand.

[A traverse is drawn to reveal the scene described by Circe]

   Yon stands a hill crown'd with high waving trees 105
   Whose gallant tops each neighb'ring country sees,
   Under whose shade an hundred silvans play
   With gaudy nymphs far fairer than the day;
   Where everlasting spring with silver showers
   Sweet roses doth increase to grace our bowers; 110
   Where lavish Flora, prodigal in pride,
   Spends what might well enrich all earth beside;
   And to adorn this place she loves so dear
   Stays in some climates scarcely half the year,
   When would she to the world indifferent be 115
   They should continual April have as we.
   Midway the wood and from the levell'd lands
   A spacious yet a curious arbour stands,
   Wherein should Phoebus once to pry begin
   I would benight him ere he get his inn, 120
   Or turn his steeds awry, so draw him on
   To burn all lands but this like Phaeton.
   Ulysses near his mates, by my strong charms
   Lie there till my return in sleep's soft arms.

Then, Sirens, quickly wend we to the bower   12
To fit their welcome and show Circe's power.
Siren. What all the elements do owe to thee
In their obedience, is perform'd in me.
Circe. Circe drinks not of Lethe. Then away
To help the nymphs who now begin their lay.   1.

The second scene

While Circe was speaking her first speech and at these words Yon stands
a hill *etc. a traverse was drawn at the lower end of the hall, and gave
way for the discovery of an artificial wood so near imitating nature that
I think had there been a grove like it in the open plain birds would have* 1.
*been faster drawn to that than to Zeuxis' grapes. The trees stood at the
climbing of an hill and left at their feet a little plain which they circled
like a crescent; in this space upon hillocks were seen eight musicians in
crimson taffeta robes, with chaplets of laurel on their heads, their lutes
by them, which being by them touched as a warning to the Nymphs of* 1
the wood, from among the trees was heard this song:

The song [of the Nymphs] in the wood.

What sing the sweet birds in each grove?
    Nought but love.
What sound our echoes day and night?   1
    All delight.
What doth each wind breathe as it fleets?
    Endless sweets.
Chorus. Is there a place on earth this isle excels
Or any nymphs more happy live than we?   1
When all our songs, our sounds, and breathings be,
That here all love, delight, and sweetness dwells.
                   [Musicians retire to the wood]

*By this time Circe and the Sirens being come into the wood, Ulysses was
seen lying as asleep under the covert of a fair tree, towards whom Circe* 1
coming bespake thus:

Circe. Yet holds soft sleep his course. Now Ithacus,
  Ajax would offer hecatombs to us,
  And Ilium's ravish'd wives and childless sires
  With incense dim the bright aetherial fires   160
  To have thee bound in chains of sleep as here.
  But that thou may'st behold and know how dear
  Thou art to Circe, with my magic deep
  And powerful verses, thus I banish sleep.

The charm   165

      Son of Erebus and night
      Hie away; and aim thy flight
      Where consort none other fowl
      Than the bat and sullen owl,
      Where upon the limber grass   170
      Poppy and mandragoras,
      With like simples not a few,
      Hang for ever drops of dew.
      Where flows Lethe, without coil
      Softly like a stream of oil.   175
      Hie thee thither, gentle sleep,
      With this Greek no longer keep;
      Thrice I charge thee by my wand,
      Thrice with moly from my hand
      Do I to touch Ulysses' eyes,   180
      And with the jasper. Then arise
      Sagest Greek...

Ulysses, as by the power of Circe, awaking thus began:

Ulysses. Thou more than mortal maid
  Who when thou lists canst make, as if afraid,   185
  The mountains tremble and with terror shake
  The seat of Dis; and from Avernus lake
  Grim Hecate with all the Furies bring
  To work revenge; or to thy questioning
  Disclose the secrets of th'infernal shades   190
  Or raise the ghosts that walk the under-glades.

191

To thee, whom all obey, Ulysses bends.
But may I ask, great Circe, whereto tends
Thy never-failing hand? Shall we be free?
Or must thine anger crush my mates and me?   195
Circe. Neither, Laertes' son; with wings of love
To thee and none but thee my actions move.
My art went with thee, and thou me may'st thank
In winning Rhesus' horses ere they drank
Of Xanthus stream; and when with human gore   200
Clear Hebrus channel was all stained o'er;
When some brave Greeks companions then with thee
Forgot their country through the Lotos tree;
I tyn'd the firebrand that, beside thy flight,
Left Polyphemus in eternal night;   205
And lastly to Æaea brought thee on
Safe from the man-devouring Laestrygon.
This for Ulysses' love hath Circe done;
And if to live with me thou shalt be won
Aurora's hand shall never draw away   210
The sable veil that hides the gladsome day
But we new pleasures will begin to taste,
And better still those we enjoyed last.
To instance what I can: music, thy voice,
And of all those have felt our wrath the choice,   215
Appear; and in a dance 'gin that delight
Which with the minutes shall grow infinite.

Here one attired like a woodman in all points came forth of the wood
and, going towards the stage, sung this song to call away the first   220
anti-masque.

Song

Come ye whose horns the cuckold wears,
The wittol too with ass's ears;
    Let the wolf leave howling,
    The baboon his scowling,   225
      And Grillus hie
      Out of his sty;

Though grunting, though barking, though braying, ye come
We'll make ye dance quiet and so send ye home.
    No gin shall snare you, 230
    Nor mastiff scare you,
      Nor learn the baboon's tricks;
    Nor Grillus scoff
    From the hog trough,
      But turn again unto the thicks. 235

  Here's none, 'tis hop'd, so foolish scorns
That any else should wear the horns;
    Here's no cur with howling,
    Nor an ape with scowling,
      Shall mock or mow 240
      At what you show
In jumping, in skipping, in turning, or ought
You shall do to please us, how well or how nought.
    If there be any
    Among this many 245
  Whom such an humour steers,
    May he still lie
    In Grillus' sty
  Or wear for ever the ass's ears.

While the first stave of this song was singing, out of the thickets on 250
either side the boscage came rushing the anti-masque, being such as by
Circe were supposed to have been transformed, having the minds of
men still, into these shapes following:
  2 with harts' heads and bodies, as Actaeon is pictured.
  2 like Midas, with ass's ears. 255
  2 like wolves, as Lycaon is drawn.
  2 like baboons.
Grillus, of whom Plutarch writes in his Morals, *in the shape of a hog.*
The music was composed of treble violins with all the inward parts;
a bass viol, bass lute, sagbut, cornemuse, and a tabor and pipe. These 260
together dancing an antic measure, towards the latter end of it missed
Grillus who was newly slipped away, and whilst they were at a stand
wondering what was become of him, the Woodman stepped forth and
sung this song:

Song   2

Grillus is gone, belike he hath heard
The dairy-maid knock at the trough in the yard;
 Through thick and thin he wallows,
 And weighs nor depths nor shallows.
  Hark how he whines!   2
  Run all ere he dines;
  Then serve him a trick
  For being so quick,
 And let him for all his pains
  Behold you turn clean off   2
   His trough,
 And spill all his wash and his grains.

*With this the triplex of their tune was played twice or thrice over and
by turns brought them from the stage; when the Woodman sung this
other stave of the last song and then ran after them.*   2

Song

And now 'tis wish'd that all such as he
Were rooting with him at the trough or the tree;
 Fly, fly, from our pure fountains
 To the dark vales or the mountains.
  List! someone whines
  With voice like a swine's,
  As angry that none
  With Grillus is gone,
 Or that he is left behind.   2
  O let there be no stay
   In his way
To hinder the boar from his kind.   [*Exit*]

Circe. How likes Ulysses this?
Ulysses.   Much like to one   2
 Who in a shipwreck being cast upon
 The frothy shores, and safe, beholds his mates
 Equally cross'd by Neptune and the Fates.

You might as well have ask'd how I would like
A strain, whose equal Orpheus could not strike,   300
Upon a harp whose strings none other be
Than of the heart of chaste Penelope.
O let it be enough that thou in these
Hast made most wretched Laertiades.
Let not the sad chance of distressed Greeks   305
With other tears than sorrow's dew your cheeks!
Most abject baseness hath enthrall'd that breast
Which laughs at men by misery opprest.
Circe. In this, as lilies or the new-fall'n snow,
Is Circe spotless yet. What though the bow   310
Which Iris bends appeareth to each sight
In various hues and colours infinite?
The learned know that in itself is free
And light and shade make that variety.
Things far off seen seem not the same they are,   315
Fame is not ever truth's discoverer;
For still where envy meeteth a report
Ill she makes worse, and what is good come short.
In whatsoe'er this land hath passive been,
Or she that here o'er other reigneth queen,   320
Let wise Ulysses judge. Some, I confess,
That tow'rds this isle not long since did address
Their stretched oars, no sooner landed were,
But, careless of themselves, they here and there
Fed on strange fruits, invenoming their bloods,   325
And now like monsters range about the woods.
If those thy mates were, yet is Circe free
For their misfortunes have not birth from me;
Who in th'apothecary's shop hath ta'en,
Whilst he is wanting, that which breeds his bane,   330
Should never blame the man who there had plac'd it
But his own folly urging him to taste it.
Ulysses. Æaea's queen and great Hyperion's pride,
Pardon misdoubts; and we are satisfied.
Circe. Swifter the lightning comes not from above   335

Than do our grants borne on the wings of love.
And since what's past doth not Ulysses please
Call to a dance the fair Nereides,
With other Nymphs which do in every creek,
In woods, on plains, on mountains, simples seek
For powerful Circe; and let in a song
Echoes be aiding, that they may prolong
My now command to each place where they be,
To bring them hither all more speedily.

*Presently in the wood was heard a full music of lutes which, descending
to the stage, had to them sung this following song, the Echoes being
placed in several parts of the boscage.*

Song [*of the Nymphs in the wood*]
Circe bids you come away,
 Echo. Come away, come away.
From the rivers, from the sea,
 Echo. From the sea, from the sea.
From the green woods every one,
 Echo. Every one, every one.
Of her maids be missing none,
 Echo. Missing none, missing none.
No longer stay except it be to bring
A med'cine for love's sting;
That would excuse you and be held more dear
Than wit or magic, for both they are here.
 Echo. They are here, they are here.

The Echo had no sooner answered to the last line of the song, They are
here, *but the second anti-masque came in, being seven Nymphs and
were thus attired:*

Four {
*in white taffeta robes, long tresses, and chaplets of flowers,
herbs, and weeds on their heads; with little wicker baskets in
their hands, neatly painted. These were supposed to be maids
attending upon Circe and used in gathering simples for their
mistress's enchantments—Pausanias,* in prioribus Eliacis.

Three {
in sea green robes, greenish hair hanging loose, with leaves of 370
coral and shells intermixed upon it. These are by Ovid
affirmed to help the Nymphs of Circe in their collections: by
these:
}

> Nereides nymphaeque simul, quae vellera motis
> Nulla trahunt digitis nec fila sequentia ducunt, 375
> Gramina disponunt sparsosque sine ordine flores
> Secernunt calathis variisque coloribus herbas;
> Ipsa, quod hae faciunt, opus exigit *etc.*

These having danced a most curious measure to a softer tune than the
first anti-masque, as most fitting, returned as they came; the Nereides 380
towards the cliffs and the other maids of Circe to the woods and plains;
after which Ulysses thus:

> *Ulysses.* Fame adds not to thy joys I see in this;
> But like a high and stately Pyramis
> Grows least at farthest. Now fair Circe grant— 385
> Although the fair-hair'd Greeks do never vaunt
> That they in measur'd paces ought have done
> But where the god of battles led them on—
> Give leave that, freed from sleep, the small remain
> Of my companions on the under plain 390
> May in a dance strive how to pleasure thee,
> Either with skill or with variety.
> *Circe.* Circe is pleased. Ulysses, take my wand
> And from their eyes each child of sleep command;
> Whilst my choice maids with their harmonious voices, 395
> Whereat each bird and dancing spring rejoices,
> Charming the winds when they contrary meet,
> Shall make their spirits as nimble as their feet.

The third scene's description

Circe, with this speech delivering her wand to Ulysses, rests on the 400
lower part of the hill; while he going up the hill and striking the trees
with his wand, suddenly two great gates flew open making as it were a
large glade through the wood, and along the glade a fair walk, two

seeming brick walls on either side over which the trees wantonly hung;
a great light, as the sun's sudden unmasking, being seen upon this 405
discovery. At the further end was descried an arbour, very curiously
done, having one entrance under an architrave borne up by two pillars
with their chapters and bases gilt, the top of the entrance beautified with
postures of satyrs, wood nymphs and other antic work, as also the sides
and corners; the covering archwise interwove with boughs, the back of it 410
girt round with a vine and artificially done up in knots towards the top;
beyond it was a wood seen in perspective. The fore part of it opening at
Ulysses his approach, the Masquers were discovered in several seats
leaning as asleep.

Their attire.   415

Doublets of green taffeta cut like oaken leaves, as upon cloth of silver;
their skirts and wings cut into leaves, deep round hose of the same, both
laid with sprig lace spangled; long white silk stockings; green pumps,
and roses done over with silver leaves; hats of the same stuff, and cut
narrow-brimmed and rising smaller compass at the crown; white 420
wreath hatbands, white plumes, egrettes with a green fall; ruff bands
and cuffs.

Ulysses severally came and touched every one of them with the wand
while this was sung:

Song   425

Shake off sleep ye worthy knights
Though ye dream of all delights;
Show that Venus doth resort
To the camp as well as court
   By some well-timed measure.   430
And on your gestures and your paces
Let the well-composed Graces
   Looking like and part with pleasure.

By this the Knights, being all risen from their seats, were by Ulysses
(the loud music sounding) brought to the stage. Then to the violins danced 435
their first measure, after which this song brought them to the second.

Song

On and imitate the sun,
Stay not to breathe till you have done;

Earth doth think, as otherwhere 440
Do some women she doth bear,
Those wives whose husbands only threaten
Are not lov'd like those are beaten.
   Then with your feet to suff'ring move her
   For whilst you beat earth thus you love her. 445

*Here they danced their second measure, and then this song was sung,
during which time they take out the Ladies.*

Song

Choose now among this fairest number
Upon whose breasts love would for ever slumber; 450
Choose not amiss, since you may where you will,
   Or blame yourselves for choosing ill.
Then do not leave, though oft the music closes,
Till lilies in their cheeks be turn'd to roses.
Chorus. And if it lay in Circe's power 455
   Your bliss might so persever,
That those you choose but for an hour
   You should enjoy for ever.

*The Knights with the Ladies dance here the old measures, galliards,
corantos, the brawls etc. And then, having led them again to their* 460
*places, danced their last measure. After which this song called them
away.*

Song

Who but Time so hasty were
To fly away and leave you here? 465
   Here where delight
   Might well allure
A very stoic from this night
   To turn an epicure.
But since he calls—away! And Time will soon repent 470
He stayed not longer here, but ran, to be more idly spent.
                    [Exeunt]

THE TEXT

There were no early editions of William Browne's *Inner Temple Masque*, but two MS copies exist, one in the library of Emmanuel College, Cambridge, and the other in the possession of Lt.-Col. John Chandos-Pole of Newnham Hall, Daventry. Both have the character of early seventeenth-century transcripts, possibly made shortly after the production of the masque. The Newnham Hall copy is apparently in the hand of Thomas Gell (1595–1657), a member of the Inner Temple.[1]

The Emmanuel MS is by far the more careful transcript. Neither is derived from the other; for example, the Emmanuel MS supplies lines and phrases omitted by copyist's error from the Newnham Hall MS; and the Newnham Hall MS contains some variants which are unlikely to be corrections made by a copyist working from the Emmanuel MS, considering that the copyist was hurried and inaccurate elsewhere (e.g. line 147, *Em.* us that fleets; *Newn.* as it fleets; line 397, *Em.* Harming; *Newn.* Charming. Both the Newnham Hall readings I take to be the true ones). Whether the MSS derive from different ancestral texts is uncertain since the variants between the texts could all be explained as the copyists' omissions, misreadings and sophistications of a common original. In any case, a modern edition must take the Emmanuel MS as its copy text since it is a fuller and more careful transcript. Besides, it must be sadly recorded that about one-sixth of each leaf of the Newnham Hall MS has been consumed by mice or rats. Nonetheless, the texts are of independent authority and several readings have been incorporated from the Newnham Hall MS.

The masque was first printed[2] in 1772 in T. Davies's edition of *The Works of William Browne* and subsequently in Robert Anderson, *A Complete Edition of the Poets of Great Britain* (1793), vol. 4; W. C. Hazlitt, *The Works of William Browne* (1868–9); Gordon Goodwin, *The Poems of William Browne of Tavistock*, with an introduction by A. H. Bullen (1894); Gwyn Jones, *Circe and Ulysses*, Golden Cockerel Press (1954). All except the last two editions are based solely on the Emmanuel MS.

[1] He seems to have been a diligent transcriber, for among the Gell family papers at Newnham Hall are copies of Raleigh's speech at his execution in 1618 and of two speeches of Francis Bacon in parliament. These pieces together with a legal notebook and the masque are in the same hand, and comparison with an autograph letter of the civil war period from Thomas to Sir John Gell suggests that Thomas was the copyist. I am indebted for this clue as to the copyist to P. J. Croft.

[2] T. Warton's remark, 'I have been informed, that a few copies [of *Ulysses and Circe*] were printed soon after the presentation', remains opaque (ed. of Milton's *Poems upon Several Occasions*, 1791, p. 136).

COLLATION

59 scaled] *Davies*; scalded *Em.*, *Newn.*; scalled *Hazlitt*.
74 greater hand her power] *Em.*; greater power her hand *Newn.*
81 hest] *Em.*; heat *Newn.*; haste *Davies*.
98 enough] *Newn.*; ynouk *or* ynouh *Em.*
147 as it fleets] *Newn.*; us that fleets *Em.*
194 hand] *Newn.*; hands *Em.*
313 that] *Em.*; it *Newn.*
340 on plains] *Davies*; *Em. is ink-stained here*; in plains *Newn.*
397 Charming] *Newn.*; Harming *Em.*
413 *his approach*] *Em.*; approach *Newn.*

COMMENTARY

Title-page *nec semper...nervo*] 'not for ever does the Cretan aim his bow, but, freeing its string, he relaxes its horns' (*Laus Pisonis*, 142–3 (Minor Latin Poets, 1934, Loeb Classical Library)). Authorship doubtful. The quotation is apt for a student at law, being an exhortation to Piso to indulge in the pleasures of poetical composition after his graver eloquence in court and senate.

14–15 *Iamque...albos*] 'And now, onward borne, it (the fleet of Aeneas) was nearing the cliffs of the Sirens, perilous of old and white with the bones of many men' (*Aeneid*, v, 864–5 (Loeb Classical Library)).

16–18 *Upon...hen*] C. Julius Hyginus, *Fabularum Liber* cxxv; Servius, *Commentarii in Virgilium*, v, 864. For an illustration see A. Nicoll, *Stuart Masques*, etc., p. 172. Browne follows classical authority; the emblems of Alciati (1551) and Whitney (1586) endow the Sirens with the tails of mermaids.

18–19 *One of these...*] The two Sirens are usually described as singing in unison.

19–20 *as lascivious proper*] appropriately lascivious. Odd constructions and usages, such as this, are not uncommon in Browne.

22 Δεῦρ'...'Αχαιῶν] 'Come hither, as thou farest, renowned Odysseus, great glory of the Achaeans' (*Odyssey*, xii, 184 (Loeb Classical Library)).

27–8 Perfumes...nest] According to Pliny's version of the myth the Phoenix builds himself a scented nest with sprigs of cinnamon and frankincense in which to die (*Nat. Hist.* x, 2).

29 Fear not your ships] Fear not for your ships, i.e. shipwreck.

34 *Triton*] Son of Poseidon and Amphitrite. Apollonius (1610–16) describes him as god-like to the waist but with the tail of a sea-monster. Pausanias (ix, 21, 1) gives a colourful account which includes gills and green hair and eyes.

38 Your...mandrakes be] The mandrake is a fork-rooted herb formerly renowned chiefly as a narcotic and aphrodisiac. Prominent among the many superstitions associated with the mandrake (see Sir Thomas Browne, *Pseudodoxia Epidemica*, ii, vi) was that the groan or shriek emitted by the herb on eradication caused death or madness in the gatherer unless elaborate precautions were taken. The connexion here with the Sirens and Circe is especially appropriate since a tradition stemming from Dioscorides (*Materia Medica*, iv, 76) also calls the mandrake Circaea, as being the source of the potion with which Circe enamoured and transformed her victims.

42 By wiles whose policies] *Policies* probably refers back to Circe's *wiles*, but the antecedent of *whose* could be *him* from the previous line, the reference being to the traditional cunning of Ulysses. For examples of awkward

separation of antecedent and relative see below, lines 70–1, and *Pastorals*, II, song 4, 109–10.

55–6 scarce...thunderbolts] Jupiter.

58–73 she...dainties] *Metamorphoses*, XIV, which Browne consulted for its version of the Circe–Ulysses story, relates also the Circe–Picus episode as illustrative of her magical powers. In lines 403–11 there are notable similarities with this passage in Browne.

59 scaled fish] The 'scalded fish' of the MSS is colourful, but an easy misreading of a possible 'scalled' in the original. 'Scaly fish' and 'scaly train' are found in the *Pastorals*.

67 A prospect...antipodes] A view to the opposite side of the earth.

76 Nereus' daughter] A marginal note here (partly cropped) reads 'Hom: ἀλλά ἑ Νηρῆος θυγάτηρ etc.'. Browne over-reaches himself in this pedantic reference to *Hymn to Apollo*, 319, for there we are told that the daughter of Nereus is Thetis; he has confused Tethys with her granddaughter Thetis.

89 ring] Presumably the outer circumference of the compass on which the points were marked. As a technical term *ring* referred not to the compass but was the name for the mariner's astrolabe, an instrument for taking altitudes.

91 tell] count, note.

94–6 At the...hand] This simple description is in keeping with Browne's pastoralism rather than with the ornate Circe found in the emblem books and in Inigo Jones's designs for *Tempe Restored* (1632).

95 anadem] chaplet, garland.

103 Æaea] Circe's island.

108 gaudy] Brilliant in appearance; an unexpected choice of adjective since in the seventeenth century it was normally used pejoratively as today.

115 indifferent] impartial, fair.

120 ere he get his inn] before due sunset time. Browne lodges Phoebus in his 'inn' twice in the *Pastorals*.

122 To...Phaeton] Phaeton, son of Helios, drove his father's chariot, but the horses bolted and the earth was in danger of being burnt up. *Phaeton* is trisyllabic.

127–8 What...me] Her obedience to Circe matches that of the elements.

129 Circe drinks not of Lethe] A claim to alacrity in action; she has nothing of the lethargy associated with the river of forgetfulness.

136 Zeuxis] A Greek painter whose skill was so great that birds are said to have pecked at a bunch of grapes he had painted.

136–7 at the climbing] on the slope.

157 Ithacus] Ulysses, king of Ithaca.

158 hecatombs] great public sacrifices.

166 Son of Erebus] Somnus, Sleep.

170 limber] pliant.

179 moly] a herb of magical properties. In Homer it was given by Mercury to Ulysses to protect him from the enchantments of Circe.

181 jasper] Medieval lapidaries attribute to this stone various healing properties and virtues, amongst which that it affords protection against fiends, Jews and Saracens. See J. Evans and M. S. Sergeantson, *English Medieval Lapidaries* (E.E.T.S., 1933).

187 The seat of Dis] the underworld.

188–9 Grim Hecate...revenge] In *Metamorphoses*, XIV, Circe takes revenge upon Glaucus by transforming his beloved Scylla into a monster with the aid of Hecate's spells.

198–207 and thou me may'st thank...] Circe is her own authority for this claim. Browne traces the adventures of Ulysses's party from the departure from Troy to the arrival at Æaea (*Odyssey*, IX and X).

199–200 Rhesus' horses...stream] Diomedes and Ulysses intercepted the forces of Rhesus, king of Thrace, to prevent the fulfilment of an oracle which declared that Troy would never be taken if the horses of Rhesus drank the waters of the Xanthus (Scamander) which flowed just north of Troy (*Iliad*, X).

201 Hebrus channel] Ulysses plundered the city of Ismarus at the mouth of the river Hebrus in Thrace, but delayed departure and suffered severe losses in a battle with reinforcements which subsequently arrived.

204–5 I tyn'd...night] *tyn'd*, kindled; *beside*, in addition to. The *eternal night* of the one-eyed giant Polyphemus was sorrow at the escape of his human prey as well as his blindness.

213 better still] always improve upon.

214 what I can] 'what I am skilled in' or 'what I can do'.

215 the choice] the choicest.

223 wittol] acquiescent cuckold.

226 Grillus] a hog. See note below at line 258.

231–2 Nor mastiff...tricks] The main burthen of the song is a reassurance to the creatures of the anti-masque that they will not be mocked at, so the most likely interpretation of these two lines is that no dog will be allowed to mimic the dancing and tumbling of the baboon. In Elizabethan and Jacobean times both dogs and monkeys were taught such tricks for the purpose of entertainment.

235 thicks] thicket.

236–7 Here's none...horns] No-one should be so foolish as to laugh at a cuckold.

240 mow] grimace.

243 nought] badly.

245 many] Either elliptical, 'many people', or a substantive by confusion with meinie, 'company'.

246 steers] governs.

254 *Actaeon*] He was transformed by Artemis into a stag. The emblem books 'picture' him with the head of a stag and the body of a man.

255 *Midas*] Apollo changed his ears to those of an ass for judging that Pan was a superior flute-player to Apollo.

256 *Lycaon*] Jupiter changed Lycaon into a wolf for offering the god human flesh to eat.

258 *Grillus*] The reference is to a dialogue between Circe, Ulysses and Grillus, entitled 'Beasts are Rational' (Plutarch, *Moralia*, Loeb Classical Library, XII, 492–533). Grillus, who is one of the Greeks transformed by Circe into a hog, triumphantly argues to Ulysses that animals are more rational than men, more virtuous, and happier. Plutarch's intention is satire of the morals of men through the intelligent Grillus, but Browne treats him as merely swinish. Spenser mentions Grillus (*F.Q.* II, xii, 86–7) as one of the men transformed by Acrasia into beasts. The Book of Temperance, Phaedria and Acrasia, with their Circe–Siren affinities, must have been known to Browne, but he takes only Spenser's imaginative colouring and not his moral interpretation.

259 *inward parts*] Parts intermediate between the highest and lowest of the harmony.

260 *sagbut*] trombone.

260 *cornemuse*] bagpipe.

269 weighs] considers.

275 turn clean off] completely overturn. *Turn off* in this sense is not recorded in *N.E.D.*

278 *triplex*] 'triple time' or 'treble, melody'.

299–302 You...Penelope] Such music could not be equalled by Orpheus, but it would be hateful to Ulysses.

319–21 In whatsoe'er...judge] This is awkwardly expressed. Circe asks Ulysses to judge whether she and her land have not been innocent (*passive*) in everything (*whatsoe'er*).

340 simples] herbs.

343 now] present. Common seventeenth-century usage.

363–71 *and were thus attired...*] Inigo Jones's drawings of nymphs and naiads for Daniel's *Tethys' Festival* (1610) show far heavier costumes than Browne's description suggests, though similar in some details (Simpson and Bell, *Designs*, plates V and VI).

369 *Pausanias*] Elis. I, xix, 7. A merely pedantic reference to Pausanias's description of a cedar chest in the temple of Hera in Elis, carved in part with figures supposed to be Ulysses, Circe and her four handmaidens. Their picturesque dress is Browne's invention.

370 *greenish hair*] Browne supplies a marginal reference here to Horace, *Odes*, Book III. Ode xxviii, 10 authorizes green hair for Nereids.

372–3 *by these*] in these words/lines.

374–8 Nereides...exigit] 'Her attendants were Nereids and nymphs, who card no fleece and spin no woollen threads with nimble fingers; their only task, to sort out plants, to select from a jumbled mass and place in separate baskets flowers and herbs of various colours. She herself oversees the work they do' (*Metamorphoses*, XIV, 364–8, Loeb Classical Library).

390 on the under plain] on earth, i.e. still alive.

417 *skirts and wings*] The *skirt* was the lower part of the doublet; the *wing* was a flat tab stitched round the arm-hole to mask the juncture of the detachable sleeve.

417 *deep round hose*] full, padded trunks or breeches.

418 *laid with sprig lace spangled*] embroidered with lace worked in the form of sprigs and sewn over with eyelets of gold or silver.

421 *egrettes with a green fall*] egrettes = aigrettes. Jewelled tufts or sprays with green hangings, a common ornament for head-dress.

421 *ruff bands*] stiff, multi-pleated collars.

459 *the old measures*] Presumably referring to the two measures already danced and not a characterizing of galliards, corantos and brawls; these were fashionable dances in the Stuart period.

459–60 *galliards, corantos, the brawls*] The galliard and the coranto were lively dances in triple time; the brawl was a French dance resembling a cotillon.

470–1 But since...spent] punctuation and interpretation of these lines, this edition.

LOVERS MADE MEN

BY BEN JONSON

Edited by Stanley Wells

INTRODUCTION

Lovers Made Men was performed at a great reception given in
London on Saturday, 22 February 1617. The host was Lord Hay
(later Viscount Doncaster and Earl of Carlisle), a favourite of
James I, and notorious for his extravagance. In 1616 he had been
sent to France on a diplomatic mission; he made a public entry of
great magnificence into Paris, and was lavishly entertained. So it was
natural that when, in the following year, Charles Cauchon, Baron
du Thour et de Maupas,[1] came on an embassy to England, Hay
should have been one of those who entertained him. The party was
held in Blackfriars at the Wardrobe, of which Hay was Master. On
the same day John Chamberlain wrote to Sir Dudley Carleton: 'this
night he [du Thour] is solemnly invited by the Lord Haye to the
wardrobe to a supper and a maske.' Chamberlain disapproved of the
extravagance:

this feasting begins to grow to an excessive rate the very provision of cates
for this supper arising to more then 600[li] wherin we are too apish to
imitate the French monkeys in such monstrous waste: for supping with
Master Controller [Sir Thomas Edmondes] on Thursday...he told me
that the Lord Hay at his last beeing in Fraunce among many other great
bankets made him had three wherof the least cost 1000[li] sterling, the rest
1300[li] and 1500[li]. But yf there fall out any thing at these bankets worth the
knowlege you shall have yt by my next. Sir Edward Sackevile, Sir Harry
Rich, Sir George Goring and Sir Thomas Badger are the principall persons
in his masque (*Letters*, II, 55–6).

The last three had all accompanied Hay on his French embassy.[2]
Chamberlain had learned more gossip about the occasion, including
the culinary arrangements, by the time he wrote again to Carleton
on 8 March:

[1] Herford and Simpson (*Ben Jonson*, X, 566) identify the 'Baron de Tour' with the
Duc de Bouillon; but see, e.g., *Mémoires du Cardinal de Richelieu, 1616–19* (Paris,
1909), XI, 134.
[2] *Letters from George Lord Carew to Sir Thomas Roe*, ed. J. Maclean (Camden
Society, 1860), p. 38.

The Frenchmen are gon after theyre great entertainment, which was too great for such pettie companions, specially that of the Lord Hayes which stoode him in more then 2200[li], beeing rather a profusion and spoyle then reasonable or honorable provision, as you may guesse at the rest by this scantling, of seven score feasants, twelve partridges in a dish thoroughout, twelve whole samons, and whatsoever els that cost or curiositie could procure in like superfluitie: besides the workemanship and inventions of thirtie cookes for twelve dayes (pp. 57–8).

George, Lord Carew, who was present, was impressed by the masque as well as by the food and company; he wrote to Sir Thomas Roe:

Before the departure of Monsieur de la Tour, the Frenche Kinges Extra-ordinarye Ambassador, the Lord Hay feasted him att the Wardrobe, which, in a word, was the most magnificent feast thatt ever I have seene in my life without exception; and after supper a maske equall to those which you have seene att Whitehall, whereatt most of the Englishe and Scottishe Lords and great ladies then in town were present.[1]

In spite of the general lavishness of the occasion, the masque that Jonson composed for the guests' entertainment is among his least elaborate. A single set is employed throughout, and no stage machinery is required. Following a precedent set by Campion in his wedding masque for Lord Hay (1607), Jonson had the anti-masque performed by the masquers themselves,[2] so the number of per-formers was unusually small. This relative austerity, while it may have disappointed some of the spectators, is an advantage to the reader, for *Lovers Made Men* is more of a realized work of literary art than many of its fellows: it has, as Herford and Simpson say (II, 302), a 'harmony of total effect in which it surpasses many

---

[1] Carew, in *op. cit.* pp. 91–2. *Note.* A passage from Sir Anthony Weldon's *The Court and Character of King James* (1651, pp. 19–20; quoted, e.g., by Bentley, *Jacobean and Caroline Stage*, IV, 651) is often associated with the performance of *Lovers Made Men*. The passage is both confused and confusing, and it is possible that Weldon is mingling information about more than one occasion, but since he states that the masque was held at Essex House (not the Wardrobe) and that the King was present, there are no grounds for supposing that his primary reference is to *Lovers Made Men*. Weldon is more likely to have had in mind the masque, now lost, per-formed on 8 January 1621 (see Chamberlain, *op. cit.* II, 333–4).

[2] Welsford, *The Court Masque*, p. 204, sees a possible trace of French influence in this device. Jonson used it again in *The Gipsies Metamorphosed* (1621).

Masques of greater magnificence'. The simple moral scheme that forms the core or 'device' of the stage action is anticipated by the emblematic representation on the triumphal arch framing the stage. On top of the arch the figure of Humanity 'sits with her lap full of flowers, scattering them with her right hand, and holding a golden chain in her left, to show both the freedom and the bond of courtesy'. This description is based closely on that given in one of Jonson's favourite source books, Cesare Ripa's *Iconologia*. In the 1611 (Padua) edition of this work (p. 232) Humanity is described as

a beautiful woman who carries various flowers in her lap, and in her left hand holds a chain of gold. Humanity, which we commonly call courtesy, is a certain inclination of spirit, which shows itself in pleasing others. Hence she is painted with flowers that are ever pleasing to see; and with the chain of gold she nobly binds the souls of persons who perceive in themselves friendly courtesy for others.

This seems to have provided the hint for the controlling idea of the masque: that, in the civilized life, pleasure must be directed by wisdom—a theme similar to that of *Pleasure Reconciled to Virtue*. In *Lovers Made Men* the idea is specifically applied to conduct in love. In the anti-masque we see lovers, besotted by Cupid, in a state of living death in which they fancy themselves dead indeed. Mercury sympathetically leads them on to taste the waters of Lethe so that they may reach 'the fields of rest'. But the Fates, examining their records, assure Mercury that the lovers are in fact alive, and Mercury realizes that they have been deluded by Love (i.e. Cupid). He therefore urges them to drink of Lethe's waters, this time not to secure oblivion but to be cured of their error. They do this and, as the anti-masque, perform dances characteristic of the delusions they have been suffering. The Chorus urges the lovers to return 'Like lights to burn|On earth|For others' good'; they will serve as a warning to others in similar case. The metamorphosed lovers then perform the first dance of the Main Masque. Cupid, entering to them, claims their dance as a tribute to his power, but Mercury warns them against falling victims for a second time to Cupid's blandishments, which are renewed after the main dance as Cupid urges the Masquers to 'take forth' the ladies for the revels. An altercation between Cupid and Mercury follows, Mercury renewing his warnings and Cupid claiming that he is ready to disarm completely as a guarantee that his intentions are innocent. Mercury succeeds in persuading the lovers to remove themselves from Cupid's influence, and 'they dance their going out'. In a graceful coda Mercury relents somewhat. For the sake of the ladies in the audience the lovers may 'remain still such' on condition that Cupid will promise never to influence their actions without calling in Mercury too. Cupid agrees, and the work is rounded off by the Chorus:

> All then take cause of joy; for who hath not?
> Old Lethe, that their follies are forgot;
> We, that their lives unto their fates they fit;
> They, that they still shall love, and love with wit.

The complaint has been made that *Lovers Made Men* 'lacks the impact of the masques performed for the king because the audience and the masquers are peers and there is no real difference in rank which Jonson can turn into a symbol of some greater universal order'; it 'is an amusing fable illustrating pleasantly a commonplace about love; it lacks the emotional power that the presence of royalty gives to the other masques'.[1] This is true; nevertheless, the work is perfectly successful on its own level. The action moves easily and naturally, the dances are well integrated, the verse has a lucidity and grace characteristic of Jonson at his best, and, while Jonson observes 'that rule of the best artist, to suffer no object of delight to pass without his mixture of profit and example' (*Masque of Queens*, Introduction), his ethical point, being a natural outcome of the action, serves as a fitting conclusion rather than a gratuitous admonition to virtue.

The Folio text provides the information that 'the whole Masque was sung after the Italian manner, *stilo recitativo*, by Master Nicholas Lanier, who ordered and made both the Scene and the music'. *Lovers Made Men* is therefore often referred to as 'the first English opera', i.e. the first dramatic text of which the whole was sung.

[1] W. Todd Furniss, 'Ben Jonson's Masques', in *Three Studies in the Renaissance* (Yale, 1958), p. 168.

Grove's Dictionary of Music and Musicians (ed. Blom, 1954, *s.v.* 'masque') calls it 'an epochal work from the musical standpoint'. Lanier (1588–1666), though born in England, was a member of a French family of musicians associated with the Court; he was appointed Master of the King's Musick in 1625. His interest in painting, evident in the fact that he 'ordered and made...the Scene', receives further confirmation from the fact that he was responsible for the purchase in Italy of the paintings that went to form the nucleus of King Charles's great collection. Unfortunately none of his music for *Lovers Made Men* survives. However Andrew J. Sabol has constructed a score from music by Lanier and his contemporaries.[1]

Jonson printed the masque without annotation; its classical background has been investigated by C. F. Wheeler (*Classical Mythology in the Plays, Masques and Poems of Ben Jonson*, Princeton, 1938). Many of the allusions for which Wheeler gives precise classical references probably reached Jonson through Renaissance intermediaries, and some were common knowledge. Wheeler suggests that the anti-masque may derive from Lucian's *Voyage to the Lower World*, 6 and 14,

in which among those being transported by Charon were 'seven who killed themselves for love. Also Theagenes, the philosopher, for love of the Megarian courtesan.' Some on this voyage 'turn about, and must ever be looking back at what they have left behind them, far off though it be,— like men that are sick for love'.

Herford and Simpson, however, find a possible 'faint suggestion' for this part of the masque in Virgil's *Aeneid*, VI, 442–4. Though the masque could not have been written without Jonson's knowledge, direct and otherwise, of classical literature, the only direct sources that can be pointed to (apart from the quotations from Virgil and Ovid) are Ripa's *Iconologia* (first printed in 1593) and, probably, the post-classical Latin poem *Pervigilium Veneris* (see lines 140–7 n.).

[1] *A Score for 'Lovers Made Men'* (Brown University Press, 1963); Sabol's introduction is especially informative about the musical situation.

[DRAMATIS PERSONAE

Mercury
Three Fates
Lethe
Cupid
Anti-masquers, who are also the Masquers
Chorus]

LOVERS MADE MEN

A masque presented in the house of the Right Honourable the Lord Hay by divers of noble quality, his friends, for the entertainment of Monsieur le Baron de Tour, extraordinary ambassador for the French King, on Saturday, the 22 of February, 1617.

Martial: *Quid titulum poscis? Versus duo tresve legantur.*

* * *

The Front before the Scene an arch-triumphal, on the top of which Humanity, placed in figure, sits with her lap full of flowers, scattering them with her right hand, and holding a golden chain in her left, to show both the freedom and the bond of courtesy; with this inscription: Super omnia vultus.

On the two sides of the arch, Cheerfulness and Readiness, her servants: Cheerfulness in a loose-flowing garment, filling out wine from an antique piece of plate, with this word: Adsit laetitiae dator; *Readiness a winged maid with two flaming bright lights in her hands, and her word:* Amor addidit alas.

The Scene discovered is, on the one side, the head of a boat, and in it Charon putting off from the shore, having landed certain imagined ghosts whom Mercury there receives and encourageth to come on towards the River Lethe, who appears lying in the person of an old man, the Fates sitting by him on his bank. A grove of myrtles behind them, presented in perspective, and growing thicker to the outer side of the Scene. Mercury, perceiving them to faint, calls them on and shows them his golden rod. And the whole Masque was sung after the Italian manner, stilo recitativo, *by Master Nicholas Lanier, who ordered and made both the Scene and the music.*

> *Mercury.* Nay, faint not now, so near the fields of rest.
> Here no more furies, no more torments dwell
> Than each hath felt already in his breast:
> Who hath been once in love, hath prov'd his hell.

215

Up then, and follow this my golden rod   2

    That points you next to aged Lethe's shore,

Who pours his waters from his urn abroad,

    Of which but tasting, you shall faint no more.

Lethe. Stay; who, or what fantastic shades are these

    That Hermes leads?   3

Mercury.   They are the gentle forms

    Of lovers, toss'd upon those frantic seas

        Whence Venus sprung.

Lethe.   And have rid out her storms?

Mercury. No.   3

Lethe. Did they perish?

Mercury.   Yes.

Lethe.   How?

Mercury.   Drown'd by Love,

    That drew them forth with hopes as smooth as were   4

Th'unfaithful waters he desir'd 'em prove.

Lethe. And turn'd a tempest when he had 'em there?

Mercury. He did, and on the billow would he roll,

    And laugh, to see one throw his heart away;

Another, sighing, vapour forth his soul;   4

    A third to melt himself in tears, and say,

'O Love, I now to salter water turn

    Than that I die in'; then a fourth to cry

Amid the surges, 'O, I burn, I burn!';

    A fifth laugh out, 'It is my ghost, not I'.   5

And thus in pairs I found 'em. Only one

    There is, that walks, and stops, and shakes his head,

And shuns the rest, as glad to be alone,

    And whispers to himself he is not dead.

Fates. No more are all the rest.   5

Mercury.   No?

1 Fate.   No.

Mercury.   But why

    Proceeds this doubtful voice from Destiny?

Fates. It is too sure.   6

Mercury.   Sure?

2 Fate.   Ay. Thinks Mercury
  That any things or names on earth do die
  That are obscur'd from knowledge of the Fates,
  Who keep all rolls?   65
3 Fate.   And know all nature's dates?
Mercury. They say themselves they're dead.
1 Fate.   It not appears,
  Or by our rock—
2 Fate.   our spindle—   70
3 Fate.   or our shears.
Fates. Here all their threads are growing, yet none cut.
Mercury. I 'gin to doubt that Love with charms hath put
  This fant'sy in 'em, and they only think
  That they are ghosts.   75
[*1*] *Fate.*   If so, then let 'em drink
  Of Lethe's stream.
[*2*] *Fate.*   'Twill make 'em to forget
  Love's name.
[*3*] *Fate.*   And so, they may recover yet.   80
Mercury. Do, bow unto the reverend lake,
  And having touch'd there, up, and shake
  The shadows off, which yet do make
  Us you, and you yourselves mistake.

Here they all stoop to the water, and dance forth their anti-masque in 85
*several gestures, as they lived in love; and retiring into the grove, before
the last person be off the stage, the first couple appear in their posture
between the trees, ready to come forth, changed.*

          Mercury. See, see, they are themselves again!
          1 Fate. Yes, now they are substances, and men.   90
          2 Fate. Love at the name of Lethe flies.
          Lethe. For, in oblivion drown'd, he dies.
          3 Fate. He must not hope, though other states
            He oft subdue, he can the Fates.
          Fates. 'Twere insolence, to think his powers   95
            Can work on us, and equal ours.
          Chorus. Return, return,

Like lights to burn
On earth
For others' good.   10
Your second birth
Will fame old Lethe's flood,
And warn a world
That now are hurl'd
About in tempest, how they prove   10
Shadows for Love.
Leap forth; your light it is the nobler made
By being struck out of a shade.

Here they dance forth their entry, or first dance; after which Cupid,
appearing, meets them.   1

Cupid. Why, now you take me; these are rites
That grace Love's days, and crown his nights!
These are the motions I would see,
And praise, in them that follow me!
Not sighs, nor tears, nor wounded hearts,   1
Nor flames, nor ghosts: but airy parts
Tried and refin'd as yours have been;
And such they are, I glory in.
Mercury. Look, look unto this snaky rod,
And stop your ears against the charming god;   1
His every word falls from him is a snare:
Who have so lately known him, should beware.

Here they dance their main dance, which ended:

Cupid. Come, do not call it Cupid's crime
You were thought dead before your time.   1
If thus you move to Hermes' will
Alone, you will be thought so still.
Go, take the ladies forth, and talk,
And touch, and taste too; ghosts can walk.
'Twixt eyes, tongues, hands, the mutual strife   1
Is bred that tries the truth of life.
They do, indeed, like dead men move,
That think they live, and not in love.

Here they take forth the ladies, and the Revels follow; after which:

Mercury. Nay, you should never have left off,   135
  But stay'd, and heard your Cupid scoff
  To find you in the line you were.
Cupid [*to Mercury*]. Your too much wit breeds too much fear.
Mercury. Good fly, good night.
Cupid [*to the dancers*]. But will you go?   140
  Can you leave Love, and he entreat you so?
  Here, take my quiver, and my bow,
  My torches too, that you, by all, may know
  I mean no danger to your stay.
  This night I will create my holiday,   145
  And be yours, naked and entire.
Mercury. As if that Love, disarm'd, were less a fire?
  Away! away!

They dance their going out, which done:

  Mercury. Yet lest that Venus' wanton son   150
    Should with the world be quite undone,
    For your fair sakes (you brighter stars,
    Who have beheld these civil wars)
    Fate is content these lovers here
    Remain still such, so Love will swear   155
    Never to force them act to do
    But what he will call Hermes, too.
Cupid. I swear; and with like cause thank Mercury,
  As these have to thank him and Destiny.
Chorus. All then take cause of joy; for who hath not?   160
  Old Lethe, that their follies are forgot;
  We, that their lives unto their fates they fit;
  They, that they still shall love, and love with wit.

THE END

THE TEXT

Lovers Made Men was first printed, privately and without attribution to author, publisher or printer, in 1617 in a quarto probably intended for use by the performers and as a souvenir for the spectators. The only known copy is in the Bodleian Library. The masque was reprinted in the Second Folio edition of Jonson's *Works*, where the title is omitted. All later editions derive from the Folio.[1] Gifford, not knowing the quarto, renamed the piece *The Masque of Lethe*; it has often been referred to by this title. Discussing Herford and Simpson's choice of F as their copy-text, W. W. Greg objected that Q should be the basis for a critical text since 'the changes made [in F in this and certain other masques] were sporadic and could easily have been introduced into a text based on the quarto'.[2] Evelyn M. Simpson defended the choice of F as it 'showed definite revision'.[3] It is in fact demonstrable that F was based on a copy of Q on which someone, perhaps Jonson himself, had made alterations. The description of the 'Front before the Scene' was changed from the present to the past tense, and stage directions were somewhat expanded. There are some changes in punctuation and spelling, a few corrections, and some stylistic alterations. Since these changes are, as Greg wrote, 'sporadic', and do not amount to systematic revision, I have taken Q as my copy-text. To it I have added insertions made in F when these provide additional information. I have not included insertions made for stylistic reasons (e.g. 'The Front before the Scene [was] an arch-triumphal'). Similarly, I have adopted other Folio variants when they seemed to be deliberate corrections of errors, but rejected those that are probably stylistic revisions (e.g. 'them' for 'hem'). All readings adopted from F are noted in the Collation.

[1] Bentley states that in the 1692 Folio, *Lovers Made Men* 'is reprinted under the quarto title', but this is not so in the copies that I have seen, in which the text clearly derives from the 1640 Folio.

[2] 'Jonson's Masques—Points of Editorial Principle and Practice', *Review of English Studies* (April 1942), pp. 144–66.

[3] 'Jonson's Masques: A Rejoinder', *Review of English Studies* (July 1942), pp. 291–300.

COLLATION

16 *in perspective*]   F; *not in* Q.
16 *outer*]   F; other Q.
17–20 *Mercury...music*]   F; *not in* Q.
96 and]   Q; or F.
136 your Cupid]   F; your generall Cupid Q.
138 Your]   F; Hermes, your Q.

COMMENTARY

Title Martial...*legantur*]   from Martial's *Epigrams*, XII, iii. The next line is: '*clamabunt omnes te, liber, esse meum*'—'Why do you require a title? Let two or three verses be read: all will cry that you, O book, are mine.'

1 *Front*]   frontispiece; proscenium arch. (*N.E.D.* does not distinguish the theatrical sense; in the sense of 'frontispiece', the word is first recorded in 1647.)

2 *Humanity*]   see Introduction, p. 211.

2 *in figure*]   in emblematic representation.

4 *freedom...bond*]   parallel to the figures of Cupid and Mercury in the action.

4–5 Super...vultus]   Ovid, *Metamorphoses*, VIII, 677–8: '*super omnia vultus | accessere boni*'—'besides all this, pleasant faces were at the board.'

6 *Cheerfulness*]   'Compare Euphrosyne or Gladness in the *King's Entertainment*, 128–36. Ripa, p. 12, has a woodcut of "Allegrezza" with wine in her right hand and a gold cup in her left' (Herford and Simpson, X, 567).

7 *filling out*]   pouring out.

8 *word*]   motto.

8 Adsit...dator]   Virgil, *Aeneid*, I, 734: 'May the giver of joy be present' —referring to Bacchus.

9 *Readiness*]   Herford and Simpson point out the resemblance to Prothymia or Promptitude in the *King's Entertainment*, pp. 150–7, itself based on Ripa's 'Prontezza' (p. 439).

10 Amor...alas]   'Love added wings'—adapted from Virgil, *Aeneid*, VIII, 224: '*pedibus timor addidit alas.*'

15 *myrtles*]   sacred to Venus.

16 *outer*]   F's reading appears to correct Q's.

18 *golden rod*]   the caduceus (cf. line 119).

19 *Lanier*]   see Introduction, pp. 212–13.

21 fields of rest]   Elysium.

24 prov'd]   experienced.

69 rock]   distaff. This, the spindle and the shears are the conventional attributes of the Fates.

81 Do]   Whalley (1756) plausibly reads 'Go'.

81 lake]   could be used of a stream (*N.E.D.* sb.³).

86 *several*]   different for each.

87 *posture*]   position.

96 and]   F's 'or' is probably a revision rather than a correction.

109 *entry*]   a dance introduced between the parts of an entertainment.

111 take]   probably 'charm', 'delight'.

222

120 charming] enchanting, bewitching.

136 and 138 your Cupid *and* Your] Herford and Simpson (VII, 450) comment: 'Did the line run at first "heard your Generall scoff"—i.e. Cupid as commander-in-chief of the masquers—and Jonson, feeling an ambiguity in this vague phrase, decide to insert Cupid's name, but forgot [sic] to cancel "generall"? Similarly, the over-long line 187 [i.e. 138]...is shortened in the Folio by omitting "Hermes".' This seems a satisfactory explanation of the metrical irregularities in the quarto.

137 line] perhaps 'occupation' (*N.E.D.* V, 28): or the line of the dance.

139 fly] contemptuous word for 'spirit', 'familiar'; 'familiar demon'.

140–7] Herford and Simpson (X, 568) draw attention to the parallel with the *Pervigilium Veneris*, lines 29–35:

> *It puer comes puellis; nec tamen credi potest*
> *esse Amorem feriatum si sagittas vexerit.*
> *Ite, Nymphae, posuit arma, feriatus est Amor:*
> *iussus est inermis ire, nudus ire iussus est,*
> *neu quid arcu neu sagitta neu quid igne laederet.*
> *Sed tamen, Nymphae, cavete, quod Cupido pulcher est.*
> *Est in armis totus idem quando nudus est Amor.*

152 your...stars] i.e. the ladies among the spectators.

157 But what] unless (*N.E.D.* 'but' IV, 30: 'for *but that* in various senses'; first recorded in 1662).

157 Hermes, too] Herford and Simpson (X, 568) say 'In modern punctuation "Hermes' too"'. Presumably they would paraphrase 'except such as he would name an act of Hermes, too'. I interpret 'without his calling in Hermes, too'.

PLEASURE RECONCILED TO VIRTUE

BY BEN JONSON

Edited by R. A. Foakes

INTRODUCTION

The masque was staged on 6 January 1618, Twelfth Night, before King James I, and again a few days later for the benefit of the Queen, who had missed the first performance because of illness. It was revived on Shrove Tuesday, 18 February, in the same year, with a substantial addition, called *For the Honour of Wales*, in which the mountain Atlas, the scene of the main masque, became Snowdon, and a long, mildly comic prose induction spoken by Griffith, Jenkin and Evan preceded songs and dances celebrating Welsh hills, Welsh products, and Welshmen. This addition, with its 'newe Conceites & ante maskes & pleasant merry speeches',[1] seems to have pleased, but it has no real connexion with *Pleasure Reconciled to Virtue*, is much inferior to it, and is not printed here.

The masque raised high expectations, for it was to be the first court masque in which Prince Charles would have a part, and indeed it became known as the 'Prince's masque'.[2] Moreover, King James was considering a marriage between Charles and the Infanta of Spain, and, to further his policy, invited the Spanish ambassador to attend the first performance. In the event, it disappointed, as several letter-writers of the time testify; one remarked that 'Inigo Jones has lost his reputation in regard to some extraordinary device was looked for', and another commented that 'the poet is grown so dull that his device is not worthy the relating'.[3] Perhaps a more splendid revelation of Charles was looked for than his entry leading the masquers from the 'lap of the mountain' (line 197). Certainly the main device of Inigo Jones, designer of the masque, was not new; the mountain or rock with a cave opening for some discovery was by 1618 a commonplace of the masque, and already in 1613

[1] Sir Gerard Herbert writing to Sir Dudley Carleton on 22 February 1618; cited in Herford and Simpson, x, 577.
[2] It is so called, for instance, by John Chamberlain and Sir Gerard Herbert in letters of 10 January and 22 February 1618 to Sir Dudley Carleton; cited in Herford and Simpson, x, 576–7.
[3] Edward Sherburn and Nathaniel Brent in letters to Sir Dudley Carleton on 10 January 1618; cited in Herford and Simpson, x, 576.

George Chapman had opened his *Masque of the Middle Temple and Lincoln's Inn* with the character Plutus 'surveying the work', and commenting, 'Rocks? Nothing but rocks in these masquing devices? Is invention so poor she must needs ever dwell amongst rocks?'[1] Pigmies, too, had been seen before,[2] and only the antimasque of men dressed as bottles seemed original, and was 'not ill liked' at the time.[3] It is also likely that the elevated tone of the later part of the masque was not enjoyed by a court bent on revelry, though it was not Jonson's words, but a dull Spanish dance, that bored the King and made him cry out, 'Why don't they dance? What did they make me come here for? Devil take you, dance.'[4] The printed text ends with a note, 'This so pleased the King as he would see it again', and perhaps this is not merely Jonson putting on a brave front; many observers seem to have been irritated less by the dances than by the literary and serious nature of this masque.

Soon after the first performance, Edward Sherburn sent to Sir Dudley Carleton a 'little book' of the masque,[5] and one manuscript copy of it has survived, made no doubt either for a participant, or for some spectator or patron. It is a small octavo of two gatherings of eight leaves, measuring $4\frac{1}{16}$ in. by $6\frac{1}{16}$ in.[6] The masque occupies 24 pages, and four leaves are blank. It is in the hand of the well-known professional scribe Ralph Crane,[7] and shows a number of his habitual usages and favourite spellings.[8] In particular, the punctua-

---

[1] *The Comedies of George Chapman*, edited T. M. Parrott (1914), p. 446; see also Nicoll, *Stuart Masques*, pp. 83–4.

[2] Enid Welsford, *The Court Masque*, p. 163, describes a màsque of 1594 which had a rock that opened, and pigmies.

[3] Sir Edward Harwood, writing to Sir Dudley Carleton on 7 January 1618; cited in Herford and Simpson, x, 576.

[4] So wrote Orazio Busino, a Venetian who saw the masque and sent home a description of it (see below, p. 234).

[5] On 10 January 1618; cited in Herford and Simpson, x, 574.

[6] The manuscript is now in the collections of the Duke of Devonshire at Chatsworth House, Derbyshire.

[7] His career was discussed by F. P. Wilson in *The Library*, 4th series, VII (1926), 194–215; the same scholar first identified Crane's hand in this masque in a note in the *Times Literary Supplement*, 8 November 1941.

[8] These have been discussed by W. W. Greg, 'Some Notes on Crane's Manuscript of *The Witch*', *The Library*, 4th series, XXII (1942), 208–19, but see also the editions of Thomas Middleton's *The Witch*, by W. W. Greg and F. P. Wilson (Malone Society Reprints, 1948 (1950)), pp. xiii–xv, and of John Fletcher's *Demetrius and*

tion is heavy and over-elaborate, with a marked use of colons. The stage directions are all in the present tense, which indicates closeness to a performance. *Pleasure Reconciled to Virtue* was first printed in Jonson's *Works* (1641), in which folio it occupies signatures D3ᵛ–E3ʳ, pp. 22–9, in the section of masques. The manuscript does not contain *For the Honour of Wales*, which follows the masque in the printed text. This text was derived from a manuscript, perhaps the author's, which also had stage directions in the present tense; for though most of the directions in the folio report action in the past tense, two verbs in the first entry are in the present tense.[1] The printed text also has some odd spellings and usages in common with Crane's copy, and these may well derive from Jonson.[2] Both texts are good; the printed text omits two words that were presumably illegible in the copy, and has some errors that can be corrected from the manuscript, but its punctuation is lighter and more readily intelligible than Crane's. It seems to have been Jonson's custom to put stage directions into the past tense for printing, and he did so, too, in the manuscript of *The Masque of Queens* which he presented to Prince Henry. I have therefore used the folio version as copy-text, the rather because Herford and Simpson reprint the manuscript exactly in their edition.[3]

Jonson used a variety of sources for this masque, but relied chiefly on four for the principal allegory. His basic idea was that of Hercules at the crossroads, choosing between Virtue and Vice (Pleasure), two women who, in an allegory set forth in Xenophon's *Memorabilia*, II, i, seek to tempt him to follow a hard or an easy path. This story was well known in the Renaissance, and provided an emblem for some compilers of emblem-books (see Plate 48 (*b*)), which in turn affected the composition of masques.[4] It is employed

Enanthe, by Margaret Cook and F. P. Wilson (Malone Society Reprints, 1950 (1951)), pp. ix–xi. Crane was fond of parentheses, used a heavy and fussy punctuation, liked hyphens, and preferred certain spellings, such as *theis* for *these*, *beuty* for *beauty*, *ck* in words like *thank*, and some others that occur in the manuscript of the masque.

[1] See Collation, lines 5 and 7.   [2] See Collation, lines 77, 82, 170, 289.   [3] VII, 479–91.

[4] See Rosemary Freeman, *English Emblem-Books* (1948), pp. 9 ff., and, for the theme in general, E. Panofsky, *Hercules am Scheidewege und andere antike Bildstoffe in der neueren Kunst* (1931). The importance of Hercules as a type of the heroic figure in classical and Renaissance literature has recently been examined by Eugene Waith in *The Herculean Hero* (1962), and the first two chapters of this book illustrate the

in Jonson's masque to exhort Prince Charles, and all present, to follow Virtue, but the pill is sugared over in the clever idea of reconciling Pleasure and Virtue, and making both of them enemies of Vice. Vice is represented first by Comus, a figure described originally by Philostratus in his *Imagines*, I, 2, as the youthful spirit of revelry. Jonson made him obese, older, more like Bacchus, whom he seems to resemble in the drawing by Inigo Jones of the anti-masque, reproduced as Plate 14. Jonson's alteration of the figure owes much to the sketch of Gaster, the god of the belly, in Rabelais's *Pantagruel*, Book IV. The secondary representatives of Vice are the pigmies, brothers of Antaeus, who attack the sleeping Hercules, an incident also taken from the *Imagines* of Philostratus. Vice thus appears as deformed, in the gross Comus, and his rout of men turned to bottles or tuns, in the pigmies, with their petty spites, and in the giant Antaeus, whose overthrow was shown in the masque.[1]

At the end of the anti-masque, Mercury appears, as in the *Imagines*, to crown Hercules, and to introduce Pleasure and Virtue, two female figures whose radiance contrasts with the deformity of Vice. Here Atlas, the mountain which functions appropriately as the setting of the first part, being the legendary location of Hercules's fight with Antaeus, becomes the 'hill of knowledge' (line 186); Jonson uses a passage from Diodorus Siculus, *Bibliotheca*, IV, 27, to emphasize the wisdom of Atlas as man-god, and to make him the brother of Hesperus, 'the glory of the west' (line 174), who symbolizes King James, chief patron and instigator of the masque. The troop of masquers, led by Prince Charles, emerge from the mountain, resplendently dressed as princes in crimson, white and blue, with gold and silver trimmings, descend in the shape of a pyramid,[2] and, guided in their dancing by Daedalus, the great artificer, they enact the union of Pleasure and Virtue which concludes the masque.

If the setting, and the device of revealing the masquers from within the mountain, were commonplace, nevertheless Jonson's allegory was finely conceived, and is embodied in poetry that rises,

significance of Jonson's choice of subject in this masque. See also the chapter on 'Virtue Reconciled with Pleasure' in Edgar Wind, *Pagan Mysteries in the Renaissance* (1958), pp. 78–88. [1] As Busino noted; see below, p. 233.

[2] Busino reports this, and his account of the costumes is confirmed by the payments for masquing suits recorded in Audit Office accounts; see Herford and Simpson, x, 578.

in the songs of Daedalus, to a graceful and impassioned utterance. John Milton, who must have had access to a manuscript of this masque, paid his tribute to its power in his own *Comus*, which ends, like *Pleasure Reconciled to Virtue*, with an eloquent lyric in praise of virtue. In *Comus*, as in Xenophon's allegory, pleasure is hardly to be distinguished from vice, and Jonson's conception is more subtle in this respect, in that the grosser vices are dismissed as deformities of mind and body in the anti-masque, so that pleasure may appear as linked with virtue. The dances of the masquers represent, in the first place, the pleasures of activity, courtliness and splendour, but the pattern of the dance also suggests, for Jonson, a labyrinth which is emblematic of the perplexities of human life, here resolved, as it were, in a rhythmic and intelligible pattern. In this harmony the maze of life becomes, in the second and third songs, a labyrinth of beauty and of love, as the ladies are taken into the dance. The dance of the masquers, then, becomes the main metaphor of the poetry, which seizes on its various possibilities of implication, and reaches beyond the pleasure of the moment to figure forth the pattern of human life as ideally it might be, and to suggest the harmony of heaven, where Virtue 'hath her right of birth' (line 318). Perhaps Milton again recalled this when he wrote, in *Paradise Lost*, of the dances of the angels in heaven, who move

> In song and dance about the sacred Hill,
> Mystical dance, which yonder starry sphere
> Of planets and of fixed in all her wheels
> Resembles nearest, mazes intricate,
> Eccentric, intervolved, yet regular
> Then most, when most irregular they seem:
> And in their motions harmony divine.   (v, 619–25)

This heavenly harmony is the final wisdom of the dance, as prefigured in the 'sacred harmony' of the teaching of Daedalus (line 222). The whole makes a nice compliment to the King, for he is imaged as Hesperus, a star in the heavens, and therefore part of the 'unalter'd law, and working of the stars' (line 170).[1] Compliments

---

[1] W. Todd Furniss, 'Ben Jonson's Masques', in *Three Studies in the Renaissance: Sidney, Jonson, Milton* (1958), pp. 169–76, lays stress on the King's presence as giving a meaning to the masque as a whole, and certainly it was an important function of the masque to compliment James I and Prince Charles.

to his royal patrons, however, are subsidiary in Jonson's writing to his main theme, the celebration of Virtue as the final conqueror of chance (line 312), and unraveller of the maze of life. It is to this wisdom that the dancer, and the spectator, may come, if they can understand what they are doing,

> For dancing is an exercise
>   Not only shows the mover's wit,
> But maketh the beholder wise,
>   As he hath power to rise to it.   (244–7)

The conception seems to have been too subtle, or too serious, for the spectators at the court of King James; their interest, as Jonson complained in his *Expostulation with Inigo Jones*, was all in shows, not words. They did not look for wisdom in a masque, and it was left to Milton and later readers to value the power of Jonson's writing, which gives distinction to *Pleasure Reconciled to Virtue*.

THE FIRST PERFORMANCE

A description of the first performance of *Pleasure Reconciled to Virtue* was sent to Venice on 24 January 1618 by Orazio Busino, chaplain to the Venetian embassy in London. The translation of the extract which follows is taken from *Calendar of State Papers, Venetian*, XV (1909), 111–14.

A large hall is fitted up like a theatre, with well secured boxes all round. The stage is at one end and his Majesty's chair in front under an ample canopy. Near him are stools for the foreign ambassadors...Whilst waiting for the king we amused ourselves by admiring the decorations and beauty of the house with its two orders of columns, one above the other, their distance from the wall equalling the breadth of the passage, that of the second row being upheld by Doric pillars, while above these rise Ionic columns supporting the roof. The whole is of wood, including even the shafts, which are carved and gilt with much skill. From the roof of these hang festoons and angels in relief with two rows of lights. Then such a concourse as there was, for although they profess only to admit the favoured ones who are invited, yet every box was filled notably with most noble and richly arrayed ladies, in number some 600 and more according to the general estimate; the dresses being of such variety in cut and colour as to be indescribable; . . . On entering the house, the cornets and trumpets to the number of fifteen or twenty began to play very well a sort of recitative, and then after his Majesty had seated himself under the canopy alone, the queen not being present on account of a slight indisposition, he caused the ambassadors to sit below him on two stools, while the great officers of the crown and courts of law sat upon benches. The Lord Chamberlain then had the way cleared and in the middle of the theatre there appeared a fine and spacious area carpeted all over with green cloth. In an instant a large curtain dropped, painted to represent a tent of gold cloth with a broad fringe; the background was of canvas painted blue, powdered all over with golden stars. This became the front arch of the stage, forming a drop scene, and on its being removed there appeared first of all Mount Atlas, whose enormous head was alone visible up aloft under the very roof of the theatre; it rolled up its eyes and moved itself very cleverly. As a foil to the principal ballet and masque they had some mummeries performed in the first act; for instance, a very chubby Bacchus appeared on a car drawn by four gownsmen, who sang in an undertone before his Majesty. There was another stout individual on foot, dressed in red in short clothes, who made a speech, reeling about like a drunkard, tankard in hand, so that he resembled Bacchus's cupbearer. This first scene was very gay and burlesque. Next followed twelve extravagant masquers, one of whom was in a barrel, all but his extremities, his companions being similarly cased in huge wicker flasks, very well made. They danced awhile to the sound of the cornets and trumpets, performing various and most extravagant antics. These were followed by a gigantic man representing Hercules with his club, who strove with Antaeus and performed other feats. Then came twelve masked boys in the guise of frogs. They danced together, assuming sundry grotesque attitudes. After they had all fallen down, they were driven off by Hercules. Mount Atlas then opened, by means of two doors, which were made to turn, and from behind the hills of a distant landscape the day was seen to dawn, some gilt columns being placed along either side of the scene, so as to aid the perspective and make the distance seem greater. Mercury next appeared before the king and made a speech. After him came a guitar player in a gown, who sang some trills, accompanying himself with his instrument. He announced himself as some deity, and then a number of singers, dressed in long red gowns to represent high priests, came on the stage, wearing gilt mitres. In the midst of them was a goddess in a long white robe and they sang some jigs which we did not understand. It is true that, spoiled as we are by the graceful and harmonious music of Italy, the composition did not strike us as very fine. Finally twelve cavaliers, masked, made their appearance, dressed uniformly, six having the entire hose crimson with plaited doublets of white satin trimmed with gold and silver lace. The other six wore breeches down to the knee, with the half hose also crimson, and white shoes. These matched well their corsets which were cut in the shape of the ancient Roman corslets. On their heads they wore long hair and crowns and very tall white plumes. Their faces were covered with black masks. These twelve descended together from above the scene in the figure of a pyramid, of which the prince formed the apex. When they reached the ground the violins, to the number of twenty-five or thirty, began to play their airs. After they had made an obeisance to his Majesty, they began to dance in very good time, preserving for a while the same pyramidical figure, and with a variety of steps. Afterwards they changed places with each other in various ways, but ever ending the jump together. When this was over, each took his lady, the prince pairing with the principal one among those who were ranged in a row ready to dance, and the others doing the like in succession, all making obeisance to his Majesty first and then to each other. They performed every sort of ballet and dance of every country whatsoever such as passamezzi, corants, canaries, Spaniards and a hundred other very fine gestures devised to tickle the fancy (*fatte a pizzego*). Last of all they danced the Spanish dance, one at a time, each with his lady, and being well nigh tired they began to lag, whereupon the king, who is naturally choleric, got impatient and shouted aloud Why don't they dance? What did they make me come here for? Devil take you all, dance. Upon this, the Marquis of Buckingham, his Majesty's favourite, immediately sprang forward, cutting a score of lofty and very minute capers, with so much grace and agility that he not only appeased the ire of his angry lord, but rendered himself the admiration and delight of everybody. The other masquers, thus encouraged, continued to exhibit their prowess one after another, with various ladies, also finishing with capers and lifting their goddesses from the ground. We counted thirty-four capers as cut by one cavalier in succession, but none came up to the exquisite manner of the marquis. The prince, however, excelled them all in bowing, being very formal in making his obeisance both to the king and to the lady with whom he danced, nor was he once seen to do a step out of time when dancing, whereas one cannot perhaps say so much for the others. Owing to his youth he has not yet much breath, nevertheless he cut a few capers very gracefully.

PLEASURE RECONCILED TO VIRTUE

A Masque
As it was presented at Court before
King James, 1618.

*   *   *

The scene was the mountain Atlas, who had his top ending in the figure of an old Man, his head and beard all hoary and frost, as if his shoulders were covered with snow; the rest wood and rock. A grove of ivy at his feet, out of which, to a wild music of cymbals, flutes and tabors, was brought forth Comus, the god of cheer or the belly, riding in triumph, his head crowned with roses and other flowers, his hair curled: they that waited upon him crowned with ivy, their javelins done about with it; one of them going with Hercules his bowl borne before him, while the rest presented him with this Hymn.

Room, room, make room for the bouncing belly,
First father of sauce, and deviser of jelly;
Prime master of arts, and the giver of wit,
That found out the excellent engine, the spit,
The plough and the flail, the mill and the hopper,
The hutch and the bolter, the furnace and copper,
The oven, the bavin, the mawkin, the peel,
The hearth and the range, the dog and the wheel.
He, he first invented both hogshead and tun,
The gimlet, and vice too, and taught 'em to run;
And since, with the funnel, an hippocras bag
'Has made of himself, that now he cries swag;
Which shows, though the pleasure be but of four inches,
Yet he is a weezle, the gullet that pinches
Of any delight, and not spares from his back
Whatever to make of the belly a sack!
Hail, hail plump paunch, O the founder of taste,
For fresh meats, or powder'd, or pickle, or paste,

Devourer of broil'd, bak'd, roasted, or sod,
And emptier of cups, be they even or odd;
All which have now made thee so wide i'the waist,   30
As scarce with no pudding thou art to be lac'd,
But eating and drinking until thou dost nod,
Thou break'st all thy girdles, and break'st forth a god.

To this the Bowl-bearer.

Do you hear, my friends? To whom do you sing all this now? 35
Pardon me only that I ask you, for I do not look for an answer;
I'll answer myself: I know it is now such a time as the saturnals for
all the world, that every man stands under the eaves of his own hat,
and sings what please him; that's the right, and the liberty of it.
Now you sing of god Comus here, the belly-god; I say it is well, 40
and I say it is not well: it is well as it is a ballad, and the belly
worthy of it, I must needs say, and 'twere forty yards of ballad
more, as much ballad as tripe. But when the belly is not edified by
it, it is not well; for where did you ever read or hear that the belly
had any ears? Come, never pump for an answer, for you are 45
defeated; our fellow Hunger there, that was as ancient a retainer to
the belly as any of us, was turned away for being unseasonable, not
unreasonable, but unseasonable; and now is he, poor thin gut, fain
to get his living with teaching of starlings, magpies, parrots, and
jackdaws, those things he would have taught the belly. Beware of 50
dealing with the belly; the belly will not be talked to, especially
when he is full; then there is no venturing upon venter, he will
blow you all up, he will thunder, indeed la. Some in derision call
him the father of farts; but I say he was the first inventor of great
ordnance, and taught us to discharge them on festival days; would 55
we had a fit feast for him i'faith, to show his activity. I would have
something now fetched in to please his five senses, the throat, or
the two senses, the eyes: pardon me for my two senses, for I, that
carry Hercules' bowl i'the service, may see double by my place; for
I have drunk like a frog to-day. I would have a Tun now brought 60
in to dance, and so many Bottles about him. Ha! You look as if
you would make a problem of this; do you see? a problem: why
Bottles? and why a Tun? and why a Tun? and why Bottles to

dance? I say that men that drink hard, and serve the belly in any place of quality (as the jovial tinkers, or the lusty kindred), are 65 living measures of drink, and can transform themselves, and do every day, to Bottles or Tuns when they please: and when they ha' done all they can, they are, as I say again (for I think I said somewhat like it afore), but moving measures of drink; and there is a piece i'the cellar can hold more than all they. This will I make 70 good, if it please our new god but to give a nod, for the belly does all by signs; and I am all for the belly, the truest clock i'the world to go by.

Here the first Anti-masque, after which Hercules.

What rites are these? Breeds Earth more monsters yet?   75
Antaeus scarce is cold: what can beget
This store? And stay,—such contraries upon her?
Is Earth so fruitful of her own dishonour?
Or 'cause his vice was inhumanity,
Hopes she, by vicious hospitality,   80
To work an expiation first? And then—
Help Virtue!—these are sponges, and not men:
Bottles? Mere vessels? Half a tun of paunch?
How, and the other half thrust forth in haunch?
Whose feast? The belly's? Comus? And my cup   85
Brought in to fill the drunken orgies up?
And here abus'd, that was the crown'd reward
Of thirty heroes after labour hard?
Burdens, and shames of nature, perish, die!—
For yet you never liv'd, but in the sty   90
Of vice have wallow'd, and in that swine's strife
Been buried under the offence of life.
Go, reel and fall under the load you make,
Till your swollen bowels burst with what you take.
Can this be pleasure, to extinguish man,   95
Or so quite change him in his figure? Can
The belly love his pain, and be content
With no delight but what's a punishment?
These monsters plague themselves, and fitly too,

238

For they do suffer what, and all they do.   100
But here must be no shelter, nor no shroud
For such: sink grove, or vanish into cloud!

After this, the whole grove vanished, and the whole Music was dis-
covered, sitting at the foot of the mountain, with Pleasure and Virtue
seated above them. The Choir invited Hercules to rest with this song. 105

    Great friend, and servant of the good,
    Let cool a while thy heated blood,
    And from thy mighty labour cease.
        Lie down, lie down,
    And give thy troubled spirits peace,   110
        Whilst Virtue, for whose sake
    Thou dost this god-like travail take,
    May of the choicest herbage make
      (Here on this mountain bred)
        A crown, a crown   115
      For thy immortal head.

Here Hercules being laid down at their feet, the second Anti-masque,
which was of Pigmies, appeared.

1 Pigmy. Antaeus dead, and Hercules yet live?
  Where is this Hercules? What would I give   120
  To meet him now? Meet him? Nay, three such other
  If they had hand in murder of our brother.
  With three? With four? With ten? Nay, with as many
  As the name yields. Pray anger there be any
  Whereon to feed my just revenge, and soon.   125
  How shall I kill him? Hurl him 'gainst the moon,
  And break him in small portions? Give to Greece
  His brain, and every tract of earth a piece?
2 Pigmy. He is yonder.
1 Pigmy.   Where?   130
3 Pigmy. At the hill foot, asleep.
1 Pigmy. Let one go steal his club.
2 Pigmy. My charge, I'll creep.
4 Pigmy. He is ours.

1 Pigmy. Yes, peace. 1
3 Pigmy. Triumph; we have him, boy.
4 Pigmy. Sure, sure, he is sure.
1 Pigmy. Come, let us dance for joy.

At the end of their dance, they thought to surprise him, when suddenly, being awaked by the Music, he roused himself, [and] they all ran into 1
holes.

Song

Wake, Hercules, awake; but heave up thy black eye,
'Tis only ask'd from thee to look, and these will die,
   Or fly. 1
  Already they are fled,
  Whom scorn had else left dead.

At which, Mercury descended from the hill, with a garland of
poplar to crown him.

Mercury. Rest still, thou active friend of virtue; these 1
 Should not disturb the peace of Hercules.
 Earth's worms, and honour's dwarfs, at too great odds
 Prove, or provoke, the issue of the gods.
 See here a crown the aged hill hath sent thee,
 My grandsire Atlas, he that did present thee 1
 With the best sheep that in his fold were found,
 Or golden fruit on the Hesperian ground,
 For rescuing his fair daughters, then the prey
 Of a rude pirate, as thou cam'st this way;
 And taught thee all the learning of the sphere, 1
 And how, like him, thou mightst the heavens upbear,
 As that thy labour's virtuous recompense.
 He, though a mountain now, hath yet the sense
 Of thanking thee for more, thou being still
 Constant to goodness, guardian of the hill, 1
 Antaeus by thee suffocated here,
 And the voluptuous Comus, god of cheer,
 Beat from his grove, and that defac'd. But now
 The time's arriv'd that Atlas told thee of, how

By unalter'd law, and working of the stars,   170
There should be a cessation of all jars
'Twixt Virtue and her noted opposite,
Pleasure; that both should meet here, in the sight
Of Hesperus, the glory of the west,
The brightest star, that from his burning crest   175
Lights all on this side the Atlantic seas,
As far as to thy pillars, Hercules.
See where he shines, Justice and Wisdom plac'd
About his throne, and those with Honour grac'd,
Beauty and Love. It is not with his brother   180
Bearing the world, but ruling such another
Is his renown. Pleasure, for his delight,
Is reconcil'd to Virtue; and this night
Virtue brings forth twelve Princes have been bred
In this rough mountain, and near Atlas' head,   185
The hill of knowledge; one, and chief, of whom
Of the bright race of Hesperus is come,
Who shall in time the same that he is be,
And now is only a less light than he.
These now she trusts with Pleasure, and to these   190
She gives an entrance to the Hesperides,
Fair Beauty's garden; neither can she fear
They should grow soft, or wax effeminate here,
Since in her sight, and by her charge all's done,
Pleasure the servant, Virtue looking on.   195

*Here the whole Choir of music called the twelve Masquers forth from
the lap of the mountain, which then opened with this song.*

>   Ope, aged Atlas, open then thy lap,
>   And from thy beamy bosom strike a light,
>   That men may read in thy mysterious map   200
>   All lines
>   And signs
>   Of royal education, and the right.
>   See how they come, and show,
>   That are but born to know;   205

Descend,

Descend,

Though Pleasure lead,

Fear not to follow;

They who are bred

Within the hill

Of skill

May safely tread

What path they will;

No ground of good is hollow.

In their descent from the hill, Daedalus came down before them, of whom Hercules questioned Mercury.

> *Hercules.* But Hermes, stay a little, let me pause;
>   Who's this that leads?
> *Mercury.*   A guide that gives them laws
>   To all their motions, Daedalus the wise.
> *Hercules.* And doth in sacred harmony comprise
>   His precepts?
> *Mercury.*   Yes.
> *Hercules.*   They may securely prove
>   Then any labyrinth, though it be of love.

Here, while they put themselves in form, Daedalus had his first song.

> Come on, come on; and where you go,
>   So interweave the curious knot,
> As ev'n th'observer scarce may know
>   Which lines are Pleasure's, and which not.
> First, figure out the doubtful way
> At which awhile all youth should stay,
> Where she and Virtue did contend
> Which should have Hercules to friend.
> Then, as all actions of mankind
>   Are but a labyrinth or maze,
> So let your dances be entwin'd,
>   Yet not perplex men unto gaze;
> But measur'd, and so numerous too,

242

As men may read each act you do;
And when they see the graces meet,
Admire the wisdom of your feet:
For dancing is an exercise
   Not only shows the mover's wit,   245
But maketh the beholder wise,
   As he hath power to rise to it.

       The first Dance
  After which Daedalus again;
    The Second Song   250

O, more, and more; this was so well
As praise wants half his voice to tell;
   Again yourselves compose,
And now put all the aptness on
Of figure that proportion   255
   Or colour can disclose;
That if those silent arts were lost,
Design, and picture, they might boast
   From you a newer ground,
Instructed by the height'ning sense   260
Of dignity and reverence
   In your true motions found.
Begin, begin, for look, the fair
Do longing listen to what air
   You form your second touch,   265
That they may vent their murmuring hymns
Just to the tune you move your limbs,
   And wish their own were such.
    Make haste, make haste, for this
    The labyrinth of beauty is.   270

     The second Dance.
  That ended, Daedalus;
    The third Song

It follows now you are to prove
The subtlest maze of all; that's Love,   275
   And if you stay too long,

The fair will think you do 'em wrong.
Go, choose among, but with a mind
As gentle as the stroking wind
    Runs o'er the gentler flowers;   2
And so let all your actions smile,
As if they meant not to beguile
    The ladies, but the hours.
Grace, laughter, and discourse may meet,
    And yet the beauty go not less;   2
For what is noble should be sweet,
    But not dissolv'd in wantonness.
      Will you that I give the law
        To all your sport, and sum it?
      It should be such should envy draw,   2
        But ever overcome it.

*Here they danced with the Ladies, and the whole Revels followed;
which ended, Mercury called to him in this following speech; which was
after repeated in song by two Trebles, two Tenors, a Bass, and the
whole Chorus.*   2

The fourth Song

An eye of looking back were well,
Or any murmur that would tell
    Your thoughts, how you were sent,
      And went   3
    To walk with Pleasure, not to dwell.
These, these are hours by Virtue spar'd
Herself, she being her own reward,
    But she will have you know
      That though   3
    Her sports be soft, her life is hard.
You must return unto the hill,
    And there advance
With labour, and inhabit still
    That height and crown,   3
From whence you ever may look down
    Upon triumphed Chance.

She, she it is in darkness shines,
'Tis she that still herself refines
By her own light to every eye,   315
More seen, more known when Vice stands by;
And though a stranger here on earth,
In heaven she hath her right of birth;
     There, there is Virtue's seat.
    Strive to keep her your own;   320
      'Tis only she can make you great,
    Though place here make you known.

After which, they danced their last dance, [and] returned into the scene,
which closed, and was a Mountain again, as before.

THE END

COLLATION

Title 1618] *This ed.*; 1619 F.

5 *was*] *This ed.*; is F.

7 *waited*] *This ed.*; waite F.

18 both] MS; the F.

20 an] MS; and F.

24 his] *Gifford*; this F; the MS (y^e).

63 Tun? and] MS; tun? and why a tun? and F.

77 And stay,—] *This ed.*; (and stay) F, MS.

82 Help Virtue!] F, MS (Helpe vertue).

88 heroes] F; Heröes MS.

89–90 die!— | For...liv'd, but] *This ed.*; die; | (for...liv'd) but F; dye, | for...liv'd. But MS.

100 suffer what,...they do.] MS; suffer; what, ...the doe, F.

119–38 *1 Pigmy...2 Pigmy...3 Pigmy...4 Pigmy*] 1...2...3...4. F, MS.

134 He is] MS; He's F.

140 *and*] *Gifford*; *not in* F.

152 dwarfs, at...odds] MS; dwarfes (at...ods) F.

157 on] MS; in F.

170 By unalter'd] *This ed.*; B'unalterd F, MS.

197 *lap*] MS; top F.

200 thy] MS; the F.

241 you] MS; they F.

246 beholder] MS; beholders F.

262 your] MS; their F.

267 tune] MS; *not in* F.

289 sum it] F, MS (some-it).

291 ever] MS; *not in* F.

323 *and*] MS; *not in* F.

COMMENTARY

1 *Atlas*] The mountain was usually located in Libya. As a god, Atlas was fabled to have supported the world on his shoulders; he was also said to be the father of the Hesperides (see lines 157, 191), and grandfather of Mercury (see line 155). Orazio Busino said that the figure of Atlas in the masque rolled its eyes and moved; see above, p. 233.

5 *Comus*] originally a youth crowned with roses, the spirit of revelry, in Philostratus, *Imagines*, I, 2, Jonson makes him god of the belly, and gives him a paunch like Gaster in Rabelais, *Pantagruel*, Book IV, ch. 57. See line 12 and n.

8 *Hercules his bowl*] Hercules is said to have obtained a bowl from the sun in which to sail across the sea to Libya; it is sometimes depicted as shaped like a boat. Jonson has combined this legend with other accounts of the hero as a great drinker. See C. F. Wheeler, *Classical Mythology in the Plays, Masques and Poems of Ben Jonson* (1938), pp. 112–15, and A. H. Gilbert, *The Symbolic Persons in the Masques of Ben Jonson* (1948), pp. 119–20.

12 Prime...arts] a phrase from *Pantagruel*, Book IV, ch. 57. The song describing Comus is much indebted to the accounts of Gaster in chapters 57–61, where he is called the inventor of all machines and all sciences that minister to eating and drinking. His diet is also itemized, and may have suggested lines 26–9. See also lines 49–50 and n.

14 hopper] chute that feeds grain into a mill.

15 hutch] bolting-hutch, or box into which flour was sifted.

15 bolter] cloth used to sift flour.

15 copper] cooking-vessel.

16 bavin] bundle of brushwood used to give a quick blaze in bakers' ovens.

16 mawkin] mop used to clean bakers' ovens.

16 peel] baker's shovel.

17 dog...wheel] i.e. the roasting-wheel driven by a dog treading inside it, or some mechanical device for roasting.

19 vice] screw-tap.

20 hippocras bag] a conical bag used as a strainer. Hippocras was a cordial made of wine and spices; it is referred to in the account of Gaster's diet, *Pantagruel*, Book IV, ch. 60.

21 cries swag] 'proclaims himself a swag-belly with his hanging paunch' (Herford and Simpson).

23 weezle] windpipe, or epiglottis, a swelling in the throat.

29 even or odd] i.e. of any kind; all sorts included.

31 As...lac'd] i.e. that, with hardly any (more) stuffing, you need to be laced in.

247

37 saturnals] a time of general licence and revelry, alluding to the date of the masque's first performance, on Twelfth Night, 1618, at the end of the Christmas Revels corresponding roughly with the Roman Saturnalia.

38 stands...hat] i.e. keeps his hat on where he would normally go bareheaded out of respect.

43 tripe] guts, alluding to the paunch of Comus.

44–5 belly...ears] cited from *Pantagruel*, Book IV, ch. 63.

49–50 teaching...jackdaws] So Gaster is said to teach arts to brute creatures, and namely to the birds listed here, in *Pantagruel*, Book IV, ch. 57.

52 venter] Latin for belly.

56 activity] quibbling on the common meaning 'dancing and tumbling', appropriate at a Christmas feast.

65 jovial...kindred] There was a song called 'The Jovial Tinker', referred to by Jonson in *Tale of a Tub*, I, IV, 42 (Herford and Simpson, III, 19), and 'drunk as a tinker' was a common phrase; 'lusty kindred' probably had a similar reference, but is unexplained. There was, as Herford and Simpson note, a dance-tune called 'The Lusty Gallant'.

69 measures] quibbling on the sense 'dances'.

70 piece] cask.

72–3 truest...by] cited from *Pantagruel*, Book IV, ch. 64, though the phrase was proverbial, cf. M. P. Tilley, *Dictionary of Proverbs*, B 287a.

74 *Anti-masque*] danced by men cased, according to Busino, in wicker flasks, with one in a barrel.

76 Antaeus] a legendary giant in Libya, who waylaid and wrestled with all strangers who came his way, and was invincible as long as he remained in contact with his mother, Earth; Hercules killed him by lifting him and crushing him in the air. Busino reports seeing the overthrow of Antaeus mimed in the masque, but there is no indication of this in the text.

85–8 cup...hard] See above, line 8 and n. The cup becomes a chalice, devoted to the worship of Hercules as hero-god, in Virgil, *Aeneid*, VIII, 268–79. It was the custom to crown heroes with circlets of leaves, cf. lines 113–16.

88 heroes] MS 'Heröes' may preserve a Jonsonian pronunciation, for this spelling occurs in other works by him, as in *Epigrams*, CXXXIII, line 143.

90–2 never...life] Herford and Simpson cite the 'Epithalamion' in *Underwood* (*Works*, VIII, 257), lines 153–6: 'Th'ignoble never liv'd, they were awhile | Like Swine, or other cattle here on earth: | Their names are not recorded on the file | Of life.'

100 suffer...do] perhaps 'they are pained by what they are doing now, and by all that they do'; F has 'the do' (do = commotion, stir), which makes poor sense, but may register a difficulty in Jonson's MS here.

104 *Pleasure and Virtue*] See Xenophon, *Memorabilia*, II, i, 21–34, and above, Introduction, p. 229; in the original allegory the two women represented Vice and Virtue, Vice tempting Hercules with a life of pleasure.

Busino saw at some point in the performance a goddess in a long white robe in the midst of musicians clothed in red like priests and wearing gold mitres; cf. line 208 and n.

115 crown] In the *Imagines*, II, 21, Hermes (Mercury) comes to crown Hercules after his conquest of Antaeus.

117–41] The incident of the pigmies attacking Hercules is derived from the *Imagines*, II, 22; see Introduction, p. 230.

124 As...yields] As Herford and Simpson note, several local heroes were absorbed into the cult of Hercules, and the name was liable to be attached to any unusually strong man.

127 Greece] presumably because Hercules was a Greek hero.

139 *dance*] Busino reports seeing not pigmies, but twelve boys who looked like frogs.

148 *Mercury*] See line 115 and n. In the *Imagines*, Mercury comes as the messenger of the gods, who have watched the fight with Antaeus, but Jonson makes him come from Atlas (line 155).

149 *poplar*] especially associated with Hercules, cf. Virgil, *Aeneid*, VIII, 276.

152 Earth's worms] In the *Imagines*, II, 22, they are said to be the children of Earth, their mother.

153 Prove] make trial of.

155–62] The story of Hercules rescuing the Hesperides from pirates, and of Atlas teaching him astronomy, is taken from Diodorus Siculus, *Bibliotheca*, IV, 27. Here, and in the *Imagines*, II, 20, there is reference also to the legend of Hercules taking over or sharing the burden of Atlas. See also line 191 and n.

174 Hesperus] the evening star, that appears in the west; hence an appropriate emblem of Britain, and so of James I.

177 pillars] the cliffs of Ceuta and Gibraltar, reputed to have been set up by Hercules; an account of them is given in Diodorus Siculus, IV, 18.

180 brother] Diodorus Siculus, IV, 27, makes Hesperus the brother of Atlas.

186 knowledge] Diodorus Siculus, III, 60 and IV, 27, depicts Atlas as a learned astronomer; but the idea was familiar, and Jonson describes the achieving of truth in the image 'Monte potiri, to get the hill' in *Discoveries* (*Works*, VIII, 628).

186 one] Prince Charles, chief masquer.

191 Hesperides] The gardens were often located in Libya, and the three sisters, the Hesperides, who guarded Juno's golden apples there, were commonly identified as the daughters of Atlas. Hercules had to obtain these apples as one of his twelve labours.

195–7, 208] It is not clear what happens here. Mercury says, line 184, that Virtue 'brings forth' the masquers, but line 195 suggests that Virtue remains seated as an onlooker, and it seems from line 208 that Pleasure leads the way. Busino reports seeing a goddess robed in white among musicians (p. 233 above), and the text suggests that this may have been Pleasure, not, as Herford and Simpson think, Virtue. See line 104 and n.

212 skill]   knowledge.

216 *Daedalus*]   in Greek legend, the great artist or inventor, whose labyrinth, built in Crete for Minos, suggested lines 236–9, 270, 275.

229 knot]   design formed of crossing lines.

239 unto gaze]   into bewilderment.

240 numerous]   harmonious.

253 yourselves compose]   take positions and attitudes (for the dance).

255 figure]   bodily shape and bearing; or perhaps movement in the dance (*N.E.D.* first records in 1636). Jonson may have had both senses in mind, and he leapt to the further idea of 'figure' as the human form in painting in lines 254–6.

259 ground]   fundamental principle of knowledge; also, in painting, a basis (background) to work from.

263 the fair]   the ladies, waiting to be 'taken out' into the dance, the usual culmination of a masque; cf. line 292.

265 touch]   presumably grouping, hand to hand, for the dance.

289 sum]   epitomize; sum up.

297–301]   Although Mercury 'called'(line 293) these lines to Daedalus, they are addressed to the masquers, and prepare for their return into the mountain.

312 triumphed]   triumphed over.

313–22]   Cf. Milton's *Comus*, lines 1018–23.

THE INNER TEMPLE MASQUE

OR
MASQUE OF HEROES

BY THOMAS MIDDLETON

Edited by R. C. Bald

INTRODUCTION

Middleton's *Inner Temple Masque, or Masque of Heroes*, was performed some time between 6 January and 2 February 1619. Kirsmas was 'very lusty a' Twelfth Night' (line 71) but he is 'drawing on' (line 69) and 'may linger out till Candlemas' (line 112). Perhaps the actual date of performance was nearer Candlemas than Twelfth Night; a performance in the second half of January seems reasonably certain. The records of the Inner Temple do not seem to throw any light on the masque or when it was given; they mention a play at Candlemas for which £7 was paid, but nothing more.[1] The costs of such an entertainment as this were probably defrayed from a special fund collected by the officers for Christmas and were not included in the accounts of the Inn itself.

The list of performers prefixed to the masque shows that Prince Charles's Men were called in to help the Templars. All five actors whose names are given were at that date members of the Prince's company. Joseph Taylor joined the King's Men a few months later, just after Burbage's death, and remained their leading actor until the closing of the theatres. William Rowley, Middleton's friend and collaborator, was also with the King's Men for the last three years of his life, but the careers of the other three, Newton, Atwell, and Carpenter, are associated almost entirely with the Prince's Men. Rowley was rotund, and generally played rollicking parts; he is also known to have played the Fat Bishop in *A Game at Chess*; so it was natural to cast him as Plumporridge. By contrast Newton as the Fasting Day must have been spare of figure and easily made up to look cadaverous. Taylor naturally took the leading role, and Atwell was cast as the juvenile lead. He was, according to Rowley, who wrote some lines to his memory, a 'little man', but he must have compensated for his lack of size by the grace of his action. Altogether this is one of the more revealing actor lists of its period.

According to Middleton's prefatory verses, 'This nothing owes to any tale or story'. In a sense this is true; nevertheless, it is easy to

---

[1] *Calendar of Inner Temple Records*, II, 116.

see the origins of most of the device. The almanac itself provided the central idea for the characters, the dialogue, and the anti-masques. The first anti-masque was a dance of the six days liable (though Lent is an uneasy exception) to bring disturbance or trouble of one kind and another, between the time of performance and the hottest time of the year. The second anti-masque of good, bad, and indifferent days comes directly from the almanacs. Not all of them ended with a table of good and evil days in the month, but one which did so was Bretnor's, to which Middleton alludes. There is, in fact, little doubt that Middleton had Bretnor's almanac for 1618 before him. The prognostications for the year contain tables for each month showing the positions of the planets and the quarters of the moon, followed by predictions of the weather; then comes the list of good and evil days. Each day had some phrase—a motto or proverb, often cryptic in tone—assigned to it, which was supposed to characterize it. The list for one of the months (October) which did not provide Middleton with any materials is given by way of illustration:

Good dayes	Euill dayes
1, 2, 6. Hold fast and feare not.	3, 4, 5. Wast and want.
13, 14. First come, first serud.	7, 8, 9, A meer cheater.
17, 18, 19. *Vsque ad aras.*	10, 11, 12. Crosse carding.
20, 21, 22. Good in the wearing.	15, 16. Busie about nothing.
24, 26, 27. Better then nothing.	23, 25. From pomp to pouerty.
29, 31. Countenance will carry it.	28, 30. More hast worse speed.

All Middleton's examples except one ('Faint heart never') are to be found scattered through the months. The indifferent days, it will be seen, were a class of his own making, but he found their mottoes distributed under good and bad.

Ianuarie	Euill dayes.	22, 23, 24.	Post for puddings.
February	Euill daies.	7.	Neither full nor fasting.
March	Good daies.	3, 5.	It fals into thy mouth.
	Euill daies.	9, 12.	Nihil in a bagge.
Iune	Euill dayes.	16, 17, 21.	Gape after gudgins.
Iuly	Good daies.	23, 26, 28.	It cottens well.

August	Good daies.	7, 8, 9.	In docke out nettell.
	Euill daies.	26, 28, 29.	Put vp thy Pipes.
September	Good daies.	16, 17, 18.	Make hay betime.
	Good daies.	19, 22.	Cocke oth hoope.
November	Good daies.	13, 14, 17, 18.	Ply the boxe.
	Euill daies.	28, 29.	Rods in pisse.[1]

It is difficult to believe, too, that Middleton was unacquainted with Jonson's *Christmas his Masque*, performed at Court in 1616; perhaps he had seen it, or perhaps a manuscript had come his way. Jonson's piece, as R. J. A. Tiddy points out,[2] follows the pattern of the typical mummers' play rather than of the masque proper, with Christmas presenting the other characters in turn. In this piece they are his children, and among them are Gambol and Wassall, and (the youngest) Baby-Cake, whose usher bears 'a great cake with a bean, and a pease',—the last-mentioned objects being the instruments for 'choosing King and Queen' on Twelfth Night. Even the dialogue had its implications for Middleton:

Gambol. Here's one o' Friday-street would come in.
Christmas. By no means, nor out of neither of the Fish-streets, admit not a man; they are not Christmas creatures. Fish and fasting days, foh![3]

Finally, that the departing season should make his will was an old folk motif; it was prominent in Tallboyes Dymock's play of the death of the Summer Lord;[4] it not only figured in, but provided the title for, Nashe's *Summer's Last Will and Testament*.

Middleton, who consistently wrote 'Antemasque' for 'Antimasque', seems to have thought of it as a dance preceding the main masque. The 'device', with its dialogue incorporating the two antimasques, is admirably coordinated, although its relation to the masque of heroes, with which the entertainment concludes, is slight. It is difficult not to identify the heroes, since they were nine in

[1] It is perhaps worth adding that the earlier section 'Certaine Physicall observations' in the 1618 Bretnor has some vigorous remarks about the physician's inability to diagnose solely by urine. These comments Middleton, for the purposes of his dialogue, saw fit to ignore.
[2] *The Mummers' Play*, p. 131. [3] Herford and Simpson, VII, 440.
[4] See Norreys Jephson O'Conor, *Godes Peace and the Queenes*, part VI, and C. L. Barber, *Shakespeare's Festive Comedy*, ch. I.

number, with the Nine Worthies; significantly, Middleton has a dance of the Nine Worthies in *The World Tossed at Tennis*, though there each of the nine is named and distinguished from the others in a speech that accompanies their entry. The earlier part of *The Inner Temple Masque* was performed in front of some sort of static background; the adornments of music, song, and moving scenery were reserved for the masque proper. When the preliminary part of the entertainment was over, the first cloud 'vanished' to disclose Harmony and her choir; then the scenery opened again to discover the masquers 'sitting in arches of cloud'. Here the influence of the court masque was most apparent. Yet, in spite of all accretions, the masque itself still retained its primitive form: the masquers in disguise make their entrance, dance, seize partners from among the ladies, and dance again.

The Inner Temple Masque, slight as it is, has all the marks of Middleton's maturity in its manipulation of incident and its ease of dialogue. The anti-masque of the Days, with their mottoes culled from the almanacs, brings to mind Middleton's early interest in the *impresa*, of which he had made effective use in *Your Five Gallants*, but his skill in handling allegorical personifications, here and in *The World Tossed at Tennis*, with humour and irony, anticipates the triumphs yet to come in *A Game at Chess*.

[DRAMATIS PERSONAE]

THE PARTS	THE SPEAKERS
Dr. Almanac	Jos. Taylor
Plumporridge	W. Rowley
A Fasting Day	J. Newton
New Year	H. Atwell
Time	W. Carpenter
Harmony	A Boy

Two Anti-masques
In the first, six Dancers

1. Candlemas Day
2. Shrove Tuesday
3. Lent
4. Ill May Day
5. Midsummer Eve
6. The First Dog Day

The second Anti-masque, presented by

eight Boys

Good Days - - - - - - - - -3
Bad Days - - - - - - - - - -3
Indifferent Days - - - - - 2

The Masque itself receiving its illustration
from nine of the Gentlemen of the House

THE INNER-
Temple Masque.

OR

MASQUE OF
HEROES.

Presented (as an Entertainment for
many worthy LADIES:)

By GENTLEMEN of the same
Ancient and Noble
HOUSE.

*   *   *

This nothing owes to any tale or story,
With which some writer pieces up a glory;
I only made the time they sat to see
Serve for the mirth itself, which was found free
And herein fortunate (that's counted good),   5
Being made for ladies, ladies understood.   T.M.

*Enter Doctor Almanac coming from the funeral of December,
or the Old Year.*

Doctor. I have seen the Old Year fairly buried,
Good gentleman he was, but toward his end
Full of diseases; he kept no good diet,
He loved a wench in June (which we count vild)
And got the latter end of May with child.
That was his fault, and many an old year smells on't.

[*Enter a Fasting Day.*]   1

How now, who's this? Oh, one o' th' Fasting Days
That followed him to his grave.
I know him by his gauntness, his thin chitterlings;
He would undo a tripe-wife. Fasting Day,
Why art so heavy?   20
Fasting Day.   O sweet Doctor Almanac,
I have lost a dear old master; beside, sir,
I have been out of service all this Kirsmas;
Nobody minds Fasting Day;
I have scarce been thought upon a' Friday nights,   25
And because Kirsmas this year fell upon't
The Fridays have been ever since so proud
They scorn my company; the butchers' boys
At Temple Bar set their great dogs upon me;
I dare not walk abroad, nor be seen yet,   30
The very poulters' girls throw rotten eggs at me,
Nay, Fish Street loves me e'en but from teeth outward,
The nearest kin I have looks shy upon me
As if 't'ad forgot me. I met Plumporridge now,
My big-swollen enemy; he's plump and lusty,   35
The only man in place. Sweet Master Doctor,
Prefer me to the New Year, you can do't.
Doctor. When can I do't, sir? You must stay till Lent.
Fasting Day. Till Lent! You kill my heart, sweet Master Doctor.
Thrust me into Candlemas Eve, I do beseech you.   40
Doctor. Away; Candlemas Eve will never bear thee i' these days;
'tis so frampole, the Puritans will never yield to't.

Enter Plumporridge.

Fasting Day. Why, th'are fat enough.
Doctor. Here comes Plumporridge.   45
Fasting Day. Ay, he's sure of welcome; methinks he moves like
one of the great porridge tubs going to the Counter.
Plumporridge. O killing cruel sight, yonder's a Fasting Day, a lean
spiny rascal with a dog in's belly, his very bowels bark with
hunger. Avaunt, thy breath stinks; I do not love to meet thee 50
fasting; thou art nothing but wind, thy stomach's full of farts, as

if they had lost their way, and thou made with the wrong end
upward, like a Dutch maw, that discharges still into th' mouth!

Fasting Day. Why, thou whoreson breakfast, dinner, nuncheons,
supper and bever, cellar, hall, kitchen and wet-larder!

Plumporridge. Sweet Master Doctor, look quickly upon his water,
That I may break the urinal about his pate.

Doctor. Nay, friendship, friendship!

Plumporridge.   Never, Master Doctor,
With any Fasting Day, persuade me not;
Nor anything belongs to Ember week;
And if I take against a thing, I'm stomachful;
I was born an Anabaptist, a fell foe
To fish and Fridays; pig's my absolute sweetheart,
And shall I wrong my love, and cleave to saltfish,
Commit adultery with an egg and butter?

Doctor. Well, setting this apart, whose water's this, sir?

Plumporridge. Oh, thereby hangs a tale; my master Kirsmas's,
It is his water, sir, he's drawing on.

Doctor. Kirsmas? why, let me see;
I saw him very lusty a' Twelfth Night.

Plumporridge. Ay, that's true, sir, but then he took his bane
With choosing King and Queen;
H'as made his will already, here's the copy.

Doctor. And what has he given away? Let me see, Plumbroth.

Plumporridge. He could not give away much, sir; his children have
so consum'd him beforehand.

Doctor. (*reads*) The last Will and Testament of Kirsmas, irre-
vocable.

Imprimis, I give and bequeath to my second son, In-and-In, his
perpetual lodging i' the King's Bench, and his ordinary out of the
basket.

Plumporridge. A sweet allowance for a second brother.

Doctor. (*reads*) *Item,* I give to my youngest sons Gleek and
Primivist the full consuming of nights and days and wives and
children, together with one secret gift, that is, never to give over
while they have a penny.

Plumporridge. And if e'er they do, I'll be hang'd.

Doctor. (*reads*) For the possession of all my lands, manors, manor houses, I leave them full and wholly to my eldest son Noddy, 90 whom during his minority I commit to the custody of a pair of knaves and one and thirty.

Plumporridge. There's knaves enow a' conscience to cozen one fool.

Doctor. (*reads*) *Item,* I give to my eldest daughter, Tickle-me-quickly, and to her sister My-Lady's-Hole, free leave to shift for 95 themselves either in court, city, or country.

Plumporridge. We thank him heartily.

Doctor. (*reads*) *Item,* I leave to their old aunt, My-Sow-has-Pigged, a litter of courtesans to breed up for Shrovetide.

Plumporridge. They will be good ware in Lent, when flesh is forbid 100 by proclamation.

Doctor. (*reads*) *Item,* I give to my nephew Gambols, commonly called by the name of Kirsmas Gambols, all my cattle, horse, and mare, but let him shoe 'em himself.

Plumporridge. I ha' seen him shoe the mare forty times over. 105

Doctor. (*reads*) Also, I bequeath to my cousin german Wassail-Bowl, born of Dutch parents, the privilege of a free denizen, that is, to be drunk with Scotch ale or English beer; and lastly, I have given by word of mouth to poor Blindman-Buff a flap with a fox tail.

Plumporridge. Ay, so h'as given 'em all for aught I see. 110
But now what think you of his water, sir?

Doctor. Well, he may linger out till Candlemas,
But ne'er recover it.

Fasting Day.　　　Would he were gone once,
I should be more respected. 115

Enter New Year.

Doctor.　　　　　Here's New Year!

Plumporridge. I have ne'er a gift to give him; I'll be gone.

[*Exit.*]

Doctor. Mirth and a healthful time fill all your days. 120
Look freshly, sir.

New Year.　　　I cannot, Master Doctor.
My father's death sets the spring backward i' me.
For joy and comfort yet, I'm now between

261

Sorrow and joy, the winter and the spring,   12

And as time gathers freshness in its season

No doubt affects will be subdued with reason.

Doctor. Y'ave a brave mind to work on; use my rules

And you shall cut a caper in November,

When other years, your grandfathers, lay bedrid.   13

New Year. What's he, that looks so piteously and shakes so?

Doctor. A Fasting Day.

New Year.   How's that?

Doctor.   A foolish Fasting Day,

An unseasonable cockscomb, seeks now for a service;   13

H'as hunted up and down, h'as been at court,

And the long porter broke his head across there;

He had rather see the devil, for this he says:

He ne'er grew up so tall with fasting days.

I would not for the price of all my almanacs   14

The guard had took him there,

They would ha' beat out his brains with bombards.

I bade him stay till Lent, and now he whimpers

He would to Rome forsooth, that's his last refuge,

But would try a while   14

How well he should be used in Lancashire.

New Year. He was my father's servant,

That he was, sir.

Doctor.   'Tis here upon record.

Fasting Day. I serv'd him honestly, and cost him little.   15

Doctor. Ay, I'll be sworn for that.

Fasting Day.   Those were the times, sir,

That made your predecessors rich, and able

To lay up more for you, and since poor fasting days

Were not made reckoning on, the pamper'd flesh   15

Has play'd the knave; maids have had fuller bellies;

Those meals that once were sav'd, have stirr'd and leapt

And begot bastards, and they must be kept.

Better keep fasting days, your self may tell ye,

And for the profit of purse, back, and belly!   16

Doctor. I never yet heard truth better whin'd out.

New Year. Thou shalt not all be lost, nor for vainglory
  Greedily welcom'd; we'll begin with virtue.
  As we may hold with't, that does virtue right.
  Set him down, sir, for Candlemas Eve at night.   165
Fasting Day. Well, better late than never.
  This is my comfort, I shall come to make
  All the fat rogues go to bed supperless,
  Get dinners where they can.   *[Exit.]*

            [Enter Time.]   170

New Year.   How now, what's he?
Doctor. 'Tis old Time, sir, that belong'd
  To all your predecessors.
New Year.   Oh, I honour
  That reverend figure; may I ever think   175
  How precious thou'rt in youth, how rarely
  Redeem'd in age.
Time.   Observe, you have Time's service.
  There's all, in brief.

       Enter the first Anti-masque.   180

New Year.   Ha, Doctor, what are these?
Time. The rabble that I pity. These I have serv'd too,
  But few or none have ever observ'd me
  Amongst this dissolute rout. Candlemas Day!
  I'm sorry to see him so ill associated.   185
Doctor. Why, that's his cause of coming to complain,
  Because Shrove Tuesday this year dwells so near him;
  But 'tis his place, he cannot be remov'd.
  You must be patient, Candlemas, and brook it.
  This rabble, sir, Shrove Tuesday, hungry Lent,   190
  Ill May Day, Midsummer Eve, and the first Dog Day,
  Come to receive their places due by custom,
  And that they build upon.
New Year.   Give 'em their charge,
  And then admit 'em.   195
Doctor.   I will do't incony.

Stand forth, Shrove Tuesday, one o' the silenc'd bricklayers;
'Tis in your charge to pull down bawdy houses,
To set your tribe a-work, cause spoil in Shoreditch
And make a dangerous leak there, deface Turnbull
And tickle Codpiece Row, ruin the Cockpit—
The poor players ne'er thriv'd in't, o' my conscience,
Some quean piss'd upon the first brick.
For you, lean Lent, be sure you utter first
Your rotten herrings and keep up your best
Till they be rotten, then there's no deceit
When they be all alike. You, Ill May Day,
Be as unruly a rascal as you may
To stir up Deputy Double-Diligence
That comes perking forth with halberts;
And for you, Midsummer Eve, that watches warmest,
Be but sufficiently drunk, and y'are well harness'd.
You, Dog Day!
Dog Day. Woh!
Doctor. A churlish maund'ring rogue,
You must both beg and rob, curse and collogue,
In cooler nights the barn with doxies fill,
In harvest lie in haycock with your Jill.
They have all their charge.
New Year. You have gi'en't at the wrong end.
Doctor. To bid 'em sin's the way to make 'em mend,
For what they are forbid they run to headlong—
I ha' cast their inclinations. Now your service,
To draw fresh blood into your master's cheeks, slaves!

The first Dance, and first Anti-masque,
consisting of these six rude ones.

Exeunt.

New Year. What scornful looks the abusive villains threw
Upon the reverend form and face of Time!
Methought it appear'd sorry, and went angry.
Doctor. 'Tis still your servant.

[*Enter the second Anti-masque.*]

264

New Year.   How now, what are these?
Doctor. These are your good days and your bad days, sir,
  Those your indifferent days, nor good nor bad.   235
New Year. But is here all?
Doctor.   A wonder there's so many,
  How these broke loose; everyone stops their passage
  And makes enquiry after 'em.
  This farmer will not cast his seed i'th' ground   240
  Before he look in Bretnor; there he finds
  Some word which he hugs happily, as 'Ply the box',
  'Make hay betimes', 'It falls into thy mouth'.
  A punctual lady will not paint forsooth
  Upon his critical days—'twill not hold well—   245
  Nor a nice City wedlock eat fresh herring
  Nor periwinkles,
  Although she long for both, if the word be that day
  'Gape after gudgeons' or some fishing phrase.
  A scrivener's wife will not entreat the money-master   250
  That lies i'th' house and gets her husband's children
  To furnish a poor gentleman's extremes
  If she find 'Nihil in a bag' that morning;
  And so of thousand follies. These suffice
  To show you good, bad, and indifferent days,   255
  And all have their inscriptions. Here's 'Cock-a-Hoop',
  This 'The Gear Cottons', and this 'Faint Heart Never';
  These, noted black for badness, 'Rods in Piss',
  This 'Post for Puddings', this 'Put up thy Pipes';
  These black and white indifferently, inclining   260
  To both their natures, 'Neither Full nor Fasting',
  'In Dock, out Nettle'.—Now to your motion,
  Black knaves and white knaves, and you parcel rascals,
  Two hypocritical parti-coloured varlets,
  That play o' both hands.   265

> *Here the second Dance, and last Anti-*
> *masque; eight boys, habited according*
> *to their former Characters.*

The three Good Days, attired all in white garments, sitting close to their bodies, their inscriptions on their breasts. 27

> *On the first.*
> Cock-a-Hoop.
> *On the second.*
> The Gear Cottons.
> *On the third.* 27
> Faint Heart Never.

The three Bad Days all in black garments, their faces black, and their inscriptions.

> *On the first.*
> Rods in Piss. 28
> *On the second.*
> Post for Puddings.
> *On the third.*
> Put up thy Pipes.

The Indifferent Days in garments half white, half black, their faces 2
seamed with that parti-colour, and their inscriptions.

> *The first.*
> Neither Full nor Fasting.
> *The second.*
> In Dock, out Nettle. 2

These having purchased a smile from the cheeks of many a beauty by their ridiculous figures, vanish, proud of that treasure.

Doctor. I see these pleasures of low births and natures
  Add little freshness to your cheeks; I pity you,
  And can no longer now conceal from you 2
  Your happy omen, sir; blessings draw near you.
  I will disclose a secret in astrology:
  By the sweet industry of Harmony,
  Your white and glorious friend,
  Ev'n very deities have conspir'd to grace 3
  Your fair inauguration. Here I find it—
  'Tis clear in art—

The minute, nay, the point of time's arriv'd;
Methinks the blessings touch you, now they're felt, sir.

At which loud music heard; the first cloud vanishing, Harmony is 305
discovered with her sacred choir.

The first song

Harmony.   New Year, New Year, hark, hearken to me!
                  I am sent down
                          To crown   310
                  Thy wishes; with me
          Thy fair desires in Virtue's court are fil'd.
                  The goodness of thy thought
                  This blessed work hath wrought,
                          Time shall be reconcil'd.   315
          Thy spring shall in all sweets abound,
          Thy summer shall be clear and sound,
          Thy autumn swell the barn and loft
          With corn and fruits, ripe, sweet, and soft,
          And in thy winter, when all go,   320
          Thou shalt depart as white as snow.

Then a second cloud vanishing, the Masquers themselves discovered,
sitting in arches of clouds, being nine in number, Heroes deified for their
virtues.

The song goes on   325

          Behold, behold, hark, hearken to me!
                  Glories come down
                          To crown
                  Thy wishes, with me,
          Bright heroes in lasting honour spher'd   330
                  Virtue's eternal spring,
                  By making Time their king,
                          See, they're beyond Time rear'd.
                  Yet in their love to human good,
                  In which estate themselves once stood,   335
                  They all descend to have their worth

267

Shine to imitation forth;
And by their motion, light, and love,
To show how after times should move.

Then the Masquers descending, set to their first dance.

The second song

Harmony.   Move on, move on, be still the same,
        You beauteous sons of brightness;
You add to honour spirit and flame,
        To virtue, grace and whiteness;
        You, whose every little motion
        May learn strictness more devotion,
        Every pace of that high worth
        It treads a fair example forth,
        Quickens a virtue, makes a story,
        To your own heroic glory;
May your three times thrice blest number
Raise Merit from his ancient slumber.
        Move on, move on, &c.

Then they order themselves for their second dance, after which

The third song

[*Harmony.*] See whither Fate hath led you, Lamps of Honour,
        For goodness brings her own reward upon her;
        Look, turn your eyes, and then conclude, commending,
        And say, you have lost no worth by your descending.
        Behold a heaven about you, spheres more plenty,
            There, for one Luna, here shines ten,
            And for one Venus, twenty;
        Then heroes, double both your fame and light,
        Each choose his star, and full adorn this night.

At which, the Masquers make choice of their ladies, and dance.

Time, thus closing all.

Time.   The morning grey
Bids come away;
Every lady should begin   370
To take her chamber, for the stars are in.

Then making his honour to the ladies.

Live long the miracles of times and years
Till with those heroes you sit fix'd in spheres.

FINIS

THE TEXT

The piece was published by the author not long after its first performance. It was entered in the Stationers' Register on 19 July 1619 as 'The Temple Masque Anno 1618' by John Browne, with a licence from Sir George Buc and with consent of the wardens. Browne was one of the stationers who had their shops in the churchyard of St Dunstan-in-the-West, just across Fleet Street from the Temple; his shop was obviously much frequented by lawyers and law students. On the basis of the ornaments used Greg concluded that the printer of the little book was William Stansby. It consists of three quarto gatherings, A–C, with first and last leaves blank; the title page is on A2, the verses headed 'The Masque' on A3, the list of characters on A3ᵛ, and the text on A4 [mis-signed A3]–C3. According to W. A. Jackson,[1] twelve copies in all are known to have survived.

Five copies of the original edition have been consulted for this edition: the two in the British Museum, and those in the Folger, Huntington, and Boston Public Libraries. No significant variants were discovered. The masque has twice been edited previously: by Alexander Dyce (1840) and A. H. Bullen (1885–6) in their editions of Middleton's *Works*. Like the present one, both these editions give a modernized text. The original quarto is well printed, containing very few errors, so that an editor's problems are few. The present edition, however, is somewhat more conservative than its predecessors, in that it preserves a greater number of Middleton's incomplete lines, and takes no liberties with the original elisions in order to fit the words into the conventional blank verse pattern.

[1] *The Carl H. Pforzheimer Library*, II, 116.

COLLATION

9 *Doctor*] *omitted in* Q.
16 this] *Dyce*; t'is Q.
24–5 Nobody...nights] *all one line in* Q.
33 The nearest kin I have] (The nearest Kin I haue) Q.
56–7] *as prose in* Q.
59–60 Never...not] *all one line in* Q.
78 *Doctor. (reads)*] Q *omits here and at lines 84, 89, 94, 98, 102, 106.*
78–9 The last...irrevocable.] *printed as a heading in* Q, *and followed by* Read.
132 *Doctor.*] *so Dyce*; *Fast.* Q.
141–2] *All one line in* Q.
143 whimpers] whimpers; Q.
159 ye] *Dyce*; you Q.
194–5 Give...'em] *all one line in* Q.
196 incony.] in Cone. Q.
201–2] Cockpit, the | Poor Players...Cōscience some | Queane Q.
237 many,] many. Q.
238 loose;] loose, Q.
257 Never';] neuer- Q.
285 *The Indifferent Days in garments*] *The Indifferent Dayes.* | In Garments Q.

COMMENTARY

18 chitterlings]   here used of the intestines generally.

23 Kirsmas]   colloquial form of Christmas.

26 this year]   In 1618 Christmas fell on a Friday.

29 Temple Bar]   Butcher Row was just outside Temple Bar on the north side of the Strand.

32 Fish Street]   the main fish market of London.

40 Candlemas]   the feast of the purification of the Virgin, celebrated on 2 February.

42 frampole]   disagreeable, peevish.

47 porridge tubs]   containing gruel for the prisoners.

53 Dutch maw]   (unexplained).

54 nuncheons]   snacks.

55 bever]   afternoon snack.

55 wet-larder]   where moist or liquid provisions were stored.

61 Ember week]   a period of three-day fasting, occurring four times a year.

62 take against]   oppose.

62 stomachful]   obstinate, resentful.

64 pig]   On the Puritan fondness for pork, see Jonson's *Bartholomew Fair*, I, vi, etc.

71 Twelfth Night]   the climax of the Christmas revels.

73 choosing King and Queen]   a Twelfth Night sport. The King was the person who found a bean in his slice of Christmas cake, the Queen the person who found a pea.

80 In-and-In]   a gambling game played with dice.

82 basket]   used for collecting food for the poor prisoners.

84 Gleek]   a card game.

85 Primivist]   'a game at cardes called Prime, Primero, or Primauista', Florio, 1598 (*N.E.D.*).

90 Noddy]   another card game.

94–9 Tickle-me-quickly...My-Lady's-Hole...My-Sow-has-Pigged]   all card games.

101 proclamation]   the annual proclamation issued at the beginning of Lent against the eating of flesh without dispensation. Cf. Middleton's *A Chaste Maid in Cheapside*, II, ii.

102 Gambols]   'certain Sports or Tumbling Tricks in use about Christmas-time', Phillips, ed. Kersey, 1706 (*N.E.D.*).

105 shoe the mare]   Shoeing the wild mare was a Christmas game, in which one of the players was pursued by the others in order to be shod.

106 Wassail-Bowl.] Drinking from the wassail-bowl was a custom on New
Year's Eve. Sometimes it was offered by a host to his guests; sometimes it
was taken from door to door by young women who collected what they could
from the drinkers.

109 a flap with a fox tail] figuratively, a rebuke.

112 linger out till Candlemas] 'With some Christmas ends with the twelve
day, but with the generality of the vulgar, not till Candlemas' (Brand,
Popular Antiquities).

118 ne'er a gift to give him] Presents were given not at Christmas but on
New Year's day.

127 affects] natural feelings.

137 the long porter] An account of him is to be found in Fuller's *Worthies*,
sub Staffordshire. His name was Walter Parsons and he was over seven
feet tall.

142 bombards] leather jugs. Apparently the guards had a habit of hurling
them about, for in *The Martyred Soldier* Shirley refers to 'the black Jacks |
Or Bombards tossed by the King's Guard'.

146 Lancashire] the county in which recusants were most numerous.

187 dwells so near him] In 1619 Shrove Tuesday fell on 9 February, just a
week after Candlemas.

191 Ill May Day] a day of riots against foreign artisans, 1 May 1517. Some
of its events are dramatized in the play of *Sir Thomas More*.

191 Midsummer Eve] celebrated with bonfires and other forms of merri-
ment.

191 the first Dog Day] 'In current almanacs the dog days are said to begin
3 July and end 11 August' (*N.E.D.*).

196 incony] rarely, skilfully.

197 silenc'd bricklayers] meaning uncertain; perhaps refers to unordained
Puritan preachers who had been forbidden to preach.

199 Shoreditch] a neighbourhood with a bad reputation outside the City
jurisdiction on the north-east.

200 leak] A Mrs Leak was the keeper of a bawdy house. Dyce quotes from
The Owles Almanacke, 1618: 'Shroue-tuesday falls on that day, on which
the prentices plucked downe the cocke-pit, and on which they did always
vse to rifle Madame Leakes house at the vpper end of Shoreditch.'

200 Turnbull] Turnbull Street was notorious for its brothels.

201 Codpiece Row] a court of Petty France in Westminster, also frequented by prostitutes.

201 Cockpit] the theatre in Drury Lane, looted during the Shrove
Tuesday riots of 1617, just after the Queen's players had begun using it.

215 maund'ring] grumbling.

216 collogue] wheedle.

241 Bretnor] Thomas Bretnor was an astrologer whose almanacs appeared
between 1605 and 1630.

242 Ply the box] wield vigorously.

244 punctual] punctilious.

246 wedlock] wife.

249 Gape after gudgeons] swallow greedily and credulously.

253 Nihil] a trifle of no value.

256 Cock-a-Hoop] exultant.

257 The Gear Cottons] The matter goes on prosperously.

258 Rods in Piss] to have punishment in store for someone.

259 Post] hurry.

259 Put up thy Pipes] come to an end, desist.

262 In Dock, out Nettle] 'This phrase, which was originally a charm to cure nettle stings by dock leaves, became a proverbial expression for changeableness and inconstancy' (Tilley).

263 parcel] partly, in portions.

THE TRIUMPH OF PEACE

BY JAMES SHIRLEY

Edited by Clifford Leech

INTRODUCTION

A magnificent formal gesture from the four Inns of Court, *The Triumph of Peace* was a declaration of continuing loyalty to Charles I. Prynne's *Histriomastix* had appeared in November 1632, with the author described on the title-page as 'an *Vtter-Barrester of* Lincolnes Inne': its first dedication was 'To His Mvch Honovred Friends, the Right Worshipfvll Masters of the Bench of the Honourable flourishing Lavv-Society of Lincolnes-Inne'; its second 'To the Right Christian, Generovs Young Gentlemen-Students of the 4 famous Innes of Court, and especially those of Lincolnes Inne'. The book attacked performances of plays and those who countenanced them: in the index it was easy to find the entries '*Women-Actors*, notorious whores...' and '*Kings*... infamous for them to act or frequent Playes, or favour Players'. Both Charles and his Queen thus seemed to be personally attacked: the book was suppressed and Prynne was sent to the Tower, where he awaited trial and (in 1634) cruel punishment. Early in October 1633 the hint came from the King that the gentlemen of the Inns should present a masque at court: it was an obvious opportunity for them to show that Prynne, whom Lincoln's Inn had expelled, was in no way their spokesman. Preparations were quickly put in hand. There would be not only a sumptuous masque but a procession through the city, starting at the adjoining Ely and Hatton Houses in Holborn and making its way as far east as Aldersgate Street before arriving at Whitehall. G. Garrard, writing to Strafford in Ireland on 9 January 1634, referred to £20,000 as the rumoured cost: that may have been rumour's exaggeration, but the Inner Temple records, under the date 12 November 1633, indicated that every bencher had to provide £5, with lesser sums for those of lower standing, and, under the date 9 February 1634, that the 'stock of the House' was to be drawn on to make up the deficiency between the sum raised and the sum spent.

A strong team was employed for the devising of the masque. Inigo Jones, inevitably, was in charge of scenes and costumes.

James Shirley (1596–1666) may have been chosen as the poet for his condemnation of Prynne in his verses for Ford's *Love's Sacrifice* (1633) and the ironic dedication of his own *The Bird in a Cage* (1633) to Prynne in the Tower. In any event, Jonson not being available for further collaboration with Jones, Shirley was as good a choice as could be made. The music was by William Lawes (1602–45) and Simon Ives (1600–62). Lawes was also to write the music for Davenant's masque *The Triumph of the Prince d'Amour* in 1635: it was his brother Henry Lawes who collaborated with Milton in *Comus* (1634) and with Carew in *Coelum Britannicum* (1634).

The performance took place on 3 February 1634, and, at the request of the King and Queen, it was repeated at Merchant Taylors' Hall on 13 February, with the Lord Mayor as host.

Shirley was admitted to membership of Gray's Inn on 23 January 1634, doubtless in recognition of his work on the masque.

Three accounts of the procession are extant—that given in the printed text of the masque, one included in the Manuscripts of Richard Cholmondeley of Condover Hall, Shropshire (*Hist. MSS. Com.*, Fifth Report, part 1 (1876)), and one given by Bulstrode Whitelocke, who was a member of the committee in charge of the preparations (*Memorials of the English Affairs*, published 1732). The names of the masquers are given in Francis Lenton's *The Inns of Court Anagrammatist; or The Masquers Masqued in Anagrammes* (1634). The documents relating to the performances are quoted extensively in G. E. Bentley's *Jacobean and Caroline Stage*, v, 1154–63. Several of Jones's designs for the occasion are at Chatsworth, and the music of Lawes and Ives has been said to be preserved at Oxford (Bentley, p. 1163).

Shirley's text was to express loyalty to the King and Queen. There was an inevitable irony in this, as loyalty was slipping away in 1634, and the irony was increased in the choice of a theme. The basic setting is the Forum or Piazza of Peace, with representations on either side of Minos and Numa, the legendary figures embodying respectively Greek and Roman ideas of Law and Justice. Presenters of the masquers are Irene (Peace), Eunomia (Law) and Dice (Justice, sometimes, as here, identified with Astrea)—the three Hours, daughters of Zeus and Themis, according to Hesiod the tutelary goddesses of agriculture and the guardians of order in society. They and a Genius present to Charles and Henrietta Maria the masquers from the Inns of Court (sons of Peace, Law and Justice), and praise the blessed and orderly condition of the kingdom. Just before the presentation the King and Queen are momentarily taken to be the divine parents of the Hours.

Because of its occasion, *The Triumph of Peace* had to outdo its predecessors in scenic splendour and in variety of device. The anti-masque had never been used so freely as here: there were twelve separate anti-masques preceding the entry of the presenters, and an additional anti-masque came between the main masquing dance and the revels. The anti-masques had their own presenters— a group of abstractions of which Fancy was appropriately the leader. After the revels, the masque was brought to a close with the impressive appearance of Amphiluche, ushering in the morning and the festivity's end. Dancing both grotesque and solemn ran through the whole, and there were nine songs.

Shirley's work on the text has not been much praised, and indeed it would be difficult to find great felicity in his words. But if he was responsible for the general planning (as 'invented' on the title-page lets us assume that he was), his achievement was considerable. The multiplicity of anti-masques might indeed have been dull, but Shirley has avoided that first by his method of presentation through Fancy and his associates, and then by the variety of material. After Fancy and the rest have themselves danced, he proceeds to a series of dances from common life, centred on a tavern-scene. Then a topical touch is introduced with the projectors' anti-masque, harmless in its satire because these would-be monopolists are crazed inventors of impossibilities. After a brief return to the tavern, there are anti-masques of bird-mimicry,[1] of a merchant with thieves and officers of the law, of nymphs and satyrs and huntsmen, of dotterels and their catchers, and then suddenly an anti-masque of Don Quixote and Sancho Panza. This is the second literary reference of the anti-masques, for the fourth projector has been compared to a 'chimera out of Rabelais'. More ordinary country pastimes are

---

[1] One wonders if the Owl, mocked by the other birds, was a caricature of Prynne.

returned to in the appearance of four bowlers. But Fancy and the rest are chastened and driven away by the music that heralds the entrance of the masque-presenters. Nevertheless, the note of anti-masque returns when various common persons who have been associated with the preparations for the masque show themselves before the revels begin, and insist on seeing the entertainment: this glimpse of court-life behind the scenes takes us back to many an Elizabethan and Jacobean play, perhaps most especially to the court-scenes of Fletcher, who knew, and could display, the disorder behind the ceremony. There is an irony too in this sudden incursion of the common people. *The Triumph of Peace* was out of key with general feeling in the country, and here was a glimpse of a world that did not belong to the court: for the moment the incursion could be taken as a harmless jest.

But the most impressive moment comes at the end. *Comus* always apart, it is doubtful whether there is a more striking termination in masque-literature than the appearance of Amphiluche here. At what hour the performance ended we cannot know, yet the idea that the night was done, that the relentless beauty of a new half-light was banishing night-splendour, not only gave a fitting termination to this most elaborate of all masques but, perhaps again with unconscious irony, splendidly foreran the coldness of common day that would come to the court in a few years' time.

Note

Since this introduction was written (in 1962), our knowledge of the performance of *The Triumph of Peace* has been considerably added to by Murray Lefkowitz's article 'The Longleat Papers of Bulstrode Whitelock; New Light on Shirley's *Triumph of Peace*', *Journal of the American Musicological Society*, XVIII (1965), 42–60. The records preserved at Longleat include the names of the singers and musicians, and several diagrams showing the arrangement of singers and musicians at some key-moments in the performance. Mr Lefkowitz announces that he will publish an edition of *The Triumph of Peace* in a volume to be called *Three Caroline Masques*.

[DRAMATIS PERSONAE

Presenters of the Anti-masques:

Opinion	Confidence	Novelty	Admiration
Fancy	Jollity	Laughter	

Persons in the Anti-masques ii–xii:

Master of the Tavern	Two Thieves
His Wife	A Constable
Servants	Officers
Maquerelle	Four Nymphs
Two Wenches	Three Satyrs
Two Wanton Gamesters	Four Huntsmen
A Gentleman	Three Dotterels
Four Beggars	Three Dotterel-catchers
Six Projectors	A Windmill
An Owl	A Fantastic Knight
A Crow	His Squire
A Kite	A Country Gentleman
A Jay	His Servant
A Magpie	Four Bowlers
A Merchant	

Presenters of the Masque:

Irene	Eunomia	Dice	Genius

Masquers: Sixteen Sons of Peace, Law and Justice

Persons in Anti-masque xiii:

A Carpenter	An Embroiderer's Wife
A Painter	A Feather-maker's Wife
One of the Black Guard	A Property-man's Wife
A Tailor	Two Guards
The Tailor's Wife	

The Figure that ends it all: Amphiluche

Singers and Musicians.]

THE TRIUMPH OF PEACE

A MASQUE
PRESENTED BY THE FOUR HONOURABLE
HOUSES OR INNS OF COURT,
BEFORE THE KING AND QUEEN'S MAJESTIES,
IN THE BANQUETING HOUSE AT WHITEHALL,
FEBRUARY THE THIRD, 1633
INVENTED AND WRITTEN BY JAMES SHIRLEY,
OF GRAY'S INN, GENT.

—Primum
Hunc Arethusa mihi—

*   *   *

To the Four Equal and Honourable Societies,
the Inns of Court

I want words to express your cheerful and active desires, to present your duties to their royal Majesties, in this masque; to celebrate, by this humble tender of your hearts and services, the happiness of our kingdom, so blest in the present government, and never so rich in the possession of so many and great pledges of their parents' virtue, our native Princes.

Your clear devotions already offered, and accepted, let not me want an altar for my oblation to you. This entertainment, which took life from your command, and wanted no motion or growth it could derive from my weak fancy, I sacrifice again to you, and under your smile to the world. Let it not repent you to look upon what is the second time made your own, and, with it, the heart of the sacrificer, infinitely bound to acknowledge your free and noble souls, that have left no way for a poet to satisfy his ambition how to thank you, but with thinking he shall never be able to satisfy it.

I dare not rack my preface to a length: proceed to be yourselves (the ornament of our nation), and when you have leisure to converse with imaginations of this kind, it shall be an addition to your many favours, to read these papers and oblige, beside the seals of your other encouragement,

The humblest of your honourers,
JAMES SHIRLEY.

282

The Masque of the Gentlemen of the Four Honourable Societies or Inns of Court

At Ely and Hatton Houses, the gentlemen and their assistants met, and in this manner prepared for the Court.

The Anti-masques were ushered by a Hornpipe and a Shawm, riding in coats and caps of yellow taffeta, spotted with silver, their feathers red, their horses led by men in coats of blue taffeta (their wings red, and part of their sleeves yellow), caps and feathers; all the Torchbearers in the same habit appointed to attend and give plentiful light to the whole train.

Fancy, in a suit of several-coloured feathers, hooded; a pair of bats' wings on his shoulders, riding alone as sole presenter of the Anti-masques.

After him rode Opinion and Confidence together; Opinion in an old-fashioned doublet of black velvet and trunk hose, a short cloak of the same with an antique cape, a black velvet cap pinched up, with a white fall, and a staff in his hand; Confidence in a slashed doublet parti-coloured, breeches suitable with points at knees, favours upon his breast and arm; a broad-brimmed hat, tied up on one side, banded with a feather; a long lock of hair, trimmed with several-coloured ribbons; wide boots, and great spurs with bells for rowels.

Next rode Jollity and Laughter; Jollity in a flame-coloured suit, but tricked like a morris-dancer, with scarfs and napkins, his hat fashioned like a cone, with a little fall; Laughter in a long side-coat of several colours, laughing vizards on his breast and back, a cap with two grinning faces, and feathers between.

Then followed variety of antic music, after which rode six Projectors, one after another, their horses led by Torchbearers.

The first a jockey with a bonnet on his head, upon the top of it a whip; he seeming much to observe and affect a bridle which he had in his hand.

The second a country fellow in a leather doublet and grey trunk hose, a wheel with a perpetual motion on his head, and in his hand a flail.

The third a grim philosophical-faced fellow in his gown (furred, and girdled about him), a furnace upon his head, and in his hand a lamp.

The fourth in a case of black leather, vast to the middle and round on the top, with glass eyes, and bellows under each arm.

The fifth a physician, on his head a hat with a bunch of carrots, a capon perched upon his fist.

The sixth like a seaman, a ship upon his head, and holding a line and plummet in his hand.

Next these rode so many Beggars in timorous looks and gestures, as pursued by two Mastiffs that came barking after them.

Here variety of other antic music, counterfeiting the voices of birds; and after these rode a Magpie, a Crow, a Jay, and a Kite, in a quadrangular figure, and in the midst an Owl. These were followed by three Satyrs, two abreast and one single, sided with Torchbearers. Then three Dotterels in the same manner and attendance.

After these a Windmill, against which a fantastic Knight with his lance and his Squire, armed, seemed to make their attempts.

These moving forward in ridiculous show and postures, a Drummer followed on horseback, in a crimson taffeta coat, a white hat and feather, tipped with crimson, beating two kettle-drums.

Then fourteen Trumpeters, in crimson satin coats, white hats and feathers, and rich banners.

The Marshal followed these, bravely mounted, attended with ten Horse and forty Foot, in coats and hose of scarlet trimmed with silver lace, white hats and feathers, their truncheons tipped with silver: these upon every occasion moving to and fro, to preserve the order of their march and restrain the rudeness of people, that in such triumphs are wont to be insolent and tumultuary.

After these an hundred Gentlemen, gloriously furnished and gallantly mounted, riding two and two abreast, every Gentleman having many Pages, richly attired, and a Groom to attend him.

Next after these a Chariot drawn by four horses, two and two together, richly furnished and adorned with gold and silver, the Charioteer in a Polonian coat of green cloth of silver. In this were advanced Musicians like priests and sibyls, sons and daughters of Harmony, some with coronets, other with wreaths of laurel and myrtle, playing upon their lutes; three Footmen on each side in blue satin wrought with silver, and every one a flambeau in his hand.

In the next Chariot, of equal glory, were placed on the lowest stairs four in sky-coloured taffeta robes seeded with stars, mantles ash-coloured, adorned with fringe and silver lace, coronets with stars upon their heads. In a seat a little more elevate sat Genius and Amphiluche.

On the highest seat of this Chariot sat the three Hours or heavenly sisters, Irene, Dice and Eunomia, all whose habits shall be described in their proper places; this Chariot attended as the former.

After these came the four Triumphals or Magnificent Chariots, in which were mounted the Grand Masquers, one of the four Houses in every Chariot, seated within an half-oval, with a glorious canopy over

their heads, all bordered with silver fringe, and beautified with plumes of
feathers on the top: 100

> The first Chariot silver and orange;
> The second silver and watchet;
> The third silver and crimson;
> The fourth silver and white.

All after the Roman form, adorned with much embossed and carved 105
works, and each of them wrought with silver and his several colour. They
were mounted on carriages, the spring-trees, pole and axle-trees, the
Charioteer's seat and standers, wheels, with the fellies, spokes and naves,
all wrought with silver and their several colour.

They were all drawn with four horses a-front, after the magnificent 110
Roman Triumphs, their furniture, harness, head-stall, bits, reins and
traces, chamfron, cronet, petronel and barb of rich cloth of silver, of
several works and colours answerable to the linings of the Chariots.

The Charioteers in Polony-coats of the same colour of the Chariots,
their caps, feathers and buskins answerable.   115

The two out-horses of every Chariot led by two men in habits wrought
with silver and conformable to the colour of the other furniture, four
Footmen on either side of every Chariot, in rich habits also wrought with
silver, answerable to the rest, every one carrying a flambeau in his hand.

Between every of these Chariots four Musicians, in their robes and 120
garlands, were mounted, riding two abreast, attended with Torchbearers.

The habit of the Masquers gave infinite splendour to this solemnity,
which more aptly shall be expressed in his place.

This Masque was presented in the Banqueting House at Whitehall before
the King and Queen's Majesties and a great assembly of Lords and Ladies 125
and other persons of quality, whose aspect, sitting on the degrees prepared
for that purpose, gave a great grace to this spectacle, especially being all
richly attired.

At the lower end of the room opposite to the State was raised a stage
with a descent of stairs in two branches landing into the room. This base- 130
ment was painted in rustic work.

The border of the front and sides that enclosed all the Scene had first a
ground of arbour-work intermixed with loose branches and leaves, and in
this was two niches, and in them two great figures standing in easy
postures in their natural colours, and much bigger than the life. The one, 135
attired after the Grecian manner, held in one hand a sceptre and in the

other a scroll, and a picked antique crown on his head; his cuirass was of
gold richly enchased, his robe blue and silver, his arms and thighs bare,
with buskins enriched with ornaments of gold, his brown locks long and
curled, his beard thick but not long; and his face was of a grave and jovial 14
aspect. This figure stood on a round pedestal, feigned of white marble,
enriched with several carvings; above this in a compartment of gold was
written MINOS. The figure on the other side was in a Roman habit,
holding a table in one hand and a pen in the other, and a white bend or
diadem about his head. His robe was crimson and gold, his mantle yellow 14
and silver, his buskins watchet trimmed with silver, his hair and beard
long and white with a venerable aspect; standing likewise on a round
pedestal answerable to the other. And in the compartment over him was
written NUMA. Above all this in a proportionate distance hung two great
festoons of fruits in colours, which served for finishing to these sides. The 15
upper part in manner of a large frieze was adorned with several comparti-
ments with draperies hanging down, and the ends tied up in knots, with
trophies proper to feasts and triumphs, composed of masquing vizards and
torches. In one of the lesser compartments was figured a sharp-sighted
eye, and in the other a golden yoke; in the midst was a more great and rich 15
compartment on the sides of which sat naked children in their natural
colours, with silver wings, in action of sounding golden trumpets, and in
this was figured a *Caduceus* with an olive-branch; all which are hieroglyphics of Peace, Justice and Law.

A curtain being suddenly drawn up, the Scene was discovered, repre- 16
senting a large street with sumptuous palaces, lodges, porticos, and
other noble pieces of architecture, with pleasant trees and grounds.
This, going far from the eye, opens itself into a spacious place adorned
with public and private buildings seen afar off, representing the Forum
or Piazza of Peace. Over all was a clear sky with transparent clouds 16
which enlightened all the Scene.

The spectators having entertained their eyes awhile with the beauty
and variety of this Scene, from one of the sides of the street enters
Opinion, etc.

      Enter Opinion. Confidence meets him. They salute.   1?

Confidence. Most grave Opinion!
Opinion.   Confidence, most welcome!
  Is Fancy come to Court?

Confidence.   Breaking his way
  Thorough the guard.   175
Opinion.   So violent?
Confidence.   With jests
  Which they are less able to resist:
  He'll crack a halbert with his wit.
Opinion.   A most   180
  Strong Fancy, yet we ha' known a little engine
  Break an ingenious headpiece. But your master—
Confidence. Companion, sir. Fancy will keep no servants,
  And Confidence scorns to wait.
Opinion.   Cry mercy, sir.   185
  But is this gentleman, this Signor Fancy,
  So rare a thing, so subtile as men speak him?
Confidence. He's a great prince of th' air, believe it, sir,
  And yet a bird of night.
Opinion.   A bird!   190
Confidence.   Between
  An owl and bat, a quaint hermaphrodite,
  Begot of Mercury and Venus, Wit and Love.
  He's worth your entertainment.
Opinion.   I am most   195
  Ambitious to see him, he is not
  So nimble as I wish him. Where's my wife,
  My Lady Novelty?
                  Enter Lady Novelty.

Novelty.   Your wife? You might   200
  Have fram'd a newer word. They can but call
  Us so i' th' country.
Opinion.   No exception,
  Dear Madam Novelty, I must prepare you
  To entertain a gentleman. Where's Admiration,   205
  Our daughter?
                  Enter Admiration.

Admiration.   Here, sir. What gay man is this?
Opinion. Please you honour us, and bring in your friend, sir.
Confidence. I'll do 't, but he prevents me.   210

287

Enter Fancy, Jollity and Laughter.

Opinion.   Sir, I am ignorant
  By what titles to salute you, but y'are welcome to Court.
Fancy. Save yourself, sir. Your name's Opinion?
Opinion. And yours Fancy?
Fancy.   Right.
Jollity.   Mine Jollity.
Laughter. Mine Laughter, ha, ha, ha.
Novelty. Here's a strange shape.
Admiration.   I never saw the like.
Fancy. I come to do you honour with my friends here,
  And help the Masque.
Opinion.   You'll do a special favour.
Fancy. How many Anti-masques ha' they? Of what nature?
  For these are Fancies that take most; your dull
  And phlegmatic inventions are exploded;
  Give me a nimble Anti-masque.
Opinion.   They have none, sir.
Laughter. No Anti-masque? I'd laugh at that, i' faith.
Jollity. What make we here? No Jollity?
Fancy.   No Anti-masque!
  Bid 'em down with the Scene, and sell the timber,
  Send Jupiter to grass, and bid Apollo
  Keep cows again, take all their gods and goddesses
  (For these must farce up this night's entertainment),
  And pray the Court may have some mercy on 'em,
  They will be jeer'd to death else for their ignorance.
  The soul of wit moves here, yet there be some,
  If my intelligence fail not, mean to show
  Themselves jeer-majors; some tall critics have
  Planted artillery and wit-murderers.
  No Anti-masque! Let 'em look to 't.
Opinion.   I have heard, sir,
  Confidence made them trust you'd furnish 'em.
  I fear they should have made their address earlier
  To your invention, but your brain's nimble.

288

Pray, for the expectation that's upon 'em,
Lend them some witty Fancies, set some engines
In motion, that may conduce to the design.
I am their friend against the crowd that envy 'em,   250
And since they come with pure devotions
To sacrifice their duties to the King
And Queen, I wish 'em prosper.
Fancy.   You have charm'd me,
I'll be their friend to-night, I have a Fancy   255
Already.
Laughter. Let it be ridiculous.
Confidence. And confident.
Jollity.   And jolly.
Fancy.   The first Anti-masque   260
We will present ourselves in our own persons,
What think you on 't? Most grave Opinion,
You shall do well to lead the dance, and give it
Authority with your face; your Lady may
Admire what she finds new.   265
Novelty.   I shall applaud
The Novelties.
Admiration.   And I admire.
Fancy.   They tumble,
My skull's too narrow.   270
Laughter.   Now his Fancies caper.
Fancy. Confidence, wait you upon Opinion,
Here Admiration, there Novelty,
This is the place for Jollity and Laughter,
Fancy will dance himself too.   275

[Anti-masque i] *The first Anti-masque, the dance expressing the
natures of the Presenters.*

Fancy. How like you this device?
Opinion. 'Tis handsome, but—
Laughter.   Opinion will like nothing.   280
Novelty. It seems new.
Confidence.   'Twas bold.

Jollity.   'Twas jocund.
Laughter. Did I not do the fool well?
Admiration.   Most admirably.   285
Laughter. Nay, and the ladies do but take
  My part, and laugh at me, I am made, ha, ha.
Opinion. I could wish something, sir, of other nature
  To satisfy the present expectation.
Fancy. I imagine, nay, I'm not ignorant of proprieties   290
  And persons: 'tis a time of peace, I'll fit you,
  And instantly make you a representation
  Of the effects.
Opinion.   Of peace? I like that well.
Fancy. And since in nothing they are more express'd   29
  Than in good fellowship, I'll present you with
  A tavern.

*The Scene is changed into a tavern, with a flaming red lattice, several
drinking-rooms, and a back door, but especially a conceited sign and an
eminent bush.*   30

Novelty. A spick and span new tavern.
Admiration. Wonderful, here was none within two minutes.
Laughter. No such wonder, lady, taverns are quickly up. It is
  but hanging out a bush at a nobleman's door, or an alderman's
  gate, and 'tis made instantly.   30
Confidence. Will 't please you ladies to accept the wine?
Jollity. Well said, Confidence.
Novelty.   It will be new for ladies
  To go to th' tavern, but it may be a fashion.
  Follow me, Admiration.   3
Laughter.   And the fool:
  I may supply the absence of your fiddlers.
Jollity. If we can, let's leave Opinion behind us,
  Fancy will make him drunk.
            Exeunt to the tavern [all except Fancy and Opinion].   3

[Anti-masque ii] *Another Anti-masque of the Master of the Tavern,
            his Wife, and Servants. After these—*

[Anti-masque iii]   *A Maquerelle,*   ⎫ *These, having danced and*
              Two Wenches,   ⎪ *expressed their natures,*
              Two Wanton   ⎬ *go into the tavern. Then—* 320
                  Gamesters. ⎭

[Anti-masque iv]   *A Gentleman,* ⎫ *The Gentleman first danceth alone;*
              Beggars 4.   ⎬ *to him the Beggars; he bestows his*
                           charity; the cripples, upon his
                           going off, throw away their legs, 325
                           and dance [and exeunt].

Opinion. I am glad they are off. Are these effects of peace?
  Corruption, rather.
Fancy.   O the beggars show
  The benefit of peace.   330
Opinion.   Their very breath
  Hath stifled all the candles, poison'd the
  Perfumes. Beggars a fit presentment? How
  They cleave still to my nostril! I must tell you,
  I do not like such base and sordid persons,   335
  And they become not here.
Fancy.   I apprehend,
  If these distaste you, I can fit you with
  Persons more cleanly. What think you of Projectors?
Opinion. How, Projectors!   340
Fancy.   Here's one already.

[Anti-masque v]   *Enter a Jockey.*
                         This is a Jockey.
  He is to advance a rare and cunning bridle
  Made hollow in the iron part, wherein   345
  A vapour subtly convey'd, shall so
  Cool and refresh a horse, he shall ne'er tire.
  And now he falls to his pace.
                         Jockey dances.
Opinion.   This other?   350

      Enter a Country Fellow.

Fancy.   His habit speaks him
A country fellow, that has sold his acres
To purchase him a flail, which by the motion
Of a quaint wheel, shall without help of hands
Thresh corn all day, and now he lays about him.

The Country Fellow dances.

Enter another Projector.

This with a face philosophical and beard
Hath with the study of twenty years found out
A lamp, which plac'd beneath a furnace shall
Boil beef so thoroughly that the very steam
Of the first vessel shall alone be able
To make another pot above seethe over.
Opinion. A most scholastic project; his feet follow
The motions of his brain.

The third Projector dances.

[*Enter the fourth Projector.*]

But what thing's this?
A chimera out of Rabelais?
Fancy.   A new project,
A case to walk you all day under water,
So vast for the necessity of air,
Which, with an artificial bellows cool'd
Under each arm, is kept still from corruption.
With those glass eyes he sees, and can fetch up
Gold, or whatever jewels ha' been lost,
In any river o' the world.

The fourth Projector dances.
Opinion.   Strange water-rat!

Enter another Projector.

Fancy. This grave man, some years past, was a physician,
A Galenist, and parcel Paracelsus,
Thriv'd by diseases, but quite lost his practice,
To study a new way to fatten poultry

With scrapings of a carrot, a great benefit
To th' commonwealth.

The fifth Projector dances.

Opinion.   He will deserve a monument.

Enter the sixth Projector.   390

Fancy. This is a kind of seagull too, that will
Compose a ship to sail against the winds.
He'll undertake to build a most strong castle
On Goodwin Sands, to melt huge rocks to jelly,
And cut 'em out like sweetmeats with his keel,   395
And thus he sails.

[*The sixth Projector dances.*]

All the Projectors dance after their Anti-masque. Then—

[Anti-masque vi] *Maquerelle,* ⎱ *return as from the tavern. They*
            Wenches, ⎰ *dance together. The gallants are* 400
            Gentlemen ⎰ *cheated, and left to dance in, with a*
            drunken repentance.

Opinion. I know not, sir, how this may satisfy,
But might we be beholding to your Fancy
For some more quaint variety, some other   405
Than human shapes, would happily delight
And reach the expectation. I ha' seen
Dainty devices in this kind, baboons
In quellios, and so forth.
Fancy.   I can furnish you.   410
Opinion. Fancy will much oblige us.
Fancy.   If these objects
Please not, Fancy can present a change.
What see you now?

[Anti-masque vii] *The Scene becomes a woody landscape with low* 415
            grounds proper for hunting, the furthest part
            more desert, with bushes and by-ways repre-
            senting a place fit for purse-taking.
            In the furthest part of the Scene is seen an ivy-bush,
            out of which comes an Owl.   420

293

Opinion.   A wood, a broad-fac'd Owl,
An ivy-bush, and other Birds about her.
Fancy. These can imagination create. Silence, observe.

> *An Owl,*
> *A Crow,*
> *A Kite,* ⎫ *The Birds dance and wonder at the Owl.*   42⁵
> *A Jay,* ⎬ *When these are gone, enter—*
> *A Magpie.* ⎭

[Anti-masque viii] *A Merchant, a-horseback, with his portmanteau.*
                   Two Thieves set upon him and rob him: these by 43⁰
                   A Constable ⎫
                   and ⎬ *are apprehended and carried off.*
                   Officers ⎭ *Then—*

[Anti-masque ix] *Four Nymphs enter dancing with their javelins.*
                 Three Satyrs spy them, and attempt their persons; 43⁵
                         one of the Nymphs escapeth; a noise
                         of Hunters and their horns within,
                         as at the fall of a deer. Then enter—
                 Four Huntsmen ⎫ *These drive away the Satyrs, and*
                 and ⎬ *having rescued the Nymphs,* 44⁰
                 One Nymph. ⎭ *dance with them [and exeunt].*

Opinion. This all you will present?
Fancy.   You speak as if
  Fancy could be exhaust. Invention flows
  From an immortal spring: you shall taste other   44⁵
  Variety, nimble as thought. We change the scene.

[Anti-masque x] *A Landscape the Scene. And enter—*
                Three Dotterels,
                Three Dotterel-catchers.
Opinion. What are these?   45⁰
Fancy.   Dotterels. Be patient, and expect.

After the Dotterels are caught by several imitations, enters—

294

[Anti-masque xi] A *Windmill,* ⎫ *The Fantastic Adventurer with*
     A *Fantastic Knight* ⎮ *his lance makes many at-*
     and ⎬ *tempts upon the Windmill,* 455
     His Squire armed. ⎮ *which his Squire imitates. To*
         ⎭ *them enter—*

     A *Country Gentleman* ⎫ *These are assaulted by the*
     and ⎮ *Knight and his Squire, but*
     His Servant. ⎬ *they are sent off lame for* 460
        ⎭ *their folly.*

[Anti-masque xii]   *These having expressed their folly and gone off,*
      enter
     Four Bowlers, who show much variety of sport in
         their game and postures, and 465
         conclude the Anti-masque.

 Enter Confidence, Jollity, Laughter, Novelty, Admiration.

Opinion. Madam, accuse your absence—
Novelty.   Come, we know
 All your devices, sir; but I will have   470
 An Anti-masque of my own, in a new place too.
Opinion. Ha, what's the matter?
 Confidence, Jollity, Laughter, Admiration,
 And Madam Novelty, all drunk! These are
 Extremes indeed.   475
Admiration.   Admirable Opinion!
Confidence. Be confident.
Laughter.   And foolish.
Jollity.   I am as light now.
Fancy. Let 'em enjoy their Fancies.   480
Opinion.   What new change
 Is this? These strains are heavenly.
       Fancy and the rest go off fearfully.

The Anti-masquers being gone, there appears in the highest and fore-
most part of the heaven by little and little to break forth a whitish 485
Cloud, bearing a Chariot feigned of goldsmith's work, and in it sat
Irene, or Peace, in a flowery vesture like the spring, a garland of olives

on her head, a branch of palm in her hand, buskins of green taffeta,
great puffs about her neck and shoulders.

She sings. 4⟨

> *Irene.* Hence ye profane, far hence away,
> Time hath sick feathers while you stay.
> Is this delight
> For such a glorious night,
> Wherein two skies 4⟨
> Are to be seen,
> One starry, but an aged, sphere,
> Another here,
> Created new and brighter from the eyes
> Of King and Queen? 5⟨
> *Chorus.* Hence you profane, far hence away,
> Time hath sick feathers while you stay.

Song 2

> *Irene.* Wherefore do my sisters stay?
> Appear, appear, Eunomia, 5⟨
> 'Tis Irene calls to thee,
> Irene calls.
> Like dew that falls
> Into a stream,
> I'm lost with them 5⟨
> That know not how to order me.
> *Chorus.* See where she shines, O see,
> In her celestial gaiety,
> Crown'd with a wreath of stars to show
> The evening glory in her brow. 5⟨

Here out of the highest part of the opposite side came softly descending
another Cloud, of an orient colour, bearing a silver Chariot curiously
wrought, and differing in all things from the first, in which sat Eunomia,
or Law, in a purple satin robe, adorned with golden stars, a mantle of
carnation, laced and fringed with gold, a coronet of light upon her head, 5
buskins of purple, drawn out with yellow.

296

Song 3

Eunomia. Think not I could absent myself this night,
But Peace is gentle and doth still invite
Eunomia; yet shouldst thou silent be   525
The rose and lily which thou strowest
All the cheerful way thou goest
Would direct to follow thee.
Irene. Thou dost beautify increase,
And chain security with peace.   530
Eunomia. Irene fair, and first divine,
All my blessings spring from thine.
Irene. I am but wild without thee, thou abhorrest
What is rude, or apt to wound,
Canst throw proud trees to the ground,   535
And make a temple of a forest.
Eunomia. No more, no more, but join
Thy voice and lute with mine.
Both. The world shall give prerogative to neither.
We cannot flourish but together.   540
Chori. Irene enters like a perfum'd spring,
Eunomia ripens every thing,
And in the golden harvest leaves
To every sickle his own sheaves.

At this a third Cloud, of a various colour from the other two, begins to 545
descend toward the middle of the Scene with somewhat a more swifter
motion, and in it sat a person representing Dice, or Justice, in the
midst, in a white robe and mantle of satin, a fair long hair circled with a
coronet of silver pikes, white wings and buskins, a crown imperial in her
hand.   550

Song 4

Dice. Swiftly, O swiftly, I do move too slow!
What holds my wing from making haste
When every cloud sails by so fast?
    I heard my sisters' voice, and know   555
They have forsaken Heaven's bright gate,
    To attend another state

Of gods below.
Irene! Chaste Eunomia!

Irene, Eunomia. We,   560
 Dice, have stay'd expecting thee.
 Thou giv'st perfection to our glory,
 And seal to this night's story.
 Astrea, shake the cold dew from thy wing.
Eunomia. Descend.   565
Irene.   Descend.
Eunomia.   Descend, and help us sing
 The triumph of Jove's upper court abated
 And all the deities translated.
Chorus. The triumph of Jove's upper court abated 570
 And all the deities translated.
Eunomia. Now gaze, and when thy wonder will allow,
 Tell what thou hast beheld.
Dice.   Never, till now,
 Was poor Astrea blind, O strange surprise, 57[5]
 That too much sight should take away my eyes!
 Am I in earth or Heaven?
Irene.   What throne is that,
 On which so many stars do wait?
Dice. My eyes are bless'd again, and now I see 58[0]
  The parents of us three.
 'Tis Jove and Themis! Forward move,
 And sing to Themis, and to Jove.

Then the whole train of Musicians move in a comely figure toward the
King and Queen; and bowing to their State, this following ode is sung. 5[85]

Song 5

To you great King and Queen, whose smile
Doth scatter blessings through this isle,
  To make it best
  And wonder of the rest,   5
We pay the duty of our birth,
Proud to wait upon that earth
  Whereon you move,

Which shall be nam'd,
And by your chaste embraces fam'd,   595
The paradise of love.
Irene, plant thy olives here,
Thus warm'd, at once they'll bloom and bear;
Eunomia, pay thy light,
While Dice, covetous to stay,   600
Shall throw her silver wings away
To dwell within your sight.

The Scene is changed, and the Masquers appear sitting on the ascent of an hill cut out like the degrees of a theatre, and over them a delicious arbour with terms of young men, their arms converted into scrolls, and 605 *under their waists a foliage with other carvings to cover the joining of the term from the naked, all feigned of silver. These bore up an architrave, from which was raised a light covering arched, and interwoven with branches through which the sky beyond was seen.*

The Masquers were sixteen in number, the sons of Peace, Law and 610 *Justice, who sitting in a gracious but not set form, every part of the seats made a various composition, but all together tending to a pyramidal figure.*

Their habits was mixed, between the ancient and modern, their bodies carnation, the shoulders trimmed with knots of pure silver, and scallops 615 *of white and carnation; under them the labels of the same, the undersleeves white, and a puffed sleeve full of gathering, falling down to the elbow; about their waist was a small scallop, and a slender girdle; their under-bases were carnation and white, with labels as at their shoulders, and all this in every part was richly embroidered with pure silver; their* 620 *hats carnation, low-crowned, the brim double, and cut into several quarters lined with white, and all over richly embroidered, as the rest; about their hats were wreaths of olive, and plumes of white feathers, with several falls, the longest toward the back; their long stockings were white, with white shoes and roses.* 625

Beneath these a Genius or angelical person, with wings of several-coloured feathers, a carnation robe tucked up, yellow long hair bound with a silver coronet, a small white rod in his hand, white buskins, who descending to the stage, speaketh.

Genius. No foreign persons I make known
But here present you with your own,
The children of your reign, not blood;
Of age, when they are understood,
Not seen by faction or owl's sight,
Whose trouble is the clearest light;
But treasures to their eye, and ear,
That love good for itself, not fear.
O smile on what yourselves have made:
These have no form, no sun, no shade,
But what your virtue doth create;
Exalted by your glorious fate,
They'll tower to Heaven, next which they know
And wish no blessedness but you.
That very look into each eye   *The Masquers move.*
Hath shot a soul, I saw it fly.
Descend, move nimbly, and advance
Your joyful tribute in a dance.

*Here with loud music the Masquers descend and dance their entry to the
violins, which ended, they retire to the Scene, and then the Hours and
Chori again move toward the State and sing.*

Song 6

They that were never happy Hours
Till now, return to thank the powers
       That made them so.
       The Island doth rejoice,
And all her waves are echo to our voice,
Which in no ages past hath known
       Such treasures of her own.
Live, Royal Pair, and when your sands are spent
       With Heaven's and your consent,
     Though late, from your high bowers,
     Look down on what was yours,
For till old Time his glass hath hurl'd
And lost it, in the ashes of the world,

We prophesy you shall be read, and seen,   665
In every branch, a King or Queen.

*The song ended, and the Musicians returned, the Masquers dance their
main dance, after which they again retire to the Scene, at which they no
sooner arrive, but there is heard a great noise and confusion of voices
within, some crying ' They will come in', others ' Knock 'em down, call* 670
*the rest of the guard'; then a crack is heard in the works, as if there
were some danger by some piece of the machines falling. This continued
a little time, there rush in—*

[Anti-masque xiii] *A Carpenter,   The Tailor's Wife,
                    A Painter,   An Embroiderer's Wife,*   675
                    *One of the Black   A Feather-maker's Wife,
                        Guard,   A Property-man's Wife,
                    A Tailor,   [Two Guards].*

Carpenter. D'ye think to keep us out?
1 Guard. Knock her down.   680
Tailor. Knock down my wife! I'd see the tallest beef-eater on you
  all, but hold up his halbert in the way of knocking my wife down,
  and I'll bring him a button-hole lower.
Tailor's Wife. Nay, let 'em, let 'em, husband, at their peril.
2 Guard. Complain to my Lord Chamberlain.   685
Property Man's Wife. My husband is somewhere in the works. I'm
  sure I helped to make him an Owl and a Hobby-horse, and I see no
  reason but his wife may be admitted *in forma paperis*, to see as good
  a Masque as this.
Black Guard. I never saw one afore. I am one of the Guard, though 690
  of another complexion, and I will see 't now I am here, though I be
  turned out of the kitchen to-morrow for 't.
Painter. Aye, come, be resolute, we know the worst, and let us
  challenge a privilege. Those stairs were of my painting.
Carpenter. And that timber I set up: somebody is my witness.   695
Feather-maker's Wife. I am sure my husband sold 'em most of the
  feathers; somebody promised me a fall too if I came to Court, but
  let that pass.
Embroiderer's Wife. And mine embroidered two of the best habits.

301

What though we be no ladies, we are Christians in these clothes, 700
and the King's subjects, God bless us.

Tailor. Nay, now I am in, I will see a dance, though my shop-
windows be shut up for 't. Tell us—hum? d'ye hear? Do not they
laugh at us? What were we best to do? The Masquers will do no
feats as long as we are here. Be ruled by me. Hark, everyone, 'tis 705
our best course to dance a figary ourselves, and then they'll think
it a piece of the plot, and we may go off again with the more credit
(we may else kiss the porter's lodge for 't). Let's put a trick upon
'em in revenge, 'twill seem a new device too.

Omnes. Content.   710

Tailor. And the musicians knew but our mind now!

The violins play.

Hark, they are at it! Now for a lively frisk.   *They dance.*

Now let us go off cleanly, and somebody will think this was meant
for an Anti-masque.   715

*They being gone, the Masquers are encouraged by a song, to their
Revels with the Ladies.*

Song 7

> Why do you dwell so long in clouds
>   And smother your best graces?   720
> 'Tis time to cast away those shrouds
>   And clear your manly faces.
> Do not behave yourselves like spies
>   Upon the Ladies here;
> On even terms go meet their eyes,   725
>   Beauty and love shine there.
> You tread dull measures thus alone,
>   Not satisfy delight,
> Go kiss their hands, and make your own
>   With every touch more white.   730

*The Revels being past, the Scene is changed into a plain champaign
country which terminates with the horizon, and above a darkish sky,
with dusky clouds, through which appeared the new moon, but with a
faint light by the approach of the morning; from the furthest part of this
ground, arose by little and little a great vapour, which being come about 73*
the middle of the Scene, it slackens its motion, and begins to fall down-

ward to the earth from whence it came; and out of this rose another
Cloud of a strange shape and colour, on which sat a Young Maid, with
a dim torch in her hand. Her face was an olive-colour, so was her arms
and breast, on her head a curious dressing, and about her neck a string 740
of great pearl. Her garment was transparent, the ground dark blue, and
sprinkled with silver spangles, her buskins white, trimmed with gold.
By these marks she was known to be the forerunner of the morning,
called by the ancients Amphiluche, and is that glimpse of light which is
seen when the night is past, and the day not yet appearing. 745

Song 8

Amphiluche. In envy to the Night,
 That keeps such Revels here,
 With my unwelcome light
 Thus I invade her sphere. 750
  Proclaiming wars
 To Cynthia, and all her stars,
 That like proud spangles dress
  Her azure tress.
 Because I cannot be a guest, I rise 755
 To shame the Moon, and put out all her eyes.

Amphiluche ascending, the Masquers are called from their Revels by
other voices.
Song 9

 1. Come away, away, away, 760
  See the dawning of the day,
  Risen from the murmuring streams;
  Some stars show with sickly beams
  What stock of flame they are allow'd,
  Each retiring to a cloud. 765
  Bid your active sports adieu,
  The morning else will blush for you.

 2. Ye feather'd-footed Hours run
  To dress the chariot of the Sun;
  Harness the steeds, it quickly will 770
  Be time to mount the eastern hill.

3. The lights grow pale with modest fears,
   Lest you offend their sacred ears
   And eyes that lent you all this grace;
   Retire, retire to your own place.

4. And as you move from that bless'd Pair,
   Let each heart kneel, and think a prayer,
   That all, that can make up the glory
   Of good and great, may fill their story.

Amphiluche hidden in the Heavens, and the Masquers retired, the Scene closeth.

And thus concluded this Masque, which was, for the variety of the shows, and richness of the habits, the most magnificent that hath been brought to Court in our time.

The scene and ornament was the act of Inigo Jones Esquire, Surveyor of His Majesty's Works.

The composition of the music was performed by Mr. William Lawes and Mr. Simon Ives, whose art gave an harmonious soul to the otherwise languishing numbers.

FINIS

*　　*　　*

A speech to the King and Queen's Majesties, when they were pleased to honour the city with their presence, and gave a gracious command the former triumph should attend them.

> *Genius.* Most great and glorious princes, once more I
> Present to your most sacred Majesty
> The sons of Peace, who tender you, by me,
> Their joy-exalted heart, and humble knee;
> Happy in their ambition to wait,
> And pay their second duty to your state,
> Acknowledging no triumph but in you:
> The honour you have done them is so new
> And active in their souls that it must grow
> A part of them, and be immortal too.

304

These wonders you create, and every man   805
Receives as much joy as the island can;
Which shows you nearest Heaven, that can let fall
Unequal, yet a perfect bliss to all.
Dwell still within yourselves, for other place
Is strait and cannot circumscribe your grace,   810
Whilst men grow old with prayers for your bless'd reign,
Yet with your smiles shall be restor'd again.

THE TEXT

This masque presents a major textual problem, which has been sketched in Sir Walter Greg's article 'The Triumph of Peace: A Bibliographer's Nightmare' (The Library, ser. 5, 1 (September 1946), 113–26). The position as he outlined it is as follows: (1) the printer anticipated a large demand for the book, which was entered in the Stationers' Register on 24 January 1634 and was presumably to be ready by the time of the first performance; (2) the ordinances of the Stationers' Company limited the size of an edition to 1250 or 1500 copies; (3) the printer therefore set up two editions simultaneously, but in making up copies did not distinguish between the sheets of these two editions; (4) the formes properly constituting the 'second edition' were set up from copies of the 'first'; (5) in some instances type already set up for the 'first' was (illegally) used for the 'second'; (6) both 'editions' were subject to press-correction; (7) the demand was not exhausted by the two 'editions', and for a subsequent printing, called on the title-page 'The third Impression', standing type was once more to some extent used; (8) where standing type was not used, this edition was set up from already printed pages, although a manuscript source (or authorial correction) was certainly used as well; (9) there was a second issue of this third edition, containing a new speech by the Genius, delivered at the second performance.

The present editor cannot claim to have done more than the assembling of a text which takes note of Greg's findings. The text is here based on a photostat copy of the British Museum copy Ashley 1696, which includes three variant leaves (B3, C2, C3). This has been collated with a microfilm of the copy of 'The third Impression' in the Dyce Collection. In the Collation no attempt has been made to distinguish between the first two 'editions', but the symbols 'Qa', 'Qb' stand respectively for earlier and later readings (as far as it has been possible to decide on, or presume, a priority), whether in the separate printing of the first two 'editions' or as a result of proof-correcting, and 'Q3' indicates variant readings of the 'third edition'. 'Qab' indicates that for a particular reading no variant in the first two 'editions' has been traced. As Q3 readings have certainly a measure of authority, they have been freely admitted into the text wherever there is a case for regarding them as closer to the author's original (or perhaps revised) intention. The symbol 'Q' indicates a reading common to the Quartos.

When all available copies of the masque can be collated, it may be possible to approach a proper determination of the sequence of the variants which are known to exist and of others not so far traced. It will, however, be necessary to consider the following possibilities for each forme of the first two 'editions': (1) uncorrected state of Q 1, (2) corrected state of Q 1, (3) uncorrected state of Q 2 based on uncorrected state of Q 1, (4) corrected state of Q 2 based on uncorrected state of Q 1, (5) uncorrected state of Q 2 based on corrected state of Q 1, (6) corrected state of Q 2 based on corrected state of Q 1. This does not allow for the possibility of double proof-correcting, which Greg demonstrates took place in the first half-sheet. When, however, standing type was taken over for Q 2, it must have happened after the printing of the Q 1 forme was complete (Greg, p. 120). The possibility of authorial intervention at any stage will also have to be borne in mind. It should, moreover, be remembered that no extant copy of the volume is likely to represent *in toto* either Q 1 or Q 2. The possibilities for Q 3 need not be listed.

The Triumph of Peace has been three times reprinted since 1634: in the Gifford–Dyce edition of Shirley's *Dramatic Works and Poems* (1833), in Gosse's *James Shirley* in the Mermaid series (1888), and in H. A. Evans's *English Masques* (1897). These texts have been collated for the present edition: readings quoted from Gifford–Dyce are indicated by the symbol 'G'.

In the Quartos there is a use of roman and italic type for stage-directions, roman being employed especially when the direction is adjacent to one of the songs, which are in italic; roman is used for the opening descriptions of the procession and the scene.

COLLATION

Title By...Gent] Q a (*two lines*); By...Gent. | The Third Impression Q 3;
    By *James Shirley*, Gent Q 6.
Title *Primum...mihi*] Q b, 3; *one line* Q a.
18 oblige, beside] *This ed.*; *obliege beside*, Q; *oblige beside* G.
30 several-coloured] G; severall coloured Q.
35 and a] Q 3; a Q ab.
35 parti-coloured,] G; parti-coloured Q.
38 several-coloured] G; severall coloured Q.
43 laughing] Q; laughing, G.
48 bridle] Q b, 3; bride Q a.
59–60] Q 3; *not in* Q ab.
69 followed] Q 3; followeth Q ab.
73–4 ten Horse and] Q 3; *not in* Q ab.
80 many] Q 3; his two Q ab.
94 Dice] *so* Q 3 *throughout*; Diche Q ab *throughout*.
112 chamfron] G; Shaferon Q.
126 sitting] G; setting Q.
168 *street*] *This ed.*; streetes Q.
213] *This ed.*; ...to|Court Q; ...welcome|To...G.
214 Opinion?] *This ed.*; Opinion. Q.
215 Fancy?] *This ed.*; Fancy. Q.
220 *Admiration*] Q 3 (*Ad.*); *An.* Q ab.
230 Jollity?] *This ed.*; Iollity. Q.
232 sell] Q a, 3; fell Q b (*recorded* G).
242 Anti-masque!] G; Antimasque Q ab; Antimasque; Q 3.
244 them] Q ab; 'em Q 3.
274 the] Q b, 3; a Q a.
298–300] Q b; *A Taverne is discovered in the Scene.* Q a; *The Scene a Taverne.*
    Q 3.
306 you ladies] Q; you, ladies, G.
306 accept] Q b, 3; except Q a.
315 *all...Opinion*] G (*subs.*).
326 *and exeunt*] *This ed.*
339] *This ed.*; ...cleanly, | What... Q.
366 motions] Q ab; motion Q 3.
368] G (*subs.*).
398 *Then*—] Q 3 (*Then*); *The* Q ab.
423] *This ed.*; ...create, | Silence... Q.
442–7 *Opinion...enter*] Q ab; After these, Enter Q 3.

452 *are*]   Qab; be Q3.
454 *many*]   Q3; *not in* Qab.
456 *which his*]   Q3; his Qab.
456–61 *To them...folly.*]   Qab; *not in* Q3.
460 *they*]   *This ed.*
462–6]   Q3 (*continuing from 'imitates'* (line 456)); Bowlers, 4. Qab.
468 absence—]   G; absence, Q.
469–71 Come...too]   Q3; We know | All your devices sir Qab.
484 *Anti-masquers...gone*]   Qb, 3; Antimasques...past Qa.
501 you]   Q; ye G.
507 calls.]   G (*subs.*); calls, Q.
520 *carnation, laced*]   *This ed.*; carnation Lac'd, Q.
521 *yellow*]   Qb, 3; Yellow. This Chariot attended as the former. Qa.
532 blessings spring]   Qb, 3; blessing springs Qa.
570 *Chorus*]   G; CHOR. Q.
582 Themis!]   G (*subs.*); Themis Q.
598 warm'd, at once]   G; warme at once, Qa; warm'd at once, Qb; warm'd, at once, Q3.
603 *sitting*]   G; setting Q.
609 *was*]   Qb, 3; *not in* Qa.
611 *sitting*]   G; setting Q.
626–7 *several-coloured*]   G; *severall coloured* Q.
629 *descending*]   Qb, 3; *descended* Qa.
644 *The...move.*]   G; *opp. lines* 643–4 Q.
678 *Two Guards*]   *This ed.*
705 long as]   Q3; long Qab.
756 all]   Qa; *both* Qb, 3.
773 their]   Qa; *those* Qb, 3.
792–812]   Q3; *not in* Qab.
796 Majesty]   G; Maiesties Q3.
810 strait]   *This ed.*; streight Q3.

COMMENTARY

Title (motto)]   Greg provides evidence for believing that originally the printer set the motto in one line, and that, when instructed to set it in two (see following note), he removed the reference on the title-page to Shirley's membership of Gray's Inn, thus saving a line. By changes in leading, Q3 managed to reinsert the reference to the Inn.

Title (motto)]   Virgil, *Eclogues*, x, 1, has 'extremum hunc, Arethusa, mihi concede laborem': 'O grant me this last labour, Arethuse.' Shirley's motto is apparently a variation upon this, with 'first' (= most important) for 'last'. Shirley doubtless wanted the motto printed in two lines to separate his 'primum' from Virgil's words: see preceding note.

17 imaginations]   fancies.

25 Hornpipe, Shawm]   i.e. players of these: a hornpipe was a wind-instrument, a shawm an instrument of the oboe type.

27 wings]   pair of lateral projecting pieces on or near the shoulder.

35 fall]   here, a hanging cloth attached to the cap or hat.

35 slashed]   having vertical slits to show a contrasting lining.

36 suitable]   matching.

36 points]   tagged laces or cords.

36 favours]   things given as a mark of favour, e.g. ribbons, cockades.

37 banded with a feather]   with a feather encircling it.

41 tricked]   adorned.

42 side-coat]   outer coat.

48 affect]   be fond of.

53 case]   This was a sort of diving-suit: cf. line 372.

59–60]   Whitelock says that the beggars 'had their musick of keys and tongs, and the like, snapping, and yet playing in a consort before them. These Beggars were also mounted, but on the poorest leanest jades that could be gotten out of the dirt-carts or elsewhere' (Dyce).

62–3 a Magpie...an Owl]   'These', says Whitelock, 'were little boys put into covers of the shapes of those birds, rarely fitted, and sitting on small horses' (Dyce).

64 Dotterels]   a species of plover. They were said to be foolish and to be caught because they always mimicked what the fowler did.

66–7 Windmill, Knight, Squire]   an obvious reference to *Don Quixote*, whose First Part appeared in English translation in 1612.

73 Marshal]   This was Thomas Darrel of Lincoln's Inn, knighted the day after the performance at court.

78 insolent]   impertinent.

78 tumultuary]   disorderly.

79 furnished] decorated.

84 Polonian coat] *N.E.D.* gives 'Polony' (1818) as long coat or gown for young boys, with close-fitting body and loose skirt.

84 green cloth of silver] Cloth of silver is a tissue of threads, wires or strips of silver, generally interwoven with silk or wool (here perhaps green in colour); 'green cloth' is given as a kind of linen in *N.E.D.* (1769).

92 Genius] tutelary god connected with a place or institution: here, apparently, vaguely synonymous with '*angelical person*' (line 626).

92 Amphiluche] Greek *amphiluche nux*, morning-twilight (*Iliad*, VII, 433).

96 Triumphals] triumphal cars.

101–4 orange, watchet, crimson, white] Apparently each colour was appropriate to a particular Inn.

102 watchet] light blue.

106 his several colour] the colour special to the chariot: cf. lines 101–4.

107 spring-trees] bars or cross-pieces to which the ends of the traces are attached.

108 standers] upright supports.

108 fellies] outer circles of wheels.

108 naves] hubs.

111 furniture] caparison, trappings.

111 head-stall] part of bridle or halter that fits round the head.

112 chamfron] frontlet of a barded horse.

112 cronet] unidentified part of horse-armour.

112 petronel] here (apparently) the case for a pistol hanging at the horse's breast: commonly the term means the pistol thus carried.

112 barb] covering for horse's breast and flanks.

113 works] kinds of (ornamental) workmanship.

113 linings] apparently, contents.

126 degrees] steps.

129 State] raised platform for the royal seats.

130–1 basement] lowest portion of the structure.

131 in rustic work] i.e. giving the appearance of rough-hewn masonry.

137 picked] ornate.

142 compartiment] panel.

144 table] writing tablet.

144 bend] band.

155 eye, yoke] as emblems of vigilance and control: cf. lines 158–9.

158 *Caduceus*] the wand of Mercury.

163–5 *going...Peace*] Beyond the street represented in perspective, there is seen at the back of the stage the Forum of Peace.

166 *enlightened all the Scene*] Light shone through the transparent clouds.

178] i.e. less than they could resist actual violence.

181 engine] device, implement.

184 wait] be a servant.

187 subtile] (*a*) skilful; (*b*) tenuous: cf. next line.

203 No exception] Do not take exception.

210 prevents] anticipates.

230 What make we here?] What are we doing here?

235 farce up] fill out.

239 intelligence] information.

240 jeer-majors] leaders of jeering.

269–70] The 'Novelties' (line 267) are tumbling in my head, which is too narrow to contain them.

299 *conceited*] fanciful.

303–5] perhaps a topical reference.

307 Well said] well done.

318 *Maquerelle*] bawd.

336 become not] are not fitting.

346 subtly] here trisyllabic.

370 chimera out of Rabelais] monster such as one finds in Rabelais.

383 Galenist] follower of Galen, physician of second century A.D.

383 parcel Paracelsus] partly a follower of Paracelsus, Swiss scientist of fifteenth–sixteenth centuries. But Paracelsians and Galenists were opposed: the Projector would evidently have had it both ways.

406 happily] perhaps.

409 quellios] ruffs (Spanish *cuello*).

451 expect] wait.

460 *they*] It seems evident that it is the Knight and Squire who are worsted.

489 *puffs*] masses either of cloth gathered at the edges so as to look inflated, or of ribbons and feathers giving a similar effect.

517 *orient*] here rose-red, dawn-colour.

520 *carnation*] flesh-coloured, rose-pink.

521 *drawn out*] perhaps interwoven.

521 *yellow*] The reading in Qa seems to have been inserted from line 95, where it looks back to lines 87–8. The Chariot will not be so 'attended' in the masque.

541 *Chori.*] This may indicate that the choral songs were divided between two sections of the singers: cf. line 650.

545 *various*] different.

549 *pikes*] spikes, points.

605 *terms*] extremities, end-pieces.

616 *labels*] fillets, ribbons.

619 *under-bases*] here apparently equivalent to 'bases', plaited skirts reaching from waist to knee.

625 *roses*] rose-shaped knots worn on shoes.

630 foreign persons] strangers.

633–5] When seen properly, it will be evident that they are of full age, although factious spirits, light-blinded, cannot see them as such.

676–7 *Black Guard*] 'the meanest drudges in royal residences, who carried coals, etc.' (Gifford).

678 *Two Guards*] These speak at lines 680, 685, perhaps from outside the door.

681 beef-eater] well-fed menial (contemptuous).

687 Hobby-horse] doubtless used for the '*Merchant, a-horseback*' (line 429), perhaps also for the '*Fantastic Knight*' (line 454).

688 *paperis*] i.e. *pauperis*. Dyce points out that the mispronunciation was a common jest of the dramatists.

697 fall] Cf. line 35, with an obvious pun here.

706 figary] variant of fegary, vagary; here perhaps a malapropism for 'figure'.

708 porter's lodge] the place where servants were punished. But a vulgarism seems just avoided.

731–2 *champaign country*] level, open country.

756 all] i.e. the stars: '*both*' is manifestly a false emendation during printing.

773 their] i.e. the King's and Queen's: '*those*' seems a weakening.

789 *numbers*] verse.

792–812] On the occasion of the second performance this speech was presumably inserted in place of lines 630–47. Of the four Q3 copies containing the speech examined by Greg, two have it at the beginning, two at the end. Copies with this additional leaf he regards as a separate issue of Q3 (*Bibliography*, II, 634).

807–8] You resemble Heaven in blessing men in differing degrees yet giving to each the fullest blessing he is capable of receiving.

THE SPRING'S GLORY

BY THOMAS NABBES

Edited by John Russell Brown

INTRODUCTION

Thomas Nabbes's *The Spring's Glory* has probably never been performed. It was published in 1638 with the title-page:

THE
SPRINGS
GLORIE.

VINDICATING LOVE

by temperance against
the tenent,
Sine Cerere & Baccho friget Venus.
Moralized in a Maske.
With other Poems, Epigrams, Elegies, and
Epithalamiums of the Authors

THOMAS NABBES.

Among the miscellaneous poems was another masque with the title, *A Presentation Intended for the Prince his Highnesse on his Birth-day the 29 of May, 1638...*, but there is nothing to suggest so much as an 'intended' occasion for *The Spring's Glory*. Some copies included a dedication to Benedict, son of Nicholas Roberts, and the others an identical one to William, son of Peter Balle, but these brief formalities do not connect either masque with either recipient. Nor do commendatory verses, by 'C. G. Oxon.' and Robert Chamberlaine, offer any further hint of performance, speaking only of Nabbes's 'learn'd poesy' and his 'wingèd raptures, rhapsodies and lays', as if the contents were meant to be read, and there an end. All this marks *The Spring's Glory* apart from other masques, for they were customarily published with proud descriptions of the place, time and honour of their enactment. And in these matters Nabbes was unlikely to be reticent:[1] his published plays have statements about performances on their title-pages, and *The Unfortunate Mother*, which was 'Never acted: but set down according

[1] This point was made by G. E. Bentley in *The Jacobean and Caroline Stage*, IV, 940.

317

to the intention of the Author', was provided with explanatory dedication and proem, and commendatory verses by other hands which condemn the actors for lack of judgment in rejecting the tragedy.

The author was probably the Thomas Nabbes 'of co. Worcester, pleb...aged 16' who matriculated at Oxford from Exeter College on 3 May 1621. There is no record of his gaining a degree, but an autobiographical poem implies that he became 'a servant' to a lord in the country during which time he wrote this poem and probably others in the 1638 volume. It has been suggested that *The Spring's Glory* was also composed while he was in this service,[1] but when he became a playwright Nabbes lived in London and we may believe that the masque was written after the move. His 'Encomium on the leaden Steeple at Worcester' included among the collected verses was apparently written in 1628, the date of the steeple's restoration, and here Nabbes described himself as if still resident in the neighbourhood. But his three comedies set in London mark a change, having many references to streets, buildings, suburbs, behaviour and manners that speak for his first-hand knowledge of the city. *Covent Garden* was the first of these, acted in the 1632–3 season by the Queen's Men at the Phoenix or Cockpit. It was succeeded the next year by *Tottenham Court* at Salisbury Court, and this theatre also presented his 'Moral Masque', *Microcosmos*, in 1637. The Queen's Men produced *Hannibal and Scipio* 'at their Private house in Drury Lane' in 1635, and the King and Queen's Young Company a further London comedy, *The Bride*, in 1638. We know for certain that by now Nabbes was living in the parish of St Giles in the Fields —the parish of the Phoenix Theatre—for the registers of the church record the christening of his daughter, Bridget, on 27 May 1638. Further entries tell of Nabbes's own burial on 6 April 1641, and those of Bridget and his son William, in the following two years: his widow, who was also called Bridget, received poor relief in 1642.[2]

The links between *The Spring's Glory* and the years of Nabbes's residence in London are many and various. The notes of this new edition show only a few of the idiomatic phrases it has in common

---

[1] G. E. Bentley, *op. cit.* p. 939.   [2] Cf. G. E. Bentley, *op. cit.* pp. 928–9.

with the plays[1] and they draw attention to direct and oblique references to the city.[2] Its central theme is a simplification—a rewriting rather than a first draft—of that of *Microcosmos*, performed in 1637. And there are correspondences between *The Spring's Glory* and *A Presentation* intended for performance in May 1638: both seem to be indebted for minor details to Middleton's *Inner Temple Masque* (1619)[3] and both call for the same '*Symphony of Music with chirping of Birds, singing of Nightingales and Cuckoos*'.[4] This kind of music obviously fascinated Nabbes in his later years: he alludes to it in *Microcosmos*, Act III, when Sensuality promises:

> ...the airy choristers
> Shall strain their throats by art,

and he elaborated upon its cunning in his Elegy prefixed to Thomas Beedome's *Poems Divine and Humane* of 1641:

> No air doth move
> To make the boughs each other kiss in love,...
> Upon the branches perch no airy choirs,
> Whose untaught music art itself admires,
> And by an imitation of those notes,
> Strain'd from the slender organs of their throats
> Adds to itself perfection, and thereby
> Shows nature's weak to artful industry.[5]

Its publication, theme, topographical references, current phrases, indebtedness, and symphony of bird-song, all suggest that *The Spring's Glory* was written in London in 1637, or early 1638.

Perhaps it was conceived as a 'blank' masque, one written as a specimen or to be adapted to almost any occasion as required. It has many customary features: debates among mythological and 'low' characters; a representation of times of the year in due order; elaborate settings; an anti-masque dance of Beggars; the presentation of Spring, with appropriate music, song and dance, to deliver a

---

[1] See notes to lines 135, 149–57, 198–9.
[2] See notes to lines 133, 149–57, 162, 174, 188.
[3] So Enid Welsford, *The Court Masque* (1927), p. 212; see lines 149–57, note, in this edition.
[4] *A Presentation*, F 4ᵛ, s.d. and *The Spring's Glory*, lines 221, 236–9, 246–9, and 285–7.   [5] *Works*, ed. A. H. Bullen (1887), II, 277.

judgment. But it lacks two important features, which Nabbes did not omit from *A Presentation*: at her discovery Spring has no attendant masquers, and she delivers no compliments or gifts. This masque concludes with an Epilogue that might be addressed to any company of spectators at any spring-time occasion. Yet it is adaptable: appropriate masquers and a few speeches would transform *The Spring's Glory* into a celebration suitable for a wedding, anniversary, home-coming or visit, or a local seasonal holiday.

But Nabbes might have written in general terms because he intended this entertainment for a public theatre. There are numerous signs that dramatists were considering ways of adapting the court masque for a wider audience. Nabbes's own *Microcosmos* has elaborate stage-settings in which personifications of the Elements, Complexions, and Five Senses variously '*express themselves in their differences*' (II, S.D.); in conclusion, Love is '*discovered*' on '*a glorious throne*' with Justice, Temperance, Prudence and Fortitude, and with '*divers gloriously habited and alike, as* Elysii incolae; *who . . . place themselves in a figure for the dance*'. Dekker's *The Sun's Darling*, which was probably performed a year or two later, is another full-length, moral play with songs and dances, including the popular '*Morris*' (II, i, 82 ff.) and a gay spectacle of '*Country-fellows and Wenches*' (III, iv, S.D.); in its last scene, '*The Masquers [are] discovered*' immediately before the Sun enters '*above*' to give judgment. In the words of its title-page of 1620, *The World Tossed at Tennis* by Middleton and Rowley was an earlier attempt at a 'Courtly Masque' for presentation at 'divers times' by the Prince's Men; it had an 'Induction . . . prepared for his Majesty's Entertainment at Denmark House', but the action presents its own '*King*' and a prologue explains that its performance was an innovation on a public stage. Heywood's *Love's Mistress, or the Queen's Masque*, published in 1636, is another occasional piece which was subsequently 'Publicly Acted' by the 'Queen's Comedians, at the Phoenix in Drury-Lane'. This is a mythological play rather than a masque, but there are dances for Swains and Country Wenches, and for 'Love's Contrarieties'—that is, for king with beggar, young man with old woman, and '*Lean man*' with '*Fat Woman*' (III, i); immediately before the 'moral' is described and the action completed, there is a '*Dance of Cupid, Psyche, the gods and goddesses*'. Nabbes's *The Spring's Glory* is far briefer than any of these, but even in this there was some precedent: it might have formed part of a longer public entertainment, like the short, self-contained and generalized masque of Time which is the fourth of John Fletcher's *Four Plays in One*.[1]

If we consider these contemporary experiments, we may judge *The Spring's Glory* to be a more original work than it appears at first. The direction:

The Spring leads them a measure; after which they retire back to the scene
(lines 288–9)

seems to imply that the final dance involves the mythological persons already presented, in the place of the usual masquers, and so becomes an expression of the 'moderate' harmony that can be achieved between Venus, Cupid, Ceres and Bacchus. This would provide a more obviously unified dramatic performance than the regular masque form, for in this the earlier interests tend to be lost in the entirely new and more glorious spectacle that properly accompanied the revelation of the final masquers.

There is a *naïveté* in *The Spring's Glory* which must make us hesitate before claiming Nabbes as an original artist. Its versification, vocabulary and sentence-structure are sometimes weak; and it is a drastic simplification of the more elaborate treatment of the same theme in *Microcosmos* to have Venus boasting of both the rape of Proserpine and the spiritual basis of true love, and to have Spring represent both the pleasures of her season and the virtues of a 'platonic' love and 'temperance'. But boldness is an innovator more powerful than discretion, as fools are sometimes more precipitous than angels, and Nabbes's other works have plenty of originality. An Epilogue boasts that *Covent Garden* does not have a wedding or disguise, but the action of *Tottenham Court*, his next play, depends on both. His *Hannibal* attempted something like the dignity of Jonson's unfashionable and unsuccessful tragedies. *The*

---

[1] Shirley's *Contention for Honour and Riches*, published in 1633, is a morality play with a single concluding dance, but its extreme brevity and generalized theme may associate it with more obvious attempts to find a place for the masque in public theatres.

Bride was a citizen play performed at a small 'private' theatre, almost certainly designed as a novel attempt to draw a less sophisticated audience than usual during the slack weeks of the law vacation. In 1638 Nabbes undertook hack-work in compiling a continuation of Knolles's *Turkish History*, and yet about the same time he must have been writing his *The Unfortunate Mother* which was sufficiently against current formulas to be refused by the actors.

The Spring's Glory is fresh and lively: it has pace, and a persistent wit in the prose passages; and when Lent claims that he does Venus 'more credit' than Christmas or Shrovetide, it manages a significant surprise.[1] To these qualities we must add a measure of originality in contriving either a 'blank' masque adaptable to many occasions, or a masque for public entertainment.

[1] Cf. the treatment of Fasting Day in Middleton's *The Inner Temple Masque*.

[DRAMATIS PERSONAE

Venus   Ceres
Cupid   Bacchus

Christmas
Shrovetide
Lent

An Anti-Masque of Beggars

Spring]

THE SPRING'S GLORY,

vindicating love by temperance against the
tenet, 'Sine Cerere et Baccho friget Venus',
moralized in a masque.

* * *

*Within an arch of agreeable workmanship, a scene of winter presents
itself, the trees and earth covered with snow, and in the middle thereof
a prospect of a fair house as the mansion of Christmas.*

Venus and Cupid descend.

Venus. Without good meat and drink must Venus freeze?
Must I derive my flames and my desire
From Ceres and from Bacchus? shall the fire
That burns in hearts and pays me solemn rites
Kindle from fullness and gorg'd appetites?
It shall not, son. Learn of thy sea-born mother
Never to borrow power from any other.
The virtue that's our own, who dares to claim?
Are not both gods and men by thy sure aim,
When at their bosoms thou direct'st a dart,
Wounded with passion past the cure of art?
Did not the god of medicine himself want,
When he was struck by thee, a sovereign plant
To heal his hurt? nor did it rancour by
Abundance of choice cates and luxury?
'Twas merely thy effect. Why then should we
To Ceres' or to Bacchus' deity
Assign our rights?
Cupid.   In part we must; for they
Are aiders in our work, and therefore may
Share in the attributes of power. If wine
Did not the spirits and the blood refine,

Making them warm and active, I should throw
My shafts at rocks of ice, and from my bow
The winged arrows of desire would fly
With empty and successless battery.   30
If Ceres' bounties flow'd not, where should I
Find any flame to light my torches by?
Fullness and ease assist me more than all
The helps I have besides.
Venus.   And therefore shall   35
They be preferr'd? Thou art a foolish boy.
Their base effects are lust; they love to joy
In what is sensual only. Our pure heat
Borrows no activeness from drink or meat;
It moves more in the soul. God Bacchus shall   40
Have his due attributes, and Ceres call
The plough, crook'd sickle, flail and many more
Her own admir'd inventions, and the store
She gathers for men's use. But should the mind
Make these her only objects, what a blind   45
And dangerous issue of effects would grow
From such a seed! High spirits strive to know
More than a common eye sees, and aspire
Still upwards like the pyramid of fire,
When earth tends to its centre. We must move   50
More than the sense; else 'tis not perfect love.

To them Ceres and Bacchus.

Here's Ceres and Lyaeus.
Ceres.   We are told
By Maia's son that you intend to scold   55
With me and Bacchus.
Venus.   I have cause to chide.
You'd rob me of my titles, and beside
Make it a glutton's tenet, there can be
No love without you.   60
Ceres.   And your deity
Hath summon'd us for this: 'tis very good.

I must confess you made your father wood
To ravish fair Europa. Having seen
Trains of Arcadian virgins on the green   6
Tread their chaste measures, or with nimble pace
Through the Parthenian groves and thickets chase
A well-breath'd stag, one of them straightways must
Be tempted to her ruin by his lust:
And this employment, Venus, still is thine.   7

Venus. Ceres is mad still for her Proserpine:
Whose rape hath made her queen of the abyss.
Who to be so rewarded would not kiss
The black lips of hell's king? and to his bed
Bring the short pleasures of a maidenhead?   7
Repine not at it then.

Ceres.   I must whilst day
Hath any light, or heaven's bright eye a ray.
It was your son's great act to boast of; he
That suffers not th'infernals to go free   8
Of his diseases.

Bacchus.   Rather, Ceres, mine:
For if the god had never tasted wine,
Not all the heat of his infernal fire
Could e'er have thaw'd him into one desire,   8
Or kindled the least flame in his cold breast
Without my virtue.

Venus.   'Tis an idle jest.
Doth Bacchus think he can with heat of wine
Light the bright flame of love, that is divine,   9
And burns not from such causes but takes fire
From th'elemental part of pure desire
Unmix'd with grossness? Thy effects are foul,
And motions of the sense not of the soul.
Subscribe then to our power; my son and I   9
Must have the attributes.

Ceres.   Let him lay by
His quiver rather. Ceres means to be
The queen of love, and Bacchus' deity

Include all that is Cupid's.   100
Venus.   First I'll leave
To be immortal, and myself bereave
Of all that I can claim above the sky,
Or under heaven's arch'd roof, if destiny
May give it confirmation. Take a dart   105
And aim it at her proud imperious heart
To show in thy revenge what thou canst do.
Cupid. I must not, mother. We'll refer it to
Another trial, and if Bacchus can
Confirm what he so saucily began   110
To argue, by example, we'll deny
Nothing that's due unto his deity.
Bacchus. Content.

To them Christmas and Shrovetide enter.

Christmas is personated by an old reverend gentleman in a furred gown 115
and cap, etc., and Shrovetide by a fat cook with a frying-pan, etc.

                    And see occasion hath complied
Even with our wish. It cannot be denied
But these share both our bounties, have free use
Of all our gifts: and if you'll not refuse   120
A trial from them...
Venus.   Let them speak, whilst we
To their dispose refer the victory.
Shrovetide. I say, Christmas, you are past date, you are out of the
almanac. Resign, resign. Let the oven give place to the frying-pan, 125
and minced pies yield superiority to pancakes and fritters.
Christmas. Resign to thee! I that am the king of good cheer and
feasting, though I come but once a year to reign over baked, boiled,
roast, and plum-porridge, will have being in despite of thy lard-
ship. Thou art but my fag-end, and I must still be before thee.   130
Shrovetide. But thou wilt never be beforehand. Thou art a prodigal
Christmas; and Shrovetide hath seen thee many times in the
poultry.
Christmas. Dost scorn my liberality, thou reasty bacon, tallow-

faced scullion? Though thou be as fat as a Fleming, I'll have Lent
choke thee with a red herring.

Shrovetide. I'll arm myself for that. In three days I can victual my
garrison for seven weeks: and it shall go hard but I will domineer in
Lent despite of the thin-chapped surgeon that makes men skeletons.

Christmas. As how?

Shrovetide. At any nobleman's house I can lick my fingers in a
privy kitchen. Though I be out of commons in the hall, there's
flesh to be had sometimes in a chamber, besides a laundress. The
very three-penny ordinary will keep me in an upper gallery, and
I can be invisible even in the pie-house. Should all fail, the wenches
I got with child shall long, and have the physician's ticket.

Christmas. Thou get children!

Shrovetide. Yes, more than Christmas, and better too: for thine are
all unthrifts, whores, or murderers. Thy son In-and-In undid
many a citizen. Thou hast a daughter called My Lady's Hole, a
filthy black slut she is; and Put is common in every bawdy house.
'Tis thought Noddy was none of thine own getting, but an
alderman's, that in exchange cuckolded thee when thou wast a
courtier. Thou hast one son bred up in the country called Christmas
Gambols, that doth nothing but break men's necks; and many
more that would undo the commonwealth, were it not for the
groom porter.

Christmas. Dost see these, sirrah?

Shrovetide. Ceres and Bacchus: I am their worshipper. Were stews
tolerated, and Venus the grand bawd of them, without good meat
and drink your young factors would never be able to break their
masters or mistresses, nor your she-silkworm in Cheap care a
button for her foreman.

> *Ceres.* Venus being overcome, I hope will yield,
> Now she is vanquish'd in the open field
> And her weak forces scatter'd: nor can they
> Gather new head to make a second fray.

To them Lent enters.

*He is figured in a lean man, his habit like trouses, and what other antic
devices may be thought proper.*

328

Venus. Yes: with this champion and his fresh supply
I'll wage new war, and call back victory.

Shrovetide. This lean thin-gut starveling, begot by a Spaniard and
nursed at the lower end of Friday Street.

Lent. Why thou helluo of hens and bacon, thou larder-house of 175
collops and eggs; thou that makest the kitchen proclaim its
employment through the neighbourhood with the scent of thy
lard and crumpets, what canst thou boast of?

Christmas. Children, children, thou parched starveling: thou canst
get nothing but anatomies. 180

Lent. Children! I get more (I maintain not their lawfulness) than
Christmas and Shrovetide. O the virtue of oysters, lobsters,
sturgeon, anchovies, and caviare! Why thou grout-headed bladder,
puffed with the windiness of pared apples coffered in batter, for
every brawn or hog either Christmas or thyself have demolished 185
I have a thousand herrings, despite of the Dutchmen's wasteful
theft, let them rob the four seas never so often. Besides, I couple
more than the parson of Pancras—I mean, city woodcocks with
suburb wagtails.

Christmas. Thou couple! 190

Lent. Who more? Is not Saint Valentine's day mine? are not cods
mine, thou cod's head, and maids mine? Put them together thou
wilt find they are things...

Shrovetide. Thou art a thing of emptiness, and Lent was ever a Jack
by conversion. 195

Lent. Such a jack as can come aloft, and do Venus more credit than
thy fullness. Do not I share of Aries, Taurus, and Gemini, the
inns I lie at in my progress? Yet no cuckold can deny but Aries and
Taurus should follow Gemini. And it follows—or should—that I
having two fathers myself, should get most children. 200

Christmas. Who were thy fathers, prithee?

Lent. Devotion and Policy; and I have begotten Hypocrisy on a
holy sister that despite of all informers would have flesh, her belly
full. Let Christmas and Shrovetime eat and drink; I'll be for Venus,
though I feed upon nothing but herring-cobs. 205

> *Venus.* Who's now the conqueror? Will Ceres now
> Subscribe unto my power? and Bacchus bow

329

To Cupid's awful strength?
Ceres.   Not till it is
Confirm'd by better evidence than his.   21
Lent. Than mine! Observe.

*Here the scene suddenly changeth into a prospect, with trees budded, the
earth somewhat green, and at one side an old barn out of which issues a
company of Beggars, with a bapgipe.*

See you these good fellows, that prefer the warm sun before the   21
scraps which niggardly Christmas and Shrovetide feast them with,
and would get a better race under a hedge to people New England
than the Separatists that possess it. Whilst they entertain ye, I'll
summon the Spring, and she shall moderate.

The Beggars dance, [and then] Exeunt.   22

*After the dance, is heard the chirping of birds; and whilst the following
song is singing, the scene again changeth into a pleasant arbour in
which the Spring in a green robe wrought over with flowers presents
herself.*

The Song   22

See, see a metamorphosis:
The late grey field now verdant is.
The sun with warm beams glads the earth,
   And to the springing flowers
He gives a new and lively birth   22
   By th'aid of gentle showers.
The lambs no longer bleat for cold,
Nor cry for succour from the old;
But frisk and play with confidence
Like emblems of true innocence.   22
Chorus.   The cheerful birds their voices strain;
The cuckoo's hoarse for want of rain;
The nightingale doth sweetly sing,
To welcome in the joyful spring.

Spring. Thus break my glories forth that late lay hid   2
Within the icy earth, and were forbid

By winter's nipping cold to show their heads
Above the snowy cov'ring of their beds.
The winds, not rugged now, but calm and fair,
Sweep flow'ry gardens and perfume the air.   245
The wood's shrill choristers, whose frozen throats
Late wanted motion, now have found their notes
Straining their little organs to sound high,
And teach men art from nature's harmony.
Come you to welcome me?   250
Ceres.   Yes, lovely maid;
And to have judgment from you, who most aid
In love's great work.
Spring.   Is there a strife between
The goddess of desire and plenty's queen?   255
Will they subscribe, I'll moderate.
All.   Content.
Spring. First hear my reasons; then my sentence, bent
'Gainst neither's honours, for I must comply
With both as virtues. Venus' deity   260
Is powerful over all; and Ceres gives
Each that hath being that by which he lives.
Yet many times excess perverts the end
Of pure intentions, and extremes extend
Their powers to undo those acts are free   265
In their own natures from impurity.
Love ought to be platonic, and divine,
Such as is only kindled, and doth shine
With beams that may all dark effects control,
In the refin'd parts of the glorious soul.   270
Men do abuse your gifts when they delight
Only to please their sensual appetite
And heat the blood from fullness; whence there grows
No perfect love, but such as only knows
The coarsest difference and therefore must   275
Presume to own no other name but lust.
In me let temperance teach you to apply
Things to their best ends, and to rectify

331

All motions that intend effects beside
What may run clear and current with the tide   28
Of purest love: in which let all your jars
Be reconcil'd, and finish your stern wars.
All. Thus we embrace in peace.
Spring.   And I, the Spring,
Will lead a moderate measure. Chirpers sing   28
Your choicest airs; and as our ears they greet,
Unto the music we'll apply our feet.

The Spring leads them a measure; after which they retire back to the scene.

Epilogue   2

I that of all the seasons am the least,
Though first in time and usher in the rest,
Impart my pleasures freely, but desire
You'll not abuse them with excess. My choir   2
Shall sing as every fair one doth become
A chaste bride, her epithalamium.
    Though they are short be pleas'd with these; to you
    I yearly will return, and bring you new.

The Spring being received into the scene, it closeth.

THE END

THE TEXT

The text of 1638 is clean, and the accuracy with which elisions are marked in the verse-speeches on all but two occasions suggests that it was set from a carefully prepared manuscript. The stage-directions read like an author's, as in the use of '*chirping*' (line 221) which is *afterwards* found in the form 'Chirpers' in the text itself (line 285).

For this edition, by the kind co-operation of the respective librarians, microfilms of the following copies have been compared:

Issue dated 1638: Bodleian (Douce N247), British Museum (c. 34. d. 49), Dyce, Worcester College; Chapin, Chicago, Folger, Harvard, Huntington, Yale.

Issue dated 1639: Bodleian (Mal. 221 (13)), British Museum (162. d. 45), Dyce; Boston P.L., Harvard, Huntington (2 copies: 62726 and 62745), Newberry, Pforzheimer, Yale.

No significant variants were noted.

The Works of Thomas Nabbes were edited by A. H. Bullen in two volumes in 1887.

COLLATION

134 reasty] *This ed.*; rasty Q.
268–9 kindled,...beams...control,] *This ed.*;   kindled,...beames,...
controule Q.

COMMENTARY

1 *agreeable*] suitable, 'proper to the fancy of the rest' (*Microcosmos*).

5–7 Without...Bacchus] Cf. Erasmus, *Adagia*, 521 F.

16 god of medicine] Aesculapius.

20 'Twas...effect] It was all your doing.

53 Lyaeus] a name of Bacchus: Luaios, god of wine who frees men's minds from cares.

55 Maia's son] Mercury.

63 wood] furious, mad, reckless.

81 diseases] In the seventeenth century, this word could still have the basic sense of 'absence of ease'; hence, here, 'disturbances' or 'interference'.

95 Subscribe...to] concede the force of.

129 plum-porridge] porridge containing prunes, raisins, currants, etc.; a traditional Christmas dish.

131 be beforehand] have more than sufficient for present demands, have money in hand.

133 poultry] store-room for poultry and other provisions; there is also a pun on the Poultry, the location and name of one of the two lock-ups in the City of London.

134 reasty] rancid; Q's 'rasty' may have been a dialect form (cf. *N.E.D.*), but there is no other sign that Christmas speaks rustically.

135 fat...Fleming] Allusions to Flemings consuming large quantities of butter are common; cf. *Merry Wives*, III. ii. 316 and Nabbes's *Microcosmos*, v: '*Tasting*. I have converted more butter into kitchen-stuff, than would have victualled a Flemish garrison.'

142 commons] daily (communal) fare.

143 laundress] Laundresses were commonly reputed to be of easy virtue.

144 ordinary] eating-house or tavern providing meals at a fixed price.

145 pie-house] pie-shop.

146 ticket] authorization, permit; the consumption of meat was prohibited during Lent, but certain butchers were allowed to kill beasts for the sick and infirm.

149–57] This passage may be indebted to Middleton's account of Christmas's children in *The Inner Temple Masque* (pp. 260–1 above). Christmas enters with ten children in Jonson's *Masque of Christmas* (1616): like Nabbes, he has 'Gamboll' as a son. *In-and-In* was a gambling game for three players with four dice; in *Covent Garden*, I, iv, Nabbes uses the phrase in a series of bawdy innuendoes. *My Lady's Hole*, *Put* and *Noddy* were all card games, used here quibblingly: in the seventeenth century, *Put* could mean a 'thrust' or 'push', and to 'play at *Noddy*' was to fall asleep. The *groom porter* was an officer who regulated all gaming within the precincts of the court.

159–60 Were...tolerated] A statute of 1545 tried unsuccessfully to suppress brothels in London; it soon became a dead letter.

161 factors] agents, managers.

161 break] quibblingly: (1) 'bankrupt', (2) 'prevail upon'.

162 Cheap] I.e. Cheapside, London; mercers' shops were mostly in the East quarter.

169 *trouses*] close-fitting, knee-length breeches or trews.

173 Spaniard] Spaniards were reckoned to be poor feeders: cf. *Blurt Master Constable* (1602), I, ii: 'What meat eats the Spaniard? Dried pilchers and poor John', and Brome's *Northern Lass* (1632), v, viii: 'They are people of very spare diet, and therefore seldom fat.'

174 Friday Street] It ran south from Cheapside to Cannon Street, and was so called because fish was sold there.

175 helluo] glutton.

180 anatomies] skeletons, or corpses shrunken to skin and bones.

183 grout-headed] thick-headed.

186–7 Dutchmen's...theft] The Dutch were rivals with the English in fishing in the North Sea.

188 parson of Pancras] A 'pancridge Parson' was a priest who made a trade of irregular marriages; Sir Hugh of Pancras is a character in Jonson's *A Tale of a Tub* (published 1633).

191–2 cods...maids mine] The word-play depends on the use of *cods* for testicles and *maids* for young skate or thornback.

194 Jack] with word-play on 'poor *Jack*' or dried cod (see Lent's previous quibbles) and '*Jack*-a-Lent', an Aunt-Sally.

197–8 Do...progress] I.e. these are the signs of the Zodiac appropriate to my time of the year.

198–9 no...Gemini] I.e. from a cuckold's point of view, it would be more appropriate if the two horned beasts (the ram and the bull) came after the pairing (the twins). Nabbes varied the same jest in *Hannibal* and *The Bride* (ed. Bullen, I, 204 and II, 107).

203 flesh] Cf. the quibble at lines 142–3.

205 herring-cobs] heads of herrings.

215–18] Cf. the proverb, 'Beggars breed and rich men feed' (Tilley, *Dictionary of Proverbs*, B 244).

218 Separatists] Sectarians; often used derogatorily to imply pharisaism.

270 refin'd] purified, freed from gross elements.

285 moderate] I.e. exhibiting 'temperance'; cf. line 277.

SALMACIDA SPOLIA

BY INIGO JONES AND SIR WILLIAM DAVENANT

Edited by T. J. B. Spencer

INTRODUCTION

Salmacida Spolia was the last of the Court masques, produced early in 1640 with unparalleled splendour, almost in defiance of the political storm which was beginning to break. Soon the troubles throughout the kingdom were to give the Court no leisure for such entertainments. The purpose of this masque—a kind of exorcism of the spirit of Discord—is apparent from the beginning. It is

> a sullen age,
>> When it is harder far to cure
>>> The People's folly than resist their rage.   (177–9)

The King, the wise 'Lover of his People', has a hard task, for

>> 'tis his fate to rule in adverse times,
>>> When wisdom must awhile give place to crimes. (170–1)

But although 'Murmur's a sickness epidemical' (line 349), it is

>> kingly patience to outlast
>>> Those storms the people's giddy fury raise.   (345–6)

The weeks preceding 21 January had been singularly unpropitious, one might suppose, for the preparation of this brilliant entertainment at Whitehall. On 10 January there was a Council of War.[1] Thomas Lord Coventry, who had been Lord Keeper since 1625 and had tried to mediate between the King and the parliamentary leaders, had died on 14 January (Sir John Finch, who had been mainly responsible for the ship-money judgment of 1637, was by the influence of Henrietta Maria appointed to succeed him on 23 January). Sir John Coke had been dismissed from his office as Secretary of State and the appointment of his successor was awaited —on 3 February the King appointed Henry Vane, in spite of Strafford's opposition, 'by the dark contrivance of the Marquis of Hamilton and by the open and visible power of the Queen' (Clarendon). Nevertheless, amidst all the political intrigues and anxieties,

---

[1] S. R. Gardiner, *A History of England, 1603–42* (1883–4), IX, 84; S.P. Domestic, vol. 441, no. 83.

the preparations for *Salmacida Spolia* pushed forward. Algernon Percy, Earl of Northumberland, writes to the Earl of Leicester in Paris on 9 January:

102 [the King] is dayly so imployed about the Maske, as till that be over, we shall think of little ellse.[1]

It seems to have been felt that the kinds of disorders which had for long been destroying civilized life on the Continent were spreading to England. The fury, Discord, 'having already put most of the world into disorder, endeavours to disturb these parts, envying the blessings and tranquillity we have long enjoyed' (2–4), exclaims:

> How am I griev'd, the world should everywhere
> Be vex'd into a storm, save only here!   (113–14)

There was, from a point of view in England, some justification for this. The Thirty Years' War had begun in 1618 in Bohemia and 'gradually absorbed into itself all the local wars of Europe...From 1635 to 1648, the War continued its course through what may be called its Franco-Swedish stage, shifting to and from almost every part of Germany between the Alps and the Baltic, and everywhere leaving behind it desolation unutterable.'[2] These religious wars in Europe must have seemed a frightening magnification of the religious conflicts already gathering head in England and Scotland. They perhaps explain a surprising tartness of expression about religion in the masque. The Fury's recipe for promoting discord includes:

> make religion to become their vice,
> Nam'd to disguise ambitious avarice.   (133–4)

These lines might have been used by Christopher Hill in his *Society and Puritanism in Pre-Revolutionary England* (1964), in which he 'tries to suggest that there might (also) be non-theological reasons for supporting the Puritans' (Preface, p. 9). Equally interesting is the allusion to 'o'er-weening priests' (321–3) in the lines 'Inviting the King's Appearance in the Throne of Honour'. One notes that

[1] Letter of Algernon Percy, Earl of Northumberland, 9 January 1639/40, to Robert Sidney, Earl of Leicester, in Paris, printed in Arthur Collins, *Letters and Memorials of State...* (known as the *Sidney Papers*) (1746), I, 629.

[2] *Cambridge Modern History*, ed. A. W. Ward, etc., vol. IV, *The Thirty Years' War* (Cambridge, 1906), preface and p. 364.

this was 'to be printed, not sung'—presumably as rather tactless for the occasion. It seems to be directed at Laud's policy of reviving ecclesiastical power; and it is a surprising comment to be made at the centre of the King's circle, when Charles had recently (1638) expelled his own jester, Archie Armstrong, from the Court for jeering at Laud's difficulties in imposing a new prayer-book and canons in Scotland.[1]

Salmacida Spolia, then, is full of contemporary reverberations. Only in the gay series of vaudeville turns in the twenty anti-masques (181–288) are the troubles of the times forgotten. Here the lively young people of the Court, probably the younger officials or their sons, had their opportunity for, no doubt, well-rehearsed songs, dances, and jests. Exceptionally we are given their names, and some of them can be traced in the documents of the time. Thomas Arpe signs two bills authorizing payment for some of the Queen's robes in 1639, apparently as one of the chief officers of her household. William Ashton (and Sir Thomas Ashton), Atkins, Cassius Borough (or Burrowes), Edward Cholmeley, Sir Henry Newton, Henry Seymour (and Sir Edward Seymour), Sir Henry Skipwith, and Thomas Slingsby were gentlemen of the privy chamber extraordinary. Charles Cottrell, son of Sir Clement Cottrell, Groom Porter of the King's Chamber, was appointed Master of the Ceremonies in 1641. The 'Mr Hearne' may be Jeremiah Herne who had the privilege of teaching the Queen's maids of honour to dance (*C.S.P. Domestic 1641–3*, p. 422). Henry Jay was a gentleman usher to Prince Charles. There were several Murrays about the Court; Charles Murray was appointed to act as carver on the King's journey north in 1640 (Lord Chamberlain's Warrant Book 1634–41) and William Murray, later Earl of Dysart, was a favourite of Charles I, educated with him and said to have been his 'whipping-boy'. A Thomas Peart was gentleman usher to the Queen. 'Rimes' is difficult to trace and it may be a misprint for Rives (otherwise Reeves), of whom there were several in Court circles. Raphael Tartareau was the Queen's carver. The Villiers mentioned was probably one of the three younger brothers of William Villiers, Viscount Grandison—nephews of the late favourite; if it was

[1] *D.N.B.* (Laud and Armstrong).

Edward, the youngest (1620–89), he later became the husband of one of the masquers, Lady Frances Howard. Wardour was the name of a prominent family of the time: Sir Edward Wardour was clerk of the pells in the Exchequer. In Entry 18 the 'little Swiss who played the wag with' the other Swisses as they slept was performed by the famous Court dwarf, Sir Geoffrey Hudson. He had already appeared as Tom Thumb in Ben Jonson's *The Fortunate Isles* (and as Piecrocall in *Luminalia* (probably by Davenant)).

The authorization of £1,400 for expenses for the masque was made by the Lord Chamberlain (Philip Herbert, Earl of Pembroke and Montgomery) on 30 December 1639. The warrant is printed in the Malone Society *Collections*, vol. 2, part 3 (1931), pp. 391–2 (in 'Dramatic Records: the Lord Chamberlain's Office', edited by E. K. Chambers, Allardyce Nicoll and Miss E. Boswell).

The exact division of the writing between Davenant and Jones is not clear. We are told that 'the subject was set down by them both'; that 'the invention, ornament, scenes, and apparitions, with their descriptions' were by Jones; and that 'what was spoken or sung' was by Davenant (473–8). Of the introductory part (1–104), therefore, it seems that 1–18 would be of joint composition, 19–56 by Jones,[1] and 57–91 (the explanation of the title of the masque) in collaboration. We know that Davenant was later paid £40, perhaps for his contribution (*C.S.P. Domestic 1640–1*, pp. 545–6).

The use of the legend of Salmacis in this masque is unusual. The story of Hermaphroditus who lost his manhood by bathing in a pool while avoiding the love of the nymph Salmacis was well known. *Cui non audita est obscenae Salmacis undae?* asks Pythagoras in Ovid, *Metamorphoses* 15, 319: and Ovid has already told the story very cleverly in the fourth book:

> Unde sit infamis, quare male fortibus undis
> Salmacis enervet tactosque remolliat artus,
> discite. Causa latet, vis est notissima fontis.   (285–7)

Hermaphroditus utters his prayer when he finds himself bisexual:

> quisquis in hos fontes vir venerit, exeat inde
> semivir et tactis subito mollescat in undis!   (385–6)

---

[1] Nicoll, *Stuart Masques*, pp. 106–8, considers that, both in *The Temple of Love* and in *Salmacida Spolia*, the elaborate descriptions were actually written by Inigo Jones.

To Cicero was attributed a version of the phrase quoted in the 'Subject of the masque' (lines 60–1): *Salmaci, da spolia sine sudore et sanguine* (*De Officiis* 1. 18), as a typical reproach to those effeminate beings who want the rewards of life without working for them. This appears to be quoted from Ennius (see *Tragicorum Romanorum Fragmenta*, ed. Ribbeck, 1871, no. 338). There are other allusions in familiar Latin authors: *Procul hinc et fonte doloso | Salmacis* (Statius, *Silvae* 1. 5. 20); *Vidit semivirum fons Salmacis Hermaphroditum* (Ausonius, *Epigrammata* 76. 11). Strabo (14. 2. 16) explained that it was not the water of the fountain at Halicarnassus that rendered men effeminate, but riches and incontinent living.

What must have been the normal expectations of the audience when they saw the title of the masque? A comment on the notorious effeminacy of the English young nobility and the unwholesome exaltation of 'platonical love'?

In fact, the well-known aspects of the story are ignored in the masque; and Jones turned to the quite different and comparatively little-known interpretation by Vitruvius (2. 8. 11). In the 'Subject' Jones translates, without stating his source, Vitruvius's rationalizing explanation of the reputation of the Salmacian spring. In his account of the buildings of Halicarnassus, Vitruvius turned aside to mention the fountain. *Is autem locus est theatri curvaturae similis*, says Vitruvius, and there, *in cornu...summo dextro*, is the fountain ('On the top of the right horn of the hill which surrounds Halicarnassus in the form of a theatre', lines 70–1). And then Vitruvius tells the story:

Cum autem Melas et Areuanias ab Argis et Troezene coloniam communem eo loci deduxerunt, barbaros Caras et Lelegas eiecerunt. Hi autem ad montes fugati inter se congregantes discurrebant et ibi latrocinia facientes crudeliter eos vastabant. Postea de colonis unus ad eum fontem propter bonitatem aquae quaestus causa tabernam omnibus copiis instruxit eamque exercendo eos barbaros allectabat. Ita singillatim decurrentes et ad coetus convenientes e duro ferroque more commutati in Graecorum consuetudinem et suavitatem sua voluntate reducebantur. Ergo ea aqua non inpudico morbi vitio, sed humanitatis dulcedine mollitis animis barbarorum eam famam est adepta.

343

Lines 65–77 of the 'Subject' are a close translation of this passage and explain the title of the masque. The effects of the arts of civilization in taming barbarians are favourably contrasted with the victories which are gained over them by violence. The optimistic implication is that the King's political skill and powers of moral persuasion will appease his seditious enemies; whereas to quell them by armed force would give but a hollow and destructive victory.

One wonders how many of the audience were so dazzled by the pageantry of *Salmacida Spolia* as to accept the wishful thinking of its authors. Among the brilliant company of masquers, sitting on their thrones in the palm trees or in 'the upper part of the heavens', we know there were some who had private doubts. For Newport, Herbert, Fielding, Russell, and Paget were soon to oppose the King and aid the Parliamentary cause. So would Lady Margaret Howard's husband and brother and Lady Caernarvon's father, the latter the same Lord Chamberlain Pembroke who had paid the bill for the masque.

Apart from the passage of Vitruvius quoted, Davenant and Jones between them borrowed other things for the composition of this masque. The description of the globe from which emerges a Fury (92–104) is clearly derived from a passage in *La Galatée* (1625) of Abraham Remy:

Ils [Mercury and Apollo, who present the subject of the ballet] ne se furent pas plustost retirez derriere la tapisserie, que parmy le meslange confus des instrumens & de la Musique, on veit paroistre sur le theatre vn Globe de prodigieuse grandeur, remply de mille grotesques & de chimeres imparfaites, comme Lions aislez, Tygres volans, Lièvres cornus, & d'vne infinité d'animaux à demy formez. L'eau mesme & le feu, les vapeurs & les nuages sortoient pesle mesle de tous les endroicts de ce Globe, & sembloit que la confusion des instrumens & des voix s'accordast auec la diuersité des especes qu'on y auoit représentées, car on y voyoit toutes sortes de couleurs & de figures.

De ceste Boule, comme d'vn chaos remply de désordre & de meslange, sortit la Discorde, furie espouuantable, dont les regards horribles, & le visage difforme versoient de la terreur dans l'ame des plus hardis, vne cheuelure hérissée de couleuures luy venoit battre sur les espaules: elle

344

tenoit dans sa main gauche vne pomme d'or, & dans la droitte vne torche ardante, dont les noires fumées estoient suiuies d'vne infinité de feux & de serpenteaux, qu'elle faisoit voller aux enuirons du theatre.[1]

Likewise many of Wolfgangus Vandergoose's 'receipts' and 'rare secrets' are translated from the *Ballet de la Foire Saint-Germain*, printed in 1612.[2] The French originals are here given against the Vandergoose numbers:

1. Confection d'esperance et de crainte pour entretenir les amoureux.
2. Essence de dissimulation pour se faire aymer.
3. Eau de jouyssance pour soulager la fievre amoureuse.
4. Eau de baiser et attouchemens pour eschauffer un vieux courage.
5. Essence tres-subtile tirée des points et lignes mathematiquales de l'ombre du silence Pitagorique, des songes de Poliphile, avec le gros orteil du fantosme de Brutus, passez dans l'esprit d'un melancolique, pour faire engendrer les chastrez.
6. Pomade d'escorce de belle taille, de miel, de douceur, d'absinte, de gravité, pour oindre ceux qui ont mauvaise mine.
7. Esprit des caprioles de Saturne, des entrechats de Vulcan, des pirouëttes de Bacchus, pour faire bien dancer.
8. Un morceau de la premiere matiere de la roüille de la faux du Temps, avec le jus des herbes de Medée, pour rajeunir toutes sortes de vieilles gens.
10. Trocisques de l'arbre de Judas et de l'escorce de chanvre, pour consoler ceux qui ont perdu leur argent.

[1] Quoted by Jean Jacquot in 'La Reine Henriette-Marie et l'Influence française dans les Spectacles à la Cour de Charles Ier' (*Cahiers de l'Association internationale des Études françaises*, no. 9, June 1957, p. 159).
[2] *Recueil des plus excellens ballets de ce temps* (Paris, 1612); see Paul Lacroix, *Ballets et Mascarades de Cour de Henri III à Louis XIV (1581–1652)*, recueillis et publiés, d'après les éditions originales (6 vols., Genève, 1868–70), I, 224 ff.; Brotanek, *Maskenspiele*, p. 297.

SALMACIDA SPOLIA

A MASQUE

Presented by the King and Queen's Majesties at Whitehall
on Tuesday the 21 day of January 1639 [1640]

*   *   *

The Subject of the Masque

Discord, a malicious Fury, appears in a storm and by the invocation of
malignant spirits, proper to her evil use, having already put most of the
world into disorder, endeavours to disturb these parts, envying the
blessings and tranquillity we have long enjoyed.

These incantations are expressed by those spirits in an Anti-masque; 5
who on a sudden are surprised and stopped in their motion by a secret
power, whose wisdom they tremble at; and depart as foreknowing that
wisdom will change all their malicious hope of these disorders into a
sudden calm, which after their departure is prepared by a dispersed
harmony of music.   10

This secret wisdom, in the person of the King attended by his Nobles
and under the name of Philogenes or Lover of his People, hath his
appearance prepared by a Chorus, representing the beloved people, and is
instantly discovered environed with those Nobles in the Throne of
Honour.   15

Then the Queen personating the chief heroine, with her martial ladies,
is sent down from Heaven by Pallas as a reward of his prudence for
reducing the threatening storm into the following calm.

In the border that enclosed the scenes and made a frontispiece to all the
work, in a square niche on the right hand stood two figures of women: 20
one of them expressing much majesty in her aspect, apparelled in sky
colour, with a crown of gold on her head and a bridle in her hand, representing Reason; the other embracing her was in changeable silk with wings
at her shoulders, figured for Intellectual Appetite; who while she em-
braceth Reason, all the actions of men are rightly governed. Above these, 25
in a second order, were winged children, one riding on a furious lion,

which he seems to tame with reins and a bit; another bearing an antique ensign; the third hovering above with a branch of palm in his hand, expressing the victory over the perturbations. In a niche on the other side stood two figures joining hands: one a grave old man in a robe of purple, with a heart of gold in a chain about his neck, figured for Counsel; the other a woman, in a garment of cloth of gold, in her hand a sword with a serpent winding about the blade, representing Resolution, both these being necessary to the good means of arriving to a virtuous end.

Over these and answering to the other side was a round altar raised high, and on it the bird of Pallas, figured for Prudence. On either side were children with wings: one in act of adoration, another holding a book, and a third flying over their heads with a lighted torch in his hand, representing the Intellectual Light accompanied with Doctrine and Discipline, and alluding to the figures below, as those on the other side.

Above these ran a large frieze, with a cornicement; in the midst whereof was a double compartment rich and full of ornament. On the top of this sat Fame with spreaded wings, in act, sounding a trumpet of gold. Joining to the compartment in various postures lay two figures in their natural colours as big as the life: one holding an anchor representing Safety; the other expressing Riches, with a cornucopia, and about her stood antique vases of gold. The rest of this frieze was composed of children, with significant signs to express their several qualities: Forgetfulness of Injuries, extinguishing a flaming torch on an armour; Commerce, with ears of corn; Felicity, with a basket of lilies; Affection to the Country, holding a grasshopper; Prosperous Success, with the rudder of a ship; Innocence, with a branch of fern; all these expressing the several goods, followers of peace and concord, and forerunners of human felicity; so as the work of this front, consisting of picture qualified with moral philosophy, tempered delight with profit.

In the midst of the aforesaid compartment in an oval table was written:

SALMACIDA SPOLIA

The ancient adages are these: *Salmacida spolia sine sanguine sine sudore, potius quam Cadmia victoria, ubi ipsos victores pernicies opprimit.*

But before I proceed in the descriptions of the scenes, it is not amiss briefly to set down the histories from whence these proverbs took their original.

For the first: Melas and Arevanias of Argos and Troezen conducted a common colony to Halicarnassus in Asia, and there drave out the bar-

barous Carie and Lelegi, who fled up to the mountains; from whence they made many incursions, robbing and cruelly spoiling the Grecian inhabitants, which could by no means be prevented.

On the top of the right horn of the hill which surrounds Halicarnassus 70 in form of a theatre is a famous fountain of most clear water and exquisite taste called Salmacis. It happened that, near to this fountain, one of the colony, to make gain by the goodness of the water, set up a tavern and furnished it with all necessaries; to which the barbarians resorting (enticed by the delicious taste of this water, at first some few, and after 75 many together in troops) of fierce and cruel natures were reduced of their own accord to the sweetness of the Grecian customs.

The other adage is thus derived: the city of Thebes, anciently called Cadmia, had war with Adrastus, the Argive King; who raised a great army of Arcadians and Messenians and fought a battle with them near 80 Ismenia, where the Thebans were overthrown, turned their backs, and fled into their city. The Peloponnesians, not accustomed to scale walled towns, assaulting furiously but without order, were repulsed from the walls by the defendants and many of the Argives slain. At that instant the besieged, making a great sally and finding the enemy in disorder and con- 85 fusion, cut them all in pieces, only Adrastus excepted, who was saved by flight. But this victory was gotten with great damage and slaughter of the Thebans; for few of them returned alive into their city.

The allusion is that his Majesty, out of his mercy and clemency approving the first proverb, seeks by all means to reduce tempestuous and 90 turbulent natures into a sweet calm of civil concord.

A curtain flying up, a horrid scene appeared of storm and tempest. No glimpse of the sun was seen, as if darkness, confusion, and deformity had possessed the world and driven light to Heaven; the trees bending, as forced by a gust of wind, their branches rent from their trunks, and 95 some torn up by the roots. Afar off was a dark wrought sea, with rolling billows breaking against the rocks, with rain, lightning, and thunder In the midst was a globe of the Earth, which, at an instant falling on fire, was turned into a Fury, her hair upright, mixed with snakes, her body lean, wrinkled, and of a swarthy colour. Her breasts hung bagging 100 down to her waist, to which with a knot of serpents was girt red bases, and under it tawny skirts down to her feet. In her hand she brandished a sable torch, and looking askance with hollow envious eyes came down into the room.

349

Fury. Blow winds! until you raise the seas so high   10
  That waves may hang like tears in the sun's eye,
  That we, when in vast cataracts they fall,
  May think he weeps at nature's funeral.
  Blow winds! and from the troubled womb of earth,
  Where you receive your undiscover'd birth,   10
  Break out in wild disorders, till you make
  Atlas beneath his shaking load to shake.
  How am I griev'd, the world should everywhere
  Be vex'd into a storm, save only here!
  Thou over-lucky, too-much-happy isle,   10
  Grow more desirous of this flatt'ring style!
  For thy long health can never alter'd be
  But by thy surfeits on felicity.
  And I to stir the humours that increase
  In thy full body, over-grown with peace,   12
  Will call those Furies hither who incense
  The guilty and disorder innocence.

  Ascend, ascend, you horrid sullen brood
  Of evil spirits, and displace the good!
  The great, make only wiser to suspect   1
  Whom they have wrong'd by falsehood or neglect.
  The rich, make full of avarice as pride,
  Like graves or swallowing seas unsatisfied,
  Busy to help the State, when needy grown,
  From poor men's fortunes, never from their own.   1
  The poor, ambitious make, apt to obey
  The false, in hope to rule whom they betray;
  And make religion to become their vice,
  Nam'd to disguise ambitious avarice.

The speech ended, three Furies make their entry presented by: Mr Charles 1
Murray; Mr Seymour; Mr Tartareau.
  *This Anti-masque being past, the scene changed into a calm; the sky
serene; afar off Zephyrus appeared breathing a gentle gale; in the landscape were cornfields and pleasant trees, sustaining vines fraught with
grapes, and in some of the furthest parts villages, with all such things* 1

*as might express a country in peace, rich and fruitful. There came
breaking out of the heavens a silver chariot, in which sat two persons: the
one a woman in a watchet garment, her dressing of silver mixed with
bull rushes, representing Concord; somewhat below her sat the Good
Genius of Great Britain, a young man in a carnation garment, em-* 145
*broidered all with flowers, an antique sword hung in a scarf, a garland
on his head, and in his hand a branch of platan mixed with ears of corn.
These in their descent sung together:*

Song I

Good Genius of Great Britain   Concord

Concord. Why should I hasten hither, since the good   150
　　　I bring to men is slowly understood?

Genius. I know it is the People's vice
　　　To lay too mean, too cheap a price
　　　On ev'ry blessing they possess.
　　　Th'enjoying makes them think it less.   155

Concord. If, then, the need of what is good
　　　Doth make it lov'd or understood,
　　　Or 'tis by absence better known,
　　　I shall be valued when I'm gone.

Genius. Yet stay, O stay! if but to please   160
　　　The great and wise Philogenes.

Concord. Should dews not fall, the sun forbear
　　　His course, or I my visits here,
　　　Alike from these defects would cease
　　　The power and hope of all increase.   165

Genius. Stay then, O stay! if but to ease
　　　The cares of wise Philogenes.

Concord. I will! and much I grieve that, though the best
　　　Of kingly science harbours in his breast,
　　　Yet 'tis his fate to rule in adverse times,   170
　　　When wisdom must awhile give place to crimes.

*Being arrived at the earth and descended from the chariot, they sing
this short dialogue; and then departed several ways to incite the beloved
people to honest pleasures and recreations, which have ever been
peculiar to this nation.*

> *Both.* O who but he could thus endure
> To live and govern in a sullen age,
> When it is harder far to cure
> The People's folly than resist their rage?

After which there followed these several Entries of Anti-masques:

Entry 1

*Wolfgangus Vandergoose, spagyric, operator to the Invisible Lady
styled the Magical Sister of the Rosicross, with these receipts following
and many other rare secrets undertakes in short time to cure the defects
of nature and diseases of the mind:*

1. *Confection of hope and fear, to entertain lovers.*
2. *Essence of dissimulation, to enforce love.*
3. *Julep of fruition, to recreate the hot fevers of love.*
4. *Water of dalliance, to warm an old courage.*
5. *A subtle quintessence drawn from mathematical points and lines,
   filtered through a melancholy brain, to make eunuchs engender.*
6. *Pomado of the bark of comeliness, the sweetness of wormwood,
   with the fat of gravity, to anoint those that have an ill mind.*
7. *Spirit of Satyrus' high capers and Bacchus' whirling vertigos, to
   make one dance well.*
8. *One dram of the first matter, as much of the rust of Time's scythe,
   mixed with the juice of Medea's herbs; this, in an electuary, makes
   all sorts of old people young.*
9. *An opiate of the spirit of muscadine taken in good quantity to
   bedward, to make one forget his creditors.*
10. *Powder of Menippus' tree and the rine of hemp, to consolate those
    who have lost their money.*
11. *Treacle of the gall of serpents and the liver of doves, to initiate a
    neophyte courtier.*
12. *An easy vomit of the fawning of a spaniel,* Gallo-belgicus, *and the*

last coranto, hot from the press, with the powder of some lean jests, to prepare a disprovu's welcome to rich men's tables.

13. *A gargarism of* Florio's First Fruits, Diana de Montemayor, *and the scraping of* Spanish Romanzas *distilled* in balneo, *to make a sufficient linguist without travelling or scarce knowing himself* 210 *what he says.*

14. *A bath, made of a catalogue from the mart and common places, taken in a Frankfort dryfat; in his diet he must refrain all real knowledge and only suck in vulgar opinions, using the fricassee of confederacy; will make ignorants in all professions to seem and* 215 *not to be.*

Entry 2

Four old men richly attired, the shapes proper to the persons, presented by } Mr Boroughs
Mr Skipwith
Mr Pert   220
Mr Ashton

Entry 3

Three young soldiers in several fashioned habits, but costly, and presented to the life by } Mr Hearne
Mr Slingsby
Mr Chumley   225

Entry 4

A nurse and three children in long coats, with bibs, biggins, and muckenders.

Entry 5

An ancient Irishman, presented by   Mr Jay   230

Entry 6

An ancient Scottishman, presented by   Mr Atkins

Entry 7

An old-fashioned Englishman and his mistress, presented by } Mr Arpe
Mr Will. Murray   235

These three Anti-masques were well and naturally set out.

Entry 8

A country gentleman...

Doctor Tartaglia and two pedants
  of Francolin, presented by } Mr Rimes
Mr Warder
Mr Villiers   24

Entry 9

Four grotesques or drollities, in the most fantastical shapes that could
  be devised.

Entry 10

The Invisible Lady, magical sister of the Rosicross.   24

Entry 11

A shepherd, presented by   Mr Charles Murray

Entry 12

A farmer and his wife, presented by   Mr Skipwith

Entry 13   25

A country gentleman, his wife, and
  his bailiff, presented by } Mr Boroughs
Mr Ashton
Mr Pert

Entry 14

An amorous courtier richly apparelled,   25
  presented by   Mr Seymour

Entry 15

Two roaring boys, their suits answering their profession.

Entry 16

Four mad lovers, and as madly clad.   26

Entry 17

A jealous Dutchman,
  his wife, and her Italian
  lover, presented by
} Mr Arpe
Mr Rimes
Mr Tartareau

Entry 18
265

Three Swisses, one a little
Swiss who played the wag with
  them as they slept, presented by
} Mr Cotterell
Mr Newton
Mr Jeffrey Hudson

Entry 19

Four antique cavaliers, imitating
  a manage and tilting.
} Mr Arpe
Mr Jay
Mr Atkins
Mr Tartareau
270

Entry 20

A Cavallerizzo and two pages. 275

All which Anti-masques were well set out and excellently danced, and the tunes fitted to the persons.

The Anti-masques being past, all the scene was changed into craggy rocks and inaccessible mountains. In the upper parts, where any earth could fasten, were some trees, but of strange forms, such as only grow in remote parts of the Alps and in desolate places; the furthest of these was hollow in the midst and seemed to be cut through by art, as the Pausilipo near Naples, and so high as the top pierced the clouds; all which represented the difficult way which heroes are to pass ere they come to the Throne of Honour. 280
285

The Chorus of the beloved people came forth, led by Concord and the Good Genius of Great Britain, their habits being various and rich. They go up to the state and sing.

Song II

To the Queen Mother

1. When with instructed eyes we look upon
   Our blessings that descend so fast
   From the fair partner of our Monarch's throne,
   We grieve they are too great to last.

2. But when those growing comforts we survey
   By whom our hopes are longer liv'd,
   Then gladly we our vows and praises pay
   To her from whom they are deriv'd.

3. And since, great Queen, she is deriv'd from you,
   We here begin our offerings;
   For those who sacrific'd to rivers know
   Their first rights due unto their springs.

4. The stream from whence our blessings flow, you bred;
   You, in whose bosom ev'n the chief and best
   Of modern victors laid his weary head
   When he rewarded victories with rest;
   Your beauty kept his valour's flame alive;
   Your Tuscan wisdom taught it how to thrive.

Inviting the King's Appearance in the Throne of Honour

To be printed, not sung

Why are our joys detain'd by this delay?
    Unless, as in a morning overcast,
We find it long ere we can find out day;
    So, whilst our hopes increase, our time doth waste.
Or are you slow 'cause th'way to Honour's throne,
    In which you travel now, is so uneven,

Hilly, and craggy, or as much unknown
    As that uncertain path which leads to Heaven?
O that philosophers, who through those mists
    Low nature casts do upper knowledge spy,

Or those that smile at them, o'er-weening priests,
   Could with such sure, such an undoubted eye
Reach distant Heaven as you can Honour's throne!
   Then we should shift our flesh t'inhabit there,
   Where, we are taught, the heroës are gone,   325
     Though now content with earth, 'cause you are here.

*The song ended, they return up to the stage and divide themselves on
each side. Then the further part of the scene disappeared, and the
King's Majesty and the rest of the masquers were discovered sitting in
the Throne of Honour, his Majesty highest in a seat of gold and the rest 330
of the Lords about him. This throne was adorned with palm trees,
between which stood statues of the ancient heroes. In the under parts on
each side lay captives bound, in several postures, lying on trophies of
armours, shields, and antique weapons, all his throne being feigned of
goldsmith's work. The habit of his Majesty and the masquers was of 335
watchet, richly embroidered with silver; long stockings set up of white;
their caps silver with scrolls of gold and plumes of white feathers.*

Song III

*To the King when he appears with his Lords in the Throne
of Honour*   340

1. Those quarrelling winds, that deafen'd unto death
    The living and did wake men dead before,
  Seem now to pant small gusts, as out of breath,
    And fly, to reconcile themselves on shore.

2. If it be kingly patience to outlast   345
    Those storms the people's giddy fury raise
  Till like fantastic winds themselves they waste,
    The wisdom of that patience is thy praise.

3. Murmur's a sickness epidemical.
    'Tis catching, and infects weak common ears.   350
  For through those crooked, narrow alleys, all
    Invaded are and kill'd by whisperers.

357

4. This you discern'd, and by your mercy taught
   Would not, like monarchs that severe have been,
   Invent imperial arts to question thought,   355
   Nor punish vulgar sickness as a sin.

5. Nor would your valour, when it might subdue,
   Be hinder'd of the pleasure to forgive.
   Th'are worse than overcome, your wisdom knew,
   That needed mercy to have leave to live.   360

6. Since strength of virtues gain'd you Honour's throne,
   Accept our wonder and enjoy your praise;
   He's fit to govern there and rule alone
   Whom inward helps, not outward force, doth raise.

Whilst the Chorus sung this song, there came softly from the upper part 365
of the heavens a huge cloud of various colours, but pleasant to the sight;
which, descending to the midst of the scene, opened, and within it was a
transparent brightness of thin exhalations, such as the Gods are
feigned to descend in; in the most eminent place of which her Majesty
sat, representing the chief heroine, environed with her martial ladies; 370
and from over her head were darted lightsome rays that illuminated her
seat; and all the ladies about her participated more or less of that light,
as they sat near or further off. This brightness with many streaks of thin
vapours about it, such as are seen in a fair evening sky, softly descended;
and as it came near to the earth the seat of Honour by little and little 375
vanished, as if it gave way to these heavenly graces. The Queen's
Majesty and her ladies were in Amazonian habits of carnation, em-
broidered with silver, with plumed helms, baldrics with antique swords
hanging by their sides—all as rich as might be; but the strangeness of the
habits was most admired. 380

Song IV

When the Queen and her Ladies Descended

1. You that so wisely studious are
   To measure and to trace each star,
   How swift they travel and how far,   385
   Now number your celestial store,

Planets or lesser lights, and try
If in the face of all the sky
    You count so many as before.

2. If you would practise how to know   390
The chief for influence or show,
Level your perspectives below,
    For in this nether orb they move.
Each here, when lost in's doubtful art,
May by his eyes advance his heart,   395
    And through his optic learn to love.

3. But what is she that rules the night,
That kindles ladies with her light
And gives to men the power of sight?
    All those who can her virtue doubt   400
Her mind will in her face advise;
For through the casements of her eyes
    Her soul is ever looking out.

4. And with its beams she doth survey
Our growth in virtue or decay,   405
Still lighting us in Honour's way.
    All that are good she did inspire.
Lovers are chaste, because they know
It is her will they should be so.
    The valiant take from her their fire.   410

*When this heavenly seat touched the earth, the King's Majesty took
out the Queen, and the Lords the Ladies, and came down into the room
and danced their entry; betwixt which and the second dance was this
song:*

Song V

After the First Dance

1. Why stand you still, and at these beauties gaze,
     As if you were afraid,
       Or they were made
     Much more for wonder than delight?
   Sure those whom first their virtue did amaze
     Their feature must at last invite.

2. Time never knew the mischiefs of his haste,
     Nor can you force him stay
       To keep off day.
     Make then fit use of triumphs here!
   It were a crime 'gainst pleasant youth to waste
     This night in over-civil fear.

3. Move then like Time, for Love as well as he
     Hath got a calendar,
       Where must appear
     How ev'nly you these measures tread;
   And when they end, we far more griev'd shall be
     Than for his hours when they are fled.

The second dance ended, and their Majesties being seated under the state, the scene was changed into magnificent buildings composed of several selected pieces of architecture. In the furthest part was a bridge over a river, where many people, coaches, horses, and such like, were seen to pass to and fro. Beyond this on the shore were buildings in prospective, which shooting far from the eye showed as the suburbs of a great city.

From the highest part of the heavens came forth a cloud far in the scene, in which were eight persons richly attired representing the spheres. This, joining with two other clouds which appeared at that instant full of music, covered all the upper part of the scene; and at that instant, beyond all these, a heaven opened full of deities; which celestial prospect, with the Chorus below, filled all the whole scene with apparitions and harmony.

Song VI

To the King and Queen, by a Chorus of All   450

So musical as to all ears
Doth seem the music of the spheres,
Are you unto each other still,
Tuning your thoughts to either's will.

All that are harsh, all that are rude,   455
Are by your harmony subdued;
Yet so into obedience wrought,
As if not forc'd to it, but taught.

Live still, the pleasure of our sight,
Both our examples and delight;   460

So long, until you find the good success
Of all your virtues in one happiness;

Till we so kind, so wise, and careful be,
In the behalf of our posterity,

That we may wish your sceptres ruling here,   465
Lov'd even by those who should your justice fear,
When we are gone, when to our last remove
We are dispatch'd, to sing your praise above.

*After this song the spheres passed through the air, and all the Deities
ascended; and so concluded this Masque, which was generally approved* 470
*of, especially by all strangers that were present, to be the noblest and
most ingenuous that hath been done here in that kind.*

*The invention, ornament, scenes, and apparitions, with their
descriptions, were made by Inigo Jones, Surveyor General of his
Majesty's Works.*   475

*What was spoken or sung, by William Davenant, her Majesty's
Servant.*

The subject was set down by them both.

*The music was composed by Lewis Richard, Master of her Majesty's
Music.*   480

FINIS

The Names of the Masquers

The King's Majesty	The Queen's Majesty	
Duke of Lennox	Duchess of Lennox	
Earl of Carlisle	Countess of Caernarvon	485
Earl of Newport	Countess of Newport	
Earl of Lanerick	Countess of Portland	
Lord Russell	Lady Andover	
Lord Herbert	Lady Margaret Howard	
Lord Paget	Lady Kellymekin	490
Lord Fielding	Lady Frances Howard	
Master Russell	Mistress Cary	
Master Thomas Howard	Mistress Nevill	

THE TEXT

The quarto edition of 1640 (1639 on the title-page) was the only contemporary printing of the *Salmacida Spolia*. It was, for some reason, not included in the collected edition, *The Works of Sir William Davenant Kt, Consisting of Those which were formerly Printed, and Those which he design'd for the Press* (1673). It has been reprinted in the following volumes: *A Select Collection of Old Plays*, edited by W. R. Chetwood (Dublin, 1750); *The Dramatic Works of Sir William Davenant*, edited by J. Maidment and W. H. Logan (5 vols., Edinburgh, 1872–4; New York, 1964), vol. 2; *English Masques*, edited by H. A. Evans (1897).

COLLATION

The following copies of the 1640 (1639) quarto have been collated: Bodleian; Henry Huntington Library; Library of Congress.

84 many] Q may.

136, 264, 273 *Tartareau*] Q Tartarean.

148 *descent*] Q dissent.

157 lov'd] Q lov'd; *Maidment, Evans* lev'd (probably a misreading of a damaged letter).

193 *mind*] Q mine.

194 *Satyrus'*] Q Saturus; *Maidment, Evans* Saturn's.

275 *Cavallerizzo*] Q Cavaleritro.

316 travel] Q travaile.

378 *baldrics*] Q Bandrickes.

426 triumphs] Q Tiumphs.

487 Lanerick] Q Leimricke; *Chetwood* Limerick.

COMMENTARY

12 Philogenes] cf. 161, 167. There is apparently no ancient authority for the word as an honorific, but it occurs as a proper name (e.g. a freedman of Atticus in Cicero, *ad Atticum*, v. 13, 20; vi. 2, 3, etc.).

19 frontispiece] See Plate 15, for a similar representation of the border of the scene for *The Triumph of Peace*.

23 changeable silk] shot silk showing different colours in different aspects.

26 order] row, series.

39–40 Doctrine and Discipline] The two words were strongly associated: doctrine relates to articles of faith, discipline to the practice by which the conduct of the members of a church is regulated; cf. Milton, *The Doctrine and Discipline of Divorce restored. . .from the Bondage of Common Law*, 1643.

60–1 *Salmacida spolia. . .opprimit*] 'Salmacian spoils [which are gained] without bloodshed [and] without sweat, rather than Cadmian victories when destruction falls upon the victors themselves [as much as upon the vanquished].' See Introduction to this masque, p. 342.

92 *a horrid scene. . .of storm and tempest*] See Plate 22.

96 *wrought*] rough and agitated.

99 *a Fury*] Plates 30(*a*) and (*b*). The figure of Discord usually derives from the description of the appearance and behaviour of Allecto in Virgil, *Aeneid*, VII, 324 ff., with snakes in her upright hair (*pullat atra colubris* 329 . . .*erexit crinibus angues* 450), a darkened torch in her hand (*funereasque inferre faces* 337. . .*atro lumine fumantes. . .taedas* 457), in appearance a wrinkled old woman (*in vultus sese transformat aniles | et frontem obscenam rugis arat* 416), etc.

101 *red bases*] the bases were skirts (from waist to knee) and under them were the tawny petticoat skirts down to the feet.

103 *sable torch*] 'mournful' (Cawdrey), rather than dark; cf. *funereas. . . faces* in note to line 99 above.

109–10 Blow winds!. . .your undiscover'd birth] For the theory of origin of winds see Pliny 2. 44. 115; also Simeon K. Henniger, *A Handbook of Renaissance Meteorology* (Durham, North Carolina, 1960), pp. 107–8.

112 his shaking load to shake] The repetition is odd; perhaps *shaking* is a misprint for *quaking* or *aching*; or *shake* for *quake*.

113–14 the world should everywhere | Be vex'd into a storm, save only here] cf. lines 1–5, and Introduction to this masque, p. 340.

135] The introductory account of the masque (lines 6–10) gives information about what happens at this point. The spirits (or furies) that have been raised by Discord's incantation (lines 105–34) 'on a sudden are surprised. . . harmony of music'.

137 *the scene changed into a calm*]   Plate 23.

139 *trees, sustaining vines*]   this well-known image of the elms and vines indicates a Mediterranean landscape.

143 *watchet*]   sky blue.

146 *scarf*]   a band of material worn diagonally across the body from one shoulder to the opposite waist.

147 *platan*]   plane.

148 *descent*]   Q reads *dissent*, which might possibly be correct, meaning a disagreement of opinion (apparently not a musical term).

161, 167 Philogenes]   See line 12.

180 *Entries*]   dances introduced between the parts of an entertainment.

182 *Wolfgangus Vandergoose*]   Plate 31. Cf. Vangoose 'a rare artist' in Ben Jonson's *The Masque of Augurs* (1622).

182 *spagyric*]   alchemist.

182 *operator*]   a quack manufacturer of drugs, etc.

182–3 *the Invisible Lady styled the Magical Sister of the Rosicross*]   Everything about the Rosicrucians was so secret and mysterious that they were always good for a jest, here obscure.

196 *first matter*]   *materia prima*, the Aristotelian or scholastic *hyle* or matter without form, the original chaos.

197 *electuary*]   a medicinal paste consisting of a powder or other ingredient(s) mixed with honey or syrup.

199 *muscadine*]   muscatel wine.

201 *Menippus*]   the Cynic philosopher (first century B.C.), who amassed great wealth as a usurer but was cheated of it all and committed suicide (Diogenes Laertius, 2. 99–100).

201 *rine*]   rind.

203 *Treacle*]   theriacle, medicinal compound as antidote against venomous bites and poisons generally.

203–4 *Treacle of the gall of serpents and the liver of doves, to initiate a neophyte courtier*]   Harbage, *Davenant*, p. 54, points to the faction against *The Wits* (1634): Davenant 'was to be persecuted by a band of cleverly satirical "cavaliers" for the rest of his life'.

205 Gallo-belgicus]   a news-annual called *Mercurius Gallo-Belgicus* was published (in Latin) at Cologne, beginning in 1598 and continuing in the seventeenth century (half-yearly from 1605). Occasionally parts were translated into English, as *A relation of all matters passed, especially in the Low Countries, according to Mercurius Gallo-Belgicus*, 1614 (*S.T.C.* 20862). The untrustworthy nature of its news was frequently the object of British censure.

206 *coranto*]   gazette or newsletter (generally used in a disparaging sense).

207 *disprovu*]   presumably means 'an unprovided one', and so 'a needy man' (not in *N.E.D.*).

208 *gargarism*]   gargle.

208 Florio's First Fruits] *Florio his firste fruites: a perfect induction to the Italian and English tongues* (1578).

208 Diana de Montemayor] *La Diana* of Jorge de Montemayor (*c.* 1520–59) was translated by Bartholomew Yong in 1598.

209 *Spanish Romanças*] For the vogue of these see *The Golden Tapestry. A Critical Survey of Non-chivalric Spanish Fiction in English Translation (1543–1657)* by Dale B. J. Randall (Durham, North Carolina: Duke University Press, 1963), which contains bibliographies of both chivalric and non-chivalric fiction.

209 balneo] otherwise known as *bain-marie*, a vessel of water in which another vessel is put for warming gently.

213 *Frankfort*] apparently a slight on the book-catalogues published there.

213 *dryfat*] a large vessel used to hold dry things (as opposed to liquids).

215 *confederacy*] conspiracy.

227 *biggins*] child's cap (French *béguin*).

228 *muckenders*] handkerchiefs.

230 *Irishman*] Plate 32.

232 *Scottishman*] Plate 32.

234–5 *old-fashioned Englishman and his mistress*] Plates 32 and 33 show Elizabethan costumes. The women's parts in these Entries were taken by men. The note on this sheet of the Jones drawings reads: 'old habits of the three nations, for the music: they must be clinquant [tinselled] and rich'.

238–9 *Doctor Tartaglia and two pedants of Francolin*] Plate 35 (*a*). The allusion is obscure. Niccolò Tartaglia (*c.* 1506–59) was a celebrated Italian mathematician, who took the name Tartaglia because of an impediment in his speech.

242 *grotesques or drollities*] Plate 34.

245 *Invisible Lady*] See line 182.

258 *roaring boys*] swaggering fellows.

270 *antique cavaliers*] Plate 35 (*b*) shows them in medieval armour.

271 *manage*] the action and paces of a trained horse.

275 *Cavallerizzo*] a riding-master.

278–9 *the scene was changed into craggy rocks and inaccessible mountains*] Plate 24.

282–3 *Pausilipo near Naples*] The tunnel under Posilipo made in the time of Augustus was one of the sights of Italy. It is described by, among others, George Sandys (1610) and by Evelyn (about 8 February 1645).

290 *the Queen Mother*] Maria de' Medici (1573–1642), widow of King Henri IV of France and mother of Queen Henrietta Maria, had arrived in England in October 1638.

295 those growing comforts] the three surviving children of King Charles and Queen Henrietta Maria (aged 9, 6, and 3): Charles (later Charles II), born 29 May 1630; James (later James II), born 14 October 1633; Elizabeth,

born 28 January 1636. Henry (Duke of Gloucester) was born 8 July 1640, so Henrietta Maria was nearly four months pregnant when the masque was first performed, and five months when it was repeated at Shrovetide. The '*Amazonian habits*' (line 377) would doubtless conceal her condition.

302 rights] So Q. Perhaps read 'rites'.

304–5 the chief and best | Of modern victors] King Henri IV of France, who had been assassinated in 1610.

308 Your Tuscan wisdom] Maria de' Medici was born in Florence on 26 April 1573, daughter of Francesco de' Medici, grand duke of Tuscany. Her political ambitions were notorious (and disastrous).

321 o'er-weening priests] See Introduction to this masque, pp. 340–1.

325 heroës] trisyllabic.

329 *the rest of the masquers*] the ten men listed at the end (lines 484–93).

335 *The habit of his Majesty*] Plates 36(a) and (b), 37, and 39(a).

336 *watchet*] See line 143, n.

336 *set up of white*] See *N.E.D. s.v.* 'set' sb. 154. g. 'make brilliant, heighten the lustre of'.

337 *scrolls*] (apparently) ribboned-shaped appendages or decorations.

349 Murmur] rumour.

355 imperial arts to question thought] 'devices of an autocratic ruler who wanted to control even the thoughts of his subjects'. The apparently pejorative sense of 'imperial arts' is unusual.

366–7 *a huge cloud...opened*] Plate 25 (upper part).

369–70 *her Majesty sat*] Plate 25 (lower part).

370 *environed with her martial ladies*] the ten lady masquers listed at the end (lines 484–93).

377 *Amazonian habits*] Plates 38 and 39(a) and (b).

378 *baldrics*] belts worn over one shoulder across the breast and under the opposite arm.

392 perspectives] optical instruments; here telescopes (*optic* in line 396).

396 optic] punning on *eyes* in previous line: (1) eye, (2) telescope.

402–3 through the casements of her eyes | Her soul is ever looking out] The eyes as windows had for long been an image (Shakespeare, *Love's Labour's Lost*, 5. 2. 848: 'Behold the window of my heart, mine eye'; and *The Tempest*, 1. 2. 408, 'The fringed curtains of thine eye'). Davenant seems to be the first to use the casements.

436 *the scene was changed into magnificent buildings*] Plate 26.

437 *a bridge*] Plates 26 and 29.

440 *prospective*] perspective.

444–5 *two other clouds...covered all the upper part of the scene*] Plate 27.

446 *a heaven opened full of deities*] Plate 28.

472 *ingenuous*] ingenious.

473–4 *The invention, ornament, scenes, and apparitions, with their descriptions, were made by Inigo Jones*] This presumably means that the descriptions in the text were the composition of Jones, not of Davenant (see Nicoll, *Stuart Masques*, pp. 106–8).

478 *The subject was set down by them both*] Presumably 'The Subject of the Masque' (lines 1–18) was a joint composition.

479] Lewis Richard is described in Henrietta Maria's household book (1635) as chief of the Queen's musicians, with wages and allowance of £110 a quarter 'for himself and his boys'; his name given in this document is 'Loys Richardes' (P.R.O. E/101/439/3).

484 Duke of Lennox] James Stuart (1612–55), a close relative of the King.

484 Duchess of Lennox] Mary Villiers (1622–85), daughter of the late favourite, George Villiers, Duke of Buckingham (d. 1628).

485 Earl of Carlisle] James Hay (*c.* 1612–60), son of one of James I's great favourites (d. 1636).

485 Countess of Caernarvon] Anna Sophia Herbert (d. 1695), eldest daughter of Philip Herbert, Earl of Pembroke and Montgomery, the Lord Chamberlain; wife of Robert Dormer, who was created Earl of Caernarvon in 1628, three years after their marriage.

486 Earl of Newport] Mountjoy Blount (*c.* 1597–1666), son of the conqueror of Ireland, Charles Blount, Lord Mountjoy, Earl of Devonshire, and of Penelope Devereux, Lady Rich; a privy councillor.

486 Countess of Newport] Anne Butler, or Boteler (d. 1669); she had become a Roman Catholic in 1637, much to the annoyance of her husband.

487 Earl of Lanerick] or Lanark; William Hamilton (1616–51); created an earl by Charles I on 31 March 1639.

487 Countess of Portland] Frances Stuart (1617–94); sister of the Duke of Lennox, above, and wife of James Weston, Earl of Portland, who was the son of the late Lord Treasurer (d. 1635).

488 Lord Russell] William Russell (1616–1700); son of Francis Russell, Earl of Bedford (d. 1641). His wife was Anne Carr, only child of the Earl and Countess of Somerset.

488 Lady Andover] Dorothy Savage (*c.* 1611–91); daughter of Thomas Viscount Savage, and wife of Charles Howard, Viscount Andover, the elder son of Thomas Howard, Earl of Berkshire. Berkshire, her father-in-law, was the younger brother of Theophilus Howard, Earl of Suffolk, so this lady was a cousin by marriage of the Ladies Margaret and Frances mentioned below.

489 Lord Herbert] Philip Herbert (1621–69); brother of the Countess of Caernarvon and son of the Lord Chamberlain.

489 Lady Margaret Howard and Lady Frances Howard (line 491)] Margaret (1623–89) and Frances were daughters of Theophilus Howard, Earl of Suffolk.

490 Lord Paget] William Paget (1609–78); son and heir of William Lord Paget (d. 1629); married (1632) to Frances Rich, eldest daughter of Henry Rich, Earl of Holland.

490 Lady Kellymekin] or Kynalmeaky; Elizabeth Fielding (born 1619); sister of Lord Fielding, and wife of Lewis Boyle, Lord Kynalmeaky, the eldest son of Richard Boyle, Earl of Cork.

491 Lord Fielding] Basil Fielding or Feilding (c. 1608–75); son and heir of William Fielding, Earl of Denbigh, Master of the Great Wardrobe. His mother, Susan, Countess of Denbigh, sister of the late Duke of Buckingham, was Lady of the Robes in Henrietta Maria's household.

492 Master Russell] Probably Lord Russell's younger brother, Francis Russell (d. 1641).

492 Mistress Cary] Probably the Mistress Victoria Carey, or Carew, who is mentioned in the Lord Chamberlain's records as lodging at Whitehall, first with Lady Elizabeth Fielding before that lady's marriage to Kynalmeaky and afterwards with Lady Anne Fielding.

493 Master Thomas Howard] Probably the younger brother (1619–1706) of Charles Howard, Lady Andover's husband.

493 Mistress Nevill] not identified.

CUPID AND DEATH

BY JAMES SHIRLEY

Edited by B. A. Harris

INTRODUCTION

THE FABLE AND THE STORY

The ultimate source, and final meaning, of the fable of Cupid and Death, is to be sought at the deep well-head of the pagan mysteries, in the theme of 'Amor as a God of Death'. By the Renaissance, however, the marriage of Love and Death had been long dissolved, their essential union denied, and their undeniable conjunction explained in a multitude of sacred and profane ways. Hence, as Edgar Wind reports, 'these sweet agonies of love appeared reduced to moral anecdotes, idylls and epigrams', among which, under the title 'De Morte et Amore', Alciati introduced 'the fable of Love and Death exchanging their arrows, so that young people die and the old fall in love'.[1] Erwin Panofsky calls this popular story 'a kind of Renaissance variation on the *Danse aux Aveugles*'.[2]

The story of Cupid and Death is widespread in the related literature of sixteenth- and seventeenth-century emblem and epigram books, and its main features are clear. Sometimes Love and Death set out together hunting, Death carrying the arrows, Cupid, appropriately, the bows. Being blind, they exchange arrows by mistake. Alternatively, malicious Death steals the sleeping Cupid's weapons. But whether by accident or design the fatal exchange is often a consequence of drunkenness in a tavern, and thus the ancient mysterious relationship of sleep and death, and those associations of wine with fellowship, passion and degradation, remain easily preserved.

The moral which most evidently replaces the mystery is that commonplace which Shakespeare's Venus laments; that Death, the 'Hard-favour'd tyrant, ugly, meagre, lean', whose intended 'mark is feeble age', has once more perpetrated an outrage of the ignorant

---

[1] *Pagan Mysteries of the Renaissance* (1958), pp. 136–7.

[2] See his *Studies in Iconology* (1939), pp. 124–5, for comment on thematic and visual variations of the theme, and discussion of the engraving from a lost painting by Mattheus Bril and of a woodcut from Alciati's *Emblemata*, reproduced respectively in Plates 46 and 48(*a*).

and indifferent gods, and the young and beautiful Adonis has suffered:

> Love's golden arrow at him should have fled,
> And not death's ebon dart, to strike him dead.

(Venus and Adonis, 947–8)

The fourth emblem of Francis Thynne's *Emblemes and Epigrames* (1600) makes the point generally intended by the commonplace in terms of perverted fate:

> Thus contrary to kind, and their nature,
> Cupid doth slay, and Death doth love procure.

No old story-teller had been more influential in the general popularization of such moral fables as 'Aesop the great Mythologist', as Shirley called him in commendatory verses to John Ogilby's *The Fables of Aesop paraphras'd in verse, and adorn'd with sculptures* (1651). Shirley's masque was probably composed in the same year as this translation, and its Book One, Fable 39 'Of Cupid and Death' (Sigs Gg^r–Gg2^r) was cited as a primary source in Langbaine's *An Account of the English Dramatick Poets* (1691).

Ogilby's poem tells how Cupid roved all day wounding a thousand hearts and continued his sport at a masque. Death had 'As busy been, and mighty slaughter made' at a cruel battle. Tired, these 'two great Furies' sleep at the same inn. Death, rising early, takes Cupid's arrows by mistake, and hungry flies 'To breakfast at a massacre'. Cupid follows, storming 'with deadly arrows myrtle groves', in which 'cunning lovers lose to find their loves'. Hence, 'through the world a mighty change appears'. The bedridden dance, beldames mince, and he

> Whom Death had mark'd for sudden funerals
>   Now for his viol calls,
> And old rememb'ring makes new madrigals.

Only the action of a quick-witted youth, noting Cupid's arrows 'wing'd with death, 'gainst Nature's law', and urging him to 'See in the groves what slaughter thou hast made', eventually brings to an end this 'Tragi-Comedy...Of error long'. But Death still cheats, keeping back some of Cupid's arrows, and giving him

374

others 'dipt i'th'Stygian Lake'. The final 'Moral' shows this deceit perpetuated in human life, with sombre results:

> Age burns with Love, while Youth cold ague shakes;
> And Nature oft her principles mistakes:
> So suffers Youth in Age's cold embrace,
> As living men to dead bound face to face.

Shirley's masque considerably amplifies both the story and the moral offered here, introducing the characters of the Host and Chamberlain of the inn, providing comic relief with the all too human character of Despair and the old tale of his failure to hang himself, and augmenting the company of young lovers and old folk with military gentlemen, apes, satyrs, and the dancing figures of Folly and Madness. The four major symbolic persons of his masque are evidence enough of fresh treatment and changed intentions. Ogilby's female Death is a man in Shirley's masque, counterbalanced by the figure of Dame Nature, the dramatic representation of 'Nature's law'. The errors of blind Cupid and cozened Death, occasioned here by human malice, are not only corrected but are fully compensated by Mercury, the acknowledged agent of higher deities. The introduction of a *deus ex machina* is thus appropriate both to the theatrical form in which Shirley is working, and to enlarged significances with which he becomes concerned. For to some extent the masque follows a course suggested by some of the modulations of character creation, moving from early scenes of bucolic comedy, through a central action of tragi-comedy, to a resolution of noble sentiment and operatic splendour; just as its three scenes change from the inn yard in a forest clearing, to a pleasant formal park, and then to the brief solemnity of Paradise.

Although the 1653 text specifically names only the second entry, the 1659 edition adding the first, *Cupid and Death* has a coherent dramatic structure. The first two scenes have each five entries, five songs, and five anti-masques; the final short scene provides an additional song, the grand dance of the full company, and an epilogue.

In the first entry the Host and his Chamberlain discuss preparations at the inn for the arrival of Cupid and Death as guests; there follows the first anti-masque of Cupid's arrival attended by Folly and Madness, and the first choral comment with its ironic anticipation of disaster,

> Though little be the God of love,
> Yet his arrows mighty are.

The second entry belongs to Death, whose menacing dance is properly the second anti-masque. This prepares the sardonically conceived encounter of the Chamberlain with Despair, ending in a mood of drunken elation, disappointed greed, and revenge, transformed by the second song's didactic protest against 'Victorious men of Earth'. In the third entry the Chamberlain narrates how he has revenged himself upon both Cupid and Death by changing their arrows, a hollow victory of humanly uncontrollable consequences. Death has already left the inn, Cupid now rises, and the third song is an aubade of strong foreboding,

> Stay Cupid, whither art thou flying?
> Pity the pale lovers dying.

After this lengthy expository drama the scene changes to the formal garden of slain lovers (see Plate 47 (a)). Nature makes the fourth entry to a sad spectacle, which reaches its grotesque climax in the third anti-masque of infatuated old men and women. The fourth song, upon the impotence of Death, concludes in a chorus of reconciliation, urging Death and Love to try 'Upon yourselves your sad artillery'. This is the appropriate cue for the fourth anti-masque of six armed gentlemen, who take the field to fight, are shot by Death, and stay to dance together. The fifth song takes up the encouraging theme of war and peace, and its chorus implores the gods to intervene. The plea is to be answered, but theatrical art delays the awaited epiphany while the Chamberlain makes the fifth entry and prepares for later seriousness with a comic interlude. Afraid of what he has done he has left his old job and now leads apes to fairs. Nemesis, of course, is at his heels. Death strikes the Chamberlain, who falls in love with his apes, courts them sensually, is deprived of them by a satyr, and goes off to hang himself in the noose inherited from Despair. This episode closes in a bestial anti-masque of the apes and satyrs, an explicit enough manifestation of the central theme of mistaken action and misused natural powers.

To the sound of solemn music Mercury descends upon a cloud,

stilling the ribald confusion. Nature is discovered sleeping, exhausted by her appeals to the gods. Mercury summons Cupid and Death to judgment, and Nature wakes to find her dreams come true, her sleep restorative, and the gods just. Their judgments are traditional, and here Shirley seems to draw upon the further fable of Cupid, Death, and Reputation, who attend a funeral feast for young dead lovers in Ogilby's Fable 61 of Book Four (see Plate 47 (*b*) and Commentary, pp. 402–3). The three plan to meet again, and exchange addresses. Cupid lives among shepherds, Death is found in war, Reputation has no fixed abode, and therefore suggests they should all stay together, since 'Lost Reputation hard is to be found'.

This simple morality is invoked in the denouement to the masque. Mercury banishes Cupid from palaces to peasants' cottages, and though Death's power cannot be denied, its force is limited: for men of honour and renown may 'bleed but never die'. Nature's demand for satisfaction on behalf of those who have suffered, her 'noble children in the grave', is answered when Mercury causes the scene to change 'into Elysium, where the Grand Masquers, the slain lovers, appear in glorious seats and habits'. The masque closes with this theme of compensation, whose splendour is hymned in a final song, hinting at heaven, and Nature's sight 'Grows feeble at the brightness of this glory'. The dead rise to share the ecstatic finale of the grand dance, from which Mercury triumphantly summons them back, to enchantment from entertainment, to apotheosis from an audience's applause.

PRIVATE AND PUBLIC OCCASIONS

Cupid and Death was written for private performance, between 1651 and 1653, probably by the schoolboys Shirley was then teaching. It was offered 'without any address or design of the Author' on 26 March 1653 to the Portuguese Ambassador, the Condé de Penaguião, negotiator of the Treaty of Peace and Alliance between King John IV and Oliver Cromwell, signed in 1654.

Of this unexpected second occasion a note in the subsequent first edition of 1653 tells us only that the masque was 'presented by Mr Luke Channen, &c.', that the 'Scenes wanted no elegance, or curiosity for the delight of the spectator', that 'the musical compositions had in them a great soul of harmony', and that the 'gentlemen that performed the dances...shewed themselves masters of their quality'. Luke Channen is evidently the Luke Channell mentioned by Pepys (*Diary* for 24 September 1660), and described by Downes in *Roscius Anglicanus* as assisting Priest with dances for Davenant's *Macbeth* of 1672/3, for which Matthew Locke wrote music.

Christopher Gibbons composed the music for the 1653 performance of the masque, and his setting of 'Victorious men of Earth' was printed in that year. Matthew Locke took charge of the music for a third, and more spectacular, revival of *Cupid and Death* in 1659, probably by or for the Military Company at a house in Leicester Square.[1]

The survival of Locke's autograph score for 'The Instrumentall and Vocall Musique in the Morall representation att the Millitary Ground in Lesceitre ffields' (B.M. Add. MS 17799) is undoubtedly the main reason for the stage survival of the masque itself. A transcript (Huntington Library MS. HM 601) was made by J. P. Kemble in 1786 from Malone's copy of the 1653 quarto, and another transcript (B.M. Add. MS 17800) was made by Edward Jones, with a score by Sir Henry Rowley Bishop, in the nineteenth century. But the masque was revived for the first time since the seventeenth century on 1 March 1915, when it was presented in the Cambridge Museum of Classical Archaeology to illustrate Edward Dent's celebrated lectures on English Opera. On 24 April 1919 Dent again lectured on the subject at the Easter Festival at Glastonbury, for which, on 26 April, Rutland Boughton produced a one-scene version of the latter part of the masque. The whole work was given at the Summer Festival of that year, on 18, 22 and 27 August, Dent probably conducting the music. These occasions were noticeably gynarchical. Nature was played both times by Gwen Ffrangcon-Davies; Death was presented by Alice Bostock (a role she took in *Everyman*), and then by Naomi Florence; Cupid was taken by Kathleen Blurton and by Ruby Boughton; Despair by Phyllis Jewson; but the Chamberlain was Steuart Wilson.[2]

Cupid and Death now achieved a brief repertory. Antony Bernard

[1] See R. G. Howarth, 'Shirley's *Cupid and Death*', *T.L.S.* 15 November 1934, p. 795.
[2] See Michael Hurd's 'The Glastonbury Festivals', *Theatre Notebook*, XVII (Winter 1962/3), 54–5.

produced it at the Haslemere Festival of 1925; J. A. Westrup revived
it in December 1930 at the Scala Theatre, London; and in June 1931
G. E. Sedge presented it for Shirley's old college, in the Fellows'
Garden of St Catharine's College, Cambridge.

The largest public reached by the masque was also the most
private: those who heard two B.B.C. Third Programme performances
on 14 and 16 November 1952. The occasion was again seen as an
event of interest mainly to musicologists, and Edward Dent introduced the masque afresh in *The Listener*, as a 'masculine counterpart
to *Dido and Aeneas*'. Musically, of course, the comparison works to
the disadvantage of *Cupid and Death*. But the reminder that both
works were originally written respectively for a boys' school and a
girls' school is not only a tribute to seventeenth-century education
but a just scale of evaluation of *Cupid and Death* as a work of literature. Dent rightly terms it 'a very English mixture of stateliness and
broad comedy', a poet's 'idealization of the young English gentleman—a classical sixth form with its peculiar dignity and courtliness, its
background of antique learning, and its irrepressible sense of humour'.

The early scenes offer little more than relaxed, indeed loquacious,
contemporary amusement, well suited to sixth-formers, but as the
masque engages lyrically with its central theme of Love and Death
the songs are weighted with an imagery derived from an equally
contemporary experience of civil war. The defiant conclusion
Shirley offers is that of Christian piety and an appropriately hopeful
didacticism, and his literary skill matches this growing intention.
To some extent the masque moves beyond its first intentions with
an intensity which attracted two composers and caused its two increasingly elaborate and more public presentations. There is thus
credit, and much piquancy, in the circumstance which brought
Shirley from scholarly retirement to resume his long sustained role
of court entertainer, this time to Cromwell's guest. And since J. B.
Trend perceived that 'an allegorical piece like *Cupid and Death*,
with its incidental music and symbolic dancing, has an extraordinary
suggestion of Calderón's mythological pieces of the same period',[1]
perhaps the Portuguese Ambassador's 'honorable acceptation' was
more informed than we might suppose, or can ourselves achieve.

[1] See *Seventeenth Century Studies presented to Sir Herbert Grierson* (1938), pp. 161–2.

[DRAMATIS PERSONAE

Host
Chamberlain
Cupid
Folly
Madness
Death
Despair
Mercury
Nature

Lovers
Ladies
Two Old Men
Two Old Women
Six Armed Gentlemen
Satyr
Two Apes]

CUPID AND DEATH

A MASQUE
AS IT WAS PRESENTED BEFORE
HIS EXCELLENCY THE AMBASSADOR OF
PORTUGAL UPON THE 26 OF MARCH 1653

*   *   *

A Forest; on the side of a Hill a fair House representing an Inn or
Tavern, out of which cometh an Host, being a jolly, sprightly old man,
his cap turned up with crimson, his doublet fustian, with jerkin and
hanging sleeves, trunk hose of russet, stockings yellow, cross-gartered;
after him, a Chamberlain.   5

    Host. Are all things in their preparation
      For my immortal guests?
    Chamberlain.   Nothing is wanting
      That doth concern my province, sir; I am
      Your officer above stairs. The great chamber   10
      With the two wooden monuments to sleep in
      (That weigh six load of timber, sir) are ready.
      That for the Prince D'Amour, whom we call Cupid,
      I have trimm'd artificially with roses
      And his own mother's myrtle. But I have   15
      Committed sacrilege to please the other;
      Death does delight in yew, and I have robb'd
      A church-yard for him. Are you sure they'll come
      Tonight? I would fain see this dwarf call'd Cupid;
      For t'other, I look on him in my fancy   20
      Like a starv'd goblin.
    Host.   Death, I must confess,
      Cuts not so many inches in the say
      As our last venison; 'tis a thin-chapp'd hound,
      And yet the cormorant is ever feeding.   25

Chamberlain. He is kin to the devouring gentleman
  Of the long robe—
Host.   That has bespoke a chamber
  I' the College among the Bears, and means to be
  In commons with them.   3
Chamberlain.   But, good sir, resolve me,
  Are they good-spirited guests? Will they tipple
  To elevation? Do they scatter metal
  Upon the waiters? Will they roar, and fancy
  The drawers, and the fiddles, till their pockets   3
  Are empty as our neighbours drone? And after
  Drop by degrees their wardrobe? And in the morning,
  When they have daylight to behold their nakedness,
  Will they with confidence amaze the streets,
  And in their shirts, to save their pickled credits,   4
  Pretend a race, and trip it like fell footmen?
  These rantings were the badges of our gentry,
  But all their dancing days are done, I fear.
Host. These were the garbs and motions, late in fashion
  With humorous mortals; but these guests are of   ¿
  No human race.
Chamberlain. Pray, what attendance have they?
Host.   Love has two
  Gentlemen, that wait on him in his chamber,
  Of special trust; he cannot act without them.
Chamberlain. Their names, sir, I beseech you?   9
Host.   Folly and Madness.
Chamberlain. A pair of precious instruments, and fit
  To be o' the Privy Council.
Host.   We may see   ·
  What most of our nobility are come to.
Chamberlain. Sure they are well descended, sir.
Host.   The fool
  Could ride a hundred miles in his own pedigree,
  And give as many coats—   ·
Chamberlain.   Fools' coats, there are
  Enough to wear them—

Host.   —as he had acres in
  Eleven fat lordships,
  And play'd at duck and drake with gold, like pebbles.   65
Chamberlain. Was this man born a fool?
Host.   No, but his keeping
  Company with philosophers undid him,
  Who found him out a mistress they call'd Fame,
  And made him spend half his estate in libraries,   70
  Which he bestow'd on colleges, took the toy
  Of building quadrangles, kept open house,
  And fell at last most desperately in love
  With a poor dairy-maid, for which he was begg'd—
Chamberlain. A fool?   75
Host.   —and leads the van in Cupid's regiment.
Chamberlain. What was the madman, sir?
Host. A Thing was born to a very fair *per annum*,
  And spent it all in looking-glasses.
Chamberlain. How?   80
  That's a project I never heard on, looking-glasses!
  How many did he break, sir, in a day?
Host. They broke him rather, in the right understanding;
  For nature having given him a good face,
  The man grew wild with his own admirations,   85
  And spent his full means upon flatterers
  That represented him next to an angel.
  Thus blown up, he took confidence to court
  A lady of noble blood and swelling fortune;
  Within three days fell sick of the small pox,   90
  And, on the fourth, run mad, with the conceit
  His face, when he recover'd, would be like
  A country cake from which some children had
  New pick'd the plums.
Chamberlain.   A brace of pretty beagles.   95
Host. They are here.
Chamberlain. I see not Death.
Host.   He's the last thing we look for.

383

*Enter Cupid, Folly, Madness; the Host joins with them in
a dance.*

Song

Though little be the God of love,
Yet his arrows mighty are,
And his victories above
What the valiant reach by war;
Nor are his limits with the sky;
O'er the milky way he'll fly,
And sometimes wound a deity.
Apollo once the Python slew,
But a keener arrow flew
From Daphne's eye, and made a wound
For which the God no balsam found.
One smile of Venus, too, did more
On Mars, than armies could before:
If a warm fit thus pull him down,
How will she ague-shake him with a frown!
Thus Love can fiery spirits tame,
And, when he please, cold rocks inflame.

Enter Death: he danceth the Second Entry; after which, he speaks.

Death. Holla! within!
Enter Chamberlain.

Chamberlain. You are welcome, gentlemen—ha!
Quarter, oh quarter! I am a friend, sir,
A movable belonging to this tenement
Where you are expected. Cupid is come already,
And supp'd, and almost drunk. We have reserv'd
According to order, for your palate, sir,
The cockatrice's eggs, the cold toad-pie,
Ten dozen of spiders, and the adders' tongues
Your servant Famine, sir, bespoke.
Death. Live, live. *Exit.*
Chamberlain. I thank you, sir. A curse upon his physnomy!

384

How was I surpris'd! 'Twas high time to comfort me,
I felt my life was melting downward.
[*Despair.*] Death, oh death!   *Within.* 135
Chamberlain. Who's that? I do not like the voice. What art?

Enter Despair, with a halter.

Despair. A miserable thing.
Chamberlain.   Aye, so thou seem'st:
  Hast not a name?   140
Despair.   My name, sir, is Despair.
Chamberlain. Despair? My time's not come yet: what have I
  To do with thee? What com'st thou hither for?
Despair. To find out Death: life is a burden to me;
  I have pursued all paths to find him out,   145
  And here i' the forest had a glimpse on him,
  But could not reach him with my feet, or voice;
  I would fain die, but Death flies from me, sir.
Chamberlain. I wonder you should travel in the forest,
  And among so many trees find none convenient,   150
  Having the tackling ready 'bout your neck too.
  Some great affairs take up the devil's time,
  He cannot sure attend these low employments;
  He's busy 'bout leviathans. I know not,
  There's something in't. You have not made your will, sure. 155
Despair. Yes, sir, I carry it wi' me; it wants nothing
  But his name, and my subscription.
Chamberlain.   Whose name?
Despair. His name I mean to make my heir.
Chamberlain.   Who's that?   160
Despair. That charitable man
  Will bring Death to me; there's a blank left for him,
  And if you please to do me, sir, the office,
  Even you shall be the man. I have profess'd
  An usurer these fifty years and upwards;   165
  The widows and sad orphans, whose estates
  I have devour'd, are croaking in my conscience.
Chamberlain. And shall he be your heir, that does this feat,

25   385   S M

To make you acquainted with this cannibal
You talk of?   170
Despair.   O my happiness!
Chamberlain.   I'll do it.
But I believe you're sorry for your baseness,
Your rapines and extortions—
Despair.   Mistake not,   175
I am sorry for no mischief I have done;
That would come near repentance, which you know
Cures all the achings of the soul; if I
Could but be sorry, Death were of no use to me.
Chamberlain. Keep ye of that mind, you say very right, sir;   180
I'll try what I can do
With Death, to do your conscience a courtesy;
He's now within our house. I'll bring you pen
And ink to write my name too, honest father.
Despair. Thou art my dearest child, take all my blessings.   185
Chamberlain. [*aside*] Here's like to be a fortune.   *Exit.*
Despair.   I want strength
To climb; I see a very pretty twig else,   *He climbs.*
And space for a most comfortable swing;
'Tis a hard case the devil will not help   190
At a dead lift.   *He falls.*
          O my sciatica!
I have broke my spectacles, and both my hips
Are out of joint. Help!—

Enter Chamberlain with a bottle of wine.   195

Chamberlain. Death will be with you presently, the last course
Is now on the table: that you may not think
The time long, I have brought you—ha! rise up, sir.
Despair. Alas, I have had a fall: I was endeavouring
To do the meritorious work, and hang   200
Myself, for Death methought was long a coming,
But my foot slipp'd.
Chamberlain.   Alas, what pity 'twas!
If I had thought your soul had been in such

386

Haste, I would have given you a lift before   205
I went.
Despair. It was my zeal.
Chamberlain.   Alas, it seem'd so;
  You might have took the river with more ease,
  The stream would have convey'd you down so gently   210
  You should not feel which way your soul was going.
  But against the frights Death might bring with him,
  I have brought you a bottle of wine. I'll begin, sir.   *He drinks.*
Despair. Would it were poison.
Chamberlain.   So would not I, I thank you,   215
  'Tis pure blood of the grape.
Despair. Wine?
Chamberlain.   At my charge; I know you do not use
  To pay for nectar; I bestow it, sir.
Despair. That's kindly said, I care not if I taste—   220
Chamberlain. I' the mean time please you, I'll peruse the will;
  I can put in my own name, and make it fit
  For your subscription. [*aside*] What's here?   *Reads.*
  Ha! a thousand pound in jewels, in ready money
  Ten thousand more, land—ha! preserve my senses!   225
  I'll write my name, and thank heaven afterwards.
  [*To him*] Here sir, before you can subscribe, the gentleman
  Will come, and kill you to your heart's content.
Despair. Hum! this foolish wine has warm'd me; what d'ye
  Call the name on't?   230
Chamberlain.   Sack.
Despair.   Sack! why truly, son—
Chamberlain. Nay sir, make haste, for Death will be here instantly.
Despair. At his own leisure, I would not be troublesome;
  Now I do know his lodging I can come   235
  Another time.
Chamberlain. But the will, father, you may write now—
Despair. Deeds are not vigorous without legal witnesses;
  My scrivener lives at the next town, and I
  Do find my body in a disposition   240
  To walk a mile or two. Sack, d'ye call it?

How strangely it does alter my opinion!
Chamberlain. Why, have you no mind to hang yourself?
Despair. I thank you, I find no inclination.
Chamberlain. Shall not I be your heir then?   245
Despair.   In the humour
  And spirit I now feel, in brain and body,
  I may live—to see you hang'd; I thank you heartily.
Chamberlain. But you will have the conscience, I hope,
  To pay me for the wine has wrought this miracle?   250
Despair. Your free gift, I remember: you know, 'I use not
  To pay for nectar', as you call it. Yet
  I am not without purpose to be grateful;
  Some things shall be corrected in my will.
  In the mean time, if you'll accept of a   *Gives him the halter.* 255
  Small legacy, this hemp is at your service,
  And it shall cost you nothing, 'I bestow it'.
  We men of money, worn with age and cares,
  Drink in new life from wine that costs us nothing.
  Farewell, and learn this lesson from Despair,   260
  Give not your father sack to be his heir.   *Exit.*
Chamberlain. Not a tear left! Would's brains were in the bottle!
                                                             Exit.

Song

Victorious men of Earth, no more   265
   Proclaim how wide your Empires are;
Though you bind in every shore,
   And your triumphs reach as far
As night or day,
Yet you proud monarchs must obey,   270
And mingle with forgotten ashes, when
Death calls ye to the crowd of common men.

Devouring famine, plague, and war,
   Each able to undo mankind,
Death's servile emissaries are;   275
   Nor to these alone confin'd,
He hath at will

More quaint and subtle ways to kill.
A smile or kiss, as he will use the art,
Shall have the cunning skill to break a heart.   280

Enter Chamberlain.

Chamberlain. Ho, master, master!

Enter Host.

Host.   What's the matter?
Chamberlain. Nothing but to ask you whether you be   285
  Alive or no, or whether I am not
  My own ghost, that thus walk and haunt your house.
Host. Thou lookest frighted.
Chamberlain.   Death and his train are gone,
  I thank heaven he's departed. I slept not   290
  One wink tonight, nor durst I pray aloud
  For fear of waking Death: but he, at midnight,
  Calls for a cup to quench his thirst; a bowl
  Of blood I gave him for a morning's draught,
  And had an ague all the while he drunk it.   295
  At parting, in my own defence, and hope
  To please him, I desir'd to kiss his hand,
  Which was so cold, o' the sudden, sir, my mouth
  Was frozen up, which, as the case stood
  Then with my teeth, did me a benefit,   300
  And kept the dancing bones from leaping out.
  At length, fearing for ever to be speechless,
  I us'd the strength of both my hands to open
  My lips, and now felt every word I spake
  Drop from it like an icicle.   305
Host. This cold fit will be over; what said Cupid?
Chamberlain. He was fast asleep.
Host. The boy went drunk to bed; Death did not wake him?
Chamberlain. It was not necessary in point of reckoning;
  Death was as free as any emperor,   310
  And pays all where he comes, Death quits all scores.
  I have the *summa totalis* in my pocket,

But he, without more ceremony, left
The house at morning twilight.

Host.   Ha! they knock—   31?
Get thee a cup of wine to warm thy entrails.   *Exit Chamberlain.*
Though Love himself be but a water-drinker,
His train allow themselves rich wines. Your fool
And madman is your only guests to taverns;
And to excess, this licence time affords,   32(
When masters pay, their servants drink like lords.

Enter Chamberlain.

Chamberlain. Sir, they call for you; Cupid's up and ready,
And looks as fresh as if he had known no surfeit
Of virgins' tears, for whose fair satisfaction   32?
He broke his leaden shafts, and vows hereafter
To shoot all flames of love into their servants.
There are some music come, to give his godship
Good morrow, so he means to hear one song
And then he takes his progress.   33(
Host.   I attend him.   *Exit.*
Chamberlain. But I have made my own revenge upon him,
For the hard-hearted baggage that he sent me;
And Death I have serv'd a trick for all his huffing.
They think not what artillery they carry   33?
Along with them; I have chang'd their arrows.
How Death will fret to see his fury cozen'd!
But how will Love look pale when he shall find
What a mortality his arrows make
Among the lovers! Let the god look to't,   34(
I have put it past my care, and not expect
To see them again; or should I meet with Death,
I shall not fear him now; for Cupid, if
Lovers must only by his arrows fall,
I am safe, for, ladies, I defy you all.   *Exit.* 34(

Song

Stay Cupid, whither art thou flying?
Pity the pale lovers dying.
They that honour'd thee before,
Will no more   350
At thy altar pay their vows.

O let the weeping virgins strow,
Instead of rose, and myrtle boughs,
Sad yew, and funeral cypress now.
Unkind Cupid leave thy killing,   355
These are all thy mother's doves;
O do not wound such noble loves,
And make them bleed, that should be billing.

*The Scene is changed into a pleasant Garden, a fountain in the midst of
it; walks and arbours, delightfully expressed; in divers places, ladies* 360
*lamenting over their lovers slain by Cupid, who is discovered flying in
the air.*

Enter a lover playing upon a lute, courting his mistress; they dance.

*Enter Nature in a white robe, a chaplet of flowers, a green mantle
fringed with gold, her hair loose. They start, and seem troubled at her* 365
entrance.

Nature. Fly, fly my children! Love that should preserve,
And warm your hearts with kind and active blood,
Is now become your enemy, a murderer.
This garden, that was once your entertainment   370
With all the beauty of the spring, is now,
By some strange curse upon the shafts of Cupid,
Design'd to be a grave. Look, everywhere
The noble lovers on the ground lie bleeding,
By frantic Cupid slain; into whose wounds   375
Distracted virgins pour their tears so fast,
That having drain'd their fountains, they present
Their own pale monuments. While I but relate
This story, see, more added to the dead.

391

O fly, and save yourselves! I am your parent, 38
Nature, that thus advise you to your safeties.

Enter Cupid: he strikes the lover.

He's come already.
Lover.　　　　　Ha! What winter creeps
Into my heart! 38
Nature.　　　He faints; 'tis now too late;
Some kinder god call back the winged boy,
And give him eyes to look upon his murders.
Nature grows stiff with horror of this spectacle;
If it be death to love, what will it be 39
When Death itself must act his cruelty?

Enter Death.

And here he comes; what tragedies are next?

Enter old men and women with crutches.

Two aged pair; these will be fit for death; 39
They can expect but a few minutes more
To wear the heavy burden of their lives.

Death strikes them with his arrow.　　　　　[*Exit Death.*]
They, admiring one another, let fall their crutches and embrace.

Astonishment to Nature! They throw off 4
All their infirmities, as young men do
Their airy upper garments. These were the
Effects of Cupid's shafts; prodigious change!
I have not patience to behold 'em longer.　　*Exit.*

They dance with antic postures, expressing rural courtship. 4

Song

What will it, Death, advance thy name,
Upon cold rocks to waste a flame,
Or by mistake to throw
Bright torches into pits of snow? 4

Thy rage is lost,
And thy old killing frost.
With thy arrows thou may'st try
To make the young or aged bleed,
But indeed   415
Not compel one heart to die.
  Chorus. O Love! O Death! be it your fate
Before you both repent too late,
To meet and try
Upon yourselves your sad artillery.   420
So Death may make Love kind again,
Or cruel Death by Love be slain.

Enter six gentlemen armed, as in the field, to fight three against three.
To them Death: he strikes them with his arrow, [exit] and they, pre-
paring to charge, meet one another and embrace. They dance.   425

              Song

Change, O change, your fatal bows,
Since neither knows
The virtue of each other's darts.
Alas, what will become of hearts   430
If it prove
A death to love;
We shall find
Death will be cruel to be kind:
For when he shall to armies fly,   435
Where men think blood too cheap to buy
Themselves a name,
He reconciles them, and deprives
The valiant men of more than lives,
A victory, and fame: 440
Whilst Love, deceiv'd by these cold shafts, instead
Of curing wounded hearts, must kill indeed.
  Chorus. Take pity, gods! some ease the world will find,
To give young Cupid eyes, or strike Death blind.
Death should not then have his own will,   445
And Love, by seeing men bleed, leave off to kill.

Enter Chamberlain leading two apes.

Chamberlain. O yes, O yes, O yes!
All you that delight to be merry, come see
My brace of court apes, for a need we be three.   45
I have left my old trade of up and down stairs,
And now live by leading my apes unto fairs.
Will you have any sport? draw your money, be quick, sir,
And then come aloft Jack, they shall show you a trick, sir.

Now am I in my natural condition,   45
For I was born under a wandering planet;
I durst no longer stay with my old master
For fear Cupid and Death be reconcil'd
To their own arrows, and so renew with me
Some precious acquaintance.   40

Enter Death: he strikes the Chamberlain.   [Exit Death]

O, my heart!
'Twas Death I fear: I am paid then with a vengeance.
My dear apes, do not leave me, ha! come near—
What goodly shapes they have, what lovely faces!   40
Ye twins of beauty, where were all those graces
Obscur'd so long? what cloud did interpose
I could not see before this lip, this nose,
These eyes? that do invite all hearts to woo them,
Brighter than stars, ladies' are nothing to them.   4
O let me here pay down a lover's duty;
Who is so mad to dote on woman's beauty?
Nature doth here her own complexion spread,
No borrow'd ornaments of white and red;
These cheeks wear no adulterate mixtures on them   4
To make them blush as some do—fie upon them!
Look what fair cherries on their lips do grow!
Black cherries, such as none of you can show
That boast your beauties; let me kiss your a—

Enter a satyr, that strikes him on the shoulder,   4
and takes away his apes.

394

What's that? a shot i' the shoulder too? ha!
What will become of me now? O my apes!
The darlings of my heart are ravish'd from me.

He beckons, and courts them back with passionate postures.   485

No? not yet? nor yet, hard-hearted apes?
I must despair for ever to enjoy them.
Despair? that name puts me in mind—

He looks in his pocket, and pulls out the halter.

'Tis here;   490
Welcome dear legacy; I see he was
A prophet that bestow'd it; how it fits me!
As well as if the hangman had took measure.
'Tis honour in some men to fight and die
In their fair ladies' quarrel, and shall I   495
Be 'fraid to hang myself in such a cause?
Farewell my pretty apes! when hemp is tied,
Drop tears apace, and I am satisfied.   *Exit.*

A dance of the satyrs and apes.

Upon the sudden a solemn music is heard, and Mercury seen descending 500
upon a cloud, at whose approach the others creep in amazed. In a part
of the Scene, within a bower, Nature discovered sleeping.

Mercury. Hence ye profane, and take your dwellings up
Within some cave that never saw the sun,
Whose beams grow pale and sick to look upon you;   505
This place be sacred to more noble objects.
And see where Nature, tir'd with her complaints
To heaven for Death and Cupid's tyranny,
Upon a bank of smiling flowers lies sleeping.
Cares, that devour the peace of other bosoms,   510
Have, by an overcharge of sorrow, wrought
Her heart into a calm, where every sense
Is bound up in a soft repose and silence;
Be her dreams all of me. But to my embassy.

Cupid, whereso'er thou be,⁵
The gods lay their commands on thee,
In pain of being banish'd to
The unfrequented shades below,
At my first summons to appear:
Cupid, Cupid!⁵

Enter Cupid.

Cupid.   I am here.
  What send the gods by Mercury?
Mercury. Thy shame and horror. I remove
  This mist.   *He unblinds him.*⁵
            Now see in every grove
What slaughter thou hast made. All these,
Fond Cupid, were thy votaries.
Does not their blood make thine look pale?
All slain by thee; 'twill not prevail⁵
To urge mistakes, thy fact appears:
Jove and the gods have bow'd their ears
To groaning Nature, and sent me
From their high crystal thrones to see
What blood, like a dire vapour rise,⁵
Doth spread his wings to blind the eyes
Of heaven and day; and to declare
Their justice and immortal care
Over the lower world; but stay—
Another must his fate obey.⁵

    Death, heretofore the look'd-for close
    To tedious life, the long repose
    To wearied Nature, and the gate
    That leads to man's eternal fate,
    I, in the name of every god,
    Command thee from thy dark abode,⁵
    As thou wilt fly their wrath, appear
    At my first summons—

Enter Death.

Death.   I am here.   550
Mercury. Nature awake, and with thy sleep
  Shake off the heavy chains that keep
  Thy soul a captive.
Nature.   Mercury?
  Or am I still in dreams?   555
Mercury.   Thy eye
  Take truce with tears; see, much abus'd
  Nature, whom thou hast long accus'd.
  Leave thy wonder, and attend
  What the gods by Hermes send.   560
  But first I charge you to resign
  Your fatal shafts.   *They change.*
Cupid.   Aye, these are mine.
Mercury. Cupid, the gods do banish thee
  From every palace; thou must be   565
  Confin'd to cottages, to poor
  And humble cells; Love must no more
  Appear in princes' courts; their heart,
  Impenetrable by thy dart,
  And from softer influence free,   570
  By their own wills must guided be.
Cupid. I shall obey.
Mercury. Death, thou may'st still
  Exercise thy power to kill;
  With this limit, that thy rage   575
  Presume not henceforth to engage
  On persons in whose breast divine
  Marks of art or honour shine;
  Upon these if thy malice try,
  They may bleed but never die;   580
  These are not to be overcome
  Above the force of age or tomb.
  Is Nature pleas'd?
Nature.   The gods are just.

397

Mercury. To this you both submit?   5

Cupid. ⎱
Death. ⎰   We must.

Mercury. Ye are dismiss'd.   *Exeunt.*

Nature.   But Mercury,
What satisfaction shall I have   5
For noble children in the grave,
By Cupid slain?

Mercury.   They cannot be
Reduc'd to live again with thee,
And could thy fancy entertain   5
In what bless'd seats they now remain,
Thou would'st not wish them here.

Nature.   Might I
With some knowledge bless my eye,
Nature would put on youth.   6

Mercury.   Then see
Their bless'd condition.

*The Scene is changed into Elysium, where the Grand Masquers, the
slain lovers, appear in glorious seats and habits.*

Nature. Where am I?   6
The world no such perfection yields.

Mercury. These are the fair Elysian fields.

Song

Open bless'd Elysium grove,
Where an eternal spring of love   6
Keeps each beauty fair; these shades
No chill dew or frost invades.
Look how the flowers, and every tree
Pregnant with ambrosia be;
Near banks of violet, springs appear,   6
Weeping out nectar every tear;
While the once-harmonious spheres,
(Turn'd all to ears)

Now listen to the birds, whose quire
Sing every charming accent higher.   620
Chorus. If this place be not heaven, one thought can make it,
  And gods, by their own wonder led, mistake it.
Nature. O who shall guide me hence? Old Nature's sight
  Grows feeble at the brightness of this glory.
Mercury. I will be Nature's conduct.   625
Nature. Mercury, be ever honour'd.   *Exeunt.*

The grand dance.

Enter Mercury.

Mercury. Return, return you happy men,
  To your own blessed shades again,   630
  Lest staying long, some new desire
  In your calm bosoms raise a fire.
  Here are some eyes, whose every beam
  May your wandering hearts inflame,
  And make you forfeit your cool groves,   635
  By being false to your first loves.
    Like a perfuming gale o'er flowers,
    Now glide again to your own bowers.

The masquers retreated, the curtain falls.

FINIS

THE TEXT

Cupid and Death was first printed in a quarto of 1653 (Wing 3464), immediately after the March performance. There is no reason to doubt the title-page statement that it was 'Printed according to the Author's own Copy'. A second quarto of 1659 (Wing 3465) followed the performance of that year. Some copies of this edition have a variant title-page, and may represent another issue (see Greg, *Bibliography*, II, 829–30).

The present edition has been prepared from the first quarto of 1653, of which copies in the British Museum (Thomason Collection), Huntington, Newberry, and Yale Libraries have been collated. Further collation with the British Museum and Huntington Library copies of the 1659 quarto shows that the latter is an edited reprint, making two slight omissions (see Collation and Commentary, pp. 401–3). The modernized editions of A. Dyce, *The Dramatic Works and Poems of James Shirley* (1833), vol. VI, and of E. J. Dent, '*Cupid and Death*', *Musica Britannica*, II (1951), have been consulted. Dent offers a modernized score of the music of Matthew Locke and Christopher Gibbons.

Cupid and Death presents no serious textual problems, though Shirley's fondness for feminine endings, loose writing, and extra-metrical feet means that much lineation is a matter of opinion. In modernizing the punctuation I have retained more marks of exclamation than might seem justified or customary; but speeches which became recitative in 1659 are still strong declamation in 1653, and the heavier pointing seems required.

COLLATION

5]   Q2 *adds* FIRST ENTRY.
26–30 He is kin...commons with them]   Q2 *omits.*
53–6 and fit...come to]   Q2 *omits.*
71   bestow'd on colleges] bestowed Colleges Q1; bestowed on Colledges Q2.
144 burden]   Q1; burthen Q2.
232 why truly]   Q1; my truly Q2.
270 Yet]   *Tet* Q1; *Yet* Q2.
295 an ague]   Q1; and Ague Q2.
295 drunk]   Q1; drank Q2.
368 blood]   Q1; Q2 *omits (? imperfect).*
439 than]   Q1; then Q2.
447 *Chamberlain*]   Q1; Chamberlin Q2.
461 *Chamberlain.*]   Q1; Chamberlin Q2.
469 woo]   *wo* Q1; *wooe,* Q2.
470 than]   *than* Q1; *then* Q2.
475 wear]   *wear* Q1; *were* Q2.
480 *him on the*]   on the him Q1; *him on the* Q2.
500 *heard,*]   heard, Q1; heapd, Q2.
639 *The masquers retreated*]   Q1; Q2 *omits.*
639 *the*]   Q1; *The* Q2.

COMMENTARY

13 the Prince D'Amour]   probably a reference to Davenant's masque *The Triumphs of the Prince d'Amour* (1636).

23 Cuts...in the say]   Say = assay. *N.E.D.*, Sb.² 5, Venery, trial of grease, cites Chapman's *Iliad*, XIX, 246,

> There, hauing brought the Bore
> Atrides with his knife tooke sey.

29 College among the Bears]   Cf. 'I landed him at the Beares Colledge on the Bankside, alias Paris Garden', *Taylors Wit & Mirth*, reprinted in *Shakespear Jest Books*, ed. W. C. Hazlitt, p. 9. The 1659 quarto omits lines 26–30 ('He is kin...commons with them') perhaps for obscurity.

53–6 and fit...come to]   The 1659 quarto omits this allusion to the Privy Council, presumably because of increased sensitivity to political conduct.

58–95 The fool...brace of pretty beagles]   These references seem unlikely to represent specific individuals, and Shirley's social comedies yield many comparably generalized passages. It is possible that Folly, the Fame-smitten snob, and Madness, the gullible projectionist, had identifiable appearances.

154 leviathans]   Capitalized in both 1653 and 1659 quartos, and evidently referring to Hobbes's *Leviathan* (1651).

238 vigorous]   capable of being enforced.

328 music]   musicians.

334 huffing]   rage.

402 airy]   light.

425 *They dance*]   In Locke's autograph score this dance is termed 'The Hectors' Dance', which suggests that its performance in 1659 was probably given a fresh prominence for the Military Company.

447 *Enter Chamberlain*]   The scene draws upon some reminiscence of the love of Bottom and Titania.

500 *Mercury*]   In Shirley's *Triumph of Beauty*, much influenced by *A Mid-summer-Night's Dream*, Mercury intervenes in similar, though less solemn, fashion, to drive off the anti-masque of shepherds, led by the Bottom-inspired character of the roistering Bottle.

503–84 Hence ye...gods are just]   For the influence of the moralizing emblematic tradition upon this scene of the judgments upon Cupid and Death, see Ogilby's *Fables of Aesop*, Fourth Book, The One and Sixtieth Fable, 'Of Cupid, Death, and Reputation' (sigs. Aaaaʳ–Aaaa2ᵛ). Here Cupid claims to reside not in courts or cities, but among shepherds, Death boasts that his habitation is not of this world, but that he can be found 'where in mighty war, | Against his King, some valiant general stands' (surely a contemporary touch), and the moral derives reputation from honour, and condemns 'the Matchivellian'. The anecdote of 'Reputation, Love, and Death' is employed by Ferdinand in admonishment of his sister (*The Duchess of Malfi*, III. 2. 120–34), as Shirley may well have remembered.

525 *He unblinds him*]   The reference to 'mist' makes clear that this is blind, not blindfold, Cupid.

594 Reduc'd]   brought back.

639 *the curtain falls*]   Since the 1659 quarto retains this direction, and omits '*The masquers retreated*', it seems obvious that the performances of both 1653 and 1659 were given within the normal confines of private house entertainment.

'THESE PRETTY DEVICES'

A Study of Masques in Plays

By Inga-Stina Ewbank

> *A Dancer.* A masque will be delightful to the ladies.
> *Caperwit.* Oh, sir, what plays are taking without these
> Pretty devices? Many gentlemen
> Are not, as in the days of understanding,
> Now satisfied without a jig, which since
> They cannot, with their honour, call for after
> The play, they look to be serv'd up in the middle:
> Your dance is the best language of some comedies,
> And footing runs away with all; a scene
> Express'd with life of art, and squared to nature,
> Is dull and phlegmatic poetry.

These lines are spoken in Shirley's comedy *Changes, or Love in a Maze* (1631/2; IV, ii).[1] They can hardly be taken to express Shirley's thoughts on the use of masques in plays, for he drew heavily on masque materials both in his comedies and in his tragedies; nor are they very meaningful as a representation of Caperwit's own opinion, for in the last scene he engineers a masque which resolves the love-intrigues of the play. They are, rather, a conventional gesture towards the purist's scorn of a hybrid art form, such as voiced by Jonson twenty years earlier, when he spoke of 'Plays: wherein, now, the concupiscence of dances and antics so reigneth as to run away from nature, and be afraid of her, is the only point of art that tickles the spectators'.[2] Both Caperwit and Jonson profess to see the masque within a play as of mere entertainment value, and as a regrettable departure from 'nature'—i.e. from realism in action and speech. What Jonson ignores, despite his own achievement in *Cynthia's Revels*, and what Caperwit has to forget in order to make a satirical point, are the important dramatic functions that 'these pretty devices' are made to perform in many plays. In what follows I hope to explore and exemplify some of those functions.

The 'days of understanding' whose passing Caperwit laments

---

[1] The dates attributed to plays in this essay are, unless otherwise indicated, those given in E. K. Chambers, *The Elizabethan Stage*, and G. E. Bentley, *The Jacobean and Caroline Stage*. Quotations, whether from early texts or from the modern editions to which reference is made, have been modernized.

[2] *The Alchemist*, address 'To the Reader' (ed. Herford and Simpson, v, 291).

can only be envisaged as an undefined Golden Age, for it is well known that throughout the period of Tudor and Stuart drama there was a close and lively interaction between masque and dramatic forms.[1] At either end of the period the two kinds appear inextricably intermingled: Lyly turns the court-entertainment into drama;[2] while some fifty years later Shirley turns drama into masque. Linking these two chronological extremes is a whole row of plays— Peele's *The Arraignment of Paris*, Dekker's *Old Fortunatus* and his and Ford's *The Sun's Darling*, Beaumont and Fletcher's *Four Plays in One* and *Cupid's Revenge*, to mention only some of the most obvious—which in various ways owe as much to masque as to dramatic traditions. Narrative material combines with pageantry, songs and dances, in a frank disregard of dramatic illusion. *Old Fortunatus* and *The Arraignment of Paris* even have the complimentary denouement of the court masque proper. Moreover, in many of these plays the masque becomes a vehicle of moral allegory, Vices and Virtues appear in Morality fashion; and so the allegorical masque can be seen as a vital link between the drama of the Middle Ages and that of the seventeenth century. Nabbes's *Microcosmos* (1637), a 'Moral Masque' in five acts, is an outstanding example of the marriage between the spectacular and the didactic, and *Comus* could hardly be seen as a 'failure in artistic compromise'[3] if its kinship with such eclectic forms were fully realized.

But works such as these, while giving the lie to Caperwit's 'days of understanding', present a special problem, for in them masque and drama have entered into a formal union. What Caperwit and Jonson had in mind were, presumably, plays which have masque-elements in them but whose structure as a whole is primarily dramatic. Now, in trying to deal with such plays, one runs directly into questions of terminology, for in modern critical parlance terms such as 'masque-like' and 'masque-elements' are used with a fair degree of looseness. They may be used to indicate the presence of

[1] This has been dealt with by most writers on the masque, particularly by Enid Welsford in *The Court Masque* (Cambridge, 1927), ch. x, 'The Influence of the Masque on the Drama'.

[2] See G. K. Hunter, *John Lyly* (1962), esp. pp. 114–16.

[3] See Don Cameron Allen, 'Milton's *Comus* as a Failure in Artistic Compromise', *ELH* xvi (1949), 104–19.

any one, or all, of the devices which Thomas Heywood prided himself on not using:

> ...no drum, nor trumpet, nor dumb show;
> No combat, marriage, not so much today,
> As song, dance, masque, to bumbaste out a play.[1]

Or, as in Miss Welsford's interesting discussion of the masque-within-a-play as a symbolical mode of expression, the use of the term may be so widened as to make it refer to any non-realistic element.[2] To avoid confusion—and because it is impossible to deal, in the space allotted here, with every aspect of masques in plays—I am therefore going to limit myself to plays in which an entertainment with the essential features of the court masque is definitely put on by one or more of the dramatis personae before other dramatis personae. By the essential features, I mean a ritual in which masked dancers, with or without a presenter, arrive to perform a dance, sometimes to sing, and nearly always to 'take out' members of the stage audience. For several obvious reasons (lack of time, lack of machinery, lack—in the case of the adult companies—of singers, etc.) the inserted masque is briefer and less elaborated than the court masque proper. As E. K. Chambers points out,[3] it generally represents the masque as practised at the court of Elizabeth rather than that of James; sometimes it goes back to even earlier forms of 'disguising'. Yet, as is natural when many of the authors of plays with masques in them were also masque writers, the brevity is a matter of compression rather than lack of sophistication: for example, while keeping to the simple processional form, the inserted masque often utilizes the anti-masque/masque contrast.

In all the plays we shall turn to, then, the inserted masque has some plot motivation: it is performed on the pretext of a wedding (most frequently) or other celebration, such as a royal accession, the return of a victorious general, or just a banquet. Even Prospero has the social occasion of a betrothal to justify his masque. As Elizabethan comedy and tragedy became more realistic—approaching, however remotely, the well-made play—masque elements were

---

[1] Prologue to *The English Traveller* (c. 1627?).
[2] See *The Court Masque*, pp. 294–301.   [3] *Elizabethan Stage*, I, 189.

gathered up and made part of the play's structure as a plausibly motivated entertainment. This kind of device would seem much more realistic to an Elizabethan audience, more used to expect theatricals as 'part of a civilized way of life'.[1] This helps to account for the naturalness with which the masque occurs, from the 1590s onwards, in plays which seem structurally least related to the masque: domestic and satirical comedy, domestic and revenge tragedy. It also argues against the remarkably persistent notion that the masque-within-the-play only entered the drama seriously after 1608, via the Beaumont and Fletcher romances and through authors writing with an eye to the scenic facilities of the Blackfriars theatre.[2] A survey of inserted masques[3] shows that playwrights were attracted to the masque not just as a means to 'bumbaste out a play' by spectacle, but as a functional dramatic device—a way of starting, furthering and resolving plots and of adding meanings to plots.

In one sense, however, spectacle is the essential attribute of the inserted masque. If masques of this kind have hitherto received relatively little critical attention, it may be because so much of their effect is purely visual-theatrical, and therefore lost in reading. In many cases a masque exists to the reader only in a few brief stage-directions, such as '*Enter a Masque of Soldiers, and dance*' (Shirley, *The Maid's Revenge*, IV, 3). Indeed the elements which are charac-teristic of the masque, and which playwrights draw most heavily on,

---

[1] Arthur Brown, 'The Play within the Play: An Elizabethan Dramatic Device', *Essays and Studies* (1960), p. 37.

[2] This notion was put forward most emphatically by A. H. Thorndike, in 'The Influence of the Court-Masques on the Drama, 1608–15', *P.M.L.A.* XV (1900), 114–20, and *The Influence of Beaumont and Fletcher on Shakespeare* (Worcester, Mass., 1901); and, though it has been refuted by E. K. Chambers (*Elizabethan Stage*, I, 187) and others, it keeps reappearing in works on Beaumont and Fletcher—see, e.g., L. B. Wallis, *Fletcher, Beaumont and Company* (New York, 1947), p. 109. It may seem to have received new support in G. E. Bentley, 'Shakespeare and the Blackfriars Theatre', *Shakespeare Survey 1* (1948), 38–50; but Professor Allardyce Nicoll, in a recent article on 'Shakespeare and the Court Masque', *Shakespeare Jahrbuch* XCIV (1958), 51–62, points out how Shakespeare used masque devices long before Beau-mont and Fletcher and the Blackfriars entered the picture, and how, in any case, it was not the spectacular devices of the masque which most interested Shakespeare.

[3] As aids to such a survey, there are lists of plays which contain masques in Paul Reyher, *Les Masques Anglais* (Paris, 1909), pp. 497–8, and in R. S. Forsythe, *The Relations of Shirley's Plays to the Elizabethan Drama* (New York, 1914), pp. 79–80, the latter fuller than the former, but neither quite exhaustive.

are not adequately reflected in words—they are moments of pure
theatrical effects. There is first the arrival of the masquers: the
sudden intrusion on a festive company of grotesquely or handsomely
masked beings is bound to bring the thrill of the unexpected, or even
the fearsome. We, the audience, have usually been well briefed by
watching the conception and planning of the masque, but the stage
audience is conventionally taken by surprise; and this surprise is
utilized by many playwrights, particularly and ironically in Revenge
plays where the delighted surprise of the person 'honoured' by the
masque is soon to be turned into horror and death. Then there is the
dance, which usually leaves no more trace in the text than a laconic
'They dance', or 'ist strain', but which, together with the music,
could by discord or harmony form an emblematic comment on the
action of the play. The taking-out is perhaps the most obviously
functional aspect of the masque,[1] for by mingling performers with
audience it becomes a way of bringing people together and achieving
actions otherwise impossible—whether it means abduction (for a
tragic or comic end), the ballet-like pairing-off which often com-
poses the denouement of a comedy, or the murder that closes many
a Revenge tragedy. The sudden confrontations that take place during
the taking-out dance tend, from *Love's Labour's Lost* onwards, to
be handled with a kind of cinematic focusing device: couple after
couple are brought in turn to the fore, in a pattern which governs
dialogue as well as intrigue. Thus ironies due to misapprehension
(real or pretended) of identity are highlighted, and often the central
comic idea of the play epitomized: apart from *Love's Labour's Lost*,
v, 2, Chapman's *May-Day* (c. 1609), v, 1, contains a good example.[2]
This form of patterned encounter seems soon to have become a
conventional technique for furthering the plot directly and rapidly
—examples can be seen in Beaumont and Fletcher's *Wit at Several
Weapons* (before 1610?), v, 5, and Field's *A Woman is a Weathercock*

---

[1] It is above all the taking-out, with its intermingling of stage audience and performers, that distinguishes the masque-within-a-play from the play-within-the-play
and gives the former quite different dramatic possibilities from the latter. The analytic
value of Arthur Brown's above-mentioned essay is somewhat lessened by his un-
willingness to make this distinction.

[2] The same technique is of course employed in the exchanges between four
different couples in the masked dance in *Much Ado about Nothing*, ii, 1.

(1609), v, 2—while on a more serious level it is used to spotlight the reunion of long-lost partners, as at the end of *The Malcontent* (1604). Usually, the social range of the play is also epitomized in this pattern: the masked confrontations start with the hero and heroine and run through to the servants (again *The Malcontent* is typical). And, finally, the moment of unmasking, when it occurs, is generally a climactic point not only in the masque but in the play as a whole. It concentrates into one shocked moment the happy solution of an intrigue (as in *A Woman is a Weathercock*, Fletcher's *Women Pleased* (1619–23), or Shirley's *Changes*) or the striking of Nemesis (as in Marston's *Antonio's Revenge* (1599) and *The Malcontent*).

It can be said, then, that in some cases the 'fable' or 'device' of the inserted masque does not play much part in its dramatic effect. What the playwright is relying on is the moments of non-verbal theatre which the masque provides: surprise, shock, discovery, revelation, contrast, irony, occurring singly or in a pattern. It would also be true to say that these moments are very often central in the structure of the play where they occur. Indeed, in a great number of plays the inserted masque provides the crucial point in the action, the climax, the denouement, or even the centre of moral insight. (In a few cases, like Marston's *The Insatiate Countess* (*c.* 1610) and Shirley's *The Cardinal* (1641), it sets off the mounting action.) It would seem that a profitable way of looking at masques in plays would be to see them from the point of view of their contributions to the dramatic structure of the plays in which they are contained.

I. THE MASQUE AS ENTERTAINMENT AND ALLEGORY

If we set out to look for masques which are mere divertissements, we shall find surprisingly few. Even where the chief function of the masque is to provide pomp and circumstance, that is often in itself important to the sense of social occasion which the play is trying to evoke. The masque seems rapidly to have become a shorthand device for dramatizing festivity and solemnity. Often, too, it is part of an attempt at historical reconstruction. When in *Henry VIII*, I, 4 the King arrives in a pastoral masque at Cardinal Wolsey's banquet, Shakespeare is following his historical sources closely, and the masque is rightly of the form practised at the court of Henry VIII. But its pattern is also very typical of fictional masques in plays: surprise arrival of disguised strangers, who proceed directly to take out the ladies (and during this dance the King meets and falls in love with Anne Boleyn, which triggers off the main action of the play), followed by unmasking and revelation. Less functional from the point of view of intrigue, but no less intent on creating historical atmosphere, is the masque in Ford's *Perkin Warbeck* (1622–32?), III, 1. It is an economical way of sketching in the festivities around the wedding of Perkin Warbeck and the Lady Catherine before the wars which are the main business of the play begin, but no doubt it may have been suggested by a passage in Gainsford's *True and Wonderful History of Perkin Warbeck*:

...as the time, business and place afforded, shows, masques and sundry devices invited him to his contentment.[1]

Its form certainly indicates an attempt at evoking the early Tudor masque:

Enter at one door four Scotch Antics, accordingly habited; enter at another four wild Irish in Trowses, long-haired, and accordingly habited.
     Music. The masquers dance. (ed. Struble, III, 1, 231)

Such a masque commonly consisted of 'figures typical of different countries, trades or social classes'.[2] Ford may, too, by his choice of masquers, have wanted to emphasize the Scottishness of his setting. Geographical, rather than historical, atmosphere is also one aim of the masque in Fletcher and Massinger's play about Caesar and Cleopatra, *The False One* (c. 1620). In III, 4 Ptolemy puts on before Caesar and Antony a masque of the riches of the Nile, with Isis as presenter, three Labourers as masquers and Nilus as *deus ex machina*:

    Make room for my rich waters' fall,
      And bless my flood;
    Nilus comes flowing to you all
      Increase and good.

[1] Cf. Mildred Clara Struble, *A Critical Edition of Ford's 'Perkin Warbeck'* (*University of Washington Publications in Language and Literature*, III, 1926), p. 140.
[2] Welsford, *The Court Masque*, p. 145.

> Now the plants and flowers shall spring,
> And the merry ploughman sing.
> In my hidden waves I bring
> Bread, and wine, and ev'ry thing.
>
> (ed. Waller and Glover, III, pp. 342–3)

Though to us the effect may seem pastoral rather than exotic, the masque achieves its intrigue purpose, which is to 'dazzle Caesar with excess of glory'; and Caesar abruptly leaves the masquing hall:

> The wonder of this wealth so troubles me,
> I am not well.

No device could better provide the sense of social occasion around a marriage than the masque, and any play which contains a wedding is almost bound to contain a marriage masque. Hymen in *As You Like It*, v, 4 shows that the drama knew of the allegorical wedding-masque before it was fully developed at court; on the other hand more elaborate and less integrated masques in Jacobean plays observe all the formal features of the court masque. Chapman's *The Widow's Tears* (before 1609) has, in III, 2, one of the best examples of the marriage masque, brief but complete in structure. Upon the traditional call for clearance of the masquing room— 'A hall, a hall! let no more citizens in there'—Hymen descends, to music, from the heavens, '*and six Sylvans enter beneath, with torches*'. Hymen explains the device and its flattering reference to the bridal couple:

> to delight
> Your frolic eyes, and help to celebrate
> These noblest nuptials; which great destiny
> Ordain'd past custom and all vulgar object,
> To be the readvancement of a house
> Noble and princely, and restore this palace
> To that name that six hundred summers since
> Was in possession of this bridegroom's ancestors,
> The ancient and most virtue-famed Lysandri.
>
> (ed. Parrott, III, 2, 96–104)

The Sylvans then take out the bride and others and dance with them, and the whole is concluded by a speech in which Hymen invokes 'the blessings of your nuptial joys' over the bride and bridegroom.

Due solemnity is thus created around the marriage of Tharsalio and Eudora, the widow Countess, and it is fitting that this should have been one of the plays acted at court during the royal wedding celebrations in February 1613. The masque has no vital plot function in the play, but it is thematically apt in a comedy which, in its two plots, is much concerned with marriage, nuptial joys and faithfulness.

A similar lack of intrinsic connexion with the plot, and a similar thematic relevance, can be seen in the marriage masque in Fletcher's *A Wife for a Month* (1624), II, 1, but here the 'celebration' is given a sinister twist. Frederick, the usurping Duke of Naples, referred to—not unfairly—as 'unnatural and libidinous', has tried but failed to seduce Evanthe, who is chastity personified. He decrees that Evanthe and her lover Valerio shall marry and that Valerio shall die after a month, and so shall Evanthe, unless she can find another husband on the same monthly terms. The masque, then, celebrates this macabre marriage (the consummation of which is to be prevented by Frederick through one monstrous trick after another) in a dismal setting; even the usual merry thronging of the citizens outside the hall is replaced by a reference to gloating sensationalists:

> . . . how they flock hither,
> And with what joy the women run by heaps
> To see this marriage.   (ed. Waller and Glover, v, p. 22)

Fittingly, in a play of black and white contrasts, the masquers are personified vices, virtues and emotions; they are what Cupid, the presenter, calls his 'servants, the effects of love'. Some of them are the emotions and vices which lie behind the harrowing twists of the plot, and so the masque is used, as it were, to comment on the intrigue and anticipate some of its developments. The appearance of the masquers as personified abstracts is in itself an anticipation of the 'moral masques' of the 1630s, which will be discussed presently.

The most elaborate of all inserted marriage masques is that in Beaumont and Fletcher's *The Maid's Tragedy* (before 1611), I, 2. It is artistically finished: its exposition is conducted by dialogue rather than by the simpler device of the presenter; it has a full mythological plot, acted and spoken by Night, Cynthia, Neptune, Aeolus and other elemental deities, and a complimentary climax; it has two songs and two 'measures'. It is completely set off from the rest of the action in that the characters in it are not any of the regular dramatis personae, nor is there any taking-out of spectators at the end (in that respect it is more like a play-within-a-play). It looks, then, like a self-contained piece of entertainment, and most critics seem agreed that it is only a 'pièce de circonstance'.[1] Clearly Beaumont and Fletcher were interested in the theatrical and spectacular effects that they could get out of the masque as such. Yet it also has a peculiar, strongly ironical, bearing on the action of the play. Its themes are highly conventional—the benevolent forces of nature are bidden to wait on the bridal couple, the wedding-night (which should ideally never change into day) is made much of, and so are the bride's virginity, her pretended reluctance to give it up, and the bridegroom's ardour—and this very conventionality is used as a foil to the actual marriage-night in II, I. Much of the imagery of the masque is recalled in the later scene, and throughout the first part of the scene the contrast between the floridness of Amintor's conventional adoration and the cynical realism of Evadne's brief retorts is most effectively managed:

> *Amintor.* The vapours of the night will not fall here.
> To bed, my love; Hymen will punish us
> For being slack performers of his rites.
> Com'st thou to call me?
> *Evadne.* No.

Or:

> *Amintor.* I cannot find one blemish in thy face,
> Where falsehood should abide...
> *Evadne.* A maidenhead, Amintor, at my years?

Even Amintor's first outbursts after the truth has begun to dawn on him are couched in terms of the earlier marriage masque:

> Are these the joys of marriage? Hymen keep
> This story (that will make succeeding youth
> Neglect thy ceremonies) from all ears;

but gradually his rhetoric is whittled down to common, cowardly but pathetic, humanity:

[1] Reyher, *op. cit.* p. 315.

...and it is some ease
To me in these extremes, that I knew this
Before I touched thee;

or:

Be careful of thy credit, and sin close;
'Tis all I wish; upon thy chamber-floor
I'll rest tonight, that morning visitors
May think we did as married people use.
(ed. Waller and Glover, I, pp. 17–22)

The pathos of these lines is made ironical by the fact that the masque-
songs are still ringing in our ears:

Joy to this great company,
    And no day,
Come to steal this night away,
Till the rites of love are ended,
And the lusty bridegroom say,
' Welcome light of all befriended'.   (p. 11)

The same kind of irony lies in the contrast between what the
masque-song anticipates:

Stay, stay, and hide
The blushes of the bride.
Stay gentle night, and with thy darkness cover
The kisses of her lover.
Stay, and confound her tears, and her shrill cryings,
Her weak denials, vows and often dyings;

and Evadne's actual words:

Alas Amintor, think'st thou I forbear
To sleep with thee, because I have put on
A maiden's strictness? Look upon these cheeks,
And thou shalt find the hot and rising blood
Unapt for such a vow.   (pp. 21–2)

Irony, too, is achieved by the masque's handling of royal flattery. In
the opening lines of the play we hear that masques

must commend their King, and speak in praise of the assembly, bless the
bride and bridegroom, in person of some God; th'are tied to rules of
flattery;   (p. 1)

and the masque ends in the conventional compliment to the King as
a greater Sun, ironical in that the King, who has married his own
mistress off to the unsuspecting Amintor, is soon to be known as the
villain of the piece, and that in watching the masque he is so far
from being the ideal monarch as to be in the midst of perpetrating
his worst villainy. The scene of the masque ends on what must
surely be the most effective example of the ethical dative in Elizabethan drama, as the King hurries the bridal couple off to bed to
'get me a boy'. In *The Maid's Tragedy*, then, the authors have
seized on the assumptions of the traditional marriage masque—
pre-nuptial chastity, bridal bliss and royal integrity—and contrasted
them with a corrupt reality; and so, albeit in an obvious way, the
masque is used dramatically rather than as mere spectacular padding.

Perhaps the most far-reaching use of the masque as social symbol
is in *Timon of Athens*. The masque of Amazons in 1, 2 is indeed
'tied to rules of flattery'; it gathers into itself symbolically all the
elements of Timon's earlier life: lavish expenditure, social grace,
ceremony and ostentation. From the opening of Cupid's presenting
speech,

Hail to thee, worthy Timon, and to all that of his bounties taste,

(ed. Oliver, 1, 2, 118–19)

Timon at the banquet is seen as a king in his court:

*The Lords rise from table, with much adoring of Timon, and to show their
loves each single out an Amazon, and all dance, men with women, a lofty
strain or two to the hautboys, and cease.*

'Dancing to song is a thing of great state and pleasure' says Bacon
in his essay 'Of Masques and Triumphs'; here it is also an emphatic
image of the excessive adulation given to Timon. Meanwhile the
precariousness of this adulation is kept before us by the words of
Apemantus:

I should fear those that dance before me now
Would one day stamp upon me. 'T'as been done.

(lines 139–40)

Apemantus is in this scene in the most literal sense an anti-masquer.
As Cupid brings in the masquers, '*with lutes in their hands, dancing
and playing*', he undercuts the value of the masque:

Hoy-day!
What a sweep of vanity comes this way.
They dance? They are madwomen.
Like madness is the glory of this life,
As this pomp shows to a little oil and root.   (lines 127–31)

The second banquet (in III, 6) realizes his words. Here Timon is the presenter of his own show:

Gentlemen, our dinner will not recompense this long stay. Feast your ears with the music awhile, (lines 31–3)

and his words are deliberately made to echo those of Cupid:

> Th'ear,
> Taste, Touch, Smell, pleas'd from thy table rise;
> They only now come but to feast thine eyes.
> (ed. Alexander, I, 2, 120–22)

The effective contrast between the two scenes is obvious. The later banquet represents the 'stripping' and rejection of flattery, as the first represented the acceptance of it. The staged 'discovery' of the contents of the dishes, the throwing of water in the guests' faces to the accompaniment of abuse,

> Live loath'd and long,
> Most smiling, smooth, detested parasites,
> Courteous destroyers, affable wolves, meek bears,
> You fools of fortune, trencher-friends, time's flies,

and their scrambled exit, can be seen as an inversion of the ritual of flattery in I, 2. In Shakespeare's hands here the masque as social symbol has become an important dramatic tool.

In *The Tempest* the ultimate function of the masque is as a symbol of evanescence rather than of social ethics. We see in this play Shakespeare's uniqueness in being able to use the masque on so many levels at once. First, it relates to the plot by celebrating the betrothal of Ferdinand and Miranda—Prospero is thus, through his magic, creating a social occasion in the wilderness for his daughter. Secondly, the mythological device of the masque, as exhibited in the expository dialogue of Iris, Ceres and Juno, in the songs and in the dances of Nymphs and Reapers, is bound thematically to the whole play, through its stress on nature and fertility. And thirdly, the very idea of the masque is seized on for a comment on all reality. Prospero's speech about 'this insubstantial pageant' is too well known to need quoting, but the point needs to be made that Shakespeare is here drawing on a tendency of the court masque to turn on itself, philosophizing. In the masque, perhaps more than in any other art form, the paradox seems to hold that 'in the very temple of Delight | Veil'd Melancholy has her sovran shrine'. The very delight of the masque provokes the thought of its own short-livedness and hence of the impermanence of all things, as poignantly expressed at the end of Jonson's masque *Love Freed from Ignorance and Folly*,

> What just excuse had aged Time
>   His weary limbs now to have eased,
> And sat him down without his crime,
>   While every thought was so much pleased!
> But he so greedy to devour
>   His own and all that he brings forth,
> Is eating, every piece of hour,
>   Some object of the rarest worth.

Daniel's solution of the dilemma—'Pleasures are not, if they last'— in *Tethys' Festival* is the exception rather than the rule. Even the marriage masque, for all its hymeneal joy, tends to be deeply time-conscious. Often, of course, Time in the final, epithalamic lines of a marriage masque is just a question of the impatiently awaited marriage-bed; but equally often the concern goes deeper than that: the conflict between Love, or Life, and Time is sensed. This happens not only in the more thoughtful masques of Jonson; even, for example, a conventional conceit in Beaumont's *Masque of the Inner Temple and Gray's Inn* gets a sting of urgency:

> Away! Alas that he that first
> Gave Time wild wings to fly away,
> Hath now no power to make him stay.
>
> .   .   .   .
>
> I would this pair, when they are laid,
>   And not a creature nigh them,
> Could catch his scythe, as he doth pass,
> And cut his wings, and break his glass,
>   And keep him ever by them.   (lines 352–60)

Shakespeare, then, is not unique when he lets the realization of the *ars brevis* of the masque expand to the thought of *vita brevis*, but he is unique in working into a play a masque which becomes an allegory of life.

Other playwrights use the masque of entertainment for much more limited allegorical ends. We have already seen in *A Wife for a Month* a masque with an allegorical bearing on the action. In some cases this allegorical implication is made very obvious. An example is the court entertainment in Chapman's *Byron's Tragedy* (1608), II, I. The weight of this lies in the exceedingly long speech of Cupid as presenter, where the reconciliation of the Queen and the King's mistress is allegorically presented:

> This on the right hand is Sophrosyne,
> Or Chastity, this other Dapsile,
> Or Liberality; their emulation
> Begat a jar, which thus was reconcil'd.
> I (having left my Goddess mother's lap,
> To hawk and shoot at birds in Arden groves)
> Beheld this princely nymph with much affection,
> Left killing birds, and turn'd into a bird,
> Like which I flew betwixt her ivory breasts
> As if I had been driven by some hawk
> To sue to her for safety of my life.

(ed. Parrott, II, I, 16–26)

The masque has much the same combination of sensuous detail, personified abstracts, morality and narrative which characterizes Baroque allegorical painting. Rubens's series of Maria de' Medici paintings (1621–5) would provide a parallel; interestingly, it was this Queen who appeared as Chastity in the prototype of Chapman's masque, which was played at the French court in 1602.[1]

---

[1] See Grimestone's *A General Inventory of the History of France* (1607), p. 958, where, in the middle of the material relating to Biron, we have an account of 'The Queen's Masque': 'This winter, the Court was full of jollity and sports, the Queen having made a very rich and sumptuous masque, calling fifteen Princesses and Ladies of the Court unto her, which represented sixteen Virtues, whereof the Queen made the first. The Duke of Vendôme being attired like Cupid, marched before the Queen...' The excision of passages in the play preparing for the masque by describing the quarrel between the Queen and the King's mistress has led to the truncated state of the extant text (cf. Parrott's notes on the play in his edition of *The Tragedies of George Chapman*, p. 592).

The main use of the allegorical masque seems to have been in plays belonging to the 1630s and notably in the plays of Shirley. In both *The Coronation* (1634/5) and *The Traitor* (1631) a masque is arranged by one character to point a lesson to another. Allegory in *The Coronation*, IV, 3 is a mere excuse for theatricality: the masque does not comment on the meaning of the play but only makes spectacular one character's idea of what is going on, and a mistaken idea at that. The masque in *The Traitor*, III, 2 is used in a similar fashion. Alexander, Duke of Florence, desires Amidea; Sciarrha, her brother, plans to murder the Duke, to save his sister's honour. To accomplish this, he invites the Duke to feast at his house. After the banquet he puts on a 'moral masque', the presenter of which is Lust, attended by the Pleasures. The central figure of the masque is 'a young man richly habited and crowned', and he gaily dances the first measure together with Lust and the Pleasures. As in *The Coronation*, the stages in the masque alternate with interpreting comments, some of them self-consciously directed towards the form of the masque—

> *Lorenzo.* Me thinks they [the furies]
>   Should have been first, for th'anti-masque.
> *Sciarrha.* Oh no!
>   In hell they do not stand upon the method,
>   As we at court; the grand masque and the glory
>   Begin the revels—   (ed. Gifford and Dyce, II, p. 136)

and some towards its moral contents:

> [*Sciarrha*]   does not
>   That death's head look most temptingly? the worms
>   have kiss'd the lips off.   (p. 137)

That death's head is in fact pursuing the young man, as are 'a large train of Furies', and the second measure becomes a Dance of Death:

> *Enter Furies who join in the dance, and in the end carry the young Man away.*
>   (p. 137)

Sciarrha's brother, to make assurance double sure, tells us that 'the duke himself was personated', but evidently the moral masque does not have much effect on the Duke, who is all the time preoccupied with Amidea:

My eyes so feasted here, I did not mark it,
But I presume 'twas handsome.   (p. 137)[1]

What exactly is the dramatic purpose of the masque is difficult to say because, if the Duke had caught on, Sciarrha would hardly have been able to pursue his aim. Shirley is after theatrical effect: in a play full of posturing (see, e.g., Amidea's speech on death as a bridegroom, IV, 2, or Amidea's death, V, 1), morality itself is here turned to posturing. The obvious source of the masque is the skull-scene in *The Revenger's Tragedy*, but Shirley elaborates and gives a set-piece quality to what in *The Revenger's Tragedy* is completely interwoven in structure and language. The skull in *The Revenger's Tragedy* gives a further dimension to the action; the moral masque of death here merely makes more self-conscious the steps in the plot. Devices have become more important than the meaning they carry. However, the Duke is eventually (V, 3) killed, as a direct consequence of his lust, which means that the masque is an allegorical anticipation of the action. It thus performs one function of the dumb-show, and can be compared, for example, to the dumb-show at the end of Act III of *The Spanish Tragedy*.

We may be able to take this use of the masque with more respect than Shirley's can command, if we remember that Milton contemplated it when he was planning a drama on the theme of Paradise Lost. The plan for *Adam Unparadised*—the fourth draft in the Cambridge MS—has the following passage:

The Angel is sent to banish them out of Paradise; but, before, causes to pass before his eyes, in shapes, a masque of all the evils of this life and world.[2]

Similar masques are probably envisaged in the first and second drafts, which have lists of 'mutes', such as Sickness, Discontent, Ignorance, and others, and in the pageant of such mutes which an angel presents to Adam and Eve in Act V of the third draft.

[1] A confirmation of the theory that Claudius does not see the dumb-show before the Mousetrap?

[2] Reprinted in J. H. Hanford, *A Milton Handbook* (4th ed., New York, 1946), pp. 182–6.

2. COMIC USES OF THE MASQUE

The social possibilities, not to say liberties, which the masque implied—intruding under disguise on an assembly and mixing, in the taking-out, with the guests—had made it notorious, in life as well as in literature, as a vehicle for love-intrigue. In *The Malcontent*, Malevole says that he would rather leave a lady in a bordello than in 'an Italian lascivious palace', for there she will be subjected to

soft rest, sweet music, am'rous masquerers, lascivious banquets, sin itself gilt o'er.   (ed. Harvey Wood, I, p. 179)

Milton speaks in much the same vein when he contrasts 'wedded love' with
> court amours,
> Mixed dance, or wanton masque, or midnight ball,
> (*Paradise Lost*, IV, 767–8)

and the brothers of the Duchess of Malfi warn her that

> A vizor and a masque are whispering rooms
> That were nev'r built for goodness.
> (ed. Lucas, I, 1, 373–4)

Although in *The Revenger's Tragedy* (I, 4) we are told that Antonio's wife has been carried away in a masque and raped, when playwrights actually come to use the masque for amorous intrigue they stress its less sinister and sinful aspects. A masque may provide access to the beloved,[1] for, as Lyly's Philautus says when 'entreated to make one in a masque...in the gentleman's house where Camilla lay',

It hath been a custom, fair Lady, how commendable I will not dispute, how common you know, that masquers do therefore cover their faces that they may open their affections, and under the colour of a dance discover their whole desires.   (ed. Bond, II, 103)

In this case, the sharp lady outwits the masquer:

If you build upon custom that masquers have liberty to speak what they should not, you shall know that women have reason to make them hear what they would not.   (*Ibid.* p. 105)

---

[1] A good example of this, outside comedy, is in *The Death of Robert Earl of Huntingdon* (1598), II, 2 (pp. 266–7 in Hazlitt–Dodsley, 4th ed., 1874, vol. VIII), where the King gains access to and urges his affections on the very reluctant Matilda, Robert's widow.

The situation is essentially that of *Love's Labour's Lost*, v, 2, where the King of Navarre and his followers have planned their Muscovite masque to gain access to their respective loves, only, through the ladies' counter-masking, to have it shown off for the absurd device which it is.

More commonly the access gained via a masque is a matter of consent and collusion. As a plot device in comedy, the masque is almost always a way for young people to defeat the schemings of those who oppose the course of true love. It provides a useful variation on that basic plot in New Comedy in which the children are forbidden to marry by their fathers and then find means to evade the order. Often those most involved are most passive, while a friend—descendant of the clever servant—engineers the masque. The taking-out provides means of abduction, and as such is used in a number of plays—most cleverly, perhaps, in Field's *A Woman is a Weathercock*, v, 2, and Brome's *The Mock Marriage* (1637), IV, 5.[1] Often, as in *A Woman is a Weathercock*, a hasty marriage is thereby accomplished, so that the parents are presented with a *fait accompli*. The unmasking usually leads to a comically effective denouement, where a marriage or marriages are revealed, as, for example, in Shirley's *Changes* and in his *Love Tricks* (1624/5). The deceit practised in this type of masque is harmless and even beneficial. Dramatically, it builds to a large extent on irony: the outcome is suddenly found to be the opposite of what had been expected. Thus, in *Wit at Several Weapons*, the masque in v, 5 provides an opportunity for Cunningham and the Niece to meet, steal away and be quickly married—all this happening under the very eyes of the people who most want to prevent it happening.

Shirley, at the end of a long tradition of this use of the masque, employs it superbly in *The Constant Maid* (1636–40?), where an old usurer, Hornet, is cozened so as to make possible the marriage of his Niece to her heart's choice, Playfair. Hornet is made to believe that the King has knighted him and that he has been appointed 'Controller of the masque' at a court wedding. He guards the door of the

[1] In Fletcher and Rowley's *The Maid in the Mill* (1623), where in II, 2 there is a shepherds' feast with a masque on the Paris theme, a girl, Florimel, is carried off against her will but so impresses and subdues her abductor, Gerasto, through her chastity that he eventually marries her.

hall against presumed citizens, he is presented with a copy of 'the subject of the masque', which is the arraignment of Paris, and he approvingly watches the supposed royal bride appear as Helen to join her hand with Paris's. The whole court setting is, of course, a fake, and the King and courtiers are disguised helpers of the young couple, but the fact of the marriage remains.

While the masque is a useful device for resolving a comic intrigue, it also helps formally to tighten a sprawling plot. Its use sometimes indicates an attempt to get into the more realistic comedy the kind of patterned effect which Shakespeare achieves effortlessly when handling his lovers in *A Midsummer-Night's Dream*. This becomes particularly obvious towards the end of the tradition. Shirley's comedy *Changes* is a tangle of love relationships—*A* in love with *B*, *B* with *C*, etc.—which does full justice to its subtitle, *Love in a Maze*. In terms of psychological probability no denouement would be possible, as there is little reason why anyone should marry any particular person. The Gordian knot is cut by all the lovers, paired off and married, being suddenly, in the last scene, presented in a masque to parents and audience. By this time the resolving masque has become a shorthand device. As such it is, I think, ridiculed by Ben Jonson in *A Tale of a Tub* (1633). It is well known that Jonson was satirizing Inigo Jones when he created 'Medlay the joiner, In-and-In of Islington', and the masque at the end of this comedy (v, 5), engineered by In-and-In, has to be seen in the light of the intended satire. But it also forms a nice satire of masques in plays, and, by being not only pretentious and inane but also completely ineffectual and non-functional as far as the plot goes, it surely laughs at the facile tying-up of all the threads of an intrigue in a masque.

Masques which bring about a comic denouement do not usually achieve more than a technically effective crossing and double-crossing. Perhaps the earliest of all masques which create what we may call a purgative resolution to a play is that in *Love's Labour's Lost*, where the serious effect of the ladies' counter-masking is to put off the happy ending for a purgatory of a twelvemonth and a day. It suggests the difference between a simple intrigue resolution through the masque, on the one hand, and, on the other, a masque which is used to make some kind of criticism of life. Such criticism, however, steals in unexpectedly even in the intrigue type. An example of this is *A Woman is a Weathercock*. Here the disguising which the masque demands is linked with a form of disguise which goes right back to the Moralities. Nevill, the engineer of the masque, has been disguised as a parson, but, as the 'unvizarding' of the masquers reveals the marriage of Scudmore and Bellafront, Nevill for no plot reason '*puts off the Priest's weeds, and has a devil's robe under*'. All exclaim 'A pretty emblem!', and Nevill expounds the emblem:

> Who married her, or would have caus'd her marry
> To any man but this, no better was.

(ed. Peery, V, 2, 72–3)

In other words, it was morally wrong to force Bellafront to marry for worldly wealth, and the masque has righted the wrong. Certainly the symbolical-moral function of the masque in *A Woman is a Weathercock* is less important to the play as a whole than the plot-solving function; yet it is there, and it may not be altogether irrelevant to point out that Field had acted in both *Cynthia's Revels* and Middleton's *Your Five Gallants*—plays in which the former masque function is of prime importance.

Cynthia's Revels (1600–1) contains the most important of the masques used to moral ends, and it must have been the more or less direct model of many later plays in which the denouement is a reformatory masque. The purpose of the revels before Cynthia is not merely to flatter the monarch, but to show her as a reformer of manners and morals, just as the purpose of the whole play is to show how 'a virtuous Court a world to virtue draws'.[1] Much of Act v is taken up by a masque presented to the Queen: four female 'Virtues' and four male, who are in fact disguised Follies, appear, and long presenters' speeches introduce each of these masquers, dwelling at length on their attributes of goodness:

The fourth in white, is Apheleia, a Nymph as pure and simple as the soul, or as an abrase table, and therefore called Simplicity; without folds,

---

[1] A. H. Gilbert, in 'The Function of the Masques in *Cynthia's Revels*', *P.Q.* XXII (1943), 211–30, interestingly discusses how the masques 'subserve Jonson's purpose of reforming the manners of Elizabeth's court'.

without plaits, without colour, without counterfeit: and (to speak plainly) plainness itself. Her device is no device. The word under her silver shield, *Omnis Abest Fucus*. Alluding to thy spotless self, who art as far from impurity as from mortality.

(ed. Herford and Simpson, v, 7, 51–8)

After dancing three 'strains' with each other, the masquers unmask (v, 11, 50). This is the crucial moment, visually as well as morally, for here they stand revealed as frauds. Correction is meted out to them, and we last hear them singing a palinode of penance.

A brief account of the form of this masque gives little idea of how integral it is to the play as a whole, structurally as well as thematically. It epitomizes the antithesis of good and bad that the whole play is built on, for the play's structure is composed of antithetical characters: Crites and Arete versus the rest, with Cynthia as the presiding goddess. Thus, while the masque itself is of the simple, earlier, type, the structure of the play embodies the contrast of opposites, order/disorder, virtue/vice, which Jonson's later court masques were to build on. The masque proper, moreover, here forms the vehicle for exposing the bad elements and so purging the evil out of court society. Clearly this rhythm of inflation, sudden deflation and punishment is very close to Jonson's idea of comedy as realized in, say, *Volpone*.[1] The masque enables him to explore and exhibit in a concentrated way the gap between appearance and reality, between pretended good and actual evil.

That Jonson was not just concerned with court manners in a superficial sense may be indicated already by his choice of technique. The disguise of vices as virtues on the stage was a well-known device in Moralities and Interludes. In *Respublica*, for example, Avarice, Insolence, Oppression and Adulation appear disguised as Policy, Authority, Reformation and Honesty, and similar disguises occur in Lindsay's *Ane Satyre*.[2] Apart from this, before the masque is introduced it is made quite clear that it is to be a tool of serious

---

[1] Dolora Cunningham, whose essay, 'The Jonsonian Masque as a Literary Form', *ELH* xxii (1955), 108–24, seems to me one of the best studies of Jonson's masques, somewhat surprisingly insists on Jonson's conception of comedy being firmly separate from his conception of the masque. But the masque in *Cynthia's Revels* is in intention, structure and effect nothing but a condensed satirical-didactic comedy.

[2] This point is made by Gilbert.

reformation. Even in the 1601 quarto we are told that Cynthia wishes for revels,

> That so she might more strictly, and to root,
> Effect the reformation she intends.
>
> (Fol. v, 5, 45–6; Q, IV, 6, 42–3)

The additions in the 1616 Folio expand the court satire, and part of this is a series of passages on the intention of the masque. The serious implications are made increasingly clear in the discussions between Mercury and Crites in v, 1, and v, 4, and in Crites's words the intended reformation is seen in strictly moral terms:

> T'inflame best bosoms, with much worthier love
> Than of these outward and effeminate shades:
> That these vain joys, in which their wills consume
> Such powers of wit and soul as are of force
> To raise their beings to eternity,
> May be converted on works, fitting men.
> And, for the practice of a forced look,
> An antique gesture, or a fustian phrase,
> Study the native frame of a true heart,
> An inward comeliness of bounty, knowledge,
> And spirit, that may conform them, actually,
> To God's high figures, which they have in power:
> Which to neglect for a self-loving neatness,
> Is sacrilege of an unpardon'd greatness.   (v, 4, 635–48)

Moral purgation through exhibition and humiliation is the pattern laid down by *Cynthia's Revels*.

A play which owes more to this pattern than may at first appear is Middleton's comedy *Your Five Gallants* (1607). Its denouement is engineered in a theatrically highly effective masque by which the gentlemen outwit the gallants, but the double-crossing is not the whole point here. Katherine is supposed to make her election of a husband from among the gallants who parade before her in a masque; instead they are unmasked to her—all the more effectively as they are, unwittingly, made to reveal and condemn themselves by the impreses they carry, the Latin mottoes of which they fail to understand. The gift, too, which they bring, turns out to be the chain of pearls stolen from her. Thus the villains of the piece are shown in their true moral light, and Katherine is enlightened:

> How easily may our suspectless sex
> With fair appearing shadows be deluded!
>
> (ed. Bullen, V, 2, 53–4)

Here, as in *Cynthia's Revels*, the moral unmasking (and intended reformation) concerns the masquers themselves; in other uses of the masque, it is the object of the celebration—the person before whom the masque is presented—that is being 'stripped'.[1] It is interesting that, in a play satirizing Jonson and written only shortly after *Cynthia's Revels*, Dekker should have used the masque for the purpose of reformation. In *Satiromastix* (1601) melodrama turns moralizing via a masque.

Satiromastix is a notoriously disjointed play: the satirical subplot (where Jonson is attacked in the figure of Horace) has only loosely been tacked on to a tragi-comic main plot. The latter revolves around the wedding of Sir Walter Terrill and Caelestine, at which the King is a guest. The King dances with the bride, is seized with desire for her and commands the bridegroom to bring her to that evening's court revels—obviously to become a prey to his lust on her own wedding-night. To save her from dishonour, her father gives her a poison; this done, bride, husband and father proceed to court, there to present a kind of marriage masque:

> if any ask
> The mystery, say death presents a masque.
>
> (ed. Bowers, V, 1, 177–8)

At the opening of V, 2, the scene of this macabre masque, the King is revelling in his own projected immorality—'A King in love is steward to himself' (V, 2, 20). The emotional contrast between King and subjects is pressed home by spectacle as the masquers enter,

Enter [six people], all masked, two and two with lights like masquers: Caelestine in a chair,

---

[1] The masque of rebuke in Middleton's *No Wit No Help Like a Woman's*, IV, 2 is theatrically highly effective, but non-integral to the play and morally unimpressive. It does in fact suggest Shirley's use of the masque rather than Middleton's; and, as the play may have been revised by Shirley (see Bentley, V, p. 1134), this masque could be his.

and also verbally, as the bridegroom kneels before the King, who reproaches him:

> Com'st thou the Prologue of a masque in black?   (v, 2, 43)

The formal masque structure is insisted on at each step. Terrill explains:

> only I
> Present the Prologue, she [Caelestine] the mystery.   (51–2)

The next step is the 'revelation', which is also the interpretation of the allegorical 'mystery': the King unmasks Caelestine and finds her dead. At this point, insistence on the firm masque-structure prevents the scene from becoming mere sensationalism and gives it moral direction. Terrill makes a speech which turns the conventional eulogy of masques which 'must commend their king' into its opposite:

> Now King, I enter, now the Scene is mine,
> My tongue is tipp'd with poison;...
>   ...I blush not, King,
> To call thee Tyrant: death hath set my face,
> And made my blood bold;...
> This man of men, (the King) what are not kings?
> Was my chief guest, my royal guest...   (61–71)

Even the giving of gifts to the King is ironically observed:

> here take her, she was mine,
> When she was living, but now dead, she's thine.   (82–3)

So far, then, the masque is serving the purgative purpose of shock-treating wickedness. The King is brought to repentance:

> Do not confound me quite; for mine own guilt,
> Speaks more within me, than thy tongue contains.   (84–5)

But now another step, the real transformation or discovery, is added. The moral purpose achieved, the father proves to be a master of ceremony like Paulina in *The Winter's Tale*: Caelestine comes alive. The King asks:

> Am I confounded twice?
> Blasted with wonder,   (90–1)

'wonder' being here that 'notable passion' experienced as tragedy is resolved into marvel, the passion whose outward manifestations

431

are so tellingly described by the First Gentleman in *The Winter's Tale*, v, 2, and whose inner effects are realized in the last scene of that play. The King in *Satiromastix* has been doubly affected. With the father's explanation that the presumed fatal poison was just a sleeping-potion, the play has changed from tragedy to tragi-comedy. The satirical plot here comes in to provide a kind of anti-masque:

> My Liege, to wed a comical event
> To presupposed tragic argument:
> Vouchsafe to exercise your eyes, and see
> A humorous dreadful Poet take degree,   (113–16)

and the untrussing of Horace follows. Thus is dissipated—as is the play's unity all the time dissipated—the mood of a scene which was able, at moments, to rise above sheer theatricality, to a 'wonder' strangely anticipating moments in the last scene of *The Winter's Tale*.

I have dwelt at some length on *Satiromastix* because it shows emotion controlled and directed towards moral ends through the masque. The exact opposite—a masque used to pack emotions into situations at all costs—occurs in a play where the plot situation is very similar, Fletcher and Massinger's *The Custom of the Country* (*c.* 1619–20). The custom on which Count Clodio is insisting is his *ius primae noctis*; his intended victim is Zenocia, betrothed to Arnoldo. From the moment the bride's father and his servants appear, 'in blacks; covering the place with blacks', to prepare the gruesome 'marriage-bed' of the Count and Zenocia, masque devices are used to emphasize violent emotional contrasts, epitomized in the father's inverted epithalamium which ends:

> This is no masque of mirth, but murdered honour.
> (ed. Waller and Glover, 1, p. 313)

We can easily imagine that the unspecified 'song and dance' which follow would have been a kind of mournful anti-masque, performed by the servants. It is followed by the main masque of the next scene, where Clodio on the couch, 'hot and fiery', calling for 'music and sweet airs', is surprised by the entry of '*Zenocia with bow and quiver, an arrow bent, Arnoldo and Rutilio after her, armed*'. Clodio thinks this a charming marriage masque:

> What masque is this?
> What pretty fancy to provoke me high?
> The beauteous huntress, fairer far and sweeter;
> Diana shows an Ethiope to this beauty
> Protected by two virgin knights.   (p. 315)

But, as he is about to embrace her, the device of the masque explodes
on him:

> Stand, and stand fix'd, move not a foot, nor speak not,
> For, if thou dost, upon this point thy death sits.
> Thou miserable, base, and sordid lecher,
> Thou scum of noble blood, repent and speedily,
> Repent thy thousand thefts from helpless virgins.   (p. 315)

The masquers depart and escape from the claws of the lustful Duke.
In no way is the masque essential to the plot (the lovers could
equally well have slipped away beforehand) or to the reform of
Clodio. Its function is purely that of emotional heightening: it
works up the antithesis of the lustful Duke on the one hand and the
mournful father and desperate girl on the other, and also the
ironical effects as the marriage-bed is first seen as the hearse of the
girl's honour and then as the battlefield from which she emerges a
triumphant *virgo intacta*.

If *The Custom of the Country*, then, shows more of Fletcher's
'love of the rare situation'[1] than of any interest in the masque as a
vehicle of reform, one of Massinger's unaided plays contains a good
example of denouement through a masque of moral stripping. The
aim of the masque in *The City Madam* (1632?), v, 2 is for Sir John
Frugal to reform his family. First he has to expose and convert Luke,
his evil brother, who has been appearing in a moral disguise (like the
masque characters in *Cynthia's Revels*):

> He disguis'd
> Hypocrisy in such a cunning shape
> Of real goodness, that I would have sworn
> This devil a saint;   (ed. Kirk, v, 2, 2–4)

and then he can turn to 'the physic' he intends 'to minister to [his]
wife and daughters' for their pride and their wish to move out of
their proper social sphere. Both aims are successfully effected,

---

[1] Clifford Leech, *The John Fletcher Plays* (1962), p. 57.

through shock treatment, in the climax of the masque when the 'statues' of the girls' former suitors and the 'picture' of the supposedly dead Sir John come alive. Again the pseudo-magician in charge echoes Paulina:

> Nay they have life, and motion. Descend. [*To statues*]
> And for your absent brother, this wash'd off,
> Against your will you shall know him. [*He reveals himself*][1]

(v, 3, 107–9)

We have seen the masque as morally purgative; related to this use there is the inserted masque which attempts the less moralistic and more psycho-pathological cure of some character. If the former deals in the vice/virtue opposition, the latter is more concerned with passion versus reason—a distinction which, according to Babb, would, to an Elizabethan mind, have been one without a difference.[2] The progression from disorder to order had, particularly since the introduction of the anti-masque, been the basic formal and thematic idea of the masque. In Jonson's *Hymenaei* '*the four Humours, and four Affections*' issue as an anti-masque from '*a Microcosm, or Globe, (figuring Man)*', and are eventually curbed by reason. In *Lovers Made Men* the anti-masque is made up of the 'fantastic shades' of lovers who have 'drowned by Love'—i.e. are suffering from the extreme form of love-melancholy. After achieving oblivion in Lethe the same figures emerge as main masquers, now 'themselves again', 'substances, and men'. The masque as a whole enacts much the same form of metamorphosis as is aimed at by the masque in Ford's *The Lover's Melancholy* (1628). It has been suggested that this masque has its *raison d'être* as 'an application of [Burton's] therapeutic principle that melancholy can be cured by diversion'.[3] This may be true, but not the whole truth, for Ford must also have been aware of possibilities inherent in the masque form itself. Melancholy had become a traditional form of disorder in the masque —in *The Sun's Darling* (1623/4), written at least partly by Ford himself, there is a masque of the four elements and the four com-

---

[1] My stage-directions.
[2] Lawrence Babb, *The Elizabethan Malady* (East Lansing, Mich., U.S.A., 1951), p. 150.
[3] S. Blaine Ewing, *Burtonian Melancholy in the Plays of John Ford* (Princeton, 1940), p. 38.

plexions, including Melancholy. Ford could have found a near approach to his own device for curing such disorder in two Fletcher plays, both pre-Burtonian, and both suggesting that Burton's therapeutic ideas were not needed to make dramatists use a masque to cure melancholy. The plays are *The Mad Lover* and *The Nice Valour, or The Passionate Madman*, both possibly dating from 1616.[1]

In *The Mad Lover* Memnon, 'the Generals' General', returns from the wars and falls distractedly in love with Calis, the Princess, who in her turn contracts a returned passion for Memnon's brother, Polydor. Memnon is driven by love-melancholy to such extremes of heroic absurdity as to ask for a surgeon to cut out his heart which he wants to send to Calis in a golden goblet. To cure him, Stremon puts on a masque. It opens with a song by Orpheus warning generally against loving where love is not returned, and speaking of the hell where 'they groan that died despairing'; then, in a song split between Charon and Orpheus, Memnon's specific case is taken up:

> *Orpheus.* This soldier loves, and fain would die to win;
>   Shall he go on?
> *Charon.*   No, 'tis too foul a sin.
>   He must not come aboard.
>
>   (IV, 1; ed. Waller and Glover, III, p. 49)

Memnon is obviously affected—'he bites his lip, and rolls his fiery eyes'—and there is a nice interplay between the two different personae of one character, as Stremon, playing Orpheus, steps out of his masque part to see whether the medicine is taking effect. He retires into the masque again for the second movement, which is the entry of a 'masque of beasts'. These are used directly as *exempla horrenda*; while (presumably) they dance, Orpheus details the causes of their beastliness:

> This lion was a man of war that died,
> As thou wouldst do, to gild his lady's pride:
> This dog, a fool, that hung himself for love;
>
>   (IV, 1; ed. Waller and Glover, III, p. 49)

---

[1] Reyher (*op. cit.* p. 326) thinks that *The Mad Lover* is directly based on *Lovers Made Men*, but, if we accept the date of 1616 for the play, the dependence, if any, must be in the other direction.

and so on. At this point Memnon withdraws, much moved. In the event, the masque does not turn out to have been the decisive cure.[1] Nor is it so in *The Nice Valour*, where again a main character is a mad lover, though his ailment takes a different form from Memnon's. The Passionate Madman's emotions run through a continuous cycle, from love to sadness, to anger, to mirth, and back again to love. In one love-fit he has begotten a child on a Lady, and throughout the play this unfortunate woman follows him and tries to draw him back to sanity. Her method is to use the masque. In II, 1 she impersonates Cupid in a masque, and still in this guise she continues to pursue him,

> To see if she can draw all his wild passions,
> To one point only, and that's love.
> (ed. Waller and Glover, x, p. 162)

The therapeutic masque here therefore encompasses the greater part of the play, and a great deal of low comedy is got out of the fact of a Lady with a rapidly expanding waistline acting Cupid. Despite its prominence, it is not the masque which accomplishes the final cure (which also makes an honest woman of the Lady), but a beating up which the Passionate Madman receives from a Soldier whom he has 'bastinadoed' in a fit of anger. Obviously Fletcher found the idea of the therapeutic masque dramatically useful but, ultimately, psychologically unsound.

Even in *The Lover's Melancholy*, the 'Masque of Melancholy' which Corax, the court physician, arranges for the benefit of Prince Palador, does not, as masque, cure him of his morbid melancholy, though it does, in 'Mousetrap' fashion, make it clear where the trouble lies. This entertainment consists mainly of an anti-masque, in which six madmen, representing six different Burtonian types of melancholy, introduce themselves in mad speeches and songs and then dance. Ford is here working in an anti-masque tradition which goes back to Campion's 'twelve frantics... all represented in sundry

---

[1] He needs the shock of seeing his brother (supposedly) dead: Polydor has himself carried to the Princess in a coffin along with a will in which he instructs her to marry Memnon. So, in the end, Memnon gives up Calis to Polydor, dons his armour and returns to the wars whence he came.

habits and humours' in *The Lords' Masque*, and to Webster's eight madmen in *The Duchess of Malfi*, IV, 2. The main masque is compressed into the reference to the one kind of melancholy not so far exhibited,

> 'twas not in art
> To personate the shadow of that fancy.
> 'Tis named Love-Melancholy.

Corax wants to illustrate this by reference to an actual court intrigue, so he brings forth a young stranger. At this point the Prince suddenly leaves, and Corax has thereby found out just what sort of melancholy afflicts him. What Corax does not know is that the really effective point of the masque has been the bringing together of the Prince and his long-lost love, Eroclea, who is hiding under the disguise of the young stranger. It is this reunion, when effected, which cures the Prince. In terms of diversion, or of *exempla horrenda*, the masque has achieved nothing—which seems to me another reason to suggest that in his use of the masque Ford owes more to earlier masque and dramatic tradition than to Burtonian theories.[1]

3. TRAGIC USES OF THE MASQUE

Just as the masque was a useful tool for the moves and countermoves of comic intrigue, so it offered opportunities for tragic plotting; for, as Supervacuo says in *The Revenger's Tragedy*,

> A masque is treason's licence, that build upon;
> 'Tis murder's best face when a vizard's on.

> (ed. Nicoll, v, 1, 196–7)

There were possibilities to murder in the masque-hall, under the cover of disguise, or to abduct a victim and murder him in safety.

---

[1] The therapeutic masque is more limited in period and in the number of authors who use it than any other form of the inserted masque. A late off-shoot may be Brome's *Antipodes* (1638), which closes with a masque in which Discord, attended by Folly, Jealousy, Melancholy and Madness, is overcome by Harmony, attended by Mercury, Bacchus, and Apollo—Bacchus being the specific counterforce to Melancholy! It might also be noted that, late in the tradition, Shirley's *The Ball* (1632) contains what is virtually a take-off on the transformed-lover theme in the masque. In v, 1, after a mythological masque on the common subject of the arraignment of Paris, the play's 'cynic' enters 'disguised like a Satyr, and dancing'. He wants to present, in a sort of private anti-masque, an emblem of his own transformation through love; but his device rather misfires and he exits a worse cynic than ever—the idea of the therapeutic masque thus being stood on its head.

Dramatically, the masque so used implies almost unlimited opportunities of ironic reversals: a celebration turns into a blood-bath, a wedding into a funeral.

The use of a masque as a guise for murder had historical precedents, and so would have seemed to a contemporary audience less extravagant than we may now think. Holinshed records how the supporters of the deposed King Richard II laid plans to murder Henry IV:

Thomas Walsingham and divers other...write that the conspirators meant upon the sudden to have set upon the king in the castle of Windsor, under colour of a masque or mummery, and so to have dispatched him;
(1586 ed., II, p. 515)

and the ghost of Richard repeats the same story in *The Mirror for Magistrates*:

> For when king Henry knew that for my cause
> His lords in masque would kill him if they might,
> To dash all doubts, he took no farther pause;
> (ed. L. B. Campbell, p. 117)

as does the ghost of Thomas, Earl of Salisbury (Campbell, p. 145). These plans, when revealed by the young Duke of Aumerle, directly provoked the murder of Richard II—a familiar course of events and vividly real to the Elizabethan imagination. Soergel and Brotanek would see in it the direct source of masques in a whole row of plays,[1] which seems to me unlikely, as it is much more probable that playwrights learned from each other as they went along. But it could easily have provided the model for the first notable dramatic use of a masque to commit a murder, in *Woodstock* (1591–4), a play concerned with another part of the history of Richard II.

The masque in *Woodstock* has a straightforward plot-function as well as emphasizing the contrast between Woodstock and the King. In IV, 2, Woodstock, at Pleshey House, is full of dark forebodings as to the future of the kingdom in the hands of Richard, yet he is ironically lighthearted about his own personal safety:

> May not Plain Thomas live a time, to see
> This state attain her former royalty?

[1] See R. Brotanek, *Die englischen Maskenspiele* (Vienna, 1902), p. 7, n. 4.

'Fore God I doubt it not: my heart is merry,
And I am suddenly inspired for mirth.

(ed. Rossiter, IV, 2, 277–80)

The mirth is seasonable, for a group of alleged 'country gentlemen'
have already arrived to perform a masque. Calling for a banquet,
lights and music, Woodstock prepares to receive the masquers:
'They come in love—and we'll accept it so.' To a flourish of cornets
and winding of horns, Cynthia enters as presenter, to deliver a long
allegorical speech which gives the 'device' of the masque—

> From the clear orb of our ethereal Sphere
> Bright Cynthia comes to hunt and revel here.
> The groves of Calydon and Arden Woods
> Of untamed monsters, wild and savage herds,
> We and our knights have freed, and hither come
> To hunt these forests, where we hear there lies
> A cruel tusked boar, whose terror flies
> Through this large kingdom...   (IV, 2, 102–9)

—and ushers in the masquers:

*Enter King, Greene, Bushy, Bagot, like Diana's knights, led in by four
other knights, in green, with horns about their necks and boarspears in their
hands.*

Woodstock is obtusely blind to the real meaning of that allegory:

> Ah sirrah, ye come like knights to hunt the boar indeed;
> And heaven he knows we had need of helping hands,
> So many wild boars root and spoil our lands
> That England almost is destroyed by them...
> I care not if King Richard heard me speak it.   (136–40)

The fact is, of course, that King Richard does hear, and, after the
audience has been held in suspense for the duration of a masque
dance, he reveals the device:

> This is the cave, that keeps the tusked boar
> That roots up England's vineyards uncontrolled.
> Bagot, arrest him! If for help he cry
> Drown all his words, with drums, confusedly.   (167–70)

And so Woodstock is forced into a vizard and a masquing suit and
carried out of his home and castle, to death. The masque is one of

439

the few inventions of incident by the author, who otherwise stays close to his historical sources, and it shows him fully aware of the possibilities of the masque as both a plot device and a tool of dramatic irony. The play thus forms a link between the use of a play-within-the-play to commit Revenge murder in *The Spanish Tragedy* (*c.* 1589) and the soon conventional use of a masque for this purpose in later Revenge tragedy.

It may be appropriate to deal with very much later Revenge tragedies here, for the uses of the masque in them are less complex than those in late Elizabethan and Jacobean tragedies. The masque in Shirley's *The Cardinal* (1641) follows the *Woodstock* pattern but is simpler still—a bridegroom is abducted in a masque, and his bleeding body is presently brought in (III, 2)—so simple, in fact, that it looks as if the masque of this type was by now taken for granted as a shorthand device, useful to get the action started. Neither Shirley nor Ford uses tragic masques in an elaborate fashion, or even as denouements. Thus in Ford's *Love's Sacrifice* (1632?; III. 4) the masque belongs to the subplot, although by implication it foreshadows the outcome of the main plot. Ferentes is slain by his forsaken mistresses, in revenge for his promiscuous life:

Enter, in an antic fashion, Ferentes, Roseilli, and Mauruccio at several doors; they dance a short time. Suddenly enter to them; Colona, Julia, and Morona in odd shapes, and dance; the men gaze at them; and are invited by the women to dance. They dance together sundry changes; at last Ferentes is closed in.—Mauruccio and Roseilli, being shook off, stand at different ends of the stage gazing. The women join hands and dance round Ferentes with divers complimental offers of courtship; at length they suddenly fall upon him and stab him; he falls, and they run out at several doors. The music ceases.

With its abrupt change from courtship to killing, this is a somewhat gruesome masque with which to entertain an abbot!

Equally gruesome are the festivities at Annabella's wedding in *'Tis Pity She's a Whore* (1629?–33), where Hippolita, the cast-off mistress of Annabella's husband, appears in a private vendetta, followed by *'ladies in white robes with garlands of willows'* (ed. de Vocht, l. 1650), and, after music and a dance, suddenly unmasks to confront bride and bridegroom—only to sink poisoned at their feet. The ill-fated marriage has thus begun ominously and violently, and clearly here again the subplot contributes to the atmosphere around the main plot.

But we must return to the first appearance of the masque proper in tragedy, in *Antonio's Revenge* (1599). What in *Woodstock* had been an effective plot device is now being used with a new dimension. If we want to look for a 'source' for the masque in *Antonio's Revenge*, v, 5, we are most likely to find it in Hieronimo's playlet. Marston uses the patterned action and retributive ironies of the Kydian play-within-the-play; but here, as later in *The Malcontent*, he finds the masque-within-the-play more capable of concentrated irony and of the shock of sudden discovery. In the end Marston's masque remains his own fertile and vividly original device. It is ostensibly a marriage masque, arranged to celebrate the marriage of Maria with Piero. The latter, unsuspectingly, delights in the idea of an entertainment: 'You grace my marriage eve with sumptuous pomp.' At first sight there is nothing sumptuous about the masque: the masquers have no presenter and they neither sing nor speak, as they first appear, but in ominous silence 'stand in rank for the measure', and then dance while Piero chatters on, busily ordering a banquet of 'suckets, candied delicates'. In a manner later repeated by Webster's Cardinal in *The Duchess of Malfi*, Piero absurdly aids his own undoing by complying with the masquers' wish that the rest of the assembled company should 'forbear the room'.

The moment of unmasking comes, as Piero is left alone with the masquers, and suddenly marriage celebration is turning into torture and death. The shock of this unmasking is a structural parallel to an earlier shock, in I, 3, when on Antonio's wedding morning a curtain is drawn to reveal his bride and instead discovers the murdered body of Feliche. But the masque is not finished; it continues, to shape the rest of the scene. The torture that follows is made ironical by being seen as a banquet substituting for the one that Piero had ordered. The body of his little son is presented to him as the masquers' gift, superior to the 'worthless cates' of the prepared banquet:

> Here lies a dish to feast thy father's gorge,
> Here's flesh and blood, which I am sure thou lov'st.
>
> (ed. Harvey Wood, I, p. 130)

It is a refinement on the usual Thyestean treat. The masquers are now voluble, but their speeches are controlled by the formality and stylization of the masque:

> *Pandulpho.* Was he thy flesh, thy son, thy dearest son?
> *Antonio.* So was Andrugio my dearest father.
> *Pandulpho.* So was Feliche my dearest son.
>
> *Enter Maria.*
>
> *Maria.* So was Andrugio my dearest husband.
> *Antonio.* My father found no pity in thy blood.
> *Pandulpho.* Remorse was banish'd, when thou slew'st my son.
> *Maria.* When thou empoisoned'st my loving Lord,
>   Exil'd was piety.   (p. 130)

And Antonio acts as the summing-up chorus, or indeed the presenter of masquers dehumanized into abstractions:

> Now therefore pity, piety, remorse,
> Be aliens to our thoughts: grim fire-ey'd rage
> Possess us wholly.

While the torture is counterpointed by patterned speech, the killing is accompanied by a patterned dance-movement—the climactic taking-out dance of the masquers—which should be visualized for the scene to make the right impact on us. On the line 'let him die, and die, and still be dying' they all move towards Piero, but stop suddenly short on

> And yet not die till he hath died and died
> Ten thousand deaths in agony of heart.   (p. 130)

Then each stabs him individually, in a crescendo movement of retribution,

> *Antonio.* . . . This for my father's blood.
> *Pandulpho.* This for my son.
> *Alberto.* This for them all,

which explodes in a joint attack:

> *They run all at Piero with their rapiers.*   (p. 131)

All the while the ghost of Andrugio is watching the proceedings from his place 'betwixt the music houses', thus (like Revenge and the ghost of Andrea in *The Spanish Tragedy*) providing an extra audience—one with a unique kind of involvement:

> I taste the joys of heaven,
> Viewing my son triumph in his black blood. (p. 129)

Through the use of the masque, revenge has become ritual. What this implies we may see by comparing the killing of Piero to that of Arden of Feversham. Arden, too, is stabbed by one person after another, each shouting out his or her particular grudge while stabbing. But the grudges are realistically petty ones: Mosbie's a social inferiority complex, Alice's a wifely discontent, and Shakebag's a matter of ten pounds; and the situation is realistically disorganized: Will, e.g., has to creep between Michael's legs to get at Arden and pull him down with a towel. The whole thing is just as sordid and messy as in real life, and it is dramatically inevitable that it should end in a justice-room at Feversham. What is striking in Marston is his combination and manipulation of traditionally Senecan materials towards the most theatrical effect, and the complexity of emotions he builds up through the masque ritual, with its firmly stylized pattern of ironies and retributive horrors. The whole world of *Antonio's Revenge* is one that has gone mad, and the effect of the masque is to confront the audience with a grotesquely heightened picture of such a world. Only an anticlimax is possible thereafter, and the last scene, announcing the decision of the masquers to retreat into the 'holy verge of some religious order', is the only possible anticlimax, for human activity, suffering and death itself, have, as it were, been exhausted.

A recent critic has discussed 'three plays. . .which make use of a play within a play in a more or less conventional fashion, without extending its possibilities in any way'.[1] These are *Antonio's Revenge*, *The Revenger's Tragedy* and *Women Beware Women*. It is difficult to see how *Antonio's Revenge* can be judged so unenterprisingly conventional when, in fact, it initiated a convention. Nor can I agree with the comment on the masque in *The Revenger's Tragedy* (1607) as being 'typical of a number of revenge plays which followed the course so clearly indicated by Kyd'. The device of disguising is in this play in itself particularly apposite, as much of the plotting in the play goes by disguises—Vindice's, the Bony Lady's, and others'—

[1] Arthur Brown, *Essays and Studies* (1960), p. 42.

and by disguises which are used ritualistically rather than realistically. The ironies of the masque are a fitting summing-up of the many ironic reversals in the structure of the play, and its pattern of moral retribution is an essential part of the moral structure of the play.

Instead of the single revenge masque in *Antonio's Revenge*, we have here two lots of masquers, both aiming to kill Lussurioso in masques ostensibly celebrating his accession. At the opening of v, 3 we have witnessed in a dumb-show the installation of Lussurioso as Duke, and we have also heard how he plans the death of his step-brothers and bastard brother:

> after these Revels,
> I'll begin strange ones;   (ed. Nicoll, v, 3, 13–14)

And so when the first masque arrives, his thoughts—how appropriately, he does not know—run on two kinds of revels at once:

Enter the Masque of Revengers, the two Brothers, and two Lords more.

> *Lussurioso.*   Ah tis well
> Brothers, and Bastard, you dance next in hell.   (v, 3, 52–3)

These, apart from a brief, Desdemona-like recovery, are his last words, and the dance of Vindice and his fellow-masquers is the last thing he sees:

At the end [of the dance], *steal out their swords, and these four kill the four at the table, in their chairs. It thunders.*   (v, 3, 55–6)

The next lot of masquers accordingly find themselves anticipated, as Lussurioso himself was anticipated. The absurdity of counter-plotting makes the denouement into a grim farce, where it is fitting that the disappointed would-be murderers should turn on each other in an orgy of mutual killing. It is fitting too, and the final irony of the play, that when Vindice does his last (now metaphorical) un-masking, by telling about having murdered the old Duke, he should find himself sentenced to death—

> When murders shut deeds close, this curse does seal 'em,
> If none disclose 'em, they themselves reveal 'em!
>
>   (v, 3, 115–16)

444

The masque in *The Revenger's Tragedy*, then, is typical of nothing but itself; in Tourneur's hands convention is nothing if not creative.

In *Women Beware Women* (1625?–7) it may at first seem that 'love of tortuous plots and an obsession with wholesale slaughter for its own sake now predominate',[1] for the two masques in the final scene—the interrupted pastoral main masque and the 'ante-maske' of Hymen arranged by Bianca—leave a total count of six dead bodies on the stage. Yet, upon analysis, the tissue of intrigues which reach fruition in the masques proves to have been woven with logic and precision into an exhibition of ironic retribution, in a manner which affects the whole play. Livia and Guardiano plot against Isabella and Hippolito, who in their turn counterplot. Even the individual parts in the masque thus jointly devised have been chosen ironically: Livia, the procuress of the play, is cast as 'Juno Pronuba, the marriage goddess'; Isabella, her own uncle's mistress, is a 'nymph' wooed by two shepherds, one of whom is the very same uncle. Guardiano thinks that murder in a masque will be the perfect crime, for mischiefs acted

> Under the privilege of a marriage-triumph,
> At the duke's hasty nuptials, will be thought
> Things merely accidental, all's by chance,
> Not got of their own natures.   (ed. Bullen, IV, 2, 163–7)

He speaks more truly than he realizes, for in the event all turns out as 'by chance'. Isabella who has meant to poison Livia with incense falls herself a victim to it; Guardiano falls to his death through a trap-door intended for Hippolito—though, to counterbalance this, Livia, too, eventually dies from the poisoned incense, and Hippolito is shot by the Cupids' poisoned arrows according to plan. In Bianca's anti-masque there is the same mixture of human error and chance cutting across the scheming: Ganymede by mistake presents the poisoned cup to the Duke instead of the Cardinal, and, when Bianca realizes this, she commits suicide. Thus each plotter has achieved exactly the opposite of what he or she aimed at, in an irony of what Horatio calls 'purposes mistook | Fall'n on the inventors' heads'. The supposed marriage masque turns into one

[1] *Ibid.* p. 40.

huge Dance of Death, with the Cardinal as the sole surviving main character.[1]

The purpose of this masque is not just a *coup de théâtre*, but a crystallization of the moral issues of the play. As used here, the masque becomes an image of the self-destructiveness of human vice: for all the main characters the indulgence in lust leads to death in a marriage masque. The masque functions, then, as a moralized metaphor of the action of the play as a whole.

> Lust and forgetfulness has been amongst us,
> And we are brought to nothing...

> ...vengeance met vengeance,
> Like a set match, as if the plagues of sin
> Had been agreed to meet here altogether.
>
> (ed. Bullen, v, 1, 187–200)

Thus Hippolito in his death-speech, analysing the play through the masque. We are reminded, too, that the patterned denouement is the counterpart to the earlier 'set match' in the play, the chess-game of double-entendres which makes possible and accompanies Bianca's seduction (II, 2) and thus opens a way for corruption to act in the play.

Women Beware Women is, at large, a realistic play, with characters who, like those in *The Changeling*, are 'the deed's creatures'. Up till the end of the play, there is (unlike, say, in *The Revenger's Tragedy*) no explicit moral pattern and only implicit encouragement to us, as audience, to judge the characters. But in the masque scene Middleton goes back to what must have been one of the most influential moments of theatre in the Elizabethan drama: the end of *The Spanish Tragedy*. While in theatrical performance make-believe killings are normally substituted for real ones, Middleton, like Kyd, shows us 'real' ones substituted for make-believe. Together with the

---

[1] It is a working-out in masque and dramatic terms of the dumb-show at the end of Act III in *The Spanish Tragedy*:

> The two first, the nuptial torches bore,
> As brightly burning as the mid-day's sun:
> But after them doth Hymen hie as fast,
> Clothed in sable, and a saffron robe,
> And blows them out and quencheth them with blood,
> As discontent that things continue so.

deliberate patterning which I have just discussed, this creates an effect much like the now-so-popular 'alienation', detaching us and preparing us for moral comment on the action. That is, I think, why we should not be satisfied if the play ended on Bianca's dying words of amorality—

> Yet this my gladness is, that I remove
> Tasting the same death in a cup of love—   (v, 1, 262–3)

but feel the aesthetic rightness of the Cardinal's speech which closes the play:

> Sin, what thou art, these ruins show too piteously;
> Two kings on one throne cannot sit together,
> But one must needs down, for his title's wrong;
> So where lust reigns, that prince cannot reign long.

Spoken from among 'these ruins', these lines partly turn on the word 'show', reminding us that the ironic and retributive pattern of interrelated deaths must be seen, or visualized. When the play was broadcast (a B.B.C. Third Programme production, in which the masque scene had had to be drastically simplified), it became apparent that the pattern cannot make its full impact in a purely aural performance. *Women Beware Women*, then, takes us back to the beginning of this essay, by indicating how much of an inserted masque's effect and meaning may depend on visual and non-verbal elements.

This survey in no way claims to be exhaustive; many plays and uses of masques have had to be omitted. But it has, I hope, pointed to the major uses of the masque in plays, and to the major plays in which such uses are exemplified. Clearly, the rigid division into kinds which, for purposes of analysis, I have adopted, is often artificial: we need look no further than *The Malcontent* to see a masque which all at once brings about reunion, strips villainy, and enacts revenge (albeit mildly).

From what we have seen, a few concluding points may be made. No simple chronological development in the use of the inserted masque can be traced; but, excepting Shakespeare's comedies, perhaps the finest, at once most complex and most integrated, use of the masque is in the comedies and tragedies of the first two decades of the seventeenth century. By the end of the tradition, the masque has often become a mere spectacular device. With the possible exception of the therapeutic-comic masque, no one type seems to be limited to any particular period or to any particular author. Within each type, however, we tend to find one more external kind of use—serving plot and external structure—and one more deeply related to the 'figure in the carpet', i.e. to the moral or aesthetic structure of the play.

Finally, while the inserted masque tends to have a realistic motivation, it also at the same time changes the structure of the scene where it occurs, and of the play as a whole, in a direction away from realism. The masque often gives the playwright an opportunity to introduce ritual and stylized action in a play which ostensibly is steering away from the ritualistic. The masque then becomes a kind of mediator between convention and realism. We are reminded of T. S. Eliot's grudge against the Elizabethans:

The aim of the Elizabethans was to attain complete realism without surrendering any of the advantages which as artists they observed in un-realistic conventions.[1]

Yet, in the best cases, this is not just a matter of eating one's cake and having it, too. Elsewhere I have tried to show how Webster's use of the masque in *The Duchess of Malfi* makes for a unique balance between convention and realism.[2] The masque helps other playwrights to achieve their own peculiar balance. The patterned and stylized nature of the masque may enable a playwright to make horror and sadism bearable (as in *Antonio's Revenge*) and morally meaningful (as in *Women Beware Women*). It may enrich his structure by helping him to change within one scene from topical comedy to Morality (as in *Your Five Gallants*), or from romance to Morality and then back to satire (*Satiromastix*). Masques may, then, be 'pretty devices', but they are also one of the most central, most fruitful and most useful dramatic devices open to the Elizabethan, Jacobean or Caroline dramatist.

---

[1] *Selected Essays* (New York, 1950), p. 97.
[2] 'The "Impure Art" of John Webster', *R.E.S.* IX (1958), 253–67; reprinted in *Elizabethan Drama: Modern Essays in Criticism*, ed. R. J. Kaufmann (New York, Galaxy, 1961).